Theoretical Foundations of Learning Environments

Second edition

Edited by David Jonassen and Susan Land

Routledge
Taylor & Francis Group

NEW YORK AND LONDON

Second edition published 2012
by Routledge
711 Third Avenue, New York, NY 10017

Simultaneously published in the UK
by Routledge
2 Park Square, Milton Park, Abingdon, Oxon OX14 4RN

First published in 1999 by Routledge

Routledge is an imprint of the Taylor & Francis Group, an informa business

© 2012 Taylor & Francis

Library of Congress Cataloging in Publication Data
Theoretical foundations of learning environments / [edited by] David Jonassen, Susan Land. – 2nd ed.
    p. cm.
  Includes bibliographical references and index.
  1. Learning, Psychology of. 2. Cognition. 3. Learning.
  I. Jonassen, David H., 1947– II. Land, Susan M.
  LB1060.T47 2011
  370.15´23–dc23   2011029960

ISBN 13: 978-0-415-89421-0 (hbk)
ISBN 13: 978-0-415-89422-7 (pbk)
ISBN13: 978-0-203-81379-9 (ebk)

Typeset in Sabon
by HWA Text and Data Management
Printed and bound in the United States of America on acid-free paper by Edwards Brothers, Inc.

Contents

Figures

Preface

During the 1990s, the rise of constructivism and its associated theories in psychology and education represented a paradigm shift for educators and instructional designers to a view of learning that is necessarily more social, conversational, and constructive than traditional transmissive views of learning. These contemporary learning theories are based on substantively different ontologies and epistemologies than were traditional transmissive views of learning. The first edition of *Theoretical Foundations of Learning Environments* was the first to provide a manageable overview of these new conceptions of learning environments. That edition was impelled by the convergence of learning theories that emerged in the 1990s centered by the revolution in learning psychology ushered in by constructivism and situated learning.

In the previous decade, conceptions of student-centered learning environments matured. Newer theoretical perspectives have elaborated constructivist and situated perspectives on learning. In addition to the perspectives provided in the first edition, this second edition provides an updated view of theoretical foundations to include metacognition, model-based reasoning, conceptual change, argumentation, embodied cognition, communities of learning, and communities of practice. This second edition is intended to provide an introduction to these additional theoretical foundations for student-centered learning environments for instructional designers, curriculum specialists, mathematics and science educators, learning psychologists, and anyone else interested in the theoretical state of the art.

Student-centered learning environments have provided an alternative to transmissive instruction (which remains popular), where information is transmitted from teachers (or technologies) to learners. Many educators mistakenly believe that knowledge is being transmitted, but every chapter in this book assumes that knowledge must be constructed by learners. Transmissive instruction is based on a communications model of instruction that continues to dominate practice in many settings. Educators believe that improving learning is a matter of more effectively communicating ideas to learners by improving the clarity of the message.

The assumption of most educational enterprises has always been that if teachers communicate (transmit) to students what they know, then students will know it as well. Teaching is a process of conveying ideas to students. Good teaching means more effective communication. The assumption has been that because teachers have studied ideas longer, they understand them better and are therefore better able to communicate (transmit) them. Epistemologically, it assumes knowledge is an object that can be conveyed and owned by individuals, which assumes that students can come to know the world as the teacher does.

In modern societies, being a student is a culturally accepted responsibility of the maturing process. It is a right of passage into adulthood—a way of inculcating socially accepted beliefs. Behaviorism is the theoretical foundation for amplifying the communication (submission–transmission) process by adding practice and feedback to the basic communication processes. Behaviorists assumed that if learning were a change in behavior, that behavior had to be shaped through reinforced practice. And so, various practice strategies (drill, mnemonics, mathemagenics, algorithmization, and many others) have been appended to the communication process to strengthen the students' abilities to simulate the knowledge of their teachers. Throughout the 1970s and 1980s, cognitive psychology provided internal, mentalistic explanations for these learning processes, but unfortunately those explanations were unable to systemically change the practices of education. Having more complex representations of the processes of learning did not provide enough impetus to change the processes of education. Perhaps the cognitive revolution was not revolutionary enough.

Since about 1990, education and psychology have witnessed the most substantive and revolutionary changes in learning theory in history. What makes this revolution more substantive are the shifts in the underlying ontology, epistemology, and phenomenology of learning. Contemporary situated, sociocultural, and constructivist conceptions of learning are built on different ontological and epistemological foundations than communications theory, behaviorism, and cognitivism. We have entered a new age in learning theory. Never in the relatively short history of learning theories (100+ years) have there been so many theoretical foundations that share so many assumptions and common foundations as those represented in this book. Never have alternative theories of knowledge and learning been so consonant in their beliefs and the methods they espouse.

In this book, we have collected descriptions of theories of learning and meaning making, including socially shared cognition, situated learning, model-based reasoning, conceptual change, argumentation, case-based reasoning, self-regulation, embodied cognition, everyday cognition, activity theory, communities of learners, communities of practice, and complexity theory. These conceptions of learning share many beliefs and assumptions. They are based on a similar ontology, epistemology, and phenomenology. Their theoreticians believe that learning is not a transmissive process. Rather learning is willful, intentional, active, conscious, constructive practice that includes reciprocal intention–action–reflection activities. Learning is frequently conceived as an active process. Actions are integrations of perceptions and conscious thinking. Activity theory (Chapter 10) claims that conscious learning and activity (performance) are completely interactive and interdependent (we cannot act without thinking or think without acting).

Activity is regarded as necessary but not sufficient for learning. Reflection on these perceptual and conscious actions is necessary for constructing meaning, as indicated in Chapter 7. Learning, from the perspectives presented in this book, is conscious activity guided by intentions and reflections.

There are at least three fundamental shifts in thinking that are entailed by the theories described in this book. First, learning is a process of meaning making, not of knowledge transmission. Humans interact with other humans and with artifacts in the world and naturally and continuously attempt to make sense of those interactions. Meaning making (resolving the dissonance between what we know for sure and what we perceive or what we believe that others know) results from puzzlement, perturbation, expectation violations, curiosity, or cognitive dissonance. Making meaning from phenomena and experiences involves dissonance between what we know and what we want or need to know. This dissonance ensures some ownership of the knowledge by the learner. Knowledge that is personally or socially constructed is necessarily owned by and attributed to the meaning makers. So when encountering a puzzlement or problem, learners must articulate an intention to make sense of some phenomenon and then interact with it, consciously reflecting on the meaning of those interactions. The underlying epistemological revolution here is the rejection of dualistic beliefs that mind and behavior are separate phenomena. Rather, mind and behavior and perception and action are wholly integrated. That is, we cannot separate our knowledge of a domain from our interactions in that domain. Nor can we consider the knowledge that is constructed from the activity outside the context in which it was constructed.

Second, contemporary learning theorists focus increasingly on the social nature of the meaning making process. Behavioral and cognitive theories focused on the individual as the medium of learning. Information is processed, stored, retrieved, and applied by individuals who are able to compare their representation with others but not to share them. However, just as the physical world is shared by all of us, so is some of the meaning that we make from it. Humans are social creatures who rely on feedback from fellow humans to determine their own existence and the veridicality of their personal beliefs. Social constructivists (Chapters 7 and 8) have believed for many years that meaning making is a process of social negotiation among participants in any activity. Learning, from this perspective is dialogue, a process of internal as well as social negotiation. Learning is inherently a social-dialogical process.

The third fundamental shift in assumptions relates to the locus of meaning making. Many psychologists cling to the belief that knowledge resides only in the head. Humans are the only information processors that can make meaning from experience or anything else. However, as we engage in communities of practice, our knowledge and beliefs about the world are influenced by that community and their beliefs and values. Through legitimate peripheral participation (Lave & Wenger, 1991), we absorb part of the culture that is an integral part of the community, just as the culture is affected by each of its members. As we engage in communities of discourse and practice, our knowledge and beliefs are influenced by those communities. So is our identity formation, which is also a major outcome of learning. Not only does knowledge exist in individual and socially negotiating minds, but it also exists in the discourse among individuals, the social relationships that bind them, the physical artifacts that they use and produce, and the theories, models, and methods they use to produce them. Knowledge and cognitive activity is distributed among the culture and history of their existence and is mediated by the tools they use (see Chapter 10).

This book is organized around theories. These new theories of learning and thinking have influenced education in many ways. Specifically, this book is focused on the application of these theories for the design and analysis of student-centered learning environments. For the past two decades, pedagogical research has focused increasingly on problem-based, project-based, inquiry-oriented pedagogies in the forms of open-ended learning environments, cognitive apprenticeships, constructivist learning environments, microworlds, goal-based scenarios, anchored instruction, social-mediated communication, and so on. Land, Hannafin, and Oliver (Chapter 1) describe these generically as student-centered learning environments (SCLEs).

Note that there exist lots of redundancies of ideas, perspectives, and beliefs throughout this book. That is desirable and serves only to amplify the consonance among the theories described therein. Despite the congruence and convergence of theories, as stated in Chapter 1, there is none that represents a unifying theory of learning. Together, they may provide a consonant meta-theory of constructivist learning.

David Jonassen and Susan Land

References

Lave, J., & Wenger, E. (1991). *Situated learning: Legitimate peripheral participation*. New York: Cambridge University Press.

Part 1

Overview

1 Student-Centered Learning Environments

Foundations, Assumptions and Design

Susan M. Land, Michael J. Hannafin and Kevin Oliver

Student-centered learning environments (SCLEs) "provide interactive, complimentary activities that enable individuals to address unique learning interests and needs, study multiple levels of complexity, and deepen understanding (Hannafin & Land, 1997, p. 168). This general framework is used in the learning sciences to delineate design methods that support personal sense making via problem contexts enriched with technology tools, resources, and scaffolding (Quintana, Shin, Norris, & Soloway, 2006). Such environments facilitate student- or self-directed learning by enabling students to productively engage complex, open-ended problems that are aligned authentically with the practices, culture, or processes of a domain.

During the past two decades, new frameworks for designing learning environments have emerged in response to constructivist-inspired views of learning (Jonassen, 1991). Such views represented a fundamental shift in the paradigms of learning and design during the 1990s, but few guidelines were available for designers to create learner-centered environments. Likewise, as technologies advanced, approaches evolved to integrate digital resources, tools, and connectivity to expand the designer's toolkit. These shifts in the learning–design–technology landscape required corresponding shifts in theoretical and design frameworks to capture emerging viewpoints and technologies for learning (Hannafin & Land, 1997).

The National Research Council Report (Bransford *et al.*, 2000), *How People Learn*, established principled-based approaches to designing learner-centered environments, emphasizing learning with understanding and the importance of social and cultural contexts in learning. These perspectives require very different approaches to design, teaching, and assessment, including the importance of learner preconceptions, deep, usable knowledge, and metacognition as processes that mediate individual learning. One implication for learning-environment design drawn by the NRC is that "schools and classrooms must be learner centered"

(Bransford *et al.*, p. 23). The 2006 edition of the *Cambridge Handbook of the Learning Sciences* further expanded the 2000 NRC report, aligning Learning Sciences research and development with the goals of student-centered learning outlined in that earlier work (Sawyer, 2006).

Despite the 2000 report detailing the prevailing views on how people learn, debate about the veracity of assumptions about learner-centered designs has re-emerged, with questions arising about the research evidence available in support of constructivist approaches (see for example, Hirsch, 2001; Kirschner *et al.*, 2006). Indeed, unlike for traditional instruction, no unifying theory seems to guide the design of student-centered learning environments, which creates challenges for research, scalability, and generalizability. We acknowledge the efficacy of varied approaches to teaching and design, with design decisions being a byproduct of different contexts, tasks, pragmatics, and goals. This chapter focuses on introducing the tenets of student-centered learning environments that are grounded in foundations, assumptions, and methods associated with a constructivist epistemology.

Theoretical Background

The Role of Epistemology in Learning Environments

Epistemological shifts have engendered a variety of innovative and provocative learning environments. Interest in student-centered teaching and learning, for example, has given rise to myriad approaches to provide flexible and powerful alternatives to the design of instruction (Jonassen, 1991). Student-centered environments, tacitly or explicitly, are designed to support individual efforts to negotiate meaning while engaging in authentic activities. Student-centered approaches reflecting epistemological variants have emerged including problem-based learning (Hmelo-Silver, 2004), anchored instruction (Cognition and Technology Group at Vanderbilt, 1992), cognitive apprenticeships (Collins, 2006), computer-supported collaborative learning (Stahl *et al.*, 2006), learning-by-design (Kolodner, 2006), project-based learning (Krajcik & Blumenfeld, 2006), games and simulations (D. Clark *et al.*, 2009), and open learning environments (Hannafin, Land, & Oliver, 1999). While operationalized differently, student-centered learning environments share common epistemological foundations and assumptions. SCLEs are grounded in a constructivist view of learning, where meaning is personally rather than universally defined. Such perspectives draw heavily from psychological research and theory related to areas such as situated cognition (Brown, Collins, & Duguid, 1989) with attendant assumptions emphasizing the interlacing of content, context and understanding, the individual negotiation of meaning, and the construction of knowledge (Jonassen, 1991). Pedagogically, SCLEs favor rich, authentic learning contexts over isolated, decontextualized knowledge and skill, student-centered, goal-directed inquiry over externally directed instruction, and supporting personal perspectives over canonical perspectives. Technology tools support the individual's identification and manipulation of resources and ideas (Iiyoshi, Hannafin, & Wang, 2005).

With increased popularity, however, fundamental questions have arisen related to the kinds of learning such environments support, how best to design them, and whether or not designs can be generalized across varied domains and contexts (Dick, 1991; Merrill, 1991; Kirschner *et al.*, 2006). Numerous "how to" guidelines have been offered, but they typically lack adequate theoretical or empirical framing (Hannafin & Land, 1997). Given the unique student-centered learning goals and requirements, it may be impossible to derive an inclusive design model. Rather, we need to identify frameworks for analyzing, designing, and implementing learning environments that embody and align particular foundations, assumptions, and practices.

Clark (Clark & Hannafin, 2011) recently described "pitfalls" and shortcomings of constructivist-inspired learning environments such as discovery learning research and practice, citing examples to support his assertion that fully-guided, direct instruction results in superior performance in virtually all cases. Similar arguments have been presented for constructivist-inspired learning strategies and environments including student-centered learning, inquiry-based learning, and self-directed learning (Kirschner *et al.*, 2006). Clark also suggested that empirical evidence generated from directed-learning studies is applicable to all types of learning independent of the associated epistemological roots. He suggests personal perspectives might unduly sustain the popularity of minimally-guided approaches in the absence of empirical evidence. Finally, Clark cautions "Far too many in our field are avoiding inconvenient evidence in favor of self-serving beliefs and opinions" (p. 375). He questions the preparation and motivation of non-adherents: "few people have the motivation or training necessary to invest the effort required to carefully review complex research on learning and instruction … ambivalence about research training in our instructional technology and instructional systems graduate programs is certainly a contributing factor" (p. 375). He concludes that programs that do not heed his advice "risk causing harm to people who depend on us" (p. 375).

But are the goals, assumptions, and learning contexts of these approaches really comparable to those based on learning from direct instruction? Clark *et al.*'s guidance is only occasionally viable when the circumstances and assumptions guiding design decisions are aligned. His perspectives, methods, and findings do not align with widely adopted approaches advanced by reputable theorists, researchers, and practitioners with different perspectives. Hmelo-Silver, Duncan, and Chinn (2007) challenged Kirschner *et al.*'s (2006) use of the term minimal guidance:

"problem-based learning (PBL) and inquiry learning (IL), are not minimally guided instructional approaches but rather provide extensive scaffolding and guidance to facilitate student learning" (p. 99). McCaslin and Good (1992) noted, "the intended modern school curriculum, which is designed to produce self-motivated, active learners, is seriously undermined by classroom management policies that encourage, if not demand, simple obedience" (p. 4). The authors suggest that both teachers and students require sustained opportunities and support in order to adapt and implement significant pedagogical changes. Optimal guidance is needed where learning outcomes are not or cannot be explicitly predefined.

We do not argue for inherent superiority (or inferiority) of one perspective or approach over alternatives. We do not intend to fuel what is often a rancorous ongoing debate, but to advance a more principled approach to linking teaching, learning, and technology. Since learning is the goal of design, we need to clarify the type(s) of learning we mean to facilitate. Learning systems design has evolved frameworks that provide important and useful ways to support directed learning. So, while we acknowledge that fully-guided direct instruction is often well-suited to support external learning requirements, these same methods and models cannot adequately support learning that has become increasingly spontaneous and self-directed within and across formal (e.g., independent follow-up on debates related to global warming or Jefferson's ancestry) and informal settings (e.g., learning the causes of home garden infestations or the impact of recent tax laws on personal finances). We acknowledge that different learning goals exist, recognize the implications of these perspectives on design and learning, and identify strategies that are best aligned with and appropriate for a given learning need.

Grounded Design

Grounded design is "the systematic implementation of processes and procedures that are rooted in established theory and research in human learning" (Hannafin *et al.*, 1997, p. 102). Grounded approaches emphasize the alignment of core foundations and assumptions, and the linking of methods and approaches in ways that are consistent with their corresponding epistemological perspectives. It does not advocate or presume the inherent superiority of a specific epistemology or methodology for design. Rather, grounded design provides a framework for reconciling diverse design practices with the basic tenets of their associated belief systems. We have previously outlined the importance of alignment among psychological, pedagogical, technological, pragmatic, and cultural foundations of a learning environment.

Grounded student-centered learning environments support learners as they negotiate multiple rather than singular points of view, reconcile competing and conflicting perspectives and beliefs, and construct personally-relevant meaning accordingly. Key overarching assumptions and values are reflected in seemingly diverse environments. For instance, one environment might support collaboration activities to facilitate shared meaning of scientific practices; others might rely upon individually-mediated use of technology tools to generate, test, and refine personal theories. Both environments emphasize learning as a goal-directed activity, yet each provides a somewhat different context to support learner-constructed meaning (e.g., rich technological support, rich social support). What is important from a grounded design perspective is that the design decisions, features, and sequences of the learning environment align with theoretically-grounded perspectives on learning and associated pedagogy.

Grounded design, therefore, involves the simultaneous alignment of each foundation in order to optimize coincidence across all foundations; as the intersection across foundations increases, the better grounded the design. A wide array of psychological perspectives can be drawn upon, for which a multitude of pedagogical alternatives is available. All perspectives and methods, however, are not interchangeable; in grounded design they are interdependent. By default or design, many learning environments simply do not adhere to the definition, foundations, assumptions, and methods of grounded instruction. This is the case both for designs that purport to be instruction but fail to reflect the requisite alignment as well as for learning environments that are rooted in fundamentally different perspectives. Compared with instructivist methodologies, for example, student-centered approaches support different learning goals, utilize different methods, and adopt different assumptions about the nature of knowing and understanding. However, as with instruction, not all alleged student-centered learning environments are well grounded. Many environments are rooted in appropriate foundations, yet the methods are incompatible with the associated assumptions. Gaps frequently exist between the presumed underlying constructivist epistemology and the associated affordances and activities (Perkins, 1985; Salomon, 1986). For example, learner-controlled, directed practice may be mischaracterized as a constructivist methodology despite the concurrent focus on explicit instruction; conversely, a complete absence of external support may be mistaken for student-centered learning when needed scaffolding is not provided. For constructivist as well as other learning environments, grounded educational practices align foundations, assumptions, and methods as a matter of design. Explicating alternative theories for grounding design of SCLEs is the primary purpose of this book.

We consider four conditions as basic to grounded design practice. First, designs must be rooted in a defensible and publicly acknowledged theoretical framework. Learning environments are grounded to the extent that core foundations are identified and aligned; they link corresponding foundations, associated assumptions, and methods. Next, methods must be consistent with the outcomes of research conducted to test, validate, or extend the theories upon which they are based. Grounded design methods have been evaluated in instances, cases, and research; grounded design practice builds upon tested and proven approaches. In addition, grounded designs are generalizable, that is, they transcend the individual instances in which isolated success may be evident, and can be adapted or adopted by other designers. This does not suggest a literal, algorithmic mapping of methods according to strictly defined conditions, but rather the heuristics-based application of design processes appropriate in comparable circumstances. Finally, grounded designs and their frameworks are validated iteratively through successive implementation. Methods are proven effective in ways that support the theoretical framework upon which they are based, and extend the framework itself as successive implementations clarify the approach. The design processes and methods continuously inform, test, validate, or contradict the theoretical framework and assumptions upon which they were based, and vice versa.

Key Assumptions and Methods of Student-Centered Learning Environments

Student-centered learning environments reflect several key assumptions about the nature of learning, the structure of the environment, and role of the learner (Hannafin & Land, 1997). Despite differences manifested in various student-centered designs, several core values and assumptions can be identified: (a) centrality of the learner in defining meaning; (b) scaffolded participation in authentic tasks and sociocultural practices; (c) importance of prior and everyday experiences in meaning construction; and (d) access to multiple perspectives, resources, and representations.

The Centrality of the Learner in Defining Their Own Meaning

In student-centered environments, the overarching focus is to support the learner to actively construct meaning. External learning goals may be established, but the learner determines how to proceed based on individual needs and questions that arise while generating and testing beliefs (Hannafin, Land, & Oliver, 1999). For example, the WISE project operationalizes a framework of *scaffolded knowledge integration* (Linn, 2006) in the design of computer-based, student-centered support for science learning. In the thermodynamics environment, for instance, students engage with a virtual laboratory to inquire, experiment, and compare predictions with simulated outcomes about the temperature of objects around them. Rather than simply read about thermodynamics, students are encouraged to make connections to everyday experiences, collect real data, and conduct virtual scientific investigations about fundamental thermodynamics concepts. As they conduct an investigation, such as the effects of different types of materials on rate of thermal conduction, they use simulation tools to progressively develop, test, and refine explanations of their findings. Although the environment is designed to constrain exploration of thermodynamics concepts in productive and sequenced ways, the focus is on the learner's own efforts to make sense and actively build upon what they know.

Presumably, given opportunities to make choices and pursue individual interests, learners evolve greater responsibility for their own learning. In traditional instructional environments, learners are often denied opportunities to develop the decision-making, self-monitoring, and attention-checking skills necessary to optimize learning experiences (Perkins, 1993; Sawyer, 2006). Learners become increasingly compliant in their learning, viewing the task as one of matching their meanings to those expected by external agents (McCaslin & Good, 1992). In contrast, successful learners evolve a variety of strategies to plan and pursue goals, integrate new and existing knowledge, formulate questions and inferences, and continually review and reorganize their thinking (Bransford *et al.*, 2000).

Consequently, student-centered environments scaffold student thinking and actions to facilitate ongoing management and refinement of what they know (Hannafin, Land, & Oliver, 1999). Because learners new to a domain may lack important strategic knowledge for managing the learning processes, "learners can be overwhelmed by the complexity of options available, making it difficult to direct their investigations, see what steps are relevant and productive, and make effective activity decisions" (Quintana *et al.*, 2004, p. 359). Accordingly, the process of managing inquiry (i.e., proceeding through an open-ended task by keeping track of findings, deciding what to pursue next, determining how available tools and resources are useful in a problem, and reflecting on what is being learned) are supported through structures and guidance embedded into the environment (Quintana *et al.*, 2004). The individual uniquely defines and monitors understanding to promote autonomy and ownership of the learning process, but these processes often will not occur spontaneously without explicit support.

Implications for Design

SCLE designs afford cyclical supports to engage various cycles or progressions of inquiry (Schwartz *et al.*, 1999). Designs use increasingly complex problems around a central concept, beginning with learner articulation of initial ideas. Learners progressively refine and reconstruct initial ideas through activities such as comparing ideas with experts or data, engaging in self-directed inquiry, testing ideas through experimentation, vetting formative ideas publically, and creating artifacts of their understanding. For instance, WISE design features (Linn, 2006) encourage learner-defined meaning using built-in prompts to predict outcomes before experimenting (eliciting learner preconceptions), deciding which factors to investigate, simulating outcomes of student-designed virtual experiments, and comparing and reflecting upon differences between predicted and data-based outcomes. Students are guided to search for patterns in the data to critically examine their initial ideas and to refine their explanations more scientifically.

Schwartz *et al.*'s (1999) framework for guided inquiry supports students to engage cycles of progressively complex challenges, generate their own ideas on how to address the challenges, compare ideas with others and reflect on the differences, develop, assess, and revise understanding, and ultimately present a final solution or product publically. Similar strategies are apparent in other SCLEs, such as problem-based learning (Hmelo-Silver, 2004). Although the problem or activity is structured and constrained for students, the iterative learning process is driven by students' initial ideas that are progressively refined through access to additional information, representations, experiments, or perspectives.

Scaffolded Participation in Authentic Tasks and Sociocultural Practices

Student-centered learning is rooted in situated learning theory, which explains that knowledge, thinking, and the contexts for learning are inextricably tied and situated in practice (Brown *et al.*, 1989). Barab and Duffy (2000, p. 26; Chapter 2) wrote that situativity theory "suggests a reformulation of learning in which practice is not conceived of as independent of learning and in which meaning is not conceived of as separate from the practices and contexts in which it was negotiated." A community of practice (Lave & Wenger, 1991) involves "a collection of individuals sharing mutually defined practices, beliefs, and understandings over an extended time frame in the pursuit of a shared enterprise" (Barab & Duffy, p. 36) that legitimize, use, and advance the practices of a domain. Understandings, as well as identities, are believed to develop through participation in authentic practice. The practices, situations, and processes of a community frame how knowledge is meaningfully used.

While all learning is contextually based, not all contexts support the application of knowledge equally. Knowledge acquired in decontextualized contexts, for example, tends to be inert and of little practical utility (Whitehead, 1929). For instance, learning to solve classical textbook mathematical equations independently of their authentic context tends to promote isolated, naïve, and over-simplified understanding (Brown *et al.*, 1989). Learners may successfully solve near transfer problems (e.g., other textbook problems) where the algorithm can be equivalently matched, but fail to flexibly apply or critically reason through a problem on far-transfer or novel tasks (Perkins & Simmons, 1988). In situated contexts, learning occurs as a consequence of a learner's recognizing knowledge's practical utility as well as the need to use it in an attempt to interpret, analyze, and solve real-world problems.

Implications for Design

Rather than treating knowledge as isolated content to be processed, elaborated, and retrieved, student-centered environments promote authentic practices that situate knowledge-in-use (Sawyer, 2006). In the context of schooling, Barab and Duffy (2000; Chapter 2) use the metaphor of "practice fields" to describe learning environments that engage children in "practicing" the kinds of problems and practices that may be encountered in real-world, out-of-school contexts and communities. They identify several design strategies for designing practice fields: (1) students should do domain-related practices, not just learn about them; (2) students need to take ownership of the inquiry; (3) coaching and modeling of thinking skills is needed; (4) students should be provided with explicit opportunity for reflection; (5) dilemmas are ill-structured and complex; (6) learners must be supported to engage the authentic complexity of the task, rather than simplifying the dilemma with unrealistic problems; (7) students work in teams to address contextualized problems.

Participation in authentic practices cannot be operationalized successfully without scaffolding the "gulf of expertise that lies between the novice learner and the more developed understanding or expertise embodied by an expert in the domain" (Quintana *et al.*, 2006, p. 121). Children or newcomers to a domain cannot be seen as full practitioners in the same way as professional architects, scientists, or athletes. However, Edelson and Reiser (2006) suggest that children can be supported to engage in and reflect on authentic practices, provided they are developmentally and representationally accessible. They suggest that authentic practice involves engaging students in the disciplinary practices of professional practitioners. Although children or newcomers lack the expertise to solve the same problems as practicing scientists or historians, they can engage in activities that are consistent with them and/or that have connections to real-world activities that can be directly experienced.

According to Edelson and Reiser (2006), designing to support authentic practice is complex, but has many potential benefits: (a) authentic practices may be encountered outside of school in personally consequential ways, increasing their relevance; (b) increased motivation may result from applying knowledge to meaningful contexts; and (c) the structure of knowledge, or the epistemology of the domain, can become more obvious as a result of engaging in disciplinary practices. They suggest four design heuristics to support learning in authentic contexts: (a) situate authentic practices in meaningful contexts; (b) reduce the complexity of authentic practices; (c) make implicit elements of authentic practices explicit; and (d) sequence learning activities according to a developmental progression (p. 336). Similar pedagogical strategies, well-aligned with psychological foundations of situated cognition, are commonly cited foundations for problem-based learning (Savery, 2006) and anchored instruction (Cognition and Technology Group at Vanderbilt, 1992).

Importance of Prior and Everyday Experiences

Individual beliefs and experiences provide uniquely personal frameworks for new understanding. Contemporary views on learning recognize that prior knowledge and experience form the conceptual referent from which new knowledge is organized and assimilated, and that learners' prior knowledge and beliefs influence what they perceive, organize, and interpret (Bransford *et al.*, 2000). Understanding continuously and dynamically evolves, as ideas are generated, expanded, tested, and revised (Land & Hannafin, 1996). Learners hold powerful, often naïve and incomplete, beliefs that are deeply rooted in their everyday experience. While individual models tend to be tacit and sometimes at odds with accepted notions, they provide the basis through which learners interpret and explain new concepts. Such beliefs tend to persist even in the face of contradictory evidence; simply telling children that not all heavy objects sink or that the earth is round often fails. Instead, teachers and designers must use methods of eliciting pre-existing beliefs and actively building upon them (Bransford *et al.*, 2000).

SCLEs often employ problem contexts designed to link everyday experiences and build upon what students know. When learning is anchored in everyday contexts, learners are more likely to understand how concepts are applied and why they are useful, thus facilitating transfer (Bransford *et al.*, 2000). Making connections to everyday contexts guides students to enrich and integrate schooling and life experiences and to develop meaningful, long-lasting interests and understandings (Bell *et al.*, 2009).

Implications for Design

In student-centered design practices, erstwhile tacit beliefs are frequently externalized and formalized so they can be tested. Simulations, for instance, allow learners to generate and test working models of their tacit understanding and get feedback on them (Clark *et al.*, 2009). By varying parameters and hypothesizing outcomes, learners presumably test assumptions and revise thinking based on resultant observations. Some design approaches promote a tiered or phased approach to learning that builds upon informal or everyday experiences of learners and then subsequently extends those experiences with more formalized concepts.

For instance, Clark *et al.* (2009) used video games to initially build strong intuitive knowledge of physics and later introduced more formalized concepts and representations to extend students' understanding of physics concepts. Similarly, augmented reality designs have emerged that overlay virtual media (videos, text, data) onto GPS-tagged locations (Squire & Jan, 2007) in order to extend the meaning of, or ways of experiencing or observing, familiar physical locations.

Student-centered environments often utilize familiar problems or local issues to prompt access to and deployment of personal theories and experiences. Activities and contexts that readily connect to learners' experiences are assumed to increase relevance and engagement. For instance, roller coaster simulations are designed to support children's exploration of force and motion concepts through development of a virtual roller coaster (Kirriemuir & McFarlane, 2003). The context employs a familiar referent (riding roller coasters) to assist learners in relating to-be-investigated concepts to familiar experiences. Other designs have incorporated learners' real dietary choices to investigate health and nutritional science (Land *et al.*, 2009). The everyday context is used to induce learners' related experiences to interpret, explain, and eventually formalize the related scientific knowledge.

Learning is Enriched via Access to Multiple Perspectives, Resources, and Representations

Student-centered learning environments focus on enriching and extending learning through a variety of perspectives, resources, and representations. Such environments may use teacher–student or student–student interactions to model or scaffold reflection and performance (see for example, Palincsar & Brown, 1984). Accordingly, varied perspectives from teachers, experts, or peers can be coordinated to form a knowledge base from which learners evaluate and negotiate varied sources of meaning. Varied methods and perspectives are viewed as critical to developing deeper, divergent, and more flexible thinking processes.

Computer tools are also used in SCLEs to enhance, augment, or extend thinking or perspectives (Pea, 1985). Multiple representations may be supported by visualizing ideas. By accessing alternative ways to represent "hard-to-see" concepts and to manipulate them (e.g., tools that allow learners to change the tilt of the earth's axis and distance from the sun in order to simulate the seasons), learners consider concepts and ideas in ways that would typically be inaccessible. Computing tools such as simulations, GPS data and maps, and virtual worlds allow learners to visualize and experience complex representations of concepts, thus adding to the richness of perspectives available on the topic. The externalized representations enable new forms of discourse and engagement (Roth, 1995).

Implications for Design

SCLEs promote learning via varied perspectives, representations, and resources using strategies such as structuring opportunities to integrate and share personal experiences or observations. For instance, the WISE environment described previously (Linn, 2006) uses Web technology to support sharing of learner-constructed evidence to evaluate scientific phenomena. Students can browse databases of evidence constructed by themselves, as well as with other students and teachers. Learners review the varied, and sometimes conflicting, evidence to determine whether it supports or contradicts their position. As divergent views are deliberated, learners inquire further to reconcile differences and refine explanations. Hedberg and Chang (2007) describe the G-Portal digital repository that represents a collection of geographic objects that can be represented in layers (e.g., beach profiles, vegetation). In one study, students were tasked with solving an authentic problem involving land use planning for a mock beach resort, representing data spatially and collecting resources and notes in group project spaces to inform their problem. Students presented multiple forms of argumentation during inquiry and developed presentation artifacts with recommendations regarding resort siting under specific conditions.

Design Components and Methods

SCLEs are generally comprised of four primary components, though the methods and strategies used vary depending on the goals and contexts in which they are applied (Hannafin *et al.*, 1999). *Contexts* represent the nature of the overall problems or tasks that guide and orient students to learning. They span a continuum of structure—from contexts that specify problems and outcomes, but allow for individual exploration (e.g., simulations that allow manipulation of a small number of variables around a specific set of concepts) to externally-generated problems (e.g., problem-based approaches that require solutions to an ill-defined problem) to contexts that are uniquely defined (e.g., personally-defined problems in everyday life, such as needing to learn new knowledge and skills to manage a newly-diagnosed medical condition).

Tools offer technology-based support for representing, organizing, manipulating, or constructing understanding. Hannafin *et al.* (1999) characterize three types of tools typically employed in learning environments:

- Processing tools (i.e., tools that aid in cognitive processing, information seeking, collecting, organizing, integrating, and reflecting);
- Manipulation tools (i.e., tools that function based on user input, changing and testing parameters, and visualizing effects); and
- Communication tools (i.e., tools that promote social interaction and dialog).

Visualization tools are designed to allow detailed viewing of a phenomenon that might not be visible without such representations (Clark *et al.*, 2009). Web 2.0 tools have expanded the types of tools easily available to designers to support student creation and production of artifacts. Such production tools, in combination with available downloadable software, can be integrated into a learning environment to enhance processing and reflection. For instance, students might use existing software tools to create computer games without prior programming experience (Peppler & Kafai, 2007), construct sharable concept maps to represent and organize their thinking, or create podcasts to organize and present what is being learned. Mobile computing tools have expanded the contexts for student-centered learning beyond the desktop and out into real physical surroundings. Mobile apps and handheld tools, for instance, enable GPS capability, scientific measurement, audio and video capture, as well as augmented reality of GPS-tagged locations.

Resources represent source information and content, and may range from static information resources related to the topic under study (e.g., text, video) to dynamically-evolving resources that are socially-constructed (e.g., WIKIs, blogs). Web 2.0 tools, for example, enable creation of sharable resources, and mobile tools support information to be pushed to users at the point of demand, based on GPS location (Pastore, Land, & Jung, 2011).

Scaffolds are support mechanisms designed to aid an individual's efforts to understand and are typically designed to provide the following functions (Hannafin *et al.*, 1999):

- *Conceptual* guidance on concepts related to the problem;
- *Metacognitive* guidance on how to reflect, plan, and monitor;
- *Procedural* guidance on how to use the environment's features and proceed through the environment; and
- *Strategic* guidance on how to approach the task or refine strategies.

Quintana *et al.*'s (2004) review of student-centered environments synthesized a framework characterizing three main categories of scaffolds: (a) sense-making, (i.e., scaffolds to enable learners to generate and test hypotheses, manipulate and inspect representations, make comparisons, construct explanations, or highlight disciplinary strategies); (b) process management (i.e., scaffolds to constrain and guide learners to be able to better manage the complexity of the environment); and (c) articulation and reflection (i.e., scaffolds to support reviewing, reflecting, synthesizing, and expressing). Scaffolding serves the role of helping learners to productively engage the complexity, authenticity, and open-endedness of the environment.

Types of Student-Centered Learning Environments

Student-centered learning environments draw upon a variety of design methods, tools, scaffolds, and problems, and often look very different from one another. However, despite apparent differences across learning environments, they generally follow from an overarching theoretical foundation and set of learning goals. This section categorizes and describes various student-centered learning environments to illustrate similarities and differences in foundations and designs.

Problem-based Learning

Savery (2006, p. 9) defines problem-based learning as "an instructional (and curricular) learner-centered approach that empowers learners to conduct research, integrate theory and practice, and apply knowledge and skills to develop a viable solution to a defined problem." Problem-based learning (PBL) originated within medical school curricula as a method to help medical students learn clinical problem-solving skills in a real-world context. PBL uses an authentic, ill-structured problem as the frame for learning new knowledge and skills connected to a real application. In a medical school example, students might explore a hypothetical patient case. They are then progressively supported to consider, develop, and refine explanations of important physiological concepts linked to observations from the case. Learners engage in a self-directed learning process that proceeds from generating initial explanations about possible causes of the problem (Hmelo-Silver, 2004). Students ask questions to clarify the problem and generate "learning issues" (often recorded on a whiteboard) to investigate further. Students investigate these learning issues outside of class and reconvene to discuss what was learned and to generate new learning issues. As the causes and solutions are generated, students are prompted to explain and reflect upon them according to the relevant concepts and principles.

PBL often relies on a skilled facilitator to scaffold the problem-based inquiry and use of the whiteboard as a metacognitive scaffold to guide students through the process. Resources play a prominent role, as students independently research relevant domain information to help them represent and solve the problem. The approach has been extended to both K-12 and higher education contexts, where the focus is on using realistic problems of practice or a domain as the context for learning (Savery, 2006).

Learning Communities

Learning communities (see Chapter 11) comprise groups of learners who work together to learn and model authentic, domain-related practices (Palincsar & Brown, 1984). Bielaczyc and Collins (1999, p. 271) state that "the defining quality of a learning community is that there is a culture of learning in which everyone is involved in a collective effort of understanding." They identify four characteristics of learning communities: (a) varied areas of expertise are encouraged and facilitated; (b) goals are to advance the collective knowledge of the community; (c) learning how to learn and create knowledge is emphasized; and (d) mechanisms or technologies for sharing what is learned are central.

Knowledge Forum, a well-known example of a learning community, is based on *knowledge-building* theoretical and pedagogical perspectives (Scardamalia & Bereiter, 2006). This work emphasizes collective building and improvement of ideas, and technology tools support students to post their ideas and notes, comment on and add to others' ideas, organize their own and others' ideas according to different conceptual frames, and to add varied graphical representations. Students are agents of their own understanding, and participate in a culture that generates and contributes to both individual and collective knowledge.

Stickler and Hampel (2010) describe the *Cyber Deutsch* collaborative language learning environment grounded in socioconstructivist theories, where students interacted with each other through various tools and learned language by practicing language forms and communicating authentically. Students completed various activities in both synchronous *FlashMeeting* videoconferences and asynchronous discussion forums, and leveraged Web 2.0 tools such as survey editors to question one another as well as blogs and wikis to practice writing collaboratively with ample opportunities for commenting and peer edits.

Communities of Practice (COP)

A community of practice (see Chapters 2 and 12) involves a group of individuals who share practices, beliefs, and understandings in pursuit of a shared enterprise (Barab & Duffy, 2000). In COPs, practice is not considered independent of learning and the contexts in which it is negotiated (Brown, Collins, & Duguid, 1989). The COP framework emphasizes how communities learn outside of the classroom, and emerged from research based on traditional craft apprentices (Lave & Wenger, 1991). Learning in these contexts centers on participation and the ways that newcomers progressively enter into a more central role in the community. As a result of participation, both practices and identities advance (Barab & Duffy, 2000).

Design efforts have focused on using technology with communities of practice to enhance knowledge sharing and to tighten the bonds between existing workplace communities (Hoadley & Kilner, 2005). For example, Company Command (Hoadley & Kilner) is an online COP for US Army officers that brings together company commanders across the globe to help each other advance their practice. Similarly designed COPs include those used to enhance preservice and newly practicing teacher practice (Barab *et al.*, 2002), and automobile sales and service representatives' sharing of stories and best practices (Land *et al.*, 2009).

Gaming, Virtual Worlds, and Simulation Environments

Balasubramanian and Wilson (2005) note that researchers often attempt to differentiate between games and simulations, but find "more commonalities than differences." deFreitas and Griffiths (2008) describe recent simultaneous convergences in gaming that have further blurred the boundaries with implications for education. For example, gaming has converged with cinema by employing similar software tools to create authentic 3D environments. Gaming has also converged with the Web by making collaborative multiplayer environments and virtual worlds (MUVEs) available online with Web 2.0 tools for chatting and generating content related to the experience. Further, gaming has converged with mobile devices by making handheld games accessible to more users and opening up opportunities to apply games outside of traditional classroom spaces in the field. Tools such as *Scratch* (Calder, 2010) increase opportunities for game players to design and share games that suit personal learning interests. To utilize games and simulations in education, it is necessary to plan strategies and scaffolding that will best expose students to core concepts.

Civilization III is a hybrid game/simulation environment that has been applied in some education contexts for learning about historical development and nation building. The program has rules such as the number of food units that must be produced to sustain a population of a given size, and the number of land units that can be put into production around a city. Authentic scenarios play out with students sponsoring or defending against war, and recent expansion packs allow users to pit their civilizations against others online. Charsky and Ressler (2011) applied concept maps as scaffolds for 9th grade students to focus on key concepts while interacting with *Civilization III* in a global history class. Student motivation in concept map groups, however, declined relative to no-map groups, suggesting external scaffolds imposed on a game environment may be a challenge if they decrease the autonomous nature of play.

Spires (2008) describes *Crystal Island* where students engage in virtual scientific activities at a research station to address the problem of scientists becoming ill while studying microbiology concepts. The simulation includes embedded conceptual and metacognitive scaffolds within character dialogues, and procedural scaffolds in the form of virtual lab tools for testing hypotheses. If students apply a "scattershot approach to testing hypotheses" and exceed test limits, the simulation initiates strategic scaffolds that requires students to reconsider four key components of the simulation task before they can proceed (Spires, Rowe, Mott, & Lester, in press).

Digital Repositories

In the past two decades, dramatic increases have been evident in the number of digital repositories accessible via the Web, allowing educators to access and utilize extensive data sets, maps and images, and other primary source documents featuring authentic, context-rich resources. The potential for digital repositories to support student-centered inquiry, however, is often tempered by the largely unstructured nature of these resource sets and features. Indeed, for a digital repository to support student-centered learning, appropriate learning tasks, tools, and scaffolds must be effectively integrated with the resources.

Oliver and Lee (2011) describe the Plantation Letters primary source repository that represents a collection of letters written to and from American plantation owners in the nineteenth century with a search interface to retrieve letters associated with pre-defined themes. In one lesson grounded in cognitive flexibility theory (Spiro, Feltovich, Jacobson, & Coulson, 1992), students retrieve plantation letters using health-related tags to study conditions contributing to medical problems among enslaved workers. Multiple perspectives on the concept of medical crises are supported by reading across different plantation cases presenting with chronic health problems as well as external cases of recent medical crises brought about by natural disasters. Students develop and defend a rank-ordered plan for resolving a current medical crisis with similar conditions to those described on plantations and other unhealthy sites (e.g., inadequate housing, clothing, food). Students present and discuss their plans in the Plantation Letters Ning social network to reach consensus on the most damaging conditions and the most appropriate and humane interventions.

In another more heavily scaffolded lesson created for the Plantation Letters project, students apply the SCIM-C historical inquiry strategy (Hicks, Doolittle, & Ewing, 2004), guiding their own inquiry into themes of personal interest. Students summarize information about their selected source, note contextual information within the source, make inferences about broader historical questions a teacher may pose, and monitor their assumptions and limits in interpretation. After applying SCIM to multiple sources, student then apply a fifth corroboration stage, looking for similarities or differences across sources that could further interpretations. While SCIM-C represents a scaffolded task process to inquire into digital repositories, teachers can utilize a number of emerging Web-based tools to support this work, such as *The History Engine* (HE) (Benson, Chambliss, Martinez, Tomasek, & Tuten, 2009). *The History Engine* provides students with authentic opportunities to publish their interpretations of primary sources much like historians, and engage with historical experts and other students in further analysis and corroboration.

Constructionist Learning Environments

Learning is presumed to become more meaningful and motivational when students construct designs or projects (Kafai, 2006). Constructionist environments are designed to encourage knowledge-in-use by developing physical or digital objects that represent understanding (Kolodner, 2006; Papert, 1993). Artifacts might include physical objects like a model rocket or digital objects such as student-created computer games or videos.

Web 2.0 refers to emerging, democratic Web capabilities for users to collaboratively construct and share new information online in varied forms (e.g., user-contributed videos, reflective blogs, collaborative wiki pages). Web 2.0 tools afford functionality that allows students to generate a product or solution following discussion, play, and/or research. A Web 2.0 tool by itself may not apply to all SCLEs, but educators have designed Web 2.0 learning environments that utilize collections of tools to provide rich context, collaborations with experts and/or peers for multiple perspectives and scaffolds, and constructionist projects reflecting emergent student understandings.

Lindsay and Davis' (2007) *Flat Classroom* project leverages multiple Web 2.0 tools. Middle and high school teachers around the world register their classes to discuss world-flattening concepts from Friedman's (2007) popular text examining trends that have resulted in a more connected world (e.g., Google, globalization, mobile computing, social networks). Students collaborate across schools using both asynchronous and synchronous tools such as email and Skype to compare views, and co-construct wiki spaces and video artifacts to represent their understanding in varied themes such as innovation, entrepreneurship, and play. Students must incorporate "outsourced" video segments from partner schools in their video projects to encourage further communication and collaboration. Virtual summits are convened where students share their work and receive feedback from expert judges.

Summary

This chapter provided an overview of the theoretical foundations, assumptions, and design methods that underlie many student-centered learning environments. Since the first edition of this book in 2000, significant advances have been made in articulating and researching pedagogical frameworks (Sawyer, 2006) as well as in utilizing technological capabilities to collaboratively construct, share, and represent what is learned. We have an increased understanding of the frameworks, potential problems, and design techniques associated with scaffolding the complex and open-ended nature of student-centered learning (Quintana *et al.*, 2004). Also emerging more fully in the last decade are research methodologies that have been designed to address complexities in studying interactions among teachers, learners, technology, and learning processes in the naturalistic context (Barab, 2006). Such research allows theory and design to refine simultaneously. Although considerable progress has been made to advance our understanding, many questions and issues remain. It is imperative that such efforts continue not only to ground design practices more completely but also to better understand the promise and limitations of student-centered learning environments in differentiated contexts.

References

Balasubramanian, N., & Wilson, B. G. (2005). Games and simulations. *ForeSITE, 1*. Retrieved March 25, 2011, from http://site.aace.org/pubs/foresite/

Barab, S. (2006). Design-based research: A methodological toolkit for the learning scientist. In R. K. Sawyer (Ed.), *The Cambridge Handbook of the Learning Sciences* (pp. 153–170). Cambridge, MA: Cambridge University Press.

Barab, S. A., & Duffy, T. (2000). From practice fields to communities of practice. In D. Jonassen & S. Land (Eds.), *Theoretical Foundations of Learning Environments* (pp. 25–55). Mahwah, NJ: Lawrence Erlbaum Associates.

Barab, S. A., Barnett, M. G., & Squire, K. (2002). Building a community of teachers: Navigating the essential tensions in practice. *The Journal of the Learning Sciences, 11* (4), 489–542.

Bell, P., Lewenstein, B., Shouse, A., & Feder, M. (Eds.). (2009). *Learning Science in Informal Environments: People, Places, and Pursuits.* Washington DC: National Academic Press.

Benson, L., Chambliss, J., Martinez, J., Tomasek, K., & Tuten, J. (2009). Teaching with the History Engine: Experiences from the field. *Perspectives on History, 47*(5). Retrieved March 24, 2011, from http://www.historians.org/perspectives/issues/2009/0905/

Bielaczyc, K. & Collins, A. (1999). Learning communities in classrooms: A reconceptualization of educational practice. In C. M. Reigeluth (Ed.): *Instructional-design Theories and Models: A new paradigm of instructional theory* (pp. 269–292). Mahwah, NJ: Lawrence Erlbaum Associates.

Bransford, J. D., Brown, A. L., & Cocking, R. R. (Eds.). (2000). *How People Learn: Brain, mind, experience, and school.* Washington DC: National Academy Press.

Brown, J. S., Collins, A., & Duguid, P. (1989). Situated cognition and the culture of learning. *Educational Researcher, 18*(1), 32–41.

Calder, N. (2010). Using *Scratch*: An integrated problem-solving approach to mathematical thinking. *Australian Primary Mathematics Classroom, 15*(4), 9–14.

Charsky, D., & Ressler, W. (2011). "Games are made for fun": Lessons on the effects of concept maps in the classroom use of computer games. *Computers & Education, 56*(3), 604–615.

Clark, R. & Hannafin, M. (2011). Debate about the benefits of different levels of instructional guidance. In R. Reiser & J. Dempsey (Eds.), *Trends and Issues in Instructional Design and Technology* (3rd edn), (pp. 367–382). Upper Saddle River, NJ: Pearson.

Clark, D. B., Nelson, B., Sengupta, P. & D'Angelo, C. M. (2009). *Rethinking Science Learning Through Digital Games and Simulations: Genres, Examples, and Evidence*. Invited Topic Paper in the Proceedings of the National Academies Board on Science Education Workshop on Learning Science: Computer Games, Simulations, and Education. Washington DC.

Cognition and Technology Group at Vanderbilt (1992). The Jasper experiment: An exploration of issues in learning and instructional design. *Educational Technology Research & Development, 40*(1), 65–80.

Collins, A. (2006). Cognitive apprenticeship. In R. K. Sawyer (Ed.), *The Cambridge Handbook of the Learning Sciences* (pp. 47–60). Cambridge, MA: Cambridge University Press.

deFreitas, S., & Griffiths, M. (2008). The convergence of gaming practices with other media forms: What potential for learning? A review of the literature. *Learning, Media and Technology, 33*(1), 11–20.

Dick, W. (1991). An instructional designer's view of constructivism. *Educational Technology, 31*(5), 41–44.

Edelson, D., & Reiser, B. (2006). Making authentic practices accessible to learners: Design challenges and strategies. In R. K. Sawyer (Ed.), *The Cambridge Handbook of the Learning Sciences* (pp. 335–354). Cambridge, MA: Cambridge University Press.

Friedman, T. L. (2007). *The world is flat: A brief history of the 21st century* (3rd release). New York, NY: Picador/Farrar, Straus and Giroux.

Hannafin, M. J., & Land, S. (1997). The foundations and assumptions of technology-enhanced, student-centered learning environments. *Instructional Science, 25,* 167–202.

Hannafin, M. J., Hannafin, K. M., Land, S., & Oliver, K. (1997). Grounded practice in the design of learning systems. *Educational Technology Research and Development, 45*(3), 101–117.

Hannafin, M. J., Land, S. M., & Oliver, K. (1999). Open learning environments: Foundations, methods, and models. In C. Reigeluth (Ed.), *Instructional Design Theories and Models (Vol. II)*. Mahwah, NJ: Erlbaum.

Hedberg, J. G., & Chang, C. H. (2007). The G-Portal digital repository as a potentially disruptive pedagogical innovation. *Educational Media International, 44*(1), 3–15.

Hicks, D., Doolittle, P. E., & Ewing, T. (2004). The SCIM-C strategy: Expert historians, historical inquiry, and multimedia. *Social Education. 68*(3), 221–225.

Hirsch, E. D. (2001). Romancing the child: Progressivism's philosophical roots. *EducationNext, 1*(1). Retrieved March 24, 2011, from http://educationnext. org/romancing-the-child/

Hmelo-Silver, C. E. (2004). Problem-based learning: What and how do students learn? *Educational Psychology Review, 16*(3), 235–266.

Hmelo-Silver, C. E., Duncan, R. G., & Chinn, C. A. (2007). Scaffolding and achievement in problem-based and inquiry learning: A response to Kirschner, Sweller, and Clark (2006). *Educational Psychologist, 42,* 99–107.

Hoadley, C. & Kilner, P. G. (2005). Using technology to transform communities of practice into knowledge-building communities. *SIGGROUP Bulletin, 25*(1), 31–40.

Iiyoshi, T., Hannafin, M. J., & Wang, F. (2005). Cognitive tools and student-centered learning: Rethinking tools, functions, and applications. *Educational Media International, 42*(4), 281–296.

Jonassen, D. (1991). Objectivism versus constructivism: Do we need a new philosophical paradigm? *Educational Technology Research and Development, 39,* 5–14.

Kafai, Y. B. (2006). Constructionism. In R. K. Sawyer (Ed.), *The Cambridge Handbook of the Learning Sciences* (pp. 35–46). Cambridge, MA: Cambridge University Press.

Kirriemuir, J. K. & McFarlane, A. (2003). *Use of Computer and Video Games in the Classroom.* Proceedings of the Level Up Digital Games Research Conference, Universiteit Utrecht, Netherlands. Available from: http://www.silversprite.com/

Kirschner, P. A., Sweller, J. & Clark, R. E. (2006). Why minimal guidance during instruction does not work: An analysis of the failure of constructivist, discovery, problem-based, experiential, and inquiry-based teaching. *Educational Psychologist, 41*(2), 75–86.

Kolodner, J. L. (2006). Case-based reasoning. In R. K. Sawyer (Ed.), *The Cambridge Handbook of the Learning Sciences* (pp. 225–242). Cambridge, MA: Cambridge University Press.

Krajcik, J., & Blumenfeld, P. (2006). Project-based learning. In R. K. Sawyer (Ed.), *The Cambridge Handbook of the Learning Sciences* (pp. 317–334). Cambridge, MA: Cambridge University Press.

Land, S. M., & Hannafin, M. J. (1996). A conceptual framework for the development of theories-in-action with open-ended learning environments. *Educational Technology Research & Development, 44*(3), 37–53.

Land, S., Draper, D., Ma, Z., Hsui, H., Smith, B., & Jordan, R. (2009). An investigation of knowledge-building activities in an online community of practice at Subaru of America. *Performance Improvement Quarterly, 22*(1), 1–15.

Lave, J. & Wenger, E. (1991). *Situated learning: Legitimate peripheral participation.* Cambridge: Cambridge University Press.

Lindsay, J., & Davis, V. (2007). Flat classrooms. *Learning and Leading with Technology, 35*(1), 28–30.

Linn, M. (2006). The knowledge integration perspective on learning and instruction. In R. K. Sawyer (Ed.), *The Cambridge Handbook of the Learning Sciences* (pp. 243–264). Cambridge, MA: Cambridge University Press.

McCaslin, M., & Good, T. (1992). Compliant cognition: The misalliance of management and instructional goals in current school reform. *Educational Researcher, 21*(3), 4–17.

Merrill, M. D. (1991). Constructivism and instructional design. *Educational Technology, 31*(5), 45–53.

Oliver, K., & Lee, J. (2011). Exploring history in plantation letters. *Learning and Leading with Technology, 38*(6), 24–26.

Palincsar, A., & Brown, A. (1984). Reciprocal teaching of comprehension-fostering and monitoring activities. *Cognition and Instruction, 1*(2), 117–175.

Papert, S. (1993). *The Children's Machine: Rethinking schools in the age of the computer.* New York: Basic Books.

Pastore, R., Land, S. M., & Jung, E. (2011). Mobile computing in higher education. In D. Surry, R. Gray, & J. Stefurak (Eds.), *Technology Integration in Higher Education: Social and organizational aspects* (pp. 160–173). Hershey, PA: IGI Global.

Pea, R. (1985). Beyond amplification: Using the computer to reorganize mental functioning. *Educational Psychologist, 2*(4), 167–182.

Peppler, K. A., & Kafai, Y. B. (2007). From SuperGoo to Scratch: Exploring creative digital media production in informal learning. *Learning, Media, & Technology, 32*(2), 149–166.

Perkins, D. N. (1985). The fingertip effect: How information processing technology shapes thinking. *Educational Researcher, 14*, 11–17.

Perkins, D. N. (1993). Person-plus: A distributed view of thinking and learning. In G. Salomon (Ed.), *Distributed Intelligence* (pp. 89–109). New York: Cambridge.

Perkins, D., & Simmons, R. (1988). Patterns of misunderstanding: An integrative model for science, math, and programming. *Review of Educational Research, 58*, 303–326.

Quintana, C., Reiser, B., Davis, E., Krajcik, J., Fretz, E., Duncan, R., Kyza, E., Edelson, D., & Soloway, E. (2004). A scaffolding design framework for software to support science inquiry. *Journal of the Learning Sciences, 13*(3), 337–386.

Quintana, C., Shin, N., Norris, C., & Soloway, E. (2006). Learner-centered design: Reflections on the past and directions for the future. In R. K. Sawyer (Ed.), *The Cambridge Handbook of the Learning Sciences* (pp. 119–134). Cambridge, MA: Cambridge University Press.

Roth, W.-M. (1995). Affordances of computers in teacher–student interactions: The case of Interactive Physics™. *Journal of Research in Science Teaching, 32*(4), 329–347.

Salomon, G. (1986). Information technologies: What you see is not (always) what you get. *Educational Psychologist, 20*, 207–216.

Savery, J. (2006). An overview of problem-based learning: Definitions and distinction. *Interdisciplinary Journal of Problem-based Learning, 1*(1), 9–20.

Sawyer, R. K. (2006). Introduction: The new science of learning. In R. K. Sawyer (Ed.), *The Cambridge Handbook of the Learning Sciences* (pp. 1–18). Cambridge, MA: Cambridge University Press.

Scardamalia, M., & Bereiter, C. (2006). Knowledge building: Theory, pedagogy, and technology. In R. K. Sawyer (Ed.), *The Cambridge Handbook of the Learning Sciences* (pp. 97–118). Cambridge, MA: Cambridge University Press.

Schwartz, D., Lin, X., Brophy, S., & Bransford, J. (1999). Toward the development of flexibly adaptive instructional designs (pp. 183–213). In C. Reigeluth (Ed.), *Instructional-design Theories and Models: A new paradigm of instructional theory, Volume II.* Mahwah, NJ: Lawrence Erlbaum Associates.

Spires, H. A. (2008). 21st century skills and serious games: Preparing the N generation. In L. A. Annetta (Ed.), *Serious Educational Games* (pp. 13–23). Rotterdam, The Netherlands: Sense Publishing.

Spires, H. A., Rowe, J. P., Mott, B. W., & Lester, J. C. (in press). Problem solving and game-based learning: Effects of middle grade students' hypothesis testing strategies on science learning outcomes. *Journal of Educational Computing Research.*

Spiro, R. J., Feltovich, P. J., Jacobson, M. J., & Coulson, R. L. (1992). Cognitive flexibility, constructivism, and hypertext: Random access instruction for advanced knowledge acquisition in ill-structured domains. In T. M. Duffy & D. H. Jonassen (Eds.), *Constructivism and the Technology of Instruction: A conversation* (pp. 57–76). Hillsdale, NJ: Erlbaum.

Squire, K. D. & Jan, M. (2007). Mad city mystery: developing scientific argumentation skills with a place-based augmented reality game on handheld computers. *Journal of Science Education & Technology, 16*(1), 5–29.

Stahl, G., Koschmann, T., & Suthers, D. (2006). Computer-supported collaborative learning. In R. K. Sawyer (Ed.), *The Cambridge Handbook of the Learning Sciences* (pp. 409–426). Cambridge, MA: Cambridge University Press.

Stickler, U., & Hampel, R. (2010). CyberDeutsch: Language production and user preferences in a Moodle virtual learning environment. *CALICO Journal, 28*(1), 49–73.

Whitehead, A. N. (1929). *The Aims of Education.* New York: MacMillan.

Part 2

Theoretical Perspectives for Learning Environments

2 From Practice Fields to Communities of Practice

Sasha A. Barab and Thomas Duffy

Prefatory Note

In writing this chapter we (a constructivist and a situativity theorist) struggled with the distinction between situativity and constructivism, and the implications in terms of the design of learning contexts. In clarifying (and justifying) our two sides, we created strawmen and pointed fingers with respect to the limitations of each other's perspectives. We found that although discussions of situativity and of constructivism draw on different references and clearly have specialized languages, actual interpretations of situativity and of constructivism share many underlying similarities. Further, when it comes to the design of learning contexts predicated on our respective theories, we found ourselves continuously forwarding similar principles and advocating for similar learning contexts.

We are dealing with evolving concepts—and people use new terms to include and extend old ones. Constructivism was the label used for the departure from objectivism; however, even among those who call themselves "constructivists" there are different perspectives and different sets of assumptions (see Cobb, 1994, 1995; Phillips, 1995). Now the term more commonly used is "situated," reflecting the key proposal from both the constructivist and situativity perspective that knowledge is situated through experience. In the context of this chapter, we found it trivial to distinguish among those learning theories and principles related to constructivism and those related to situativity theory. Rather, we discussed the various learning theories that have informed our understanding all under the heading of situativity learning theories. This term, and its associated assumptions and current interpretations, seemed to better capture the essence of the learning contexts we are forwarding as useful. However, even within the context of situativity theories we found it necessary to make distinctions, and it was these distinctions (not the distinction between constructivist and situativity views) that best captured the essence of this chapter.

Introduction

Currently, we are witnessing a period in which theories of learning and cognition seem to be in a state of perturbation, with numerous books and scholarly articles being published that forward radically new theories of what it means to know and learn. We have been moving from cognitive theories that emphasize individual thinkers and their isolated minds to theories that emphasize the social nature of cognition and meaning (Resnick, 1987). More recently, we have been moving to situative theories that emphasize the reciprocal character of the interaction in which individuals, as well as cognition and meaning, are considered socially and culturally constructed (Lave, 1988, 1993; Michael, 1996). In these latter situative theories (of anthropological origin), interactions with the world are viewed as not only producing meanings about the social world, but also as producing identities; that is, individuals are fundamentally constituted through their relations with the world (Lave, 1993; Lemke, 1997; Walkerdine, 1997; Wenger, 1998).

In general, situative perspectives suggest a reformulation of learning in which practice is not conceived of as independent of learning and in which meaning is not conceived of as separate from the practices and contexts in which it was negotiated. While the dominant movement over the last decade has been to a situated perspective of cognition, there has been considerable variation in our understanding of just what is meant by situated cognition or, the term we prefer, situativity theory (Greeno, 1998; Lave & Wenger, 1991; Resnick, 1987; Young, 1993). In this chapter we examine two dominant themes. First there is an approach arising from work in psychology and education that is focused on learning (or the failure to learn) in school contexts. Because of the schooling context, this work has focused on meeting specific learning objectives or content. For example, the questions that arise are how do we design learning environments to support students in learning mathematics (or learning algebra) or science (or Newtonian principles)? Here, the focus has been on situating content in authentic learner activities. In Senge's (1994) terms, we are focused on creating practice fields[1] in which students in schools engage in the kinds of problems and practices that they will encounter outside of school.

Second, parallel to the development of the psychological perspective of situativity, we have seen an "anthropological" approach,[2] reflected most heavily in the work of Lave and her colleagues. Rather than a focus on the situatedness of meaning or content, the anthropological perspective focuses on communities and what it means to learn as a function of being a part of a community. This shift in the unit of analysis from the individual's context to the community context leads to a shift in focus from the learning of skills or developing understandings to one in which, "developing an identity as a member of a community and becoming knowledgeably skillful are part of the same process, with the former motivating, shaping, and giving meaning to the latter, which it subsumes" (Lave, 1993, p. 65).

The goal of this chapter is to explore the implications of these two views of situativity for architecting learning environments. We begin with an examination of the movement from a representational view of learning to a situated perspective. We then examine the psychological perspective of situativity theories in some detail, considering the theoretical underpinnings, distinctions between this perspective and the anthropological perspective, the learning environments associated with this framework, and finally, the key principles for the design of learning environments (practice fields) associated with this group of situativity theories. We then turn to the anthropological perspective and consider how this perspective, in our view, encompasses and enriches the psychological perspective and significantly complicates the design of learning environments (from practice fields to communities of practice). We propose three characteristics of communities of practice that extend beyond those features typically found in psychologically based designs for learning. Finally, we examine in greater detail several examples of learning environments that purport to reflect the anthropological perspective on situativity, i.e., to focus on the development of self in the context of an individual's participation in a community.

Before beginning this discussion, let us emphasize two points that guide the design of this chapter. First, our focus is on schooling—we seek to understand the principles for the design of learning environments that can be utilized in schools. While the designs may require systemic change in the schools, the learning context and the motivation for learning are nonetheless framed within a school environment. Second, it is our belief that the epistemological assumptions we make and our practices are reciprocally determined. Most clearly, one's assumptions about learning and knowledge will reciprocally interact with the design of learning environments and how one participates in those environments (Bednar, Cunningham, Duffy, & Perry, 1992). It is inconceivable that a teacher or instructional designer would advocate a particular lesson or activity without at least a tacit theory of how students think and learn. In turn, however, dissatisfaction with teaching practices is likely to lead to a questioning of the epistemological assumptions on which that instruction is based. Indeed, dissatisfaction with schooling practices, along with the need for theories that account for learning that occurs outside of schools, is a major factor in the development of situativity theories.

From an Acquisition to a Participation Metaphor

Since the cognitive revolution of the 1960s, representation has served as the central concept of cognitive theory and the representational theory of mind has served as the most common view in cognitive science (Gardner, 1985; Fodor, 1975; Vera & Simon, 1993). The central tenet of the representational position is that "knowledge is constituted of symbolic mental representations, and cognitive activity consists of the manipulation of the symbols in these representations, that is, of computations" (Shanon, 1988, p. 70). Consequently, learning is "acquiring" these symbols, and instruction involves finding the most efficient means of facilitating this acquisition.

Since the late 1980s, Sfard (1998) has argued, we have been witnessing a move away from the predominant "acquisition" metaphor that has guided much of the practice in K-12 schools towards a "participation" metaphor in which knowledge is considered fundamentally situated in practice. In large measure, this epistemological shift was stimulated by a growing dissatisfaction with schooling. Learning in school was seen as resulting in inert knowledge; that is, knowledge that was "known" but simply not used outside of schools (Whitehead, 1929). Resnick (1987), in her presidential address to the American Educational Research Association, examined the practices in schools, which are predicated most strongly on the acquisition metaphor, comparing them with how we learn and use knowledge outside of schools. Her analysis focused attention on the collaborative, contextualized, and concrete character of learning outside of school, as opposed to the individual and abstract character of learning that occurs inside of schools. Arguably, it was this analysis that has served as one of the principal stimuli for the development of the participatory perspective with its emphasis on situated activity.

Shortly after Resnick's (1987) seminal work, Brown, Collins, and Duguid (1989) argued that knowing and doing are reciprocal—knowledge is situated and progressively developed through activity. Central to this theory is the contention that participation in practice constitutes learning and understanding. They further suggested that one should abandon the notion that concepts are *self-contained entities,* instead conceiving them as *tools,* which can only be fully understood through use. Reinforcing this view, Greeno and Moore (1993) argued that "situativity is fundamental in all cognitive activity" (p. 50). It is the contention from this perspective that learning involves more than acquiring understanding; instead, it involves building an "increasingly rich implicit understanding of the world in which they use the tools and of the tools themselves" (Brown *et al.,* 1989, p. 33). This understanding is framed by those situations in which it is learned and used.

The central tenets of this perspective regarding how one conceives of knowledge or of *knowing about* are the following: (a) knowing about refers to an activity—not a thing; (b) knowing about is always contextualized— not abstract; (c) knowing about is reciprocally constructed within the individual–environment interaction—not objectively defined or subjectively created; and (d) knowing about is a functional stance on the interaction—not a "truth" (see Barab, Hay, & Duffy, 1998 or Bereiter, 1994, for further elaboration on these points). This position, we feel, is consistent with the views of Clancey (1993), the Cognition and Technology Group at Vanderbilt (1990, 1993), Greeno (1997, 1998), Roschelle and Clancey (1992), Tripp, (1993), Young (1993), Resnick (1987), and Brown *et al.*, (1989). However, there is another set of discussions related to situativity theory that emphasize the situatedness of identities as well as cognitions. It is through these discussions, with their roots in anthropological circles, that we explore theories of situativity that focus on the construction of whole persons within communities of practice, not simply "knowing about" (Lave, 1997).

Discussions of situativity that have their genesis in anthropological research, including those being made by some educational psychologists (see Kirshner & Whitson, 1997, 1998), focus on learning in relation to communities of practice and provide a different perspective with respect to what is "situated" and what is constituted within an interaction. In this broadened view, what Lave (1997) referred to as *situated social practice*, there are no boundaries between the individual and the world; instead, "learning, thinking, and knowing are relations among people engaged in activity *in, with, and arising from the socially and culturally structured world*" (p. 67, italics in the original). From this "anthropological" perspective[3] it is not only meanings that are produced, but entire identities that are shaped by and shape the experience. In other words, the interaction constitutes and is constituted by all of the components—individual, content, and context. There are no clear boundaries between the development of knowledgeable skills and the development of identities; both co-arise as individuals participate and become central to the community of practice. We believe that the collection of "psychological" perspectives of situativity that were fashioned out of an interest in cognition, and the work of Resnick (1987) and Brown *et al.* (1989) in particular, constituted a decisive move away from representational theories of mind and away from didactic models of instruction. The anthropological framework further helps to enrich our conceptualization of this framework for what is meant by "situated." These two perspectives of situativity theories are described in Table 2.1. It is with this initial analysis of situativity theory that we now seek to develop principles, derived from the psychological framework, for the design of learning environments. Later in this chapter we will take a similar tack with respect to the anthropological framework.

Architecting Learning Environments: Practice Fields

Within this theoretical perspective on situativity, the unit of analysis is the situated activity of the learner—the interaction of the learner, the practices being carried out, the reasons why the learner is carrying out

Table 2.1 Focus of psychological and anthropological views of situativity theory

	Psychological views	*Anthropological views*
Focus	Cognition	Individuals' relations to community
Learners	Students	Members of communities of practice
Unit of analysis	Situated activity	Individual in community
What is produced from interactions	Meaning	Meanings, identities, and communities
Learning arena	Schools	Everyday world
Goal of learning	Prepare for future tasks	Meet immediate community/societal needs
Pedagogical implications	Practice fields	Communities of practice

particular practices, the resources being used, and the constraints of the particular task at hand. From an instructional perspective, the goal shifts from the teaching of concepts to engaging the learner in authentic tasks that are likely to require the use of those concepts or skills. As Brown *et al.* (1989) argued, concepts are seen as tools that can only be understood through use.

Designing a learning environment begins with identifying what is to be learned and, reciprocally, the real-world situations in which the activity occurs (Barab, 1999). One of those situations is then selected as the goal of the learning activity. Thus, the emphasis is on creating circumscribed "activities" or "experiences" for the learner. Consistent with Resnick (1987), these activities must be authentic; they must present most of the cognitive demands the learner would encounter in the "real world." Hence, authentic problem-solving and critical thinking in the domain is required. Learning activities must be anchored in real uses, or it is likely that the result will be knowledge that remains inert.

Senge (1994), in his discussion of the development of learning organizations, has referred to designs like this as the creation of *practice fields,* and advocates their use as a primary approach to corporate training. Practice fields are separate from the "real" field, but they are contexts in which learners, as opposed to *legitimate participants,* can practice the kinds of activities that they will encounter outside of school. Furthermore, every attempt is made to situate these authentic activities within environmental circumstances and surroundings that are present while engaged in these activities outside of school. However, these contexts are practice fields and, as such, there is clearly a separation in time, setting, and activity from them and from the life for which the activity is preparation.

Problem-based learning (PBL) is an example of one approach to creating practice fields. In the medical profession, where PBL began and is still most pervasive, the students are presented with real, historical patient cases to diagnose (Evenson & Hmelo, 2000; Koschmann, Kelson, Feltovich, & Barrows, 1996). Problem-based learning has extended well beyond the medical profession to elementary and secondary schools, business schools (Milter & Stinson, 1995), higher education (Savery & Duffy, 1996), and a host of other instructional areas. In all of these instances, the goal is to present the students with "real" societal, business, or educational problems. The PBL approach differs from studying cases in that the students are responsible for developing their own position on the issue (their solution to the problem), rather than studying someone else's solution. Thus, they are engaged "as if" they were in the real world working on this problem.

Anchored instruction, as represented in the work of the CTGV (1990, 1993), is another approach to creating practice fields. As with PBL, the goal is to capture a real problem and the context for that problem from the real world. However, in anchored instruction there is no pretense that this is an existing problem for the students. Rather, learners are invited to engage in a fictitious problem. In the Jasper Woodbury Series, rich and realistic video contexts are used to present information relevant to working on the problem. For example, in "Escape from Boone's Meadow," the students must buy into the fact that they are helping to save the eagle in the video, and in "A Capital Idea" they must adopt the idea that they are helping the students at the school develop a fall festival booth.[4] It is only when students "own" these problems that they will be engaged in the same form of problem-solving in which people in the video would engage. Of course, the method of gathering evidence and the range of distractions are considerably different from these practices in the real world. But indeed, in terms of solving the specific problems—developing the most efficient strategy for retrieving the eagle or maximizing profits from the booth at the fair—the students are engaged in solving ill-structured problems.

Cognitive apprenticeship is another approach to conceptualizing and designing practice fields (Collins, Brown, & Newman, 1989). The cognitive apprenticeship framework emphasizes learning at the elbows of experts; that is, experts are present to coach and model the cognitive activity. In reciprocal teaching (Palincsar & Brown, 1984), for example, the teacher and learner take turns in the role of student and teacher, as they seek to understand a text. Or, in the work of Schoenfeld (1996), the expert thinks aloud as he works through a novel problem and then reflects with the students on the strategies used and the paths followed.

The design of practice fields has received extensive attention over the last decade (Barab, Hay, Squire, Barnett, Schmidt, Karrigan, Johnson & Yamagata-Lynch, 2000; Barab & Landa, 1997; CTGV, 1990, 1993; Duffy and Jonassen, 1992; Duffy, Lowyck, & Jonassen, 1992; Edwards, 1995; Hannafin, Hall, Land, & Hill, 1994; Kommers, Grabinger, & Dunlap, 1996; Koschmann, 1996; Roth, 1996, 1998; Roth & Bowen, 1995; Savery & Duffy, 1996; Wilson, 1996; Young & Barab, 1999). There also have been numerous lists of principles for design since Resnick's (1987) contribution. We summarize the design principles as follows.

- *Doing domain-related practices.* Learners must be actively *doing* domain-related practices, not listening to the experiences or findings of others as summarized in texts or by teachers. The notion of an active learner has its roots in the work of Dewey (1938) who advocated for learning by doing. Schoenfeld (1996) prompted us to think further about the nature of this "doing" by considering whether students are engaged in performance dilemmas (such as getting a good grade) or domain-related dilemmas (such as finding a cure for cancer). The latter situations give rise to a more authentic appreciation for, and understanding of, the content being learned.
- *Ownership of the inquiry.* The students must be given and must assume ownership of the dilemma and the development of a resolution. That is, they must see it as a real dilemma worth investing their efforts in, and they must see their efforts as geared toward a solution that makes a difference (not a school solution). Furthermore, they must feel they are responsible for the solution. If they seek a solution from the teacher or a solution the teacher wants, they will not be engaged in the sorts of thinking in the domain that they would be engaged in outside of school (Savery & Duffy, 1996; Schoenfeld, 1996).
- *Coaching and modeling of thinking skills.* The teacher's role is not solely that of a content expert, but rather as a learning and problem-solving expert. Hence, the teacher's job is to coach and model learning and problem-solving by asking questions that students should be asking themselves. This is not directive, but rather participatory; it is based not on moving to the "right" answer, but rather, on the questions an expert problem-solver would be asking him or herself (Savery & Duffy, 1996; Schoenfeld, 1996). In part, it is the availability of coaching and modeling as well as other scaffolding (see Duffy & Cunningham, 1996), including support for reflective activities, that distinguishes practice fields from those situations in which individuals are simply doing the job.[5]
- *Opportunity for reflection.* Too often when we are engaged in work we simply do not have the opportunity to reflect on what we are doing, are going to do, or what we have done. The time demands are such that we must move forward, understanding just enough to permit progress in resolving the dilemma. However, in a practice field, opportunity for reflection must be central; indeed, it should be

central in the work environment as well. It provides the opportunity to think about why we are doing what we are doing and even to gather evidence to evaluate the efficacy of our moves. Reflecting on the experience afterwards ("debriefing" in the terminology of business) provides the opportunity to correct misconceptions and fill in where understanding was inadequate. The reflective process—an active, rigorous, and analytic process—is essential to the quality of learning (Clift, Houston, & Pugach, 1990; Schön, 1987).

- *Dilemmas are ill-structured.* The dilemmas in which learners are engaged must either be ill-defined or defined loosely enough so that students can impose their own problem frames (Roth, 1996; Savery & Duffy, 1996). It is only with ill-defined problems that students can own the problems and take ownership of the process. When working with an ill-defined problem, the quality of the solution depends on the quality of the effort in the domain. It is always possible to work a little longer in an attempt to develop a different rationale for a solution, or a more detailed solution, or to consider better alternatives. It is in this inquiry into ill-structured dilemmas that ownership and learning occurs.

- *Support the learner rather than simplify the dilemma.* The dilemma students encounter should reflect the complexity of the thinking and work they are expected to be able to do outside of the school context when this learning is completed. That is, the problem presented must be a real problem. We do not start with simplified, unrealistic problems since this would not be reflective of a practice field but rather would reflect the more traditional building-blocks approach to instruction characteristic of the representational perspective. Scaffolding is meant to support the learner in working in the practice field by providing the learner with the necessary support to undertake complex problems that, otherwise, would be beyond their current zone or proximal development (Duffy & Cunningham, 1996; Vygotsky, 1978).

- *Work is collaborative and social.* Meaning is a process of continual negotiation. The quality and depth of this negotiation and understanding can only be determined in a social environment. That is, we can see if our understanding can accommodate the issues and views of others and see if there are points of view that we could usefully incorporate into our understanding (Bereiter, 1994). The importance of a learning "community" where ideas are discussed and understandings are enriched is critical to the design of effective practice fields (Scardamalia & Bereiter, 1993).

- *The learning context is motivating.* In the educational environment, we cannot let students only pursue problems that arise in their life naturally; that is, learning issues cannot be solely self-determined. Rather, there is some need to introduce students to communities and issues or problems that engage that community. In doing so, we are faced with the problem of "bringing the issue home" to the learner (Barrows & Myers, 1993). That is, dilemmas brought to the attention of the learner are seldom engaging in and of themselves. The students must be introduced to the context of the problem and its relevance and this must be done in a way that challenges and engages the student. The importance of being challenged and engaged has a long history in education (Cordova & Lepper, 1996; Dweck & Leggett, 1988) and psychology (Csikszentmihalyi, 1990).

Extending the Participation Metaphor: Communities of Practice

Clearly, the design of practice fields, as defined above, addresses the differences of in-school learning versus out-of-school learning presented by Resnick (1987). In these contexts, learners are working in teams with concrete artifacts and examples as they address contextualized problems. The design of practice fields is consistent with the implications of situativity theory forwarded by many psychologists, and is consistent with much of the work being carried out by the authors of this chapter. More generally, this view has certainly pushed many educators' understanding of learning and cognition beyond representational views in suggesting a new contextualized emphasis to education. However, the practices that the learner engages in are still "school tasks" abstracted from the community, and this has important implications for the meaning and type of practices being learned, as well as for the individual's relations to those meanings and practices.

With respect to the practices themselves, the cultural context of schools all too often emphasizes learning and grades, not participation and use, and the identity being developed is one of student in school, not contributing member of the community who uses and values the content being taught. Lave and Wenger (1991) argued that:

> there are vast differences between the ways high school physics students participate in and give meaning to their activity and the way professional physicists do. The actual reproducing community of practice, within which schoolchildren learn about physics, is not the community of physicists but the community of schooled adults ... [As such] problems of schooling are not, at their most fundamental level, pedagogical. Above all, they have to do with the ways in which the community of adults reproduces itself, with the places that newcomers can or cannot find in such communities, and with relations that can or cannot be established between these newcomers and the cultural and political life of the community.
>
> (Lave & Wenger, 1991, pp. 99–100)

From this perspective, the main problem of practice fields is that they occur in schools rather than in the community through schools. This creates a bracketing off of the learning context from the social world through which the practices being learned are of value and of use. If one acknowledges that interactions with the world produce meaning and identity, then educators need to place more emphasis on what types of interactions and, hence, identities are being created within the context of schools. Instead of a culture emphasizing the contribution of the activity to the community, all too frequently, school culture accords knowledgeable skill a reified existence, commodifying it, and turning knowledge into something to be "acquired."

To clarify, when official channels only offer possibilities to participate in institutionally-mandated forms of commoditized activity, children develop identities in relation to their ability to engage in these commoditized activities directed towards the production of grades (Walkerdine, 1997). For some students, "good students," this helps enculturate them into the identity of a successful student (all too frequently associated with being a "nerd"), but for many others this context results in the "widespread generation of negative identities [under achievers, failures]," as well as the emergence of "institutionally disapproved interstitial communities of practice [burnouts, trouble makers]" (Lave, 1993, pp. 78–79). Indeed, in spite of the school emphasis on curriculum and discipline, it is frequently the relations to these non-curricular communities of practice that are the most personally transformative (Wenger, 1998).

While practice fields do not fully decontextualize the learning activities or the outcomes (i.e., there is a focus on more than simply the achievement of a grade), the activities are nonetheless divorced from their contribution to society—they are "practice," not "contributions." Hence, even here there is a decomposition of the activity, with the societal contribution (from which societal identity and the meaning of the activity develops) separated from the activity itself. Although this does not necessarily result in the production of negative identities, it also does not create an opportunity for membership in the community of practitioners. It is in response to these concerns that many educators are looking towards communities as an arena for learning. However, we are still in our infancy with respect to understanding the potential of, and what constitutes, a community. While Lave (1993, 1997; Lave & Wenger, 1991) has brought the most focused attention to the concept of communities of practice, this has been done through an anthropological perspective, with an examination of practices in everyday society and not environments intentionally designed to support learning.

There have been numerous efforts to introduce the concept of community into educational practice. For example, Brown and Campione (1990) proposed the design of *communities of learners and thinkers*, Lipman (1988) offered *communities of inquiry*, Scardamalia and Bereiter (1993) advanced *knowledge-building communities*, the Cognition and Technology Group at Vanderbilt (see Barron *et al.*, 1995) proposed *learning communities*, and Roth (1998) suggested *communities of practice*. However, examining these "community" efforts, we are not convinced that they do in fact capture the essence of *development of self through participation in a community*. Indeed, most appear to be in the realm of practice fields. It is for this reason that we want to re-emphasize the importance of the development of the "self," and the importance of legitimate participation as part of a community in the development of that self. We seek to promote an appreciation for the limitations of the "practice field" approach and to establish the strategic direction of making legitimate participation in the community an integral part of meeting our educational goals.

To summarize thus far, it is being argued that being a participant in a community is an essential component of the educational process, and that the community that is most clearly evident in schools is that of schooled adults, not professional practitioners who use the practices being learned. If we move toward a learning-as-participating-in-community approach, what communities are we talking about? Is this a trade school/professional school approach? How do we provide the breadth of learning experiences that our children need if they must be members of all of the communities in order to have the necessary experiences? It sounds beyond what can be managed in even a dramatic and systemic restructuring. It is with these questions in mind that we turn to a more in-depth discussion of communities of practice and their characteristics.

Characteristics of Communities of Practice

Lave and Wenger (1991) coined the term "communities of practice," to capture the importance of activity in binding individuals to communities and of communities to legitimizing individual practices. Roughly, a community of practice involves a collection of individuals sharing mutually-defined practices, beliefs, and understandings over an extended time frame in the pursuit of a shared enterprise (Wenger, 1998). Roth (1998) suggested that these communities "are identified by the common tasks members engage in and the associated practices and resources, unquestioned background assumptions, common sense, and mundane reason they share" (p. 10). Lave and Wenger defined a community of practice in the following manner:

> [Community does not] imply necessarily co-presence, a well-defined identifiable group, or socially visible boundaries. It does imply participation in an activity system about which participants share understandings concerning what they are doing and what that means in their lives and for their communities.

> (Lave & Wenger, 1991, p. 98)

Just what is a community and what characteristics of the community—of one's participation in a community—are relevant to the educational process? Predicated on research in fields such as anthropology, education, and sociology, we have found it useful to think of a community as a persistent, sustained social network of individuals who share and develop an overlapping knowledge base, set of beliefs, values, and experiences focused on a common practice and/or mutual enterprise. Building from this definition, here we discuss four features that are central to a community of practice (see Table 2.2): (1) an overlapping purpose or common enterprise, which unites, motivates, and, in part, validates the activities of the community as significant; (2) a common cultural and historical heritage, including shared goals, negotiated meanings, and practices; (3) an interdependent system, in that individuals are becoming

Table 2.2 Characteristics of a community

Common purpose or overlapping enterprise	Communities of practice tend to emerge in relation to particular purposes, with a central function of the community being to support its members in developing increasing expertise so as to more effectively realize particular goals. This purpose creates a reason for the group to function, with many of the discussions and the community learning being centered on different practices and tools that allow members to accomplish their particular purposes.
Common cultural and historical heritage	Communities go beyond the simple coming together for a particular moment in response to a specific need. Successful communities have a common cultural and historical heritage that partially captures the socially negotiated meanings. This includes shared goals, meanings, and practices. However, unlike the social negotiation of practice fields that primarily occurs on the fly, in communities of practice new members inherit much of these goals, meanings, and practices from previous community members' experiences in which they were hypothesized, tested, and socially agreed upon.
Interdependent system	Individuals are becoming a part of something larger as they work within the context and become interconnected to the community, which is also a part of something larger (the society through which it has meaning/value). This helps provide a sense of shared purpose, as well as an identity, for the individual and the larger community.
Reproduction cycle	It is important that communities have the ability to reproduce as new members engage in mature practice with near peers and exemplars of mature practice. Over time, these "newcomers" come to embody the communal practice (and rituals) and may even replace "old timers."

a part of something larger than themselves; and (4) a reproduction cycle, through which "newcomers" can become "old timers" and through which the community can maintain itself.

Overlapping Purpose

Having a shared or overlapping enterprise creates a reason for the group to function; collective discussions, practices, and tools then allow members to work towards the enterprise more effectively. Communities of practice emerge in relation to particular purposes, with a central function of the community being to support its members in developing increasing expertise so as to more effectively realize those purposes associated with the collectively-negotiated enterprise (Wenger, 1998). So, for example, a community of tailors might have as one of its purposes to make suits or to integrate technologically enhanced fabrics into designs, while a community of alcoholics might be focused on helping its members stay away from a drink (Lave & Wenger, 1991). To minimize tension inherent when members have competing agendas, the preamble in the book *Alcoholics Anonymous* (Bill W, 2002, p. 6) explicitly states: "our primary purpose is to stay sober and to help other alcoholics achieve sobriety," and tradition five further states "Each group has but one primary purpose—to carry its messages to the alcoholic who still suffers" (p. 255). In this context, the successful execution of a particular practice is not an end in itself, but instead allows members to satisfy the shared goals or purposes of the group. However, even though there might be a shared enterprise, many of the tensions in the community involve disagreements about the essential purpose of the community (and the means for carrying that out)— different members might advocate different purposes, and sometimes such disagreements result in community strife or even evolution.

To elaborate, Grossman, Wineburg, and Woolworth (2001) in their teacher education work focused on intentionally growing a teacher community, and described balancing what they refer to as the *essential tension* in building communities for learning. This tension involved balancing competing "purposes" of the community members from, for example, teachers coming together to deepen their understanding of the disciplinary content they teach versus how to best teach that content— with the former often being undervalued for teachers. In other words, the essential tension is related to balancing the two aspects of teacher development that often do not mix—one that focuses teachers' attention on improving student learning, and another on the teacher's relationship to subject matter and professional growth. The problem is that most teacher professional development does not acknowledge or support the teacher in becoming expert in the domains they teach, instead emphasizing the immediate more visible purpose of improving student learning directly and focusing professional development funds on, for example, learning how to do inquiry teaching or best practices in using technology. Such an emphasis potentially undermines the notion that teaching is a "learning profession" (cf. Darling-Hammond & Sykes, 1999) and that teachers are professionals. Instead, such a notion positions teachers as non-experts who should simply implement the textbooks as they are outlined, never engaging critically with the content or lesson.

A related danger, similar to that discussed regarding practice fields, occurs when one is intentionally designing a community to support learning—a focus of this chapter. When the focus of the community is not on supporting learners (as change agents) to have greater impact on the world, but instead on changing the learner (as objects to be changed), there is the potential to undermine the use value of the content being learned and the benefits of enlisting a community of practice model to support learning (Barab, Kling, & Gray, 2004). This is because such hybrid positioning in which members are talking about ideas, ideologies, and even purposes that are not bound up in external purpose or use scenarios creates a self-referential dialogue that lacks meaningful grounding. In this way, learning becomes a cognitive or theoretical effort, and not one that is receiving input either to constrain conceptual claims or to validate ideas and emerging expertise as having real-world relevance. Therefore, while having a shared enterprise is a core aspect of communities of practice, it is also a design challenge in that communities and their members have multiple and, at times, competing purposes—all of which can undermine the community and the power of the community model for supporting learning.

Common Cultural and Historical Heritage

A community has a significant history, a common cultural and historical heritage. This heritage includes the shared goals, belief systems, and collective stories that capture canonical practice. These shared experiences come to constitute a collective knowledge base that is continually negotiated anew through each interaction. "The negotiation of meaning is a productive process, but negotiating meaning is not constructing it from scratch. Meaning is not pre-existing, but neither is it simply made up. Negotiated meaning is at once both historical and dynamic, contextual and unique" (Wenger, 1998, p. 54). When learning as part of a community of practice, the learner has access to this history of previous negotiations as well as responsiveness from the current context on the functional value of a particular meaning.

Of course, practice fields are designed to support the development of shared goals, understandings and practices among those collaborators working on a particular problem or issue. The contrast, however, is in the embeddedness of the experiences in the community and the impact of that larger experiential context on the development of self. For example, it is through stories (narratives) that community members pass on casual accounts of their experiences to replace the impoverished descriptions frequently codified in manuals and texts. Through this telling and retelling, individuals do more than pass on knowledge. They contribute to the construction of their own identity in relationship to the community of practice and, reciprocally, to the construction and development of the community of which they are a part (Brown & Duguid, 1991).

It is also through this heritage that communities find legitimacy. When individuals become legitimate members of the community, they inherit this common heritage, which becomes intertwined with the member's identity as a community member. This is a central component in the development of self. Individuals develop a sense of self in relation to a community of practice and this can only arise by enculturation into the history of the community. They do not develop a sense of self in being a scientist simply by engaging in scientific problems, but rather through engagement in the discourse of the scientific community and in the context of the values of that community, as they become a member of the community (Bereiter, 1994, 1997). Through participation in a practice field or even as a peripheral participant to a community of practice, rules and behavior expectations may feel arbitrary, artificial, and even unnecessary. However, through participation in the community over time, one comes to accept the historical context and the importance of socially negotiated norms for defining community and one's own identity. It is only through extended participation in a community that this history and, hence, a sense of self, can develop.

Interdependent Systems

Most community members view themselves as part of something larger. It is this part of something larger that allows the various members to form a collective whole, as they work towards the joint goals of the community and its members. A community is an interdependent system in terms of the collaborative efforts of its members, as well as in terms of the greater societal systems in which it is nested. Being a member entails being involved in a fundamental way within this dynamic system (the community), which is continually redefined by the actions of its members (Barab, Cherkes-Julkowski *et al.*, 1999). In other words, the individual and the community constitute nested interactive networks, with individuals transforming and maintaining the community as they appropriate its practices (Lemke, 1997; Rogoff, 1990), and the community transforms and maintains the individual by making available opportunities for appropriation and, eventually, enculturation (Reed, 1991). Education and learning, from this perspective, involve "'taking part' and 'being a part,' and both of these expressions signalize that learning should be viewed as a process of becoming a part of a greater whole" (Sfard, 1998, p. 6).

It is through this legitimate participation in this greater community, and the community's legitimate participation in society, that communities and identities are formed. These practices, including the adoption of particular goals, belief systems, and cognitions, are ordinarily framed and valued by this greater community, and it is through the carrying out of these practices that an individual binds himself to this community. It is also in this way that learning comes to involve the building of relationships with other community members, with tools and practices, with those outcomes valued by society, and with oneself.

> Our activity, our participation, our "cognition" is always bound up with, codependent with, the participation and the activity of Others, be they persons, tools, symbols, processes, or things. How we participate, what practices we come to engage in, is a function of the whole community ecology ... As we participate, we change. Our identity-in-practice develops, for we are no longer autonomous Persons in this model, but Persons-in-Activity.
>
> (Lemke, 1997, p. 38)

However, it is not just the community members who are a part of something larger. The community itself functions within a broader societal role that gives it, and the practices of the community members, meaning and purpose.

If the community isolates itself from the societal systems of which it is a part, then both the individuals and the community become weaker— this relationship to other communities and the "products" they offer society have proven to be a central challenge for Amish and Mennonite communities, for example. "This interdependent perspective prevents communities, from small families to nations, from becoming worlds unto themselves" (Shaffer & Anundsen, 1993, p. 12). This interdependent perspective also prevents individuals from becoming worlds unto themselves. With each newly appropriated practice, individuals are becoming more central to (constitutive of) the community and, in a fundamental way, developing self—a self that is partly constituted by their participation and membership in the community of practice.

Reproduction Cycle

Lastly, a community is constantly reproducing itself such that new members contribute, support and eventually lead the community into the future. Communities are continually replicating themselves, with new members moving from peripheral participant to core member through a process of enculturation (Lave & Wenger, 1991). It is this line of thinking that led to Lave and Wenger's (1991) discussion of legitimate peripheral participation in which the primary motivation for learning involves participating in authentic activities and creating an identity that moves one toward becoming more centripetal to a community of practice. In this line of thinking, developing an identity as a member of the community and becoming able to engage in the practices of the community are one and the same (Lave, 1993; Wenger, 1998).[6]

Reproducibility, in which newcomers are able to become central to and expand the community, is essential if the community is to have a common cultural heritage. It is a process that is continually occurring in all communities of practice. Simply consider the experiences of academics: our students apprentice with us, working closely at our elbows. However, they tend to remain apprentices, seeing the world through our eyes and remaining as peripheral participants. Eventually, when they must teach others, when they must fill the role of "old timers," they enter a new level of learning and begin to expand the thinking of the community of which they are a part. They come to mentor junior faculty in the research process and in teaching. They continue to learn this process and, perhaps more importantly, grow more confident in their contributions to the community and in their sense of "self" in the community. During this process, they appropriate and contribute to the negotiation and reification of meanings. It is through this cycle that a community of practice and the individuals that constitute the community reproduce and define themselves.

It is also these reproduction cycles that define learning. In other words, the social and physical structure that defines and is defined by this cycle defines the possibilities, and what is considered legitimate participation, for learning. In fact, for Lave and Wenger (1991), legitimate peripheral participation *is* learning. Any discussions of learning, therefore, must begin within a community of practice and must consider the individual's position with respect to the hierarchical trajectory of the social and power structures of that community. Assumedly, and ignoring other social and political obstacles, it is this position in relation to the community trajectory from novice to expert that defines a particular member's ability with respect to community practices. And, "because the place of knowledge is within a community of practice, questions of learning must be addressed within the developmental cycles of that community" (Lave & Wenger, 1991, p. 100). It is in understanding how educators have supported the emergence of community trajectories and have developed scaffolds to support learners in participating in movement along these trajectories that we now move from practice fields to communities of practice.

Moving from Practice Fields to Communities of Practice

Our notion of practice fields and our notion of communities of practice have much in common, and their creation can be guided by some similar learning principles. For example, both these contexts move us away from the criticisms leveled at in-school learning by Resnick (1987). Specifically, her criticism noted that in schools there is frequently an isolated learner engaged in unaided thought using symbols that frequently have no direct connection to any real-world particulars. In contrast, while working in practice fields and in communities of practice, students are usually working collaboratively and with concrete referentials (signifieds) so that they may address contextualized problems. Further, central to both these learning contexts is the opportunity for students to actively engage in negotiating meanings through practice.

In spite of these similarities, there are also some important differences (see Table 2.1). For example, learning through participation in practice fields frequently involves students working collaboratively in a temporary (as opposed to a sustained and continuously reproducing) coming together of people (as opposed to a community of practitioners with a substantial history) around a particular task (as opposed to a shared enterprise that cuts across multiple tasks considered to be the workings of the community). Of prime importance in distinguishing practice fields from community learning contexts are: (1) whether there exists a sustainable community with a significant history to become enculturated into, including shared goals, beliefs, practices and a collection of experiences; (2) whether individuals and the community into which they are becoming enculturated are a part of something larger; and (3) whether there is an opportunity to move along a trajectory in the presence of, and become a member alongside, near peers and exemplars of mature practice—moving from peripheral participant to core member.

It is these three characteristics, which we have suggested are central to communities of practice, that determine whether there is an opportunity for learning/building identities through legitimate peripheral participation. These differences suggest the importance of supporting the emergence of communities with meaningful trajectories of participation or, at the very least, which connect learners into existing communities. Previously, we mentioned the work of the CTGV and medical fields as examples of practice fields. In this section, we will continue to examine examples to illuminate characteristics of, and differences between, practice fields and communities of practice.

The SMART Project

The work of the Cognition and Technology Group at Vanderbilt illustrates the movement from the design of practice fields to the attempt to develop a community of practice. The early work (CTGV, 1990, 1993) focused on video-based "macrocontexts" intended to overcome inert knowledge by anchoring learning within the context of meaningful problem-solving activities. In contrast to the disconnected sets of "application problems" located at the end of textbook chapters, macrocontexts refer to stories that take place in semantically rich, open-ended environments. In these anchored macrocontexts, students begin with a higher-order problem and then use top-down strategies to generate the necessary sub-goals to reach the final state. This top-down processing helps students learn the lower-level skills (i.e., mathematical algorithms and facts) in a manner that also gives them insights into the relationships between the skills being learned and the reciprocal opportunities for using them. Anchors "allow students who are relative novices in an area to experience some of the advantages available to experts when they are trying to learn new information about their area" (CTGV, 1992, p. 294).

These learning environments nicely illustrate the design of practice fields. However, through the SMART (Special Multimedia Arenas for Refining Thinking) project, the CTGV extended engagement with the problems and broke the isolation of the classroom with a learning community of 100 students (Barron *et al.*, 1995). This project, using the Jasper videodisc problems and a series of video programs, linked classrooms to each other and to the Vanderbilt community. The CTGV developed four Challenge programs composed of four segments called Smart Lab, Roving Reporter, Toolbox, and the Challenge. These segments were designed to link up the participating classrooms, grounding discussions with actual student data and video clips collected by the roving reporter as he went out to the various classrooms. At the end of the show, as a culminating event, students attempted the Big Challenge in which a problem was shown live on the local PBS-TV station. Students in the learning community were expected to call in answers to the problems and then their answers were summarized and shown at the end of the program for students to see.

The SMART program clearly moves closer to our notion of community than the isolated Jasper videos. Students are, to some degree, developing a socially-negotiated knowledge and practice base. Through the Roving Reporter, they are able to share stories about their experiences. Individuals are, to some degree, becoming a part of something larger as they see themselves and their peers as well as an expert problem-solver engaged in solving the Jasper series episodes. However, the problems are contrived and not necessarily addressing a real-world need, undermining the legitimacy of the community in terms of its interdependence with society. Further, the community itself has little common heritage. This, again, potentially limits the legitimacy of their experience in terms of being a part of something larger. Additionally, the community is formed only for the duration of the project and will not continue to reproduce. As a consequence, there is little movement over time in terms of becoming more central to the core.

In sum, while the SMART project moves toward a community concept, the key elements for the development of self in a community are absent. The project is still a school project—it does not link to or contribute to the needs of society or the on-going needs of the community itself. The students are not playing a role in society and hence do not develop a sense of their identity in society. They are not making a lasting contribution and are not developing a sense of the history of the community and all that implies. Rather, their community is a temporary one, beginning and ending with the task (or set of tasks), much as we find with practice fields. The SMART project does, however, provide a richer set of perspectives and a greater motivational context for the students to assume ownership of the task. Again, these are characteristics of practice fields.

Community of Learners

Over the last decade, Brown and Campione (Brown & Campione, 1990; Brown *et al.*, 1994) have been engineering "communities of learners." Central to this work has been the use of reciprocal teaching and jigsaw methods to engage students in collaborative work. The reciprocal teaching approach begins with the teacher modeling and coaching students in the various skills they will be expected to teach. It involves students adopting the role of a teacher, as they appropriate their practices by watching more experienced peers and teachers model the learning process. The approach is termed reciprocal teaching because the teacher and students alternate playing the role of the teacher and student.

The jigsaw method, in contrast, involves students working collaboratively and developing expertise on one component of a larger task. Then, once they have mastered their component, they use the reciprocal teaching method to share what they have learned with other group members. Using these techniques, they are able to develop repetitive structures in the classroom, so that students can gain mastery over the approaches as they perceive themselves developing mastery over time. Students participate in a research cycle lasting approximately 10 weeks. These cycles begin with a teacher or visiting expert who introduces a unit and a benchmark lesson, stressing the big picture and how the various topics can be interrelated to form a jigsaw. Students then spend the majority of the time in the research-and-teach part of the cycle. Over time, the distributed expertise begins to emerge as students become more competent in their sections. In addition to face-to-face interactions, students can use email to communicate with the wider community as well as with each other. The teacher models this practice over the course of the research cycle. At the completion of the unit, students conduct full reciprocal teaching sessions in groups where each child is an expert on one-fifth of the topic material. Two features central to Communities of Learners are distributed expertise (integral to the jigsaw method) and mutual appropriation—mutual in the sense that experts appropriate student understandings in addition to students appropriating the practices and thinking of experts.

Brown *et al.* (1994) discussed a classroom ethos in which there is an atmosphere of individual responsibility coupled with communal sharing. There is an atmosphere of respect in which students' questions are taken seriously and students listen to one another. Students also develop a community of discourse, in which "meaning is negotiated and renegotiated as members of the community develop and share expertise. The group comes to construct new understandings, developing a common mind and common voice" (Brown *et al.*, 1994, p. 200). The final aspect is that of ritual, in which participation frameworks are few and practiced repeatedly so that students develop expertise. "The repetitive, indeed ritualistic, nature of these activities is an essential aspect of the classroom, for it enables children to make the transition from one participant structure ... to another quickly and effortlessly" (Brown *et al.*, 1994, pp. 200–201).

In our mind, although the Community of Learners classrooms and the principles for community they present are exemplary, they more completely reflect the design of practice fields rather than the concept of communities that we are forwarding. There is little difference between this Communities of Learners project and problem-based learning (Barrows & Myers, 1993; Savery & Duffy, 1996) or any project-based environment where students are expected to learn collaboratively. Again, we see great value in the design of practice fields, and Brown *et al.* (1994) provided an excellent example of strategies for creating practice fields in the lower grades.

However, our goal in this section is to examine communities of practice occurring in schools in order to explore the implications of community for the design of learning environments. That is, how do we facilitate the emergence of learning environments that engage students as legitimate peripheral participants in a community, so that they develop their "self" in relation to society? The students that Brown *et al.* (1994) discussed are not engaged in tasks that contribute to a community that has a heritage or that guides practice, nor is there a community that is larger than the classroom and task. Of course the student is developing a sense of self as a learner in school and as a collaborator in school tasks and as a teacher of text information. However, we question the advantages (beyond other practice fields) of having students teach other kids, or of bringing in experts to set up a particular context when the learning occurs within the classroom context in relation to a classroom-defined task. The goal of participation in community is to develop a sense of self in relation to the society of which we are a part—a society outside of the classroom. We are not convinced that this occurs in the Communities of Learners project.

NGS Kids Network and Teleapprenticeships

The National Geographic Kids Network, a collaborative effort between the Technical Education Research Center, better known as TERC, and the National Geographic Society, is one example of a growing number of telecommunications projects that involve students in real world projects and link them to experts and other students around the world in scientific or social research. The focus in Kids Network is on socially relevant scientific issues like acid rain and solar energy.

The projects have the following design principles: (a) students can explore real and engaging scientific problems that have an important social context; (b) students do the work and engage in the discourse of scientists; and (c) the science is done collaboratively using telecommunications to link the students with others outside of their school (Tinker, 1996). Additionally, students have contact with scientists who help to interpret student-collected data and to present findings to the community. These presentations have the potential to become more than "parents' night" displays of student work, because students are talking about issues relevant to the community, and they have a rich scientific database from which to draw their conclusions.

Bradsher and Hogan, two NGS project personnel, describe the Kids Network curriculum as follows:

> Students pose and research questions about their local community, form hypotheses, collect data through experiments, and analyze results. The answers are largely unknown in advance, and the findings are of interest beyond the classroom.
>
> (Bradsher & Hogan, 1995, p. 39)

While the curriculum is considerably more structured than these descriptions suggest and the findings more prescriptive (Hunter, 1990; Karlan, Huberman, & Middlebrooks, 1997), the approach nonetheless holds potential for engaging students in real scientific problems and real scientific discourse with other students and scientists.

The Kids Network curriculum, begun in 1989, consists of eight-week curriculum units designed for fourth through sixth graders. Ten geographically dispersed classrooms (including classrooms in other countries) are linked by the Kids Network personnel to form a "research team." The students begin by reading about the curriculum area (e.g., acid rain), and discussing the issue in relation to their community. The ten classes work as a team, negotiating the approach to the research issues based on the local interests (relevance to their community) of each group. This allows for ownership and legitimacy, as well as support for the process of interdependency and social negotiation whereby groups make global comparisons. The students develop data collection tools and collect samples from their community, with experts from Kids Network available to discuss issues or offer guidance. The data are collected and submitted to Kids Network staff where they are integrated across sites. Data summaries are prepared, along with the interpretation of the data by a scientist, the latter serving to model the way scientists think (Bradsher & Hogan, 1995). The data are then sent to the classrooms. The students complete the lesson by making their own interpretation of the data, drawing conclusions relevant to the community, and preparing a presentation of the findings to a community audience.

There is considerable potential for extending the curriculum unit. As one teacher noted, "learning extends into other lessons. For language arts, students write letters to their teammates; for science they may look at ecosystems; for science and geography they use a dynamic mapping tool" (Bradsher & Hogan, 1995, p. 40). Student teams can also conduct additional experiments, collecting data on related issues and extending the web of inference. Thus, Kids Network provides a framework, and the communication technology provides the opportunity for collaboration with peers and experts on socially relevant issues. The Kids Network curriculum has been widely adopted, with more than 250,000 children from 49 different countries involved (Tinker, 1996). But, as we noted, it is only representative of a growing number of teleapprentice projects (Hunter, 1990). Two additional efforts, briefly described, follow:

- *INSITE.* This project was a joint effort among eight school districts, two universities, the Indianapolis Children's Museum, and local industry. Buchanan, Rush, and Bloede (1989, as cited in Hunter 1990) describe the goal as not creating textbook science lessons, but creating lessons that reflect current areas of concern and real-world issues. Students pose questions to the scientists (via the network) and develop cooperative experiments that require students to contact other students in the various schools. As described, this project involves students working and thinking at the elbows of experts in real-world contexts.
- *I*EARN.* Copen (1995) described the I*EARN telecommunications environment as establishing a global network, allowing "K-12 students to work on joint social and environmental projects concerning issues of international importance" (p. 44). The focus is on international linkages. Hence, classes from around the world are paired in environmental, community development, and service projects linked to their curricular goals. Clearly, the students in these projects are making significant contributions to society through their work. The practices in schools have become practices of consulting, where children can find support for their work in society. They are part of something larger—the larger community of scientists studying environmental issues and the other newcomers (other classes) to the community. And there is a heritage—the databases from their project as well as other projects.

Community of Teachers

The community of teachers (CoT) is a professional development program at Indiana University, Bloomington for pre-service teachers working towards teacher certification. It is highly field-based in that each participant is expected to commit to one school where she will do all of her fieldwork. Pre-service teachers are not assigned to a teacher, but rather spend time visiting the classes of and talking with teachers who are a part of the program. An apprentice relationship is formed with one of the teachers based on a social negotiation and a mutual determination that the relationship will be beneficial. Hence, each student is paired with a mentor teacher in their first year in the program and continues to work with that teacher for the duration.

Similarly, each student negotiates membership in a community of students who are studying to be teachers. They join an on-going community and remain a part of that community for the duration of their study. Students in the community attend seminars together and, as with any community, there are wizened veterans (seniors/students with teaching experience), newcomers (Sophomores) and levels between, mixed together in a common endeavor.

The CoT program was designed to allow students to fulfill their individual requirements for certification by becoming a part of a community. The emphasis is not on grades but on participation: "Students achieve a teaching license, not by accumulating credits and grades, but by collecting evidence that they, indeed, possess 30 qualities of good teachers that are described in CoT's Program Expectations" (Gregory, 1993, p. 1).

The CoT is founded on six principles. First is the notion of *community* and its goal is to bring a heterogeneous collection of individuals together around a shared goal. The second principle, *personalization*, has to do with students' being able to own their part in becoming good teachers. Students are also participating in *apprenticeship*s, working alongside an in-service teacher and other more competent peers. The program involves *intensive fieldwork*, with students spending approximately one full day each week with their mentor teacher. Students are engaged in *authentic performance* with the certificate predicated on their ability to accumulate a body of evidence that indicates their capacity to teach in a school. Lastly, there is a *democratic governance* with each member having the opportunity to propose a change in the program's operation that will be put to a vote.

The program involves a core seminar run by the students at all stages of preparation (from newcomer to student teacher) and supported by a university professor. The community has about 15 members who meet once a week for three hours to discuss readings, expectations, and work in the schools. Students take turns leading various seminars, planning presentations, bringing information to the group, and leading discussions related to teaching and learning. Over the course of the semester, various "issues du jour" that students are facing in the classroom are discussed. In addition to the weekly seminars, students communicate through electronic mail and the telephone. Over time, students graduate and move on and beginning teachers enter the community. Further, many former students, now teachers working nearby, return to share their experiences with the current community of teachers.

In the CoT program, students are continually negotiating goals and meanings of the community as well as the profession. Further, there is a growing collection of personal narratives that come to embody the canonical practices of the community, and students have developed a shared language to describe particular group practices (e.g., issue du jour) and group members (e.g., grizzled veterans) (T. Gregory, personal communication, July 7, 1998). The community has a tradition and heritage (seven years going) at Indiana University that captures much of the community's understandings. This heritage is continually developed and inherited by members, as they become a part of the CoT program. The community also has a trajectory that extends across multiple classrooms and multiple occasions. Individuals view themselves as becoming a part of the CoT as well as the communities (those formed by in-service teachers) in which the project is nested. Lastly, the community continually reproduces itself as "rolling cohorts" cycle from newcomers to grizzled veterans to graduated students (working teachers).

Both KidsNet and CoT characterize the sorts of communities that schools can foster and support. There is a historical context for the activity, a history of experience to be used,[7] and the results of the activity (and hence the learner/doer) contribute to the community. It is this context that keeps not only the learning but also the overall activity itself from being an end in and of itself, i.e., a commodity. As such, participants develop a sense of self in their work in society—not simply in the work of being a student. Practices are not just performances, but meaningful actions, "actions that have relations of meaning to one another in terms of some cultural system" (Lemke, 1997, p. 43). In this sense, students learn not just what and how to carry out a set of practices, but the meaning of the performance. This understanding is central to becoming a full member of the community. The fact that students have full access to the practices and outcomes, as well as a legitimate role in the functioning of the community, helps to overcome the alienation of students from the full experiences, or what Lave (1997) refers to as the "widespread generation of negative identities." It is for these reasons that we view these as exemplary models of building communities of practice in schools.

Quest Atlantis Project

An important distinction among practice fields and communities of practice, especially when intentionally designed to support learning, is in terms of what is being *situated*. We have argued that in a practice field the emphasis is on situating the content, as learners come to appreciate both the practices and concepts as well as the types of situations in which they have value—effectively converting them from facts to usable tools (Brown, Collins, & Duguid, 1989). A central tenet of this chapter is that it is just as important to position (situate) the person and the experience itself within the context of a community. Part of what makes the Community of Teachers or the NGS Kids projects so powerful is that the consequentiality of community activity is not simply theoretical or conceptual, but is bound up in a larger interdependent system that is impacted by the community practices. However, bounding up the learning process in forms that allow for the outcomes to have experiential impact or consequentiality is quite challenging to scale and to accomplish in K-12 classrooms. Further, we do not always want learners to have such impactful consequences as part of the learning process, but we do want the outcomes of learning to be meaningful beyond earning grades— potentially undermining the learners' appreciation of the content's real-world significance.

It is, in part, towards managing this challenge that the Quest Atlantis (QA) game-based learning environment was created. QA is a learning and teaching project that uses a 3D multi-user environment to immerse children ages 9–12 in educational tasks (http://QuestAtlantis.org). Combining strategies used in the commercial gaming environment with lessons from educational research on learning and motivation, QA allows children to travel to virtual spaces to perform entertaining activities (called Quests) that are also directly connected to the standards (Barab, Gresalfi, & Ingram-Goble, 2010; Barab, Thomas, Dodge, Carteaux, & Tuzun, 2005). Importantly, completion of these Quests has consequences on the game world, on one's status in the game world, and on one's positioning with other players in the multiuser environment. While the videogame world and the embedded narratives we design are clearly fictional, the dramatic agency, experiential consequentiality and multiuser environment collectively help give rise to a community of practice (Barab, Gresalfi, & Ingram-Goble, 2010). We see this environment, and the underlying design choices, as shedding important light on the challenges and opportunities of designing communities of practice to support learning in a manner that expands on the other examples in theoretically interesting ways.

The core focus of player activity is around completing Quests so as to solve fictional, yet realistic, problems and to evolve their in-game character in relation to particular conceptual ideas (e.g., water quality, measures of center, persuasive writing). Trajectories of participation and various accomplishments are structured around seven "social commitments," with the designed purpose being to foster an awareness of these critical dimensions as players make choices that simultaneously impact the virtual world as well as changing their potential (identity) to impact the virtual world (Barab, Thomas, Dodge, Carteaux & Tuzun, 2005). Bound up in this progression is set of practices, ideas, tools, and especially tasks to be solved. Each time the player solves tasks they accrue experiential currency (i.e., game lumins) and at significant junctures are able to "luminate" on the social commitments, denoting a level of expertise and at the same time unlocking new functionalities. They also become a resource for other players who they can mentor and support to solve more complex and difficult challenges.

While both practice fields and the game world as described here are somewhat removed from the real world, the game world provides important experiential consequentiality not necessary present in practice fields nor in the real world—player actions actually have consequential impact on the game space and embedded narratives (Barab, Gresalfi, Dodge, & Ingram-Goble, 2010). To be clear, player accomplishments in the virtual world actually change their own potential to accomplish more in that they unlock tools, evolve functionalities, and play-world affordances that establish a sense of transactivity (Barab, Gresalfi, & Ingram-Goble, 2010). In Dewey and Bentley's work (1949) transactivity refers to the phenomenon in which both learner and world are modified through experience, and such modification creates further possibility in a reciprocally influential set of dependencies. This transactive relationship is what bounds up communities and its members as an interdependent system and is a key experiential aspect of what we believe makes multiuser videogames like Quest Atlantis so powerful as learning environments. Additionally, in these fictional, but changeable, spaces we can support non-experts in becoming experts in the context of the game world where they are actually able to apply their emerging expertise to change situationaly relevant and personally meaningful situations even when they are still novices (Barab, Zuiker *et al.*, 2007).

As such, a videogame context can "scaffold" community membership, allowing non-experts to act a "head above themselves" (Vygotsky, 1978) as they are positioned with expert status in relation to what they can accomplish, and also to their continually growing membership status in the community. It is for this reason that Vygotsky and other activity theorists (cf. Leont'ev, 1974) described play as a "leading activity" in personal development, or why Gadamer (1989) argued that through play the individual can effectively play out consequential selves. While most child psychologists have touted the power of play and role playing in particular on emotional development (Bodrova & Leong, 2003), it is only recently and central to the "serious games" movement that we have begun to explore the power of play for cognitive development or professional growth. When we situate game play experiences in multiuser worlds where literally hundreds of thousands of members continually form multiple communities of practice, we can understand the pragmatic and theoretical power of these spaces for education and research.

Conclusions/Implications

In this chapter we have adopted a perspective of situativity theory in which meaning as well as identities are constructed within interactions. The construction of these meanings and identities is greatly influenced by the broader context in which they reside. This perspective expands previous notions of constructivism in which it was the subjective world, not the individual constructor, which was bracketed off and treated as that which was being constructed. It also expands notions of situativity theory in which, again, it was the meaning of that which was learned, and not the individual doing the learning, that was described as being constituted in the situation. Instead, the perspective being forwarded in this chapter is intended to couple individual and environment, and thereby moves beyond dualistic treatments, treating both as being constituted by and constituting the other—that is, to establish an ecology of learning (Barab, 1999; Barab, Cherkes-Julkowski *et al.*, 1999). Predicated on this assumption, we explored the notion of the communities of practice as an arena for learning that can be integrated into the practices of schools.

One difficulty with schools is that they frequently do not practice what they preach. They teach about practices of other communities, but provide students with only limited access to these external communities. As such, experience is commoditized and learners are alienated from full experiences, resulting in the bracketing off of academic performance and identity formation in relation to this performance (Lave, 1997; Lemke, 1997; Walkerdine, 1997). One attempt to address these limitations of school learning, as well as the abstract, decontextualized, and individualistic nature of school learning, is to design practice fields. In practice fields, students work as part of activity groups as they investigate and engage in practices that are consistent with the practices of real-world practitioners. Although practice fields address some of the criticisms leveled at school learning (see Resnick, 1987), they still treat knowledge as a commodity and fail to connect learners to a greater identity (i.e., a member of a community).

Lave and Wenger (1991, pp. 52–53) described a community focus as a focus on "the development of knowledgeable skill and identity—the production of persons ... [resulting from] ... long-term, living relations between persons and their place and participation in the communities of practice."[8] As such, there is no separation between the development of identity and the development of knowledgeable skill. Both reciprocally interact through a process of legitimate peripheral participation within the context of a community of practice.

This is a considerable shift in focus from the design of practice fields—a shift from a focus on the activity of an individual in a collaborative environment to a focus on the connections one has with the community and the patterns of participation in the community. It is not that a sense of self does not or cannot develop in practice fields. If successfully designed (especially in terms of developing learner ownership), the practice field not only supports the development of specific skills, but also offers the individual the opportunity to assess his or her competencies and motivation for that kind of work. Similarly, it contributes to a sense of self, as all of our experiences do. However, there is something more to membership in a community; something beyond the temporary collaborative environment of a practice field. Lave described how formal learning environments (i.e., schools) tend to commodify knowledge and learning:

> The products of human labor are turned into commodities when they cease to be made for the value of their use in the lives of their maker and are produced in order to exchange them, to serve the interests and purposes of others without direct reference to the lives of their maker.

> (Lave, 1993, p. 75)

In essence, through commodification, human activity becomes a means rather than an end in itself.

This is indeed true of practice fields. The problems, while "authentic" in the complexity they bring to the learner, are not authentic in the sense that they are an integral part of the ongoing activity of the society. This has implications both in terms of how individuals come to participate and assign meaning to the activity, as well as in terms of the identities that emerge. With the practice field, education is viewed as preparation for some later sets of activities, not as a meaningful activity in its own right. In fact, it is this reference to "something" and "someplace" else that parents, teachers, and even students use to ascribe value to that which is being taught. It is also this situation that led Dewey to criticize the educational system. Dewey (1897) argued that this is the wrong model: "I believe that education, therefore, is a process of living and not a preparation for future living" (p. 78). Further, while participating in communities of practice, the constraints on practices are present in the everyday workings of the community (e.g., more expert member practices, the demands of the clientele, contained in community-generated documents and artifacts). In classrooms, these constraints are frequently presented by one instructor (or an occasional visiting expert) who must serve as a "stand-in" for the greater community (Barab, Cherkes-Julkowski *et al.*, 1999).

In other words, a community is not simply bringing a lot of people together to work on a task. Extending the length of the task and enlarging the group are not the key variables for moving to the community concept; rather, the key is linking into society or an authentic purpose—giving the students a legitimate role (task) in society through community participation/ membership and giving the to-be-learned content consequential value. We have described communities as having four components: (a) an overlapping purpose or mutual enterprise, which unites, motivates, and, in part, validates the activities of the community as significant; (b) a common cultural and historical heritage, including shared goals, understandings, and practices; (c) individuals becoming a part of an interdependent system; and (d) the ability to reproduce work as new members alongside more competent others.

Intentionally designing community spaces to support learning as part of formal learning is not without challenges (see Barab, Kling, & Gray, 2004 for a number of such examples). Of special concern is that these spaces are often focused on producing knowledgeable users instead of producing usable knowledge. In spite of this challenge around defining purpose, as well as the more general challenge that one does not design community but instead *designs for the emergence* of community, we have found useful examples of educators enlisting the notion of community as informing a designed intervention. We also need to remember that within schools we see the emergence of many communities of practice (jocks, burnouts, musicians, etc.). In fact,

> Communities of practice sprout everywhere—in the classroom as well as on the playground, officially or in the cracks. And in spite of curriculum, discipline, and exhortation, the learning that is most personally transformative turns out to be the learning that involves membership in these communities of practice.
>
> (Wenger, 1998, p. 6)

The goals of this chapter are to further our thinking on the characteristics of communities of practice, the advantages of learning from them, and the approaches used by educators to develop them in schools. We hope that this discussion stimulates continued thinking around these questions and we look forward to educators continuing to share their work that is contextualized in learning environments that are predicated on notions of communities of practice and, just as importantly, the individual learner.

Acknowledgments

The authors would like to thank members of the Center for Research on Learning and Technology, specifically Thomas Keating and Donald Cunningham, for the valuable feedback on this chapter.

Correspondence about this chapter should be addressed to Sasha A. Barab, Learning Sciences Institute, P.O. Box 872111, Arizona State University, Tempe AZ 85287-2111.

Notes

1 Senge introduced the term "practice field" as a metaphor in relation to the practice field of sports.
2 We caution the reader to not interpret our labels "psychological" and "anthropological" as referring to disciplines or, more specifically, to individuals within disciplines; rather, we chose these labels to denote foci or the unit of analysis typically associated with the work of practitioners of these disciplines.
3 Although we will describe these contrasting alternatives as opposing views and have associated one approach more with the psychological lens and the other with the anthropological lens, it is important to note that much discussion in practice cuts across these two perspectives. For example, many psychologists rely heavily on the anthropological findings in explaining their views of situativity theory, and view whole persons (including cognitions and identities) as being created when learning. In fact, we find few explanations of situativity theory that do not reference the work of the anthropologist Jean Lave, whether these explanations are being forwarded by psychologists or anthropologists. However, many discussions of situated cognition within educational circles are still focused on contextual influences with respect to cognition and not with respect to identity creation, or the reciprocal influence of negotiated meanings, identities, and the communities through which it all emerges. Therefore, we do find the distinctions outlined in Table 2.1 to be useful in capturing some of the different interpretations of situativity theory (see Kirshner & Whitson, 1997), and in drawing out the implications for designing learning environments. We urge the reader to view these labels as denoting foci or the unit of analysis typically associated with these disciplines, and not the work of individual practitioners within these disciplines.
4 Two fictitious problems established in Jasper episodes (see CTGV, 1990, 1993).
5 But of course, decontextualizing the problem from the full community context is the overriding characteristic distinguishing a practice field from doing the job.
6 It is this opportunity to become a member of and extend the community that motivates, shapes, and gives meaning to learning the practices and negotiated meanings. This is in sharp contrast to schools in which students pass through practice fields that maintain motivation only through the exchange value (i.e., grades), not through any contribution to the community or any real-world application.
7 Let us emphasize that "experientially-based" does not mean that all learning comes from experts telling their stories. Those experts can in fact be noting what references and resources they found most useful for their own learning. It is also not that the experts have the "correct answers," but rather they have had related experiences and this is what they did (and it failed or succeeded to some degree). The main issue is that the learning is embedded not just in a task but in the history of the community.
8 Of course there is a reciprocal relation, in that through participation there is continued production and reproduction of the community. However, the present focus is on learning—the development of self—through participation in the practices of the community.

References

Barab, S. A. (1999). Ecologizing instruction through integrated units. *Middle School Journal, 30,* 21–28.

Barab, S. A., & Landa, A. (1997). Designing effective interdisciplinary anchors. *Educational Leadership, 54*, 52–55.

Barab, S. A., Gresalfi, M. S., & Ingram-Goble, A. (2010). Transformational play: Using games to position person, content, and context. *Educational Researcher, 39*(7), 525–536.

Barab, S. A., Hay, K., & Duffy, T. (1998). Grounded constructions and how technology can help. *Technology Trends, 43*(2), 15–23.

Barab, S. A., Kling, R., & Gray, J. (2004). (Eds.). *Designing for Virtual Communities in the Service of Learning.* Cambridge, MA: Cambridge University Press.

Barab, S. A., Gresalfi, M. S., Dodge, T., & Ingram-Goble, A. (2010). Narratizing disciplines and disciplinizing narratives: Games as 21st century curriculum. *International Journal for Gaming and Computer-Mediated Simulations, 2*(1), 17–30.

Barab, S., Thomas, M., Dodge, T., Carteaux, R., & Tuzun, H. (2005). Making learning fun: Quest Atlantis, a game without guns. *Educational Technology Research and Development, 53*(1), 86–107.

Barab, S. A., Cherkes-Julkowski, M., Swenson, R., Garrett. S., Shaw, R. E., & Young, M. (1999). Principles of self-organization: Ecologizing the learner-facilitator system. *Journal of the Learning Sciences, 8*(3&4), 349–390.

Barab, S. A., Hay, K. E., Squire, K., Barnett, M., Schmidt, R., Karrigan, K., Johnson, C., & Yamagata-Lynch, L. (2000). Virtual solar system project: Learning through a technology-rich, inquiry-based, participatory learning environment. *Journal of Science Education and Technology, 9*(1), 7–25.

Barab, S. A., Zuiker, S., Warren, S., Hickey, D., Ingram-Noble A., Kwon, E. J., Kouper, I., & Herring, S. C. (2007). Situationally embodied curriculum: Relating formalisms and contexts. *Science Education, 91*(5), 750–782.

Barron, B., Vye, N. J., Zech, L., Schwartz, D., Bransford, J. D., Goldman, S. R., Pellegrino, J., Morris, J., Garrison, S., & Kantor, R. (1995). Creating contexts for community-based problem solving: The Jasper challenge series. In C. Hedley, P. Antonacci, & M. Rabinowitz (Eds.), *Thinking and Literacy: The mind at work* (pp. 47–72). Hillsdale, NJ: Erlbaum.

Barrows, H. S., & Myers, A. C. (1993). *Problem based learning in secondary schools.* Unpublished monograph. Springfield, IL: Problem Based Learning Institute, Lanphier High School, and Southern Illinois Medical School.

Bednar, A. K., Cunningham, D., Duffy, T. M., & Perry, D. J. (1992). Theory into practice: How do we link? In T. Duffy & D. Jonassen (Eds.), *Constructivism and the Technology of Instruction* (pp. 17–34). Hillsdale, NJ: Erlbaum.

Bereiter, C. (1994). Implications of postmodernism for science, or, science as progressive discourse. *Educational Psychologist, 29*, 3–12.

Bereiter, C. (1997). Situated cognition and how to overcome it. In D. Kirshner & J. A. Whitson (Eds.), *Situated Cognition: Social, semiotic, and psychological perspectives* (pp. 281–300). Hillsdale, NJ: Erlbaum.

Bodrova, E., & Leong, D. J. (2003). The importance of being playful. *Educational Leadership, 60*(7), 50–53.

Bradsher, M., & Hogan, L. (1995). The Kids Network: Student scientists pool resources. *Educational Leadership, 53* (Oct.), 38–43.

Brown, A., Ash, D., Rutherford, M., Nakagawa, K., Gordon, A., & Campione, J. (1994). Distributed expertise in the classroom. In M. D. Cohen, & L. S. Sproull (Eds.), *Organizational Learning* (pp. 188–228). London, England: SAGE Publications.

Brown, A. L., & Campione, J. C. (1990). Communities of learning and thinking, or a context by any other name. *Contributions to Human Development, 21,* 108–126.

Brown, J. S., & Duguid, P. (1991). Organizational learning and communities of practice: Toward a unifying view of working, learning, and innovation. In M. D. Cohen, & L. S. Sproull (Eds.), *Organizational Learning* (pp. 59–82). London, England: SAGE Publications.

Brown, J. S., Collins, A., & Duguid, P. (1989). Situated cognition and the culture of learning. *Educational Researcher, 18,* 32–42.

Clancey, W. J. (1993). Situated action: A neuropsychological interpretation response to Vera and Simon. *Cognitive Science, 17,* 87–116.

Clift, R., Houston, W., & Pugach, M. (Eds.). (1990). *Encouraging reflective practice in education.* New York: Teachers College Press.

Cobb, P. (1994). Where is the mind? Constructivist and sociocultural perspectives on mathematical development. *Educational Researcher, 23,* 13–20.

Cobb, P. (1995). Continuing the conversation: A response to Smith. *Educational Researcher, 24,* 25–27.

CTGV, Cognition and Technology Group at Vanderbilt (1990). Anchored instruction and its relationship to situated cognition. *Educational Researcher, 19,* 2–10.

CTGV, Cognition and Technology Group at Vanderbilt (1992). The Jasper Experiment: An exploration of issues in learning and instructional design. *Educational Technology Research and Development, 40*(1), 65–80.

CTGV, Cognition and Technology Group at Vanderbilt (1993). Anchored Instruction and situated cognition revisited. *Educational Technology, 33,* 52–70.

Collins, A., Brown, J. S., & Newman, S. E. (1989). Cognitive apprenticeship: Teaching the crafts of reading, writing, and mathematics. In L. B. Resnick (Ed.), *Knowing, Learning and Instruction: Essays in honor of Robert Glaser* (pp. 453–494). Hillsdale, NJ: Erlbaum.

Copen, P. (1995). Connecting classrooms through telecommunications. *Educational Leadership, 53* (2), 44–47.

Cordova, D. I., & Lepper, M. R. (1996). Intrinsic motivation and the process of learning: Beneficial effects of contextualization, personalization, and choice. *Journal of Educational Psychology, 88,* 715–730.

Csikszentmihalyi, M. (1990). *Flow: The psychology of optimal experience.* New York: Harper and Row.

Darling-Hammond, L., & Sykes, G. (Eds.). (1999). *Teaching as the Learning Profession: Handbook of policy and practice.* San Francisco: Jossey-Bass.

Dewey, J. (1897). My pedagogical creed. *The School Journal, 543,* 77–80.

Dewey, J. (1938). *Experience & Education.* New York: Collier MacMillan.

Dewey, J., & Bentley, A. F. (1949). *Knowing and the Known.* Boston: Beacon.

Duffy, T. M., & Cunningham, D. J. (1996). Constructivism: Implications for the design and delivery of instruction. In D. Jonassen (Ed.), *Handbook of Research for Educational Communications and Technology* (pp. 170–198). New York: Simon & Schuster Macmillan.

Duffy, T. M., & Jonassen, D. H. (1992). Constructivism: New implications for instructional technology. In T. Duffy & D. Jonassen (Eds.), *Constructivism and the Technology of Instruction* (pp. 1–16). Hillsdale, NJ: Erlbaum.

Duffy, T. M., Lowyck, J., & Jonassen, D. H. (Eds.). (1992). *Designing Environments for Constructivist Learning.* Heidelberg: Springer.

Dweck, C. S., & Leggett, E. L. (1988). A social-cognitive approach to motivation and personality. *Psychological Review, 95,* 256–273.

Edwards, L. D. (1995). The design and analysis of a mathematical microworld. *Journal of Educational Computing Research, 12,* 77–94.

Evenson, D. H., & Hmelo, C. E. (Eds.). (2000). *Problem-based Learning: A research perspective on learning interactions.* Mahwah, NJ: Erlbaum.

Fodor, J. (1975). *Language of Thought.* Cambridge, MA: Harvard University Press.

Gadamer, H. G. (1989). *Truth and Method.* (2nd rev. ed.) (J. Weinsheimer & D. G. Marshall, Trans.). New York: Continuum (Original work published 1960).

Gardner, H. (1985). *The Mind's New Science.* New York: Basic Books.

Greeno, J. G. (1997). Response: On claims that answer the wrong questions. *Educational Researcher, 26,* 5–17.

Greeno, J. G. (1998). The situativity of knowing, learning, and research. *American Psychologist, 53,* 5–17.

Greeno, J. G., & Moore, J. L. (1993). Situativity and symbols: Response to Vera and Simon. *Cognitive Science, 17,* 49–61.

Gregory, T. (1993). *Community of teachers.* Unpublished manuscript, Indiana University at Bloomington.

Grossman, P., Wineburg, S., & Woolworth, S. (2001). Toward a theory of teacher community. *The Teachers College Record, 103,* 942–1012.

Hannafin, M. J., Hall, C., Land, S. M., & Hill, J. R. (1994). Learning in open-ended environments: Assumptions, methods, and implications. *Educational Technology, 34,* 48–55.

Hunter, B. (1990). *Computer-mediated communications support for teacher collaborations: Researching new contexts for teaching and learning.* Paper presented at the annual meeting of the American Educational Research Association, Boston, MA.

Karlan, J., Huberman, M., & Middlebrooks, S. (1997). The challenges of bringing the Kids Network to the classroom. In S. Raizen and E. Britton (Eds.), *Bold Ventures: Case studies of U.S. innovations in science education (Vol. 2).* Boston: Kluwer Academic Publishers.

Kirshner, D., & Whitson, J. A. (1997). Editors' introduction. In D. Kirshner & J. A. Whitson (Eds.), *Situated Cognition: Social, semiotic, and psychological perspectives* (pp. 1–16). Mahwah, NJ: Erlbaum.

Kirshner, D., & Whitson, J. A. (1998). Obstacles to understanding cognition as situated. *Educational Researcher, 27*(8), 22–28.

Kommers, P. A. M., Grabinger, R. S., & Dunlap J. C. (Eds.). (1996). *Hypermedia Learning Environments: Instructional design and integration.* Mahwah, NJ: Lawrence Erlbaum Associates.

Koschmann, T. (Ed.). (1996). *CSCL: Theory and practice of an emerging paradigm.* Mahwah, NJ: Erlbaum.

Koschmann, T., Kelson, A. C., Feltovich, P. J., & Barrows, H. S. (1996). In T. Koschmann (Ed.), *CSCL: Theory and practice of an emerging paradigm* (pp. 83–124). Mahwah, NJ: Erlbaum.

Lave, J. (1988). *Cognition in Practice: Mind, mathematics, and culture in everyday life.* Cambridge: Cambridge University Press.

Lave, J. (1993). Situating learning in communities of practice. In L. B. Resnick, J. M. Levine, & S. D. Teasley (Eds.), *Perspectives on Socially Shared Cognition* (pp. 17–36). Washington DC: American Psychological Association.

Lave, J. (1997). The culture of acquisition and the practice of understanding. In D. Kirshner & J. A. Whitson (Eds.), *Situated Cognition: Social, semiotic, and psychological perspectives* (pp. 63–82). Mahwah, NJ: Erlbaum.

Lave, J., & Wenger, E. (1991). *Situated Learning: Legitimate peripheral participation*. New York: Cambridge University Press.

Lemke, J. (1997). Cognition, context, and learning: A social semiotic perspective. In D. Kirshner & J. A. Whitson (Eds.), *Situated Cognition: Social, semiotic, and psychological perspectives* (pp. 37–56). Mahwah, NJ: Erlbaum.

Leont'ev, A. (1974). The problem of activity in psychology. *Soviet Psychology, 13*(2), 4–33.

Lipman, M. (1988). *Philosophy Goes to School*. Philadelphia: Temple University Press.

Michael, M. (1996). *Constructing Identities*. Thousand Oaks, CA: Sage.

Milter, R. G., & Stinson, J. E. (1995). Educating leaders for the new competitive environment. In G. Gijselaers, S. Tempelaar, & S. Keizer (Eds.), *Educational Innovation in Economics and Business Administration: The case of problem-based learning*. London: Kluwer Academic Publishers.

Palincsar, A. S., & Brown, A. L. (1984). Reciprocal teaching of comprehension-fostering and monitoring activities. *Cognition and Instruction, 1*(2), 117–175.

Phillips, D. C. (1995). The good, the bad, and the ugly: The many faces of constructivism. *Educational Researcher, 24*(7), 5–12.

Reed, E. S. (1991). Cognition as the cooperative appropriation of affordances. *Ecological Psychology, 3*(2), 135–158.

Resnick, L. B. (1987). Learning in school and out. *Educational Researcher, 16*, 13–20.

Rogoff, B. (1990). *Apprenticeship in Thinking: Cognitive development in social context*. New York: Oxford University Press.

Roschelle, J., & Clancey, W. J. (1992). Learning as social and neural. *Educational Psychologist, 27*, 435–453.

Roth, W.-M. (1996). Knowledge diffusion in a grade 4–5 classroom during a unit of civil engineering: An analysis of a classroom community in terms of its changing resources and practices. *Cognition and Instruction, 14*, 170–220.

Roth, W.-M. (1998). *Designing Communities*. Dordrecht: Kluwer Academic Publishers.

Roth, W.-M., & Bowen, G. M. (1995). Knowing and interacting: A study of culture, practices, and resources in a grade 8 open-inquiry science classroom guided by a cognitive apprenticeship metaphor. *Cognition and Instruction, 13*, 73–128.

Savery, J., & Duffy, T. (1996). Problem based learning: An instructional model and its constructivist framework. In B. Wilson (Ed.), *Constructivist Learning Environments: Case studies in instructional design* (pp. 135–148). Englewood Cliffs, NJ: Educational Technology Publications.

Scardamalia, M., & Bereiter, C. (1993). Technologies for knowledge-building discourse. *Communications of the ACM, 36*, 37–41.

Schoenfeld, A. (1996). In fostering communities of inquiry, must it matter that the teacher knows the "answer"? *For the Learning of Mathematics, 16*(3), 11–16.

Schön, D. A. (1987). *Educating the Reflective Practitioner.* San Francisco, CA: Jossey-Bass.

Senge, P. (1994). *The Fifth Discipline Fieldbook: Strategies and tools for building a learning organization.* New York: Doubleday.

Sfard, A. (1998). On two metaphors for learning and the dangers of choosing just one. *Educational Researcher, 27,* 4–13.

Shaffer, C. R., & Anundsen, K. (1993). *Creating Community Anywhere: Finding support and connection in a fragmented world.* Los Angeles, CA: Tarcher/ Perigee.

Shanon, B. (1988). Semantic representation of meaning: A critique. *Psychological Bulletin, 104*(1), 70–83.

Tinker, R. F. (1996). *Telecomputing as a progressive force in education.* Unpublished manuscript. Concord, MA: Concord Consortium.

Tripp, S. D. (1993). Theories, traditions, and situated learning. *Educational Technology, 33,* 71–77.

Vera, A. H., & Simon, H. A. (1993). Situated action: A symbolic interpretation. *Cognitive Science, 17,* 7–49.

Vygotsky, L. (1978). *Mind in Society: The development of higher psychological processes.* Cambridge, MA: Harvard University Press.

W, Bill (2002). *Alcoholics Anonymous: The story of how many thousands of men and women have recovered from alcoholism* (4th rev. edn). New York: Alcoholics Anonymous World Services.

Walkerdine, V. (1997). Redefining the subject in situated cognition theory. In D. Kirshner & J. A. Whitson (Eds.), *Situated Cognition: Social, semiotic, and psychological perspectives* (pp. 57–70). Mahwah, NJ: Erlbaum.

Wenger, E. (1998). *Communities of Practice: Learning, meaning, and identity.* Cambridge, MA: Cambridge University Press.

Whitehead, A. N. (1929). *The Aims of Education and Other Essays.* New York: MacMillan.

Wilson, B. (Ed.). (1996). *Constructivist Learning Environments: Case studies in instructional design.* Englewood Cliffs, NJ: Educational Technology Publications.

Young, M. (1993). Instructional design for situated learning. *Educational Technology Research and Development, 41,* 43–58.

Young, M. F., & Barab, S. (1999). Perception of the raison d'etre in anchored instruction: An ecological psychology perspective. *Journal of Educational Computing Research, 20*(2), 113–135.

3 Designing Model-Based Learning Environments to Support Mental Models for Learning

Pablo Pirnay-Dummer, Dirk Ifenthaler, and Norbert M. Seel

Introduction

Human reasoning plays a huge part in the process of learning. The principles of systematic errors, human heuristics, and reasoning itself steer the learner through content and skill (see Gilovich, Griffin, & Kahneman, 2002; Seel, 1991; Tversky & Kahneman, 1974). Of the common kinds of expertise, (1) manual, (2) cognitive, (3) academic/complex, and (4) artistic (Gruber, 1994; Gruber & Ziegler, 1993), the middle two are of particular interest for model-based and model-oriented learning environments (Pirnay-Dummer, 2006). These fields of expertise gain the most from the reasoning processes involved in the learners' model building. General psychological and epistemological principles help the learners to understand and design learning environments that are considered to have a high impact on their belief system and the development of expertise (Seel, 2003; Seel & Schenk, 2003). In this chapter we introduce the concept of mental models and how they work within the individual learning processes. We then show how learning environments may correspond to the workings of individual mental models, and we show what we believe are core design principles for model-oriented learning environments. We conclude with several different examples as characteristics for working environments from our own work to show common and specific ways to apply the design principles in practice.

Mental Models

Imagine we visit a new country, and since it does not really exist without the scope of this oversimplified example, we call it "Exampleland". As we drive in the streets we notice something odd: all the cars drive on a red traffic light and stop on a green light. This is obviously not how we expect it to be. Since we are also driving a car in local traffic, we immediately need to adapt to how the world differs from our expectations. Maybe, in Exampleland the code of the traffic lights is just inverse. Maybe, the inhabitants of Exampleland have a different perception of color (we notice, that some trees do have a red color). Maybe, they change the traffic regulations every Tuesday because they believe that rigid rules make them less flexible in their thinking. Maybe, they changed it from the international standard set of codes, because the last conqueror of their country implemented the traffic system very rigorously and the inverse traffic lights became their symbol of rebellion before they succeeded to retake their country. Maybe, stopping on the color red is highly counterintuitive for them because red culturally stands for movement, and they have far less accidents this way. This list could obviously go on indefinitely. The truth is: even in such a very simple situation that can be resolved easily, we cannot immediately know for sure why the traffic lights are encoded differently, but we can (and need to) adapt instantaneously if we do not want to get hit by the next car – despite that we cannot know the real reason for sure. To do so, we always start with what we have learned and try to reconstruct our thought and knowledge on that basis in order to adapt to new situations (see Piaget, 1976; Seel, 1991).

The above lists of solutions suggest that a non-expert in cultural anthropology tried to make sense of the situation and constructed possible solutions from his or her world knowledge: at least one mental model of the situation was created. Within the simplified example, we would not really have to know *why* the traffic lights are different as long as we know *that* they are different. But within the adaptation-process the human mind cannot circumvent the individually reconstructed reasons – they *might* be relevant to the situation. More importantly, the situation does not make much sense without at least some explanation. And once the representation of the world drops its sense, then (expectedly) the decision-making and behavior get more and more chaotic – or at least less foreseeable. The basis for the immediate adaptation of knowledge is a representation within the individual's mind. If it corresponds to something already known, we consider it a schema. In this case no adaptation is needed or done. If an adaptation of some internal aspects of the situation or task is needed, then the system creates a mental model. A mental model may consist of any kinds of knowledge, among them also existing schemata. A mental model is an idiosyncratic (specific to the individual) representation of a fact or a thing, of ideas or more generally an ideational framework about something interesting in the world. Mental representations are widely viewed as having a language-like syntax and a compositional semantic (see Carruthers, 2000; Fodor, 2003; Margolis & Laurence, 1999; Pinker, 1994; Strasser, 2010). Mental models, as types of representations, rely on language and use symbolic pieces and processes of knowledge to construct a heuristic for a situation (see Johnson-Laird, 1983; Schnotz, 1994; Schnotz & Preuss, 1997; Seel, 1991). Their purpose is heuristic reasoning which leads to either intention, planning, behavior or to a reconstruction of cognitive processes (see Piaget, 1976). Mental models may contain different sets of components and along with their purpose ranging from visual and special-analogue representations to semantic (symbolic) representations, may contain abstract and concrete aspects. In short, they provide the mind with a suitable basis (world-representation) for reasoning and decision-making. Given the task they may contain and make use of procedural and declarative knowledge. Mental models do not need to be true in an ontological sense, but they raise a sufficient amount of plausibility within the individuals who rely on their decision and act on them. People construct mental models to match the behavior of both predictable and unpredictable changes in the world in order to exercise better control and make the changes more predictable to them. This also is a key aspect of problem solving and complex problem solving (Ceci & Ruiz, 1992; Jonassen, 2000; Just & Carpenter, 1976; Seel, Ifenthaler, & Pirnay-Dummer, 2008; Spector, 2006).

The fact that the mind is incapable of not constructing representations to explain behavior in the world (see Seel, 1991) may be utilized for learning and instruction: the most interesting points of intervention are where the world does not meet parts of the learners' expectations. This goes along with the question: How do we construct a world for the learner (a model-based learning environment) that is likely to induce the model building process within the learner?

Designing Model-Based Learning Environments

In model-based and model-oriented learning environments two kinds of models need to be considered: (1) the model of the learning goal, which represents the expertise, set of skills, or, in general, the things to be learned and (2) the model within the learner that is constructed and retained in dependence on the learning environment and on the basis of the current epistemic beliefs active within the learner, i.e., whether and how the learner usually explains parts of the world. We will abbreviate the first type as the LE model (model of the learning environment) and the second as the L model (model of the learner), always assuming that the two types are closely intertwined, especially in well-designed learning environments (Figure 3.1).

The educational system (meso- and exo-system) and the learners have different influences on the learning goals at different times. The learning goals constitute the constraints for the learning environment. The learning environment is a manifestation (a derivative) of the LE model. Possible and available learning environments (technology and/or best practices) influence the system by setting the boundaries for what is possible – and decidable as regards educational planning. The learner has influence on the learning environment (as more or less pre-structured by its design). Learning takes place as soon as the LE model and the L model interact.

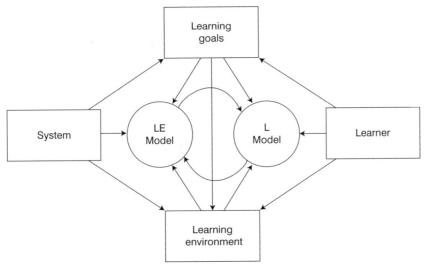

Figure 3.1 LE models and L models and instructional factors

During that time, the learning goal influences and guides the interaction between the two models.

LE model-oriented technologies usually focus on the L model while model-centered technologies concentrate more on the LE model. It is our understanding that the two (very similar) approaches will always go hand in hand and influence each other. Thus, mainly for practical reasons we decided to assume a working synthesis for this chapter.

Seven Principles

We introduce seven principles for designing model-based and model-oriented learning environments that we believe to be the most important guidelines for creating working learning environments. We herein use the above-described notion of L and LE models to distinguish between the learners' model (L) and the model driving the learning environment (LE).

1 Analytical access – proper sources for the LE model
2 Epistemic access – the matching of the L model and LE model and the processes of curiosity
3 Cognitive conflict and puzzlement – to induce change in belief
4 Diversity of surfaces – to induce generalization and transfer
5 De-contextualization – to stabilize (and limit) generalization and transfer
6 Multiplicity of goals and performance evaluation – to allow development and tracking of understanding
7 Diagnostic access to learning (i.e., to change) – to monitor the process of learning.

Analytical Access

Analytical access to the LE model is the starting point. It connects the goals to the actual states by describing either a gap or a potential, starting always with the learner and his or her prior knowledge and skills. Then, a complete construct of what is to be learned is described, as well as how it is to be learned and what the learner may take from the learning experience. Most of the time, experts are consulted at this point. Besides the explicit knowledge they can refer to, their implicit knowledge is also important. Thus, just asking them about the skills and knowledge does not suffice and yields problems, mainly during design and development later on. Acquiring knowledge from experts that is structured so it can be used for design directly is an endeavor which is often underestimated. Methods of cognitive task analysis have shown some promising results (see Means, 1993) but still leave each individual development of LE models as a complex task for LE designers. In general, four perspectives are needed from the experts:

1   Their understanding prior to the task
2   Their verbalization (e.g., by thinking-aloud protocol) during the task
3   Their reflection after the task (e.g., as a form of debriefing)
4   Their retrospective when confronted with the process of the task (i.e., their comments on a video recorded during the task or on others' behavior while they perform).

For methodological reasons, (ii) and (iv) should not use the same situation: an expert should not give a retrospective on a task for which he or she has already gone through the effort of providing a think-aloud protocol. The raw protocols of all phases need to be edited (or even translated) for the designers to gain a real understanding of the processes. Also, the experts need training in verbalizing their processes and they also need to be reminded to focus not only on the actions themselves but also on why they took them and how they came to a particular decision.

Epistemic Access

The learners' actual knowledge and skills are part of the personal episteme which is their belief network. The learners' episteme holds all the facts and things that they picture to themselves as being either true or at least valid for their actions. The fact that the learners have certain beliefs in relation to the subject matter when they enter the learning environment needs to be taken into consideration before one creates it – even more so when the learning environment is to address an inhomogeneous group, i.e., with learners who differ in their beliefs. The effects of epistemic differences can be illustrated by the following very simple example. Suppose a conspiracy theorist wants to explain his thoughts on the world to a critical audience, e.g., about UFO sightings (Figure 3.2).

Figure 3.2 UFO sightings – are they for real?

If he wants to be successful at all, he needs to start with common ground, which may take the form of a small set of common understandings. If he instead includes too many aspects that aren't there just because he considers them common knowledge, his LE model will fail. Not only will his audience still not believe what he's saying (which would probably be the case anyway), but they would most certainly also not be able to understand his perspective at all – even hypothetically: How can somebody who already makes false assumptions say anything of value? The same holds true the other way around. Imagine an astrophysicist before an audience of conspiracy theorists – also not a very unlikely event. She'd need to start with the common beliefs of her audience. By just rejecting their current thought constructions, the best she could hope for would be a weird reaction.

Of course, these are oversimplified examples that are not at all that simple in reality. New knowledge needs to be constructed on the basis of what is already there – this holds true for every learning experience. The example also shows that it is not only the knowledge itself that is important but also the way of thinking, since not all schools of thought are as strict as in science and research. Thus, an agreement – or at least mutual understanding – on that level is necessary if one wants the learner to construct something useful. It should be very clear by now why it is so important to have knowledge on where learners currently stand with their knowledge – to know about their episteme.

But the aspects of different belief sets do not only work for different everyday beliefs. A quick look at a common misunderstanding about electric current shows the same effects for school education. At some point it will become important to understand the difference between the electrical charge and the energy flow. At school, however, we are initially provided with some analogy (e.g., water pipes or air flow) that does not allow the concept of charge flowing in the opposite direction as energy. But of course the flow of charge may be changed at a high frequency and energy will still flow in just one direction (AC, single-phase alternating current). Thus, students who learned on the basis of a simple-flow analogy need to find a learning environment where they can either use or confront their initial model and find and construct new aspects by starting with their *current* beliefs. Moreover, just somebody (e.g., the teacher) stating that there is something new to be learned does not help much in the process. At best, the learners then construct a new set of ideas with only few connections to their old beliefs as a set of semantic contrasts, maybe only for the sake of passing a test. Also simply reminding them of the "old way" of looking at things – with the intention to activate their prior knowledge – would not do the trick. Then of course, in the sequence of learning events, the oldest belief-constructions are the most stable ones when it comes to reasoning, because they would then be the only ones that were constructed by the learner in order to plausibly explain behavior within the world. Thus, we could conclude that the learner necessarily needs a real-world experience in order to learn. Although there will be benefits from a real experience, this does not deplete the means of dialogue or presentations. These methods would also have to come with explicit opportunities to confront the old beliefs or to construct new aspects into them.

Model-oriented learning environments always come with a learning culture that allows for fuzziness and uncertainty with regard to decisions as well as knowledge. If learners are confronted early on with the notion that a certain set of knowledge and skills has a range of uses and can always be improved upon, changed, and reorganized, then they will also be more open towards a "date of expiry" or constraints in how what they learn can be used (Pirnay-Dummer, 2006; Seel, 1991). Also important is the role of prior and current learning experiences as well as their general and specific connotations and the particular learning instance: if the learner has had two bad experiences with simulations before, he or she may not be happy to enter into another one – no matter how well it may be designed or how appropriate for the cognitive demands.

Cognitive Conflict and Puzzlement

Now that we may know more about the learner and his or her goals, potentials, and preconditions, we want to induce learning. The third principle aims at the change of knowledge and skill within the learner. If the goals carry something really new for the learner, this means that the learner will have to let go of currently existing beliefs about the subject matter. And these situations are a key indicator for the use of model-based learning environments. They provide a good chance for knowledge change. In order to be successful in this regard, the learning environment needs to induce puzzlement or cognitive conflict (e.g., Aïmeuer, 1998; Cooper, 2007; Schnotz & Preuss, 1997) by carefully introducing a set of facts that are at first contradictory to that which the learner believes. This can be done by means of a carefully designed dilemma, a simulation, or also within cases, in short anything that might convey or support insight into the new knowledge while contradicting the learner's prior beliefs. In general, learners need puzzlement or cognitive conflict to construct new knowledge over their prior existing structures – aside from the fact that, even after a complete and successful learning cycle, the "old knowledge" stays and may still be activated by the learners should an unexpected situation arise that requires knowledge on the subject. Learners need substantial and individual feedback during the cognitive conflict. Without feedback the learner will construct just any model as long as it provides plausibility. Thus, the chances will be high that the learner will just trade one misconception for another. Sufficient learner-oriented feedback on his or her progress is the only way to lower that risk. But even with very closely monitored and applied feedback, the chance for misconceptions is still there. One reason for this is that the learner will interpret many aspects of a given environment or example as important – often too many of them. To construct a good cover story (e.g., for cases), additional circumstantial information needs to be introduced into the case in order to make the case interesting as a narrative – since there is no such thing as an interesting narrative that carries only important information but nothing circumstantial. While in cognitive conflict and with knowledge structures that are subject to change, the learners are not instantly able to distinguish between important and circumstantial aspects.

Diversity of Surfaces

Aside from feedback, multiple similar learning experiences are needed in order to consolidate the learning experience (Aebli, 1991). Thus the learning environment needs to either change the sequence of events, the perspective (e.g., through multiple roles or cover stories), the time on task, or even its immediate goals – goals inherent to the environment (e.g., "rescue a maiden" or "consult with a city planner") – while at the same time not losing sight of the learning goals. Repeating the same path through a learning environment over and over again stabilizes both the misconceptions and the intended knowledge alike and should therefore be avoided within model-based learning environments. Once more, with the proper feedback at hand learners gain a flexible use of their new knowledge if they are instructed to conduct deep comparisons of the differences and similarities between different tasks within the environment (Catrambone & Holyoak, 1989; Spiro, Feltovich, Jacobson, & Coulson, 1992). Thus, the stable aspects will be separated from the dynamic and complex ones *by the learner* – as opposed to *for the learner*.

De-contextualization

A learning environment always comes with a context. And as context is particularly important for the learning process and for the learning outcome within the puzzlement and orientation of model-based and model-oriented learning environments (Schnotz & Preuss, 1997; Seel, 2003), it needs to be considered properly. In many cases (e.g., simulations) the learning experience is not a real-life experience. Dealing with the LE models is not entirely like dealing with the real world. In fact, even in the design process there are two transfers involved (see Wein, Willems, & Quanjel, 2000):

1   The first is the transfer from the real world to the analytical knowledge that some experts have about the world. The analytical knowledge is therefore with certainty less complex than the world, due to simplifications and incompletion.
2   The second transfer has to do with the expert knowledge that makes it into the learning environment (LE model). The expert necessarily synthesizes this knowledge and offers it in abbreviated form in the LE model, because the learner cannot grasp all there is to know in a single environment, task, or simulation. Moreover, the analytical model has to be constrained to the LE model (synthesis) to run feasibly, e.g., as a simulation (see Figure 3.3). The learning experience takes place on the LE model design level. Conclusions made by the learner are made on that level. The learner then needs to take steps to reconnect his or her behavior to the real world – which is different from the learning environment.

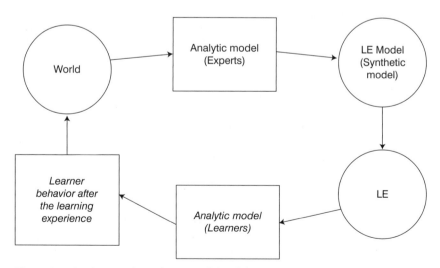

Figure 3.3 Analytic and synthetic models of the domain

Due to the two-level gap created by the designed nature of model-oriented learning environments, it is important for learners to de-contextualize what they have learned in them. De-contextualization means that the learner abstracts the knowledge during the learning experience. In contrast to *abstract knowledge* per se, which has never been interpreted before in a particular context, abstracted knowledge is not presented in an abstract way to the learner but rather *abstracted by the learner* after a concrete learning experience (e.g., Adams, 1989). The opportunity for de-contextualization needs to be embedded into a learning environment. It means that a part of the learning experience should help the learner to abstract the knowledge on his or her own. This can be done in a well-designed debriefing (e.g., for simulations), but it does not suffice to just prompt the learner to do it. In most cases, de-contextualization requires a dialogue between learners and experts in order to induce reflection, as well as a dialogue among the learners themselves focusing specifically on possible misconceptions or different interpretations. But a moderated discussion is also only an opportunity and does not necessarily mean that de-contextualization will take place. In most settings, learners need additional (meta-cognitive) training on how to conduct such reflections properly.

Multiplicity of Goals and Performance Evaluation

There are two kinds of performances within learning environments, especially within games and simulations, which may get confused during evaluation. The first is easy to predict: if an expert explores the environment, then he or she will obviously put in a good performance – unless the design has an LE model that does not correspond to the analytical model at all, a pure game of luck in other words. Once there is something systematic to the design, then experts will perform well when running the environment on their own. The second kind of performance is very similar on the behavioral level: it is the learners' performance that might improve over time. Given that the learning goals correspond to expertise, or more precisely to the experts' behavior, this design expectation, which lays the foundation of the learning environment, may create the illusion of behavior that is caused by understanding.

Unless there is no possible *other path* to successful behavior, it cannot be assumed automatically that a good performance by the learner (e.g., by means of in-game performance measures) was actually caused by real understanding. However, well-designed learning environments make use of exploration and curiosity in many ways – hopefully because this influences the learning experience, which is about more than just knowledge. Its connotations form the basis for subsequent learning experiences and also for the application of knowledge. Thus, that which would be a good design for research on ongoing understanding may not be a good learning environment: the content and the freedom to explore different approaches may make it difficult for the teacher (and researcher) to explicitly track the understanding of the learners by means of in-game performance alone and be certain that it really is based on understanding. In other words, a learner's performance may be based on understanding or on something else (e.g., trial and error or some other unintended heuristic). If the real application of the knowledge would be exactly the same as in the learning environment, the latter could still be useful – after all, who cares if a wrong or abbreviated model leads to the right behavior on the job? Considering the differences between the analytical model and the LE model, this assumption carries an underspecified danger: even in a skillfully designed LE model the abbreviations have blind spots towards the analytic model, and even more so towards the real world. Thus, even if the cause of the expert performance within the learning environment is undoubtedly experience and knowledge, the learners' actual understanding may be overstated by his or her performance.

Two aspects follow from the above assumptions:

- It does not suffice to track understanding by performance measures only.
- The learning environment needs to provide a multiplicity of possible options and goals in the same way that the surface of real-life tasks would present themselves to the future experts, especially in cases where complexity plays a key role in real-life tasks.

Simple or simplified tasks may still be used to introduce expertise to the learners. But the larger the gap between the LE model and the analytical model is, the more care is needed in tracking the understanding of the learner – to make sure that they do not base large parts of their behavior on hidden misconceptions. A closer look at the diagnostic access to learning will help to set the boundaries for a successful development of understanding.

Diagnostic Access to Learning

Mental models are constructed ad hoc (on the fly) for a given purpose, usually strongly influenced by the task and context. They are involved in the learning process and are a means of reasoning, i.e., they help the learner understand and reflect on the environment. By coming to their own conclusions, the learners learn. Because mental models are not stable mental constructions, they cannot be the ends of learning; they are rather the means of learning. They help the learning proceed from the current mental model to the knowledge and skills described in the goals – assuming that the goals are at all reachable for the learner with the given time and other resources. In many cases – and not only in research – it is mandatory

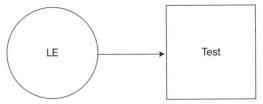

Figure 3.4 Simple post-learning test

to know something about what is going on in the learner during learning. Not only may this understanding help one to track down possible sources and concrete learning experiences that lead to misunderstanding or misconceptions on the way through the learning environment; but the insight into the process will also help tremendously with the designing and redesigning of good learning environments.

The assessment that is usually done is based on some more or less flexible criteria. In order to find out whether somebody *has learned* something, we test whether he or she *knows something*. In many cases it may suffice to know with respect to qualification and professional access whether somebody knows the right things and whether he or she can apply them. Figure 3.4 shows this simplest of all evaluations.

However, tests (e.g., exams) like this do not say anything about *what* or even *if* somebody has learned due to a learning environment. They only evaluate whether somebody knows something – or in the case of a multiple-choice test, how many errors somebody makes when given a limited set of tasks or questions. In order to circumvent this, a general strategy is to pre- and post-test a learners' abilities – which gives us a better idea of what the learner does not know. By using two measurement times, we know whether his or her abilities have changed (see Figure 3.5).

Of course, we need a control group in order to determine whether that change was due to simple development or due to the learning environment – an aspect that leads to control group designs in research settings and that should also be considered more often in evaluation. Pre-post designs are the best way to figure out if and what somebody might have learned.

If we want to say anything about what happens to the learning in the ongoing process within a learning environment, then pre-post tests do not suffice: with the pre-post procedure, we can only speculate about what happened in between. Thus, when it comes to figuring out how the learning takes place, we always need to investigate multiple time points. This is particularly true of model-oriented learning environments, where non-linear development of skill and knowledge is the rule (e.g., Ifenthaler, Masduki, & Seel, 2011).

Testing multiple times (see Figure 3.6) has its own impact on the resources needed that are – in classical settings – implemented aside from the learning experience. Outside of the research lab, it may be helpful to

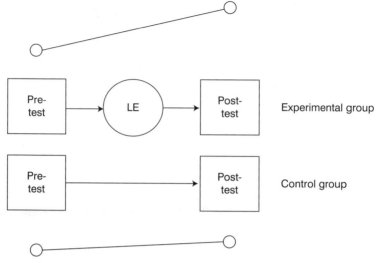

Figure 3.5 Pre-post test designs

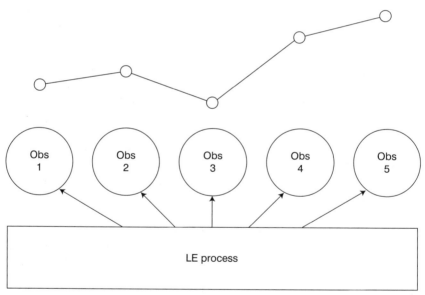

Figure 3.6 Learning process-oriented designs

incorporate the assessment into the learning experience and, moreover, to make it part of the environment and use it to support learning. Depending on the learning setting, this may be done with all kinds of non-reactive methods that are part of the environment (Zimmerman & Schunk, 2001, assessment-tasks embedded into the gaming experience). Should more complex processes need to be observed, then design experiments or various enhanced versions thereof may be helpful (see Brown, 1992; Pirnay-Dummer, 2008). With more complex assessment designs, it becomes more and more important to know about the constraints of the assessment as well – to know what can be derived from the method and data and what limits there are. At the same time, it is important to be as careful as possible with the amount of data collected: not every covariate may really be needed. The focus is provided – as very often – by the underlying theory, which needs to support the assumptions of the L model, the design of the LE model, and the evaluation of learning and transfer.

Model for Designing Model-Based Learning Environments

There are many approaches to world-like complexity. Sometimes the resources or instructional means require an approach that can be integrated into classical settings of learning. Learning tasks provide a variety of opportunities to think things through differently, especially if they require a change of reasoning or thought. In learning environments of all kinds it has always been a challenge to provide learners with the right cases and tasks to train their abilities for transfer (Biggs, 1999; Seel, 1992). There are collections of tasks available to teachers for numerous topics. Some of them are of course more oriented towards assessment (Resnick & Resnick, 1996). But there are also collections which aim at tasks that support learning (Danielson & Marquez, 1998; Willis, 2005). Complex tasks with a real surface are often needed to train a real situation (Savery & Duffy, 1996). System-oriented approaches favor a task generation with multiple analysis and design phases that correspond to both the domain and abilities or knowledge goals (Zangemeister, 1976). If the structure of such a task becomes complex, it may create illusory contradictions due to the many variables that influence the model. Resolving such contradictions and using them to construct new knowledge is considered an important factor for learning (Schnotz & Preuss, 1997; Seel, 1991, 2003).

Moreover, if the variables are not presented to the learner directly but rather create or control an environment, then they might be represented in a way that is fuzzy to the learner. This can be used to train solutions, classifications, and interpretations of feedback that would also be fuzzy in the real world. Inventing and writing down a task manually that resembles the LE model and induces enough puzzlement for the learner to make progress is always a good start. From principles 4 to 6 it can be derived that single tasks do not suffice: e.g., even with good feedback, the learners would still generalize too much while the exact task contexts would be too fixed, which then makes transfer more difficult for them – no matter how concrete the task might be. In large educational settings, there may be the necessary resources for many experts to create enough tasks with sufficient diversity among them. The more specialized a field is, the more unlikely it will be to find such a pool of comparable and yet sufficiently complex tasks that leave the task synthesis more or less to the individual instructor – with a limited amount of tasks. The need for many tasks and the lack of resources make automatic task synthesis interesting. But how can this be done without creating a whole simulation again?

One simple way of prototyping that may essentially even be implemented in Microsoft Excel, is the text-matrix approach, which utilizes both black-box and glass-box approaches from simulation. It can be developed on a much lower technological level: it creates text cases and tasks for the learner, provided that a rough simulation model can be sketched. To illustrate its simplicity and power, we will introduce it with a simplified example. Suppose we want to create tasks on learning and motivation. The first thing to do is to look at different possible motivational traits of a fictional learner. We can do so by "reverse-engineering" a common research strategy, a simple survey. Say we measure (simulated measurement) motivation on a scale from 1 to 5, where 1 is very low motivation and 5 very high motivation. To create the case for the task we randomly choose one of the possible values. At this point, we would have a case that is far too simple, but it is nonetheless already a case. A learner X has a motivation of 2. The task could then only be something like: "Explain the learner's motivation." Learners, however, do not like those kinds of cases. Thus, we can give the case a surface by reversing the measurement (see Table 3.1).

From the random number for the learner's motivation we select the proper statement from Table 3.1 and present the statement to the learner instead of the number. But a one-dimensional matrix is still neither very exciting nor complex. It can have only five different results. We now need to develop it further by constructing more layers. Thus, we may take a look at industriousness to see whether the motivation has a real effect on our fictional learner (see Table 3.2).

With the integration of Table 3.1 and Table 3.2, our case gains more complexity. The tasks could now also be changed to "Explain the

Table 3.1 Simple one-dimensional text matrix (motivation)

Motivation	1	2	3	4	5
Statement	The learner has a very low motivation and is almost unable to focus on his tasks at all.	The learner has a low motivation and can only rarely concentrate on his tasks.	The learner has a moderate motivation and is able to focus on assignments most of the time.	The learner has a high motivation and is always able to focus on assignments.	The learner has a very high motivation and participates in many additional learning activities besides the assignments.

dependency between motivation and industriousness for learner X." If we also select the measure for industriousness randomly, we now have 25 different possible cases due to the different possible combinations. The extreme cases can already invoke puzzling discussions: How is it that a highly motivated learner rarely finishes any tasks? A decent look at the Rubicon model of motivation (Heckhausen & Gollwitzer, 1987) could resolve a configuration that may at first sight be counterintuitive. While explaining the still very simple dependency between the two variables, the learner can already gain a deeper insight. Of course, there would also still be intuitively expected combinations in some of the cases. Once we know about the order of variables that are output into the final case, all the matrix texts need to fit together vertically, meaning that the text for each value of the first variable needs to fit with the text for the variable that follows. The third layer could be the gain from the learning activity for our fictional learner, providing us with cases in which somebody is highly motivated and industrious but does not learn much – maybe because he already knew everything or maybe because other traits are standing in his way, or because he has insufficient prior knowledge. All of this could then be put into layers like the one above, thus raising the complexity.

But what about the LE model? Up to now, our example works with randomly assigned numbers that are equally distributed. In the real world, variables are not connected in that way. Thus, functions other than pure random number generation could be used to select the values for the variables, e.g., if we know that motivation and industriousness have a correlation (which they do), and that they also have a distinct distribution – let's say something like a normal curve. Then, once the first variable has been randomly assigned, the others may depend on it. Thus, like in the real world, a high level of motivation would also yield a high level of industriousness in most of the cases – but not in all of them. If we have a sufficient number of layers, then some rather non-intuitive variations will also find their way into the case almost automatically, making the case more complex while still keeping to the distributions. And where do we get the distributions, correlations, and effects from? We have to

Table 3.2 Augmentation of the prior matrix (industriousness)

Industriousness	1	2	3	4	5
Statement	The learner is very rarely able to finish any task.	The learner is rarely able to finish tasks.	The learner is not always able to finish tasks.	The learner finishes tasks most of the time.	Not only does the learner finish all tasks on time, he often also completes extra assignments.

collect them from research, sometimes from multiple studies (this is the analytical model) and integrate them into the LE model afterwards.

For the L-MoSim (Learner Model Simulation) Software, Pirnay-Dummer (2010) created an LE model to train instructional design students on the individual aspects of learning about coaching for individual educational career planning (the students were being trained to be future coaches). The task synthesis was developed in a very similar way to that illustrated in the example above. It contains 24 sections (scales) with four layers each for the personality traits of the fictional learner; it comes with educational backgrounds, CVs, protocols, and also with "original quotes" from the learner. All of the variables are integrated into a multi-dimensional text layer, and the underlying model is research-driven, as introduced above. The result is a task and case document that includes 12 pages of case description. Some of the content is created dynamically depending on the output of the main model. The evaluation results were very promising once integrated properly into the course design (see Pirnay-Dummer, 2010). L-MoSim generates about 460,800,000 different cases, not counting the variations due to the educational background of the fictional learners. The solutions to the cases vary widely throughout the field of instructional design while the cases and tasks can be interesting on very different levels of expertise. The course requirements do of course need to correspond to the skill level of the learners. A non-expert learner may just find out about some dependencies and come to an initial understanding of the complexity of the field (complexity awareness, see Moxnes, 2004). A more experienced learner may be able to gain some theory-driven model insight into parts of the case, while a very well-trained expert may gain a system-analytical understanding of the individual case using the available theories. To evaluate learner performance on such complex tasks and cases and set the expectations right from the beginning with differently skilled learners, we developed the following general framework (see Figure 3.7).

The levels of learner performance start with the ability to just paraphrase what's in the case, i.e., to restate in one's own words what is in the case. The second level is the ability to identify monocausal relations, e.g., "Ah, the learner is not motivated and therefore he performs weakly in math. He probably needs motivational training." A typical indicator for this level is when the learner creates a list of independent trainings that are supposed to help the fictional person but does not interconnect them in any way. The third level can be identified most of the time when the student provides any kind of pro–con list or analysis of strengths and weaknesses, e.g., "The learner has a high level of motivation, and also high intelligence. This may be utilized to counterbalance his exam nerves (anxiety). The following ritual might use his high motivation to help him gain more control in exam situations." On the level of theory-based classifications, the students are able to use their theoretical knowledge to

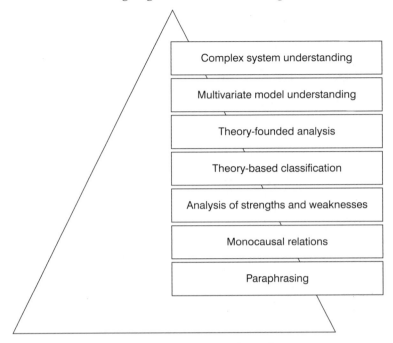

Figure 3.7 Levels of learner performance in complex tasks

find typical classes of interventions, e.g., "A high self-efficacy commonly comes with higher demands for the fellow students. For his training, we need to consider the homogeneity of his peer-group in order to help him overcome his unprofitable state of social skills. Otherwise he would probably not proceed further towards an integrated regulation." Indicators for that level are found in the theoretical rationale provided for decisions on the case. The theoretically-grounded analysis improves on this level by turning the reasoning around: instead of looking for fitting theories from the perspective of the case, theories of learning are consulted that explain in themselves what may be found in the case. Then the case is cited more in the form of empirical evidence to support the assumptions. This level may seem to be similar to the prior one at first glance, but actually requires a much improved understanding of the literature and theory. While on the first theoretical level the student uses parts of the theories to support an already existing assumption, on the latter level the whole theory is used creatively and the case becomes more and more an example of the theory. The case and task need, however, to support this option, which is only available on LE models designed on the basis of studies that are then based on theory (which is preferable anyway). The next level combines the use of theories on a multivariate level. It involves understanding on the multiplicity of interactions between different parts of the case, e.g.,

In contrast to the common visual cognitive style, this learner has an unusual overall level of attention. Usually this is not the case with this type of learner. Similar anomalies can be seen in her behavior towards authority and seniors. All three differences from what is usually expected probably point to a consistent problem. Under the circumstances, aspects of her socialization might help to shed light on her situation. Another interview may help us to clarify this particular aspect.

The example is a little vague, because multivariate model understanding is usually found in larger texts and will be found throughout the argumentation on the case. The last assessable level would then be a system understanding which includes the prior levels and adds an understanding about effects, delays of effects, cycles, and other between- or within-construct feedback. Even experts do not always reach or need this level of understanding. Finding it in a learner is rare, and it should not even be used lightly as a criterion for a veteran. It is also not very easy to judge whether an argumentation is really on this level. Given the time constraints for feedback and also grading, some argumentations may mistakenly be judged as being on this level while they in fact contain phrases that mimic this kind of understanding (not unlike those sometimes also found in the argumentation of politicians).

The levels may of course also be used in all kinds of other learning environments where learners verbalize complex aspects of their subject matter. But not only can the criteria be used as a basis for feedback and grading, they also show the applicability of the complex cases with groups of learners at different levels of advancement. Early in one's studies, learning goals may lie in identifying and using strengths and weaknesses, while more advanced students or even those in doctoral programs may have deeper theoretical understanding as their goal. On these levels, learners can find challenges depending on their current knowledge. To re-engage in the same field, learners have virtually endless cases at their disposal. The learner simulation of L-MoSim was just an example. An LE model matrix can be created for any systematically connected field of expertise once the dependencies and distributions (i.e., the mathematical model) are identified. Available complete simulation models are even more suitable (usually they are more integrated and coherent) and can be used as well.

The method for task and case synthesis introduced above is only one of many possibilities for generating tasks. It is, however, an easy one for prototyping and does not require too many resources, except to author the matrices. It is advisable to plan enough time for the revision of the text elements: not all texts fit together vertically after the first authoring.

Characteristics of Model-Based Learning Environments

Surface and Texture

The surface and textures of learning environments, simulations, and complex tasks alike are usually designed and developed as materials, media, cover stories, introductions, examples, parts of tasks, etc. Surfaces are driven by the LE model and may connect with a certain level of the individual L model. If the surfaces do not connect with the learner models or if they do not properly resemble the explanative structure of the model used for learning, they may lead the learner to draw false conclusions on the surface only. Analogies are known to be particularly prone to such errors (Gick & Holyoak, 1980, 1983; Treagust, Duit, Joslin, & Lindauer, 1992). Thus, well-designed surfaces of any kind are constructed with regard to what conclusions the supposed L model will derive from them, including the aspects that may be constructed in an unintended way (e.g., over-generalizations, over-specifications, mapping of the wrong aspects). It thus does not suffice for teachers to be able to navigate the surfaces properly, the learners also need to make the right sense out of them. Surfaces and textures need to balance out the need for simplicity and the dangers of wrong conclusions. For task surfaces this means that they need to be (see Aebli, 1991; Bruner, 1966; Spiro, Feltovich, Jacobson, & Coulson, 1991; Steiner, 2001):

- consolidated (freed from irrelevant single aspects)
- adaptable (by means of intense comparisons and diversity)
- represented in more than one way (in different representation formats)
- de-contextualized (transferability and limits thereof, abstractions of knowledge structure)
- metacognitive (allow inferences on the learner's learning activity, especially after the learning experience).

The main obstacles to designing surfaces can be categorized as either *surface dyeing* or *reverse plausibility*:

Surface dyeing is a very simple linearly creative procedure in which the surface stays completely the same for alternating tasks that are supposed to fulfill the above criteria – and only some roles and names are changed, aspects that do not play a role in the understanding of the case. In general, all kinds of textures and surfaces that take the model structure and just change the agents and roles a little are unfavorable, e.g., instead of an old man, now a young woman crosses the street, except, of course, where age and gender plays a key role in the LE model.

Reverse plausibility is a little more complex but is even worse in its effects. We illustrate this aspect with a simple ill-conceived math problem task:

Suppose a lifeguard (standing 10 meters away from the water) sees a man drowning who is 5 meters away from the shore and 20 meters to the left of the lifeguard. When he walks on the beach, he moves at 7 meters per second. In the water, he swims at 2.5 meters per second. What is the best angle for him to walk towards the water at so that he reaches the drowning man in the quickest possible way?

A student who now replies: "How long does the lifeguard need to calculate this task?" has a very valid point but will probably rarely be rewarded for such an attitude. Tasks like this are initially supposed to raise plausibility because they are embedded in a real-world context. However, the authors might have gone about it the wrong way. They may have searched inductively for a nice scenario that could convey the problem and then mapped the problem afterwards to that scene.

Although it is more time-consuming to derive every new case directly and deductively from the LE model – especially when learners are supposed to use the case for inductive learning – it is the only way to create enough model-consistent diversity (and complexity) to systematically free the learners' interpretation of their case experiences from irrelevant aspects or even misconceptions. Even the very simple task mentioned above could thus be recreated easily if instead of the beach situation it used a surface of town planning where a street needs to be constructed with a certain amount of resources. At least, these are circumstances that would really require curve sketching from calculus (identifying an extreme). However, cases, stories, and material in general get more complex the more they convey of the initial model. Thus, the need for feedback rises with the quality of the LE.

Learner Model-oriented Feedback

Feedback is of great importance in all model-based learning environments. The large body of theoretical and empirical studies on feedback provides very diverse insight into possible ways to support and regulate learning processes. Even meta-analyses have provided contradictory results (Azevedo & Bernard, 1995; Kluger & DeNisi, 1996; Schimmel, 1983). However, feedback is considered to be an elementary component for facilitating learning outcomes. As feedback can take on many forms depending on the theoretical perspective, the role of the feedback, and the methodological approach, it is important to consider which form of feedback is effective for a specific learning environment. In general, Wagner and Wagner (1985) consider feedback to be any type of information provided to learners. According to Narciss (2008), a large variety of feedback types exist, such as *knowledge of performance, knowledge of result, knowledge of correct response, multiple-try feedback,* and *elaborated feedback.*

Feedback needs to be shaped by the particular learning goals – this usually has a good practice in better learning environments (Narciss, 2008).

Moreover, it has to match the learners' current episteme, and herein we see a huge potential: learning environments rarely model the individual learner or even a group of learners appropriately, which is an important precondition in order to give feedback that fits the learners' current model.

Feedback on mental model construction, such as the use of conceptual models to help persons to build mental models of the system being studied, has also been investigated and discussed (see, for example, Mayer, 1989; Pirnay-Dummer & Ifenthaler, 2011). Conceptual models highlight the most important objects and associated causal relations of the phenomenon in question. However, not only do new developments in computer technology enable us to dynamically generate simple conceptual models and expert representations, they may also be used to generate direct responses to the learner's interaction with the learning environment (Pirnay-Dummer & Ifenthaler, 2011). We define this form of feedback as model-based feedback (Ifenthaler, 2009). An important aspect of model-based feedback is providing dynamic feedback generated purposively and individually for student-constructed models (Ifenthaler, 2009).

Newly introduced automated knowledge assessment tools (e.g., Ifenthaler, 2010c; Pirnay-Dummer & Ifenthaler, 2011) allow us to produce instant feedback on semantic and structural aspects of the student's learning progression at all times during the learning process (Ifenthaler, 2009). Such dynamic and timely feedback can promote the learner's self-regulated learning (Zimmerman & Schunk, 2001). Based on these new technologies, two intelligent and automated model-based feedback tools have been developed and implemented:

1   TASA (Text-guided Automated Self-Assessment), which generates automated feedback to learners based on natural language text input (Pirnay-Dummer & Ifenthaler, 2011). TASA is a web-based online tool for self-assessment while writing. It embeds the parts of HIMATT (Highly Integrated Model Assessment Technology and Tools; Pirnay-Dummer, Ifenthaler, & Spector, 2010) which are necessary to generate intelligent feedback from the user's text directly after the upload. With regard to the demand for instant feedback on the ongoing writing process, TASA has been developed, implemented, and empirically tested. TASA is based on mental model theory (Seel, 2003) and psycholinguistics (Frazier, 1999). To represent the underlying models of the learner's actual text, modules from the HIMATT toolset (Pirnay-Dummer & Ifenthaler, in press-a) have been adapted. A text of more than 350 words can be graphically visualized by this toolset as an association net (see Kopainsky, Pirnay-Dummer, & Alessi, 2010). It tracks the association of concepts from a text directly to a graph, using a heuristic to do so. The re-representation process is carried out automatically and uses multiple computer linguistic stages. From the

second time the learner interacts with TASA on, he or she will also get feedback on what has changed since the last upload of the written text. If two graphical representations are available – from the current and the previous version of the text – TASA gives feedback on the new associations, on the ones that are still in the model, and on the links that are no longer dominant within the texts' model (see Pirnay-Dummer & Ifenthaler, in press-b). Available measures from graph theory also make it possible to tell whether a text has gained more complexity or has been simplified since the last time (see Ifenthaler, 2010c; Tittmann, 2010). The measures are afterwards combined to form features like complexity of the written text. Additionally, TASA tracks the time the learners have already spent using the system and generates general prompts from this information.

2   iGRAF (Instant Graphical Feedback), automatically generates graphical representations based on the learner's prior knowledge (Ifenthaler, 2009, 2010a). Model-based feedback should take into account the learner's prior understanding (initial mental model, preconception), because such preconceptions are in many cases resistant to change as they have a high subjective plausibility (Ifenthaler & Seel, 2005; Seel, 1995). Past research studies lack this perspective in providing learners with conceptual models (i.e., explicit and consistent causal explanations of a given phenomenon) to improve a person's understanding of a specific problem in a given context (e.g., Mayer, 1989; Norman, 1983; Seel, 1995).

In order to fulfill the requirement of taking into account the learner's prior understanding, iGRAF not only includes an expert's solution of the given phenomenon, it also processes the learner's initial understanding of the phenomenon in question and automatically produces instant individualized feedback. Currently, two forms of model-based feedback are available: (1) cutaway model-based feedback and (2) discrepancy model-based feedback. These two forms of model-based feedback are considered as graphical re-representations constructed from a set of vertices whose relationships are represented by edges (Ifenthaler, 2010d). A cutaway re-representation includes all propositions (vertex–edge–vertex) of the individual's re-representation. Additionally, the semantically correct vertices (compared with a reference re-representation such as an expert solution) are graphically highlighted as circles (ellipses for dissimilar vertices). The discrepancy re-representation of an individual only includes propositions (vertex–edge–vertex) which have no semantic similarity to a reference re-representation. Additionally, the semantically correct vertices (compared with a reference re-representation) are graphically highlighted as circles (ellipses for dissimilar vertices). As the cutaway feedback model helps the learner to confirm the correct understanding of the phenomenon in question, the discrepancy feedback model causes a cognitive conflict, because correct propositions (vertex–edge–vertex) of the person's understanding are deleted from the re-representation (see Ifenthaler, 2010b).

Accordingly, intelligent model-based feedback helps students to monitor their individual learning process. Automated knowledge assessment tools provide the basis to produce instant feedback on semantic and structural aspects of a person's learning progression at all times during the learning process (Ifenthaler, 2009). Such dynamic and timely feedback can promote the learner's self-regulated learning (Zimmerman & Schunk, 2001).

Deep Structure and Puzzlement

Cognitive conflict can open the problem space, allowing the learner to gain access (to a window) to the structure of things. The natural result is a level of puzzlement that cannot be addressed on the task or feedback level alone. In addition to a proper configuration of task and feedback that fits both the learner's goals (LE model) and his or her state (L model), the learner needs to find – and become accustomed to – a culture of curiosity and puzzlement. In other words, the learner needs to see independently whether and how contradictions can be resolved and he or she needs confidence in that process. The latter does not come overnight; it demands an epistemic learning culture that is surprisingly similar to research and science. Thus, implicitly or explicitly, a model-oriented learning environment needs to come with an inherent philosophy of science. This may of course be a naïve one, but it needs a certain amount of transparency. Seel (2003) provides a model of intersection between philosophy of science, in particular theories and models, psychology (the learners' reality), and epistemology (the design and instruction models).

When they enter learning environments, most learners want quick answers to questions they already have. Thus, they tend to like to be provided with simple recipes and scripts – because they feel them to be of more practical value at the time. A model-based learning environment necessarily violates this quasi-need (not only) because it aims at conceptual change. The human mind does not like to change things too much (e.g., Schnotz & Preuss, 1997; Seel, 1991; van Merrienboer, Kirschner, & Kester, 2003). However, if one wishes to achieve major cognitive and complex levels of expertise, higher levels of change in beliefs are inevitable (Ifenthaler, 2006). In naturally occurring incidental learning, drastic failure is the only means to adjust for complexity and dynamics. On the other side, real-world failure too often has too many high risks to allow the expertise to emerge from failure alone (e.g., successfully teaching a class or flying an airplane). Designers of good learning environments will always need to find ways to deal with this general antipode and provide opportunities for the learners to resolve it on their side.

Summary

Environments that successfully mediate the synthetic model of the learning environment with the learners' current state and their possible future state always create multiple opportunities for thought. They thus start with three sets of assumptions: a theoretical model about what is to be learned (model-centered), a theory about the learners' models, and a theory of learning (model-oriented). If the three are integrated into the design, the learners will be able to create meaningful new insights and keep their thinking flexible at the same time. Many learning goals demand these aspects from the experts' thinking and behavior. They thus need to have the opportunity to get accustomed to the way of thinking – in general, but more importantly, also concretely – in the context of the domain. Designing and creating such environments is in itself not a very easy task. Often, blended human–environment and technical solutions offer the best trade-off as regards to resources and complementary strengths. But this is more like a current limiting factor, not a systematic one. Given the right resources and L/LE model justification, stand-alone technical solutions may be conceivable. When one follows the seven principles introduced in this chapter, well-designed model-centered and model-oriented environments have something interesting in common: the interactive learning environment is created – at least in parts – on the basis of the LE model for or during the learning process, thus providing the world's side of the adaption process and allowing the learners to use their supposedly natural tendency to strive for knowledge equilibrium.

References

Adams, M. J. (1989). Thinking skills curricula: Their promise and progress. *Educational Psychologist, 24*, 25–77.

Aebli, H. (1991). *Zwölf Grundformen des Lehrens: eine allgemeine Didaktik auf psychologischer Grundlage. Medien und Inhalte didaktischer Kommunikation, der Lernzyklus.* (6 ed.). Stuttgart: Klett-Cotta.

Aïmeuer, E. (1998). Application and assessment of cognitive-dissonance theory in the learning process. *Journal of Universal Computer Science, 4*(3), 216–247.

Azevedo, R., & Bernard, R. M. (1995). A meta-analysis of the effects of feedback in computer-based instruction. *Journal of Educational Computing Research, 13*(2), 111–127.

Biggs, J. (1999). What the student does: teaching for enhanced learning. *Higher Education Research & Development, 18*(1), 57–75.

Brown, A. L. (1992). Design experiments. Theoretical and methodological challanges in creating complex interventions in classroom settings. *Journal of the Learning Sciences, 2*(2), 141–178.

Bruner, J. S. (1966). *Toward a theory of instruction.* Cambridge, MA: The Belknap Press of Harvard University Press.

Carruthers, P. (2000). *Phenomenal consciousness: a naturalistic theory.* Cambridge: Cambridge University Press.

Catrambone, R., & Holyoak, K. J. (1989). Overcoming contextual limitations on problem-solving transfer. *Journal of Experimental Psychology, 15*(6), 1147–1156.

Ceci, S. J., & Ruiz, A. (1992). The role of general ability in cognitive complexity: A case study of expertise. In R. R. Hoffman (Ed.), *The psychology of expertise: Cognitive research and empirical AI* (pp. 218-230). Mahwah, NJ: Lawrence Erlbaum Associates.

Cooper, J. (2007). *Cognitive dissonance: 50 years of a classic theory.* London: Sage Publications.

Danielson, C., & Marquez, E. (1998). *A collection of performance tasks and rubrics: high school mathematics.* Larchmont, NY: Eye on Education.

Fodor, J. A. (2003). *Hume variations.* Oxford: Clarendon Press.

Frazier, L. (1999). *On sentence interpretation.* Dordrecht: Kluwer.

Gick, M. L., & Holyoak, K. J. (1980). Analogical problem solving. *Cognitive Psychology, 15*, 306–355.

Gick, M. L., & Holyoak, K. J. (1983). Schema induction and analogical transfer. *Cognitive Psychology, 15*, 1–38.

Gilovich, T., Griffin, D. W., & Kahneman, D. (2002). *Heuristics and biases: the psychology of intuitive judgement.* Cambridge; New York: Cambridge University Press.

Gruber, H. (1994). *Expertise Modelle und empirische Untersuchungen.* Opladen: Westdt. Verl.

Gruber, H., & Ziegler, A. (1993). Temporale Wissensstrukturierung mit Hilfe Mentaler Modelle. Temporal knowledge structures based on mental models. *Sprache & Kognition, 12*(3), 145–156.

Heckhausen, H., & Gollwitzer, P. M. (1987). Thought contents and cognitive functioning in motivational versus volitional states of mind. *Motivation and Emotion, 11*(2), 101–120.

Ifenthaler, D. (2006). *Diagnose lernabhängiger Veränderung mentaler Modelle Entwicklung der SMD-Technologie als methodologisches Verfahren zur relationalen, strukturellen und semantischen Analyse individueller Modellkonstruktionen.* Freiburg: FreiDok.

Ifenthaler, D. (2009). Model-based feedback for improving expertise and expert performance. *Technology, Instruction, Cognition and Learning, 7*(2), 83-101.

Ifenthaler, D. (2010a). Bridging the gap between expert–novice differences: The model-based feedback approach. *Journal of Research on Technology in Education, 43*(2), 103–117.

Ifenthaler, D. (2010b). Learning and instruction in the digital age. In J. M. Spector, D. Ifenthaler, P. Isaías, Kinshuk & D. G. Sampson (Eds.), *Learning and instruction in the digital age: Making a difference through cognitive approaches, technology-facilitated collaboration and assessment, and personalized communications.* New York: Springer.

Ifenthaler, D. (2010c). Relational, structural, and semantic analysis of graphical representations and concept maps. *Educational Technology Research and Development, 58*(1), 1556–6501.

Ifenthaler, D. (2010d). Scope of graphical indices in educational diagnostics. In D. Ifenthaler, P. Pirnay-Dummer & N. M. Seel (Eds.), *Computer-based diagnostics and systematic analysis of knowledge* (pp. 213–234). New York: Springer.

Ifenthaler, D., & Seel, N. M. (2005). The measurement of change: Learning-dependent progression of mental models. *Technology, Instruction, Cognition and Learning, 2*(4), 317–336.

Ifenthaler, D., Masduki, I., & Seel, N. M. (2011). The mystery of cognitive structure and how we can detect it. Tracking the development of cognitive structures over time. *Instructional Science, 39*(1), 41-61.

Johnson-Laird, P. N. (1983). *Mental models. Toward a cognitive science of language, inference and language.* Cambridge: Cambridge University Press.

Jonassen, D. H. (2000). Toward a design theory of problem solving. *Educational Technology Research and Development, 48*(4), 63–85.

Just, M. A., & Carpenter, P. A. (1976). The relation between comprehending and remembering some complex sentences. *Memory and Cognition, 4*(3), 318–322.

Kluger, A. N., & DeNisi, A. (1996). Effects of feedback intervention on performance: A historical review, a meta-analysis, and a preliminary feedback intervention theory. *Psychological Bulletin, 119*(2), 254-284.

Kopainsky, B., Pirnay-Dummer, P., & Alessi, S. M. (2010). *Automated assessment of learners' understanding in complex dynamic systems.* Paper presented at the System Dynamics Conference in Seoul, South Korea, July 25–29, 2010.

Margolis, E., & Laurence, S. (1999). *Concepts core readings.* Cambridge, MA: MIT Press.

Mayer, R. E. (1989). Models for understanding. *Review of Educational Research, 59*(1), 43–64.

Means, B. (1993). Cognitive task analysis as a basis for instructional design. In M. Rabinowitz (Ed.), *Cognitive science foundations of instruction* (pp. 97–118). Hillsdale, NJ: Lawrence Erlbaum Associates.

Moxnes, E. (2004). Misperceptions of basic dynamics: the case of renewable resource management. *System Dynamics Review, 20*(2), 139–162.

Narciss, S. (2008). Feedback strategies for interactive learning tasks. In J. M. Spector, M. D. Merrill, J. van Merrienboer & M. P. Driscoll (Eds.), *Handbook of research on educational communications and technology* (pp. 125-143). New York: Taylor & Francis Group.

Norman, D. A. (1983). Some observations on mental models. In D. Gentner & A. L. Stevens (Eds.), *Mental models* (pp. 7-14). Hilsdale, NJ: Lawrence Erlbaum Associates.

Piaget, J. (1976). *Die Äquilibration der kognitiven Strukturen.* Stuttgart: Klett.

Pinker, S. (1994). *The language instinct. The new science of language and mind.* London: Lane Penguin Press.

Pirnay-Dummer, P. (2006). *Expertise und Modellbildung – MITOCAR.* Freiburg: FreiDok.

Pirnay-Dummer, P. (2008). Rendezvous with a quantum of learning. Effect metaphors, extended design experiments and omnivariate learning instances. In D. Ifenthaler, P. Pirnay-Dummer & J. M. Spector (Eds.), *Understanding models for learning and instruction. Essays in honor of Norbert M. Seel.* (pp. 105–143). New York: Springer.

Pirnay-Dummer, P. (2010). Theory-based case simulation and automated task synthesis to support learning on learning. In M. B. Nunes & M. McPherson (Eds.), *Proceedings of the IADIS International Conference on e-Learning* (Vol. 1, pp. 299–306). Freiburg, Germany: IADIS.

Pirnay-Dummer, P., & Ifenthaler, D. (2010). Automated knowledge visualization and assessment. In D. Ifenthaler, P. Pirnay-Dummer & N. M. Seel (Eds.), *Computer-based diagnostics and systematic analysis of knowledge* (pp. 77–115). New York: Springer.

Pirnay-Dummer, P., & Ifenthaler, D. (in press-a). Reading guided by automated graphical representations: How model-based text visualizations facilitate learning in reading comprehension tasks. *Instructional Science.*

Pirnay-Dummer, P., & Ifenthaler, D. (in press-b). Text-guided automated self assessment. In D. Ifenthaler, Kinshuk, P. Isaias, D. G. Sampson & J. M. Spector (Eds.), *Multiple perspectives on problem solving and learning in the digital age.* New York: Springer.

Pirnay-Dummer, P., Ifenthaler, D., & Spector, J. M. (2010). Highly integrated model assessment technology and tools. *Educational Technology Research and Development, 58*(1), 3–18.

Resnick, D. P., & Resnick, L. B. (1996). Performance assessment and the multiple functions of educational measurement. In M. B. Kane & R. Mitchell (Eds.), *Implementing performance assessment. Promises, problems, and challenges.* (pp. 23–39). Mahwah, NJ: Lawrence Erlbaum Associates.

Savery, J. R., & Duffy, T. M. (1996). Problem based learning: An instructional model and its constructivist framework. In B. G. Wilson (Ed.), *Constructivist learning environments case studies in instructional design.* Englewood Cliffs, NJ: Educational Technology Publications.

Schimmel, B. J. (1983). A meta-analysis of feedback to learners in computerized and programmed instruction. Paper presented at the AREA 1983, Montreal.

Schnotz, W. (1994). *Aufbau von Wissensstrukturen.* Weinheim: Beltz, Psychologie-Verl.-Union.

Schnotz, W., & Preuss, A. (1997). Task-dependent construction of mental models as a basis for conceptual change. Aufgabenabhängige Konstruktion mentaler Modelle als Grundlage konzeptueller Veränderungen. *European Journal of Psychology of Education, 12*(2), 185–211.

Seel, N. M. (1991). *Weltwissen und Mentale Modelle.* Göttingen: Hogrefe.

Seel, N. M. (1992). The significance of prescriptive decision theory for instructional design expert systems. In S. Dijkstra, H. Krammer & J. van Merrienboer (Eds.), *Instructional models in computer-based learning environments* (pp. 61–81). Berlin: Springer.

Seel, N. M. (1995). Mental models, knowledge transfer and teaching strategies. *Journal of Structural Learning, 12*(3), 197–213.

Seel, N. M. (2003). Model centered learning and instruction. *Technology, Instruction, Cognition and Learning, 1*(1), 59–85.

Seel, N. M., & Schenk, K. (2003). Multimedia environments as cognitive tools for enhanceing model-based learning and problem solving: An evaluation report. *Evaluation and Program Planning, 26,* 215–224.

Seel, N. M., Ifenthaler, D., & Pirnay-Dummer, P. (2008). Mental models and problem solving: Technological solutions for measurement and assessment of the development of expertise. In P. Blumschein, J. Strobel, W. Hung & D. H. Jonassen (Eds.), *Model-based approaches to learning: Using systems models and simulations to improve understanding and problem solving in complex domains* (pp. 17–40). Rotterdam: Sense Publishers.

Spector, J. M. (2006). Introduction to the special issue on models, simulations and learning in complex domains. *Technology, Instruction, Cognition and Learning, 3*(3–4), 199–204.

Spiro, R. J., Feltovich, P. J., Jacobson, M. J., & Coulson, R. L. (1991). Knowledge representation, content specification, and the development of skill in situation-specific knowledge assembly: Some constructivist issues as they relate to cognitive flexibility theory and hypertext. *Educational Technology, 31*(9), 22–25.

Spiro, R. J., Feltovich, P. J., Jacobson, M. J., & Coulson, R. L. (1992). Cognitive flexibility, constructivism and hypertext: Random access instruction for advanced knowledge acquisition in ill-structured domains. In T. M. Duffy & D. H. Jonassen (Eds.), *Constructivism and the technology of instruction: a conversation* (pp. 57–76). Hillsdale, NJ: Lawrence Erlbaum Associates Publishers.

Steiner, G. (2001). Lernen und Wissenserwerb. In A. Krapp & B. Weidenmann (Eds.), *Pädagogische Psychologie* (pp. 137–205). Weinheim: Beltz Psychologie Verlags Union.

Strasser, A. (2010). A functional view towards mental representations. In D. Ifenthaler, P. Pirnay-Dummer & J. M. Spector (Eds.), *Computer-based diagnostics and systematic analysis of knowledge*. New York: Springer.

Tittmann, P. (2010). Graphs and networks. In D. Ifenthaler, P. Pirnay-Dummer & N. M. Seel (Eds.), *Computer-based diagnostics and systematic analysis of knowledge* (pp. 177–188). New York: Springer.

Treagust, D. F., Duit, R., Joslin, P., & Lindauer, I. (1992). Science teachers' use of analogies: observations from classroom practice. *International Journal of Science Education, 14*(4), 327–352.

Tversky, A., & Kahneman, D. (1974). Judgement under uncertainty. Heuristics and biases. *Science, 185*, 1124–1131.

van Merrienboer, J., Kirschner, P. A., & Kester, L. (2003). Taking the load off a learner's mind: Instructional design for complex learning. *Educational Psychologist, 38*(1), 5–13.

Wagner, W., & Wagner, S. U. (1985). Presenting questions, processing responses, and providing feedback in CAI. *Journal of Instructional Development, 8*(4), 2–8.

Wein, B., Willems, R., & Quanjel, M. (2000). Planspielsimulationen: Ein Konzept für eine integrierte (Re-) Strukturierung von Organisationen. In D. Herz & A. Blätte (Eds.), *Simulation und Planspiel in den Sozialwissenschaften* (pp. 275–299). Münster: Lit.

Willis, J. (2005). *A framework for task-based learning*. Harlow: Longman.

Zangemeister, C. (1976). *Nutzwertanalyse in der Systemtechnik eine Methodik zur multidimensionalen Bewertung und Auswahl von Projektalternativen.* München: Wittemann.

Zimmerman, B. J., & Schunk, D. (2001). Theories of self-regulated learning and academic achievement: An overview and analysis. In B. J. Zimmerman & D. Schunk (Eds.), *Self-regulated learning and academic achievement. Theoretical perspectives* (pp. 1–37). Mahawah, NJ: Lawrence Erlbaum Associates.

4   Conceptual Change and Student-Centered Learning Environments

David H. Jonassen and Matthew A. Easter

Introduction

At its core, conceptual change theory is concerned with how learners change their ideas or knowledge. Conceptual change occurs when learners change their understanding of the concepts they use and the conceptual frameworks that encompass them. Theories from different disciplines including cognitive psychology (Carey, 1988; Chi, 1992; Smith, di Sessa, & Roschelle, 1993; Thagard, 1992), social psychology (Eagly & Chaiken, 1993; Tesser & Shaffer, 1990), and science education (Chinn & Brewer, 1993; Strike & Posner, 1992; Vosniadou, 2002) have investigated various aspects of conceptual change including the conditions that foster change, the sources of influence on this change, the longevity and strength of the change, and the facilitation of changes (Dole & Sinatra, 1998). This research has been delineated in many different ways, but two particular demarcations are productive when considering conceptual change in student-centered learning environments (SCLEs). The first is the differences between theories that support an evolutionary conceptual change perspective (e.g., Smith *et al.*, 1993; Strike & Posner, 1992; Vosniadou, 1992) and others that take a more radical conceptual change approach (e.g., Chi, 1992; Chinn & Brewer, 1993), and the second is the "warming trend" (see Sinatra, 2005) that has more recently occurred in the conceptual change literature. After discussing these distinctions, we then describe different SCLEs that can foster primarily radical conceptual change and note how this conceptual change is warmer in some learning environments than others.

Evolutionary and Radical Conceptual Change

A major predecessor to both evolutionary and radical conceptual change theories was the work of Jean Piaget. Piaget (1950, 1952) described two processes for understanding how learners construct conceptions or knowledge and for understanding how learners could change existing knowledge to provide better explanations for new knowledge and/or experiences. Both of these processes were dependent on learners' schemas.

Piaget (1950, 1952) believed that schemas are cognitive structures consisting of organized patterns of knowledge or actions that humans develop to understand the world and cope with their surroundings.

These schemas are developed via a process termed assimilation, or the process of incorporating new knowledge into existing schemas (Piaget, 1950). However, when we find our existing schemas to be insufficient for understanding new knowledge or experiences, we will often accommodate existing schemas. Accommodation is the process of restructuring existing schemas to provide better explanations for new knowledge and/or experiences that better fit reality (Piaget, 1950, 1952). Both assimilation and accommodation occur in order to meet our needs to reach equilibration, or the desire to obtain consistency or stasis in our cognitive states (Piaget, 1950, 1952). Such desires can then lead to conceptual change, or accommodation, and it was this notion of accommodation that conceptual change theorists began to elaborate on in order to further explain how learners may experience changes in their knowledge structures at both an evolutionary and radical pace.

Conceptual change is also rooted in conceptions of cognitive structure. Similar to Piaget's assimilation–accommodation, Norman, Gentner, and Stevens (1976) claimed that reorganization of cognitive structure occurs through the processes of accretion, tuning, and restructuring. While learning, the learners' cognitive structures change to correspond more closely with the content structure or the teacher's knowledge structure (Shavelson, 1972). Cognitive structures have also been described as semantic networks, mental structures that are composed of nodes and ordered, typed relationships, or links connecting them (Quillian, 1968). The nodes are token instances of concepts or propositions and the links describe the propositional relationships among them. The resulting network of nodes and links represents a person's cognitive structure. Conceptual change may also be conceived as the reorganization of one's semantic network.

Evolutionary Conceptual Change

By using the term "evolution" a direct reference is being made to the work of Charles Darwin. In his seminal work, Darwin (1963) laid out a theory of species development that detailed a slow and gradual process for physical changes within and across species resulting from evolutionary adaptation. In much the same way, some conceptual change theories propose a more gradual and slow process of change. For instance, Smith *et al.* (1993) argue that the gradual refinement of prior knowledge should be the focus of learners' conceptual change rather than replacement or radical reorganization of prior conceptions. In this view, constructivist tenets of continuity and functionality of knowledge are used to develop a systems level of analysis regarding conceptual change. While continuity refers to the gradual process of refining old ideas by combining them with other old ideas and new ideas, functionality is concerned with the perceived utility of both old and new ideas (Smith *et al.*, 1993). By using continuity and functionality, a systems level of analysis allows for a view of conceptual change as a process of gradually refining integrated sets of knowledge as opposed to one particular misconception. Thus, conceptual change gradually occurs over time in the context of new knowledge, utility of the new knowledge, and utility of prior knowledge (Smith *et al.*, 1993).

Strike and Posner (1992) have articulated another conceptual change perspective that is more evolutionary in nature in two ways. First, their theory suggests that misconceptions interact with and are part of a broader conceptual ecology that is developed over time, and secondly, enacting change involves the more gradual process of identifying the roots of these misconceptions and replacing or refuting them. To define misconceptions, Strike and Posner's (1992) revisionist theory of conceptual change first relates that conceptions, as opposed to concepts, are not isolated and are tools of thought that function as perceptual categories within a conceptual ecology. They then note that, "a conceptual ecology consists of such cognitive artifacts as anomalies, analogies, metaphors, epistemological beliefs, metaphysical beliefs, knowledge from other areas of inquiry, and knowledge of competing conceptions" (p. 150). The interaction of these factors in the conceptual ecology is what leads to or creates misconceptions. In order to change these misconceptions, Strike and Posner (1992) suggest four conditions must be present: a dissatisfaction with current conceptions, a presence of intelligible new conceptions, a presence of plausible new conceptions, and a potential of new conceptions being productive tools of thought. These conditions are typically met by utilizing two techniques. The first involves rooting out the pieces of the conceptual ecology that foster misconceptions and replacing them, and the second involves directly challenging misconceptions or drowning them in a sea of anomalies (Strike & Posner, 1992). Thus, change tends to be a more gradual process where deeply rooted misconceptions are either directly or indirectly challenged and eventually replaced by more plausible conceptions.

A final line of research that represents a more evolutionary viewpoint of conceptual change is the research conducted by Stella Vosniadou and her colleagues in various fields of science (Vosniadou, 1992, 1994, 2002; Vosniadou & Brewer, 1992, 1994). In her view, conceptual structures are best understood as theories or mental models and restructuring of these theories is a slow and gradual process that requires many reinterpretations of conceptions and beliefs (Vosniadou, 1992). Taking a developmental approach, Vosniadou (1992) begins by noting that children typically have initial or entrenched scientific conceptual models that were developed via everyday experiences. These initial models are often inaccurate and inconsistent with adult teachings about science. When children are presented with such teachings, they often do not believe adults are wrong but also don't want to believe that their experientially informed models are wrong either (Vosniadou 1992). In their research (Vosniadou, 1992, 1994, 2002; Vosniadou & Brewer, 1992, 1994), Vosniadou and colleagues have found that students will reconcile these situations by assimilating and accommodating the adult teachings into their entrenched conceptual models creating "synthetic models" about science, and that these synthetic models become more sophisticated as children progress in school. This synthetic meaning making then is a slow process of conceptual change that involves the gradual progression towards different levels of understanding our world (Vosniadou, 1992, 2002).

Radical Conceptual Change

In much the same way that Darwin is analogous to evolutionary conceptual change, Thomas Kuhn's theories about paradigm shifts can be used as a foundation to understand radical conceptual change. Kuhn (1962) believed that scientific revolutions could be seen as epistemological paradigm shifts within the communities of practice and that these shifts lead to viewing information in fundamentally different ways. These conceptual revolutions are required when we encounter major anomalies that cannot be explained by current theories, so a new paradigm is required. The new conceptual systems are then adopted because of greater explanatory coherence of the new propositions (Thagard, 1992). However, unlike evolutionary change perspectives, Kuhn believed these paradigm shifts occur in a radical way. That is, scientific thought did not gradually lead to the adoption of Einstein's theories, instead his theories quickly and decidedly changed the way science was viewed. Some conceptual change theories view the shifting of knowledge within learners in much the same way. One such radical conceptual change perspective details the change process in terms of ontological shifts.

Chi, Slotta, and de Leeuw (1994) assume that conceptions are assigned to ontological categories by the learner, and that conceptual change occurs when concepts are reassigned to different categories. In this view, ontological categories are seen as common shared categories of knowledge (Chi *et al.*, 1994). This theory was primarily applied to learning science, positing that ontological categories in physics include material, process, and mental state ontologies. An example of an ontological shift would be a learner changing conceptual information about electricity from the matter ontology (e.g., that electricity has amounts and takes up space) to a process ontology (e.g., that electricity is the interaction of atoms). Naïve conceptions of science are often incorrect because they assign concepts to the wrong ontological category. For instance, this misconception of electricity as matter is common because most introductory texts use an analogy of water flowing through a pipe to explain the process of electricity; therefore, learners will often attribute matter-like qualities to electricity, such as that it has volume (Chi *et al.*, 1994). Such ontological shifts are seen as a radical restructuring because it requires learners to fundamentally change their knowledge of a given concept. That is, a learner brings a certain ontological category to any concept to be learned, and when this prior ontological category does not match the instructed ontological category, learners must undergo a radical shift in thinking to recategorize the concept (Chi *et al.*, 1994). Shifting ontological categories is a radical form of conceptual change.

Another theory that can be couched within the radical conceptual change framework is the one articulated by Clark Chinn and William Brewer (1993). Their theory is primarily focused on what happens when learners are presented with scientific information, or anomalous data, that does not fit their existing theories about the world. For instance:

> An individual currently holds theory A. The individual then encounters anomalous data, data that currently cannot be explained by theory A. The data may be anomalous because they clearly conflict with theory A or simply because theory A cannot be used to marshal any explanation for the data. The anomalous data may or may not be accompanied by theory B, which is intended to explain much of the body of data explained by theory A, plus the anomalous data.
>
> (Chinn & Brewer, 1993, p. 4)

When in this cognitive conflict situation, learners could conceivably have many choices regarding the anomalous data and if present, an alternative theory. However, Chinn and Brewer (1993) conceived what they believe to be an exhaustive list of seven possible learner responses to the anomalous data: 1) ignore the data, 2) reject the data, 3) exclude the data from theory A, 4) place the data in abeyance, 5) reinterpret the data while maintaining theory A, 6) reinterpret the data while making peripheral changes to theory A, or 7) accept the data and change theory A. Of these responses, only the final two represent conceptual change and they would appear to occur in a brief, more radical way. Whether the learner engages in this more revolutionary change is dependent on the learner's prior knowledge, the existence of a plausible alternative theory, the nature of the anomalous data, and the learner's processing strategies (Chinn & Brewer, 1993). For example, if the learner's prior knowledge is highly entrenched, there is no alternative theory presented, the anomalous data is ambiguous, and the learner only processes the situation in a shallow manner, then no conceptual change is likely to occur.

The theories presented represent different views on the pace and nature of conceptual changes that learners experience. Some of these theories, such as Vosniadou's (1992) synthetic meaning making and Chi *et al.*'s (1994) radical restructuring, clearly fall into their respective views of evolutionary or radical change; while others, such as Chinn and Brewer's (1993) views on cognitive conflict and Strike and Posner's (1992) views on revision, are less overtly evolutionary or radical yet still are more suited to explaining conceptual change in an evolutionary or radical way. Although both evolutionary and radical conceptual change theories have contributed to our understanding of how learners' conceptions change, many of these theories are narrowly focused. As Dole and Sinatra (1998) point out, many conceptual change theories seek to primarily explain the process and outcome of conceptual changes. More recently, conceptual change theories have begun expanding this focus to investigate how contextual influences, such as motivation and affect, can influence the change process.

Hot Conceptual Change

The theories discussed to this point, for the most part, do not address issues pertaining to learners' motivations and emotions. Pintrich, Marx, and Boyle (1993) categorized such conceptual change theories that focus solely on the cognitive processes in conceptual change and outcomes as "cold" conceptual change theories, and they argued for a need to include motivational aspects into "hot" theories of conceptual change. In her synopsis of cold conceptual change theories, Sinatra (2005) explains that these theories focused on the structural changes to knowledge, on the developmental processes in knowledge restructuring, and on the use of instruction to foster change. Such foci are of little surprise given that most of these theories were rooted in the traditions of Piaget (1950, 1952) and other schema theorists like Shavelson (1972) and Rumelhart and Ortony (1977) who had focused their efforts on structures and development of knowledge. However, the focus of the conceptual change literature was shifted soon after Pintrich *et al.*'s (1993) call for contextual factors to be considered, and this notion of including "hot" constructs has been influential in the articulation of contemporary conceptual change theories. Two theories that exemplify this new view of conceptual change are the Cognitive-Affective Model of Conceptual Change (CAMCC; Gregoire, 2003) and the Cognitive Reconstruction of Knowledge Model (CRKM; Dole & Sinatra, 1998). Both of these theories are considered part of the "warming" trend in the conceptual change literature because they include various motivational constructs in their articulation of the conceptual change process (Sinatra, 2005).

Gregoire's (2003) CAMCC proposes that cognitive processing mediates the change process, that motivation and affect mediate cognitive processing, and what gets noticed in the environment results from an individual's attitudes, goals, and prior beliefs. This theory focused on teachers' subject-matter belief change, and the change process begins when individuals are presented with reform messages in a particular environment (Gregoire, 2003). Once this reform is introduced, an individual will evaluate if the reform implicates the self, and if it does not, then positive or neutral affect is enacted and shallow processing occurs, leading to superficial or no belief change (Gregoire, 2003). If the reform does implicate the self, then the learner experiences negative affect and evaluates environmental aspects, leading to either threat or challenge appraisals of the message (Gregoire, 2003). If a threat appraisal is made, then avoidance intentions occur, leading to shallow processing and superficial or no belief change; however, if challenge appraisals are made, then approach intentions occur, leading to deep processing of the reform and to either true conceptual change or no belief change. The CAMCC borrows from cognitive theories of conceptual change as well as from theories of attitude change from social psychology (Gregoire, 2003; Sinatra, 2005). Much like the CAMCC, Dole and Sinatra's (1998) CRKM borrows from the same two fields of cognitive and social psychology; however, their model is more iterative in its view of "hot" conceptual change and can be applied to a broader variety of learners (Sinatra, 2005).

The CRKM assumes that conceptual change begins with a message that is incongruent to a learner's existing conceptions, proposing that characteristics of the learner and characteristics of the message iteratively influence cognitive change (Dole & Sinatra, 1998; Sinatra, 2005). Characteristics of the learner that influence the change process include their motivation and the nature of the existing conception. Specifically, the CRKM posits that learners will be motivated to process the message if there is dissatisfaction with their current conception, if the message is personally relevant to them, if the social context of the message presentation is persuasive, and/or if the person has a heightened need for cognition (Dole & Sinatra, 1998). If the learner's existing conception is strongly formed, coherent, and committed to, then learners may not be as likely to engage in conceptual change (Dole & Sinatra, 1998). Characteristics of the message including its comprehensibility, coherence, plausibility, and persuasiveness will also influence the likelihood of conceptual change (Dole & Sinatra, 1998). The characteristics of the learner and the congruency of the message combine to influence the engagement of the learner in processing the new information, and if this processing is high, then strong or no conceptual change is likely (Dole & Sinatra, 1998). Conversely, if this engagement is low, then weak or no conceptual change is more likely (Dole & Sinatra, 1998).

Learning Environments that Foster Conceptual Change

Many kinds of learning environments can foster conceptual change. For example, Vosniadou, Ioannides, Dimitrakopoulou, and Papademetriou (2001) constructed a rich, multi-modal learning environment to foster conceptual change. Fifth graders worked in small groups on hands-on experiments using measuring devices, vectors as symbols for the representation of forces, and models of friction. The students made predictions and then debated their findings. Students in the learning environment achieved greater cognitive gains than the control group (Vosniadou *et al.*, 2001). Like this study, most research on conceptual change in learning environments focuses on radical conceptual change. This is mainly because when interacting with learning environments, students often face cognitive dissonance from alternative perspectives that need to be resolved. As noted earlier, such cognitive conflict situations are more likely to result in radical conceptual change. However, and especially for those learners who do not initially experience radical conceptual change, longer term use of different learning environments may also support evolutionary conceptual change.

In order to most likely foster revolutionary or evolutionary conceptual change, educational activities should point out the following (Strike & Posner, 1992):

* Learners must experience dissatisfaction with an existing conception. If learners are not dissatisfied with their existing conceptions, they tend to conflate newer conflicting information with existing conceptions into incoherent theories.
* Newer conceptions must be comprehensible and integrated in a coherent set of propositions in order to avoid rote memorization.
* Newer conceptions must be plausible to the learner and preferably consistent with accepted theories.
* Newer conceptions must be applicable to solving problems.

Such suggestions do hint at not only the cold aspects of conceptual change (i.e., process and outcomes) but also at the hot aspects of conceptual change that researchers like Dole and Sinatra (1998) and Gregoire (2003) later expanded on in their respective theories. That is, qualities of the content, the context, and the learner should be considered when attempting to enact conceptual change within a learning environment. In short, any learning environment can foster conceptual change, if the learners have constructed mental models that they wish to test, apply, or debate.

Testing Simulations for Conceptual Change

Simulations are imitations of some phenomenon, state of affairs, or process. Simulations imitate phenomena by allowing learners to manipulate key characteristics or variables within a physical or abstract system that represents (simulates) the phenomenon. Because of their computational capabilities, computers are frequently used to build simulations of real-life

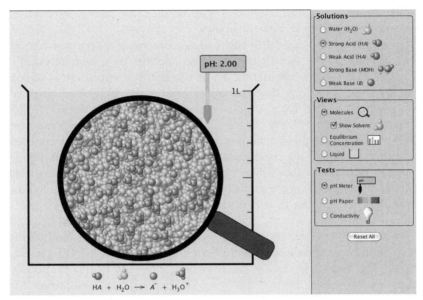

Figure 4.1 Acid–base simulation

situations. The simulation designer builds a causal model of the phenomena or processes that operationally describes how the system functions, so "the main task of the learner being to infer, through experimentation, characteristics of the model underlying the simulation" (deJong & van Jooligan, 1998, p. 179). When learners interact with the simulation, change values of (input) variables, and observe the results on the values of other (output) variables, they are testing their understanding of the phenomenon, especially the causal relationships among variables. For example, Figure 4.1 shows an acid–base reaction (phet.coloado.edu) in which learners can predict and test the pH of different acid–base reactions. Because the learner seldom has access to the underlying model, learners must induce the rules and relationships that are depicted in the model by manipulating the environment.

Simulations vary tremendously in detail, complexity, and discipline. There are hundreds of commercially available and free laboratory simulations in the science disciplines. School students also use urban simulations such as SimCity to create and test social studies problems, and in higher education, numerous business simulations have been used for decades to train strategic decision making. A large number of medical simulations also exist to support medical training. These simulations typically present a patient using video and allow the medical trainee to examine the patient, order tests, make diagnoses, and test those diagnoses (inference making) by treating the simulated patient. Those patients may be presented on a computer screen or in the form of a manipulable dummy. Some medical simulations are so complex that they allow medical personnel to conduct simulated surgery.

In commercial applications, flight simulators are an important part of pilot training. Pilots can sit in simulated cockpits that even physically move based on flight commands. These simulators can present complex and dramatic situations that the pilots must deal with. A number of planeloads of people have survived airline incidents because pilots had addressed those problems during simulator training. Simulations are used extensively in the trucking industry as well, where driver trainees encounter various road conditions and potential accident situations to navigate. Of course, the military uses simulations in numerous aspects of its training programs, especially urban warfare. Among the obvious advantages of simulation use is the ability to learn through mistakes without harming anyone.

A number of researchers early on recommended the use of simulations for fostering conceptual change (Snir, Smith, & Grosslight, 1995; Spada, 1994). The most effective simulations, they argue, are conceptually enhanced by using models that provide explicit representations for interrelated concepts. The effects of simulations on science conceptions have been examined repeatedly, and most of these investigations have focused on a more radical conceptual change process. For instance, Zietsman (1986) showed that microcomputer simulations of velocity were able to remediate misconceptions and produce significant conceptual change in students. When simulations are combined with laboratory experiments (possibly embodied cognition), students experience greater conceptual understanding than students using either simulation or laboratory activities alone (Jaakkola & Nurmi, 2008). Bell and Trundle (2008) showed that computer simulations promote conceptual change when used within a conceptual change model of instruction. However, not all the research has focused on the more radical form of change. White and Frederiksen (2000) described the results of a seven-year study using Thinker Tools, a simulation for testing understanding of force and motion. Over time, students using ThinkerTools learned how to monitor and reflect, which then facilitated conceptual change. Finally, some research has also looked at contextual factors involved in the use of simulations. Windschitl and Andre (1998) found that students who explored a computer simulation of the human cardiovascular system experienced significantly greater conceptual change than students using a procedural approach, and individuals with more sophisticated epistemological beliefs performed better when allowed to explore, whereas individuals with less sophisticated beliefs did well when given explicit directions on how to use the simulation.

What enables simulations to foster conceptual change? Though not experimentally tested, requiring students to generate hypotheses before using simulations and then reflecting on the results and explaining discrepancies between their predictions and the actual results of the simulation are most likely to affect conceptual change. Such activities are likely to enact a more radical form of conceptual change; however, studies such as the one done by White and Frederiksen (2000) do illustrate how this process can be more gradual.

Model Building for Conceptual Change

While simulations have widely been used to facilitate conceptual change in learning science, they have not consistently changed scientific conceptions (Li, Law, & Liu, 2006). Simulations enable students to explore scientific models; however, the models are immutable. Because learners have no access to the model, they cannot change it, except to manipulate a set of pre-selected variables within the model. Rather than studying others' conceptions of phenomena, students will learn more from modeling their own conceptions and comparing them with others' models (Jonassen, Strobel, & Gottdenker, 2006). Li *et al.* (2006) showed that dynamic modeling helped students adopt more scientifically acceptable conceptions. In this section, we explore the construction of models as a means for fostering radical conceptual change.

Why is model building effective? When testing simulations, students are using existing models. Learning from using simulation models depends on the extent to which we can transfer the things we learn from manipulating the model to our theory of the real world (Morgan, 1999). "We do not learn much from looking at a model – we learn a lot more from building the model and from manipulating it" (Morrison & Morgan, 1999, pp. 11–12). When learning by building models, students must discover what elements fit together in order to represent a phenomenon or a theory of it. When solving a problem or answering a complex conceptual question, learners must construct a mental model of the phenomena and use that model as the basis for prediction, inference, speculation, or experimentation. Constructing a physical, analogical, or computational model of the world reifies the learner's mental model. Model building is effective because (Jonassen *et al.*, 2006):

- Model building is a natural cognitive phenomenon. When encountering unknown phenomena, humans naturally begin to construct personal theories and models of those phenomena in order to understand them.
- Modeling is essentially constructivist – constructing personal representations of experienced phenomena.
- Modeling supports hypothesis testing, conjecturing, inferring, and a host of other important cognitive skills.
- Modeling requires learners to articulate causal reasoning, the cognitive basis for most scientific reasoning (Jonassen & Ionas, 2008).

- Modeling is important because it is among the most conceptually engaging cognitive processes that can be performed, which is a strong predictor of conceptual change.
- Modeling results in the construction of cognitive artifacts (externalized mental models).
- When students construct models, they own the knowledge. Student ownership is important to meaning making and knowledge construction.
- Modeling supports the development of epistemic beliefs. Comparing and evaluating models requires understanding that alternative models are possible and that the activity of modeling can be used for testing rival models.

Historically, much of the modeling research has focused on mathematization as the primary modeling formalism. Representing phenomena in equations is perhaps the most succinct and exact form of modeling. Although equations provide the most accurate models of phenomena, they lack conceptual meaning. However, most contemporary researchers argue that qualitative models are just as important as quantitative ones. All equations are numerical statements of causal relationships among entities; however, asking learners to unpack the concepts represented in an equation is extremely demanding and frustrating for them. In order to foster conceptual change, more qualitative, conceptually oriented modeling tools must be used. Ploetzner, Fehse, Kneser, and Spada (1999) showed that in order to successfully transfer physics problem-solving, qualitative problem representations are necessary prerequisites to learning quantitative representations.

Among the most effective qualitative modeling tools are concept maps. Concept maps consist of labeled nodes and links. Figure 4.2 illustrates one screen of a complex concept map on Macbeth produced with Semantica (www.semanticresearch.com). Double-clicking any of the concepts on the map puts that concept in the middle of the screen and shows all of the other concepts that are associated with it.

When learners construct concept maps either individually or collaboratively, they are representing their propositions connecting the concepts within any domain or problem. It is important that students be allowed to construct their own maps, which teachers may then question or perturb. Nesbit and Adesope (2006) showed that constructing concept maps results in more conceptual change than studying existing maps. Another effective strategy is to have learners compare and contrast their maps with others' maps. They quickly understand that we all construct different conceptions of phenomena, and such insights are likely to foster more rapid conceptual shifts.

One of the most powerful modeling tools is based on systems dynamics. Computer-based tools such as Stella, VenSim, and PowerSim enable users to

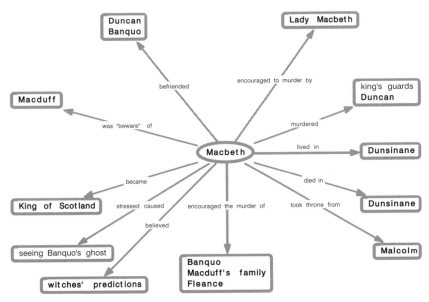

Figure 4.2 Single screen from complex concept map on Macbeth

construct qualitative models of phenomena while describing relationships among the entities quantitatively by inserting any kind of equation to describe relationships among the entities. In order to better understand conceptual change processes, Jonassen, Strobel, and Gottdenker (2006) used a systems dynamics tool, Stella, to model conceptual change processes. Figure 4.3 illustrates the model they built for representing cognitive conflict (i.e., more radical) models of conceptual change.

By constructing Stella models of the different theories of conceptual change, Jonassen, Strobel, and Gottdenker (2006) were able to test their own understanding of the theories. While building models of each theory, they reconciled their naïve personal theories with the different theoretical accounts. Realizing that such a model is always incomplete, the hot conceptual process of constructing the model required intensive negotiation about which factors in the change process are most important and how the process of conceptual change looks in an operationalized form. This experience again highlights how simulations can foster radical conceptual change as negotiating differences of opinion would likely result in conceptual change for all parties engaged in the negotiations. The experience also relates how emotions can play a crucial part in this revolutionary conceptual change. The reason for such intensity was likely related to each individual member making challenge appraisals regarding their own mental models of the phenomenon. As Gregoire (2003) explains, such challenge appraisals will lead to negative emotions and approach intentions that foster deep processing and either true conceptual change or no change.

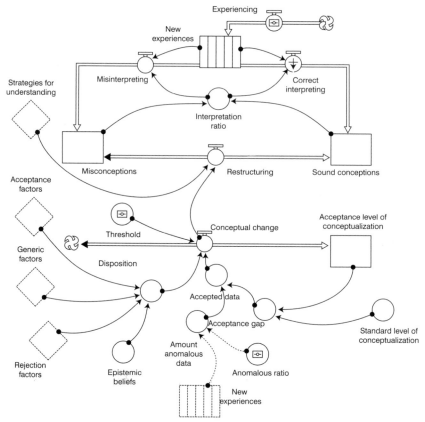

Figure 4.3 Systems dynamics model of cognitive conflict conceptual change

Arguing for Conceptual Change

Argumentation is described more completely in Chapter 5 by Nussbaum. In the following brief section, we describe the role of argumentation in supporting conceptual change. Although three different types of arguments exist (rhetorical, dialectical, and apodictic), dialectical arguments are the most likely to lead to conceptual change. Dialectical arguments represent a dialogue between proponents of alternative claims during a dialogue game or a discussion. Also known as dialogical or multi-voiced arguments, the purpose of dialectical arguments is to resolve differences of opinions (Jonassen & Kim, 2010; van Eemeren & Grootendorst, 1992). That resolution may take different forms. Dialectic arguments may be adversarial, where the goal is to convince opponents of the superiority of one's claim. They may also seek a compromise between multiple claims.

Dialectic arguments may take place within individuals (e.g., making a decision) or within social groups (Driver *et al.*, 2000). Arguments may involve small- and large-group discussions or debate about issues. Individual argumentation normally occurs in writing activities.

Dole and Sinatra (1998) have argued that promoting the level of engagement necessary to facilitate intentional conceptual change could be achieved by constructing arguments. A growing body of research has investigated the role of argumentation in fostering conceptual change and found that argumentation leads to conceptual change (Asterhan & Schwarz, 2007; Baker, 1999; Nussbaum & Sinatra, 2003; Wiley & Voss, 1999). Conceptual change occurs because argumentation emphasizes the epistemic nature of science. Inserting argumentation activities in science learning environments supports both conceptual and epistemic goals, reflecting the ways that scientists reason (Duschl & Osborne, 2002).

Most of the research on argumentation and conceptual change has explored those changes through writing activities that present ill-structured problems and issues in the sciences to learners. Mason (2001) found that reasoning and arguing collaboratively on different beliefs and ideas, as well as individual writing to express, clarify, reflect and reason on, and communicate one's own conceptions and explanations, are fruitful tools in the knowledge revision process. Individual and collaborative groups challenged to develop arguments on evolution showed greater conceptual change than students who produced more expository texts (Asterhan & Schwarz, 2007). When undergraduates were challenged to act like historians and instructed to describe historical events as arguments instead of narratives, summaries, or explanations, they produced the most integrated essays that emphasized the causal relationships among events (Wiley & Voss, 1999). Students who wrote arguments from web sources rather than merely explaining or summarizing them gained a better understanding than other students. Generating causal theories to support claims is an essential skill of argumentation (Kuhn, 1991).

Argumentation has even been applied to supporting problem solving. Undergraduates answering physics problems incorrectly who were asked to argue in favor of an alternative (correct scientific) explanation of the problem showed improved conceptions and reasoning on transfer problems than control participants who were asked to solve the problem without argumentation (Nussbaum & Sinatra, 2003). Baker (2003) showed that computer-supported collaborative argumentation enhanced students' problem-solving skills. He showed that argumentation occupies the dialectical space, which mediates the problem space and the meaning space (i.e., conceptual change).

Constructing arguments engages conceptual change because of the high conceptual engagement in students (Nussbaum & Sinatra, 2003) and helps to make scientific reasoning visible (Duschl & Osborne, 2002). Moreover, arguments provide methods for assessing student understanding of scientific concepts. Because of the social and collaborative nature of argumentation, it appears to be a warmer kind of conceptual change.

Summary

Conceptual change is a complex socio-cognitive process that results in reorganized conceptual structures. Those structures are applied when solving problems, learning new material, or attempting to explain phenomena.

We began by describing theories of evolutionary versus radical conceptual change, the former occurring more gradually as new knowledge is assimilated and accommodated into existing conceptual structures and the latter resulting from quicker change that is driven by cognitive conflict. These theories were referred to as cold conceptual change, because they focused only on the cognitive aspects of conceptual change.

More recently, scholars have begun to construct warmer theories of conceptual change that take into account the social and motivational aspects of the context in which the change is occurring. Fully understanding how minds change often involves consideration of these complex socio-cognitive components.

Any form of instruction may result in conceptual change, as long as the learners have constructed some conceptual structure and wish to test or apply their conceptual model. We described three different intentional conceptual change environments (Sinatra & Pintrich, 2003). Simulations require learners to construct some kind of model of the system represented in the simulation. Testing that theory by changing parameters in the simulation can lead to conceptual change.

Simulations are built on a model. Learners engage in significantly more conceptual change when they build models to represent their own conceptualizations. It is important that learner-constructed external models qualitatively represent their mental models.

Finally, argumentation has been shown to foster conceptual change. Clearly, more research on the effects argumentation and other learning environments on conceptual change is needed.

References

Asterhan, C. S. C., & Schwarz, B. B. (2007). The effects of monological and dialogical argumentation on concept learning in evolutionary theory. *Journal of Educational Psychology, 99*(3), 626–639.

Baker, M. (1999). Argumentation and constructive interaction. In J. Andriessen & P. Coirier (Eds.), *Foundations of argumentative text processing* (pp. 179–202). Amsterdam: Amsterdam University Press.

Baker, M. (2003). Computer-mediated argumentative interactions for the co-elaboration of scientific notions. In J. Andriessen, M. Baker, & D. Suthers (Eds.), *Arguing to learn: Confronting cognitions in computer-supported collaborative learning environments* (pp. 47–78).

Bell, R. L., & Trundle, K. C. (2008). The use of a computer simulation to promote scientific conceptions of moon phases. *Journal of Research in Science Teaching, 45*(3), 346–372.

Carey, S. (1988). Reorganization of knowledge in the course of acquisition. In S. Strauss (Ed.), *Ontogeny, phylogeny, and historical development. Human development series, Vol 2* (pp. 1–27). Westport, CT: Ablex Publishing.

Chi, M. T. H. (1992). Conceptual change within and across ontological categories: Examples from learning and discovery in science. In R. N. Giere (Ed.), *Minnesota studies in the philosophy of science:* (Vol. XV, pp. 129–186). Minneapolis, MN: University of Minnesota Press.

Chi, M. T. H., Slotta, J. D., & de Leeuw, N. (1994). From things to processes: A theory of conceptual change for learning science concepts. *Learning and Instruction, 4*, 27–43.

Chinn, C. A., & Brewer, W. F. (1993). The role of anomalous data in knowledge acquisition: A theoretical framework and implications for science instruction. *Review of Educational Research, 63*, 1–49.

Darwin, C. (1963). *On the origin of species.* London: Oxford University Press.

deJong, T., & van Joolingen, W. R. (1998). Scientific discovery learning with computer simulations of conceptual domains. *Review of Educational Research, 68*(2), 179–201.

Dole, J. A., & Sinatra, G. M. (1998). Reconceptualizing change in the cognitive construction of knowledge. *Educational Psychologist, 33*, 109–128.

Driver, R., Newton, P., & Osborne, J. (2000). Establishing the norms of scientific argumentation in classrooms. *Science Education, 84*, 287–312.

Duschl, R. A., & Osborne, J. (2002). Supporting and promoting argumentation discourse in science education. *Studies in Science Education, 38*, 39–72.

Eagly, A. H., & Chaiken, S. (1993). *The psychology of attitudes.* Fort Worth, TX: Harcourt Brace.

Gregoire, M. (2003). Is it a challenge or a threat? A dual-process model of teachers' cognition and appraisal process during conceptual change. *Educational Psychology Review, 15*, 117–155.

Jaakkola, T., & Nurmi, S. (2008). Fostering elementary school students' understanding of simple electricity by combining simulation and laboratory activities. *Journal of Computer Assisted Learning, 24*(4), 271–283.

Jonassen, D. H., & Ionas, I. G. (2008). Designing effective supports for reasoning causally. *Educational Technology: Research & Development, 56* (3), 287–308.

Jonassen, D. H., & Kim, B. (2010). Arguing to learn and learning to argue: Design justifications and guidelines. *Educational Technology: Research & Development, 58* (4), 439–457.

Jonassen, D. H., Strobel, J., & Gottdenker, J. (2006). Model building for conceptual change. *Interactive Learning Environments, 13*(1–2), 15–37.

Kuhn, D. (1991). *The skills of argument.* Cambridge, UK: Cambridge University Press.

Kuhn, T. S. (1962). *The structure of scientific revolution.* Chicago, IL: University of Chicago Press.

Li, S. C., Law, N., & Liu, K. F. A. (2006). Cognitive perturbation through dynamic modelling: A pedagogical approach to conceptual change in science. *Journal of Computer Assisted Learning, 22*(6), 405–422.

Mason, K. (2001). Introducing talk and writing for conceptual change: a classroom study. *Learning and Instruction, 11*, 305–329.

Morgan, M. S. (1999). Learning from models. In M. S. Morgan & M. Morrison (Eds.), *Models as mediators: Perspectives on natural and social science* (pp. 347–388). Cambridge, UK: Cambridge University Press.

Morrison, M., & Morgan, M. S. (1999). Models as mediating instruments. In M. S. Morgan & M. Morrison (Eds.), *Models as mediators: Perspectives on natural and social science* (pp. 10–37). Cambridge, UK: Cambridge University Press.

Nesbit, J. C., & Adesope, O. O. (2006). Learning with concept and knowledge maps: A metaanalysis. *Review of Educational Research, 76*, 413–448.

Norman, D. A., Gentner, S. & Stevens, A. L. (1976). Comments on learning schemata and memory representation. In D. Klahr (Ed.), *Cognition and instruction*. Hillsdale, NJ: Lawrence Erlbaum Associates.

Nussbaum, E. M., & Sinatra, G. M. (2003). Argument and conceptual engagement. *Contemporary Educational Psychology, 28*(3), 384–395.

Piaget, J. (1950). *The psychology of intelligence*. San Diego, CA: Harcourt Brace Jovanovich.

Piaget, J. (1952). *The origins of intelligence in children*. New York: International Universities Press.

Pintrich, P. R., Marx, R. W., & Boyle, R. A. (1993). Beyond cold conceptual change: The role of motivational beliefs and classroom contextual factors in the process of conceptual change. *Review of Educational Research, 63*(2), 167–199.

Ploetzner, R., Fehse, E., Kneser, C., & Spada, H. (1999). Learning to relate qualitative and quantitative problem representations in a model-based setting for collaborative problem solving. *Journal of the Learning Sciences, 8*(2), 177–214.

Quillian, M. R. (1968). Semantic memory. In M. Minsky (Ed.), *Semantic information processing* (pp. 227–270). Cambridge, MA: MIT Press.

Rumelhart, D. E., & Ortony, A. (1977). The representation of knowledge in memory. In R. C. Anderson, R. J. Spiro & W. E. Montague (Eds.), *Schooling and the acquisition of knowledge* (pp. 99–135). Hillsdale, NJ: Lawrence Erlbaum Associates.

Shavelson, R. J. (1972). Some aspects of the correspondence between content structure and cognitive structure in physics instruction. *Journal of Educational Psychology, 63*, 225–234.

Sinatra, G. M. (2005). The "warming trend" in conceptual change research: The legacy of Paul R. Pintrich. *Educational Psychologist 40*, 107–115.

Sinatra, G. M., & Pintrich, P. R. (2003). The role of intentions in conceptual change learning. In G. M. Sinatra, & P. R. Pintrich (Eds.), *Intentional conceptual change* (pp. 1–18). Mahwah, NJ: Lawrence Erlbaum Associates.

Smith, J. P., di Sessa, A. A., & Roschelle, J. (1993). Misconceptions reconceived: A constructivist analysis of knowledge in transition. *Journal of the Learning Sciences, 3*, 115–163.

Snir, J., Smith, C., & Grosslight, L. (1995). Conceptually enhanced simulations: A computer tool for science teaching. In D. N. Perkins, J. L. Schwartz, M. M. West, & M. S. Wiske (Eds), *Software goes to school: Teaching for understanding with new technologies* (pp. 106–129). New York: Oxford University Press.

Spada, H. (1994). Conceptual change or multiple representations? *Learning and Instruction, 4*(1), 113–116.

Strike, K. A., & Posner, G. J. (1992). A revisionist theory of conceptual change. In R. A. Duschle & R. J. Hamilton (Eds.), *Philosophy of science, cognitive psychology, and educational theory and practice* (pp. 147–176). New York: SUNY Press.

Tesser, A., & Shaffer, D. R. (1990). Attitudes and attitude change. *Annual Review of Psychology, 41,* 479–523.

Thagard, P. (1992). *Conceptual revolutions.* Princeton, NJ: Princeton University Press.

van Eemeren, F. H., & Grootendorst, R. (1992). *Argumentation, communication, and fallacies: A pragmadialectical perspective.* Hillsdale, NJ: Erlbaum.

Vosniadou, S. (1992). Knowledge acquisition and conceptual change. *Applied Psychology: An International Review, 41,* 347–357.

Vosniadou, S. (1994). Capturing and modeling the process of conceptual change. *Learning & Instruction, 4,* 45–69.

Vosniadou, S. (2002). On the nature of naive physics. In M. Limon & L. Mason (Eds.), *Reconsidering conceptual change. Issues in theory and practice* (pp. 61–76). Netherlands: Kluwer Academic Publishers.

Vosniadou, S., & Brewer, W. F. (1992). Mental models of the earth: A study of conceptual change in childhood. *Cognitive Psychology, 24,* 535–585.

Vosniadou, S., & Brewer, W. F. (1994). Mental models of the day/night cycle. *Cognitive Science, 18,* 123–183.

Vosniadou, S., Ioannides, C., Dimitrakopoulou, A., & Papademetriou, E. (2001). Designing learning environments to promote conceptual change in science. *Learning and Instruction, 11,* 381–419.

White, B. Y., & Frederiksen, J. R. (2000). Technological tools and instructional approaches for making scientific inquiry accessible to all. In M. J. Jacobson & R. B. Kozma (Eds.), *Innovations in science and mathematics education: Advanced designs, for technologies of learning* (pp. 321–359). Mahwah, NJ: Lawrence Erlbaum Associates.

Wiley, J., & Voss, J. F. (1999). Constructing arguments from multiple sources: Tasks that promote understanding and not just memory for text. *Journal of Educational Psychology, 91*(2), 301–311.

Windschitl, M., & Andre, T. (1998). Using computer simulations to enhance conceptual change: The roles of constructivist instruction and student epistemological beliefs. *Journal of Research in Science Teaching, 35*(2), 145–160.

Zietsman, A. I. (1986). Effect of instruction using microcomputer simulations and conceptual change strategies on science learning. *Journal of Research in Science Teaching, 23*(1), 27–39.

5 Argumentation and Student-Centered Learning Environments

E. Michael Nussbaum

The language is meant to serve for communication between a builder A and an assistant B. A is building with building-stones: there are blocks, pillars, slabs and beams. B has to pass the stones, and to do so in the order in which A needs them. For this purpose they use a language consisting of the words "block", "pillar", "slab", "beam". A calls them out; B brings the stone which he has learnt to bring at such-and-such a call.

(Wittgenstein, 1958/2009, p. 6e)

Auretha: I got a challenge for you, Tom, because, um ... if animal dies, she's gonna be upset with herself.

(Anderson *et al.*, 2001, p. 18)

Humans play games! These games often involve argumentation, which is the process of constructing and critiquing arguments (a chain of propositions involving inference). Games are rule-structured activities where players have specific goals. This is a broad conceptualization that covers many sorts of activities. The first quote above from Wittgenstein illustrates how two individuals are involved in a "game" of building a house. This is a cooperative game in which the first player makes moves with words and the second player make moves with actions. Argumentation is a type of language game in which both players make moves with words. The second quotation is an excerpt from a collaborative reasoning discussion (Anderson *et al.*, 2001) in which fifth graders are discussing a moral dilemma regarding a short story, *Amy's Goose* (Holmes, 1977). Here, Auretha is challenging an interpretation of another student. The children are not involved in a debate, where there are winners or losers, but are collaboratively exploring different ideas. Rather than building a house, the game here is to build the best possible argument. There are rules that structure the activity (for example, only one student should talk at a time, they should support their ideas with reasons and evidence, etc.). Walton (1996) identified various forms of argumentation (for example, persuasive discussions, negotiations, inquiries), each with its own set of rules and goals.

Argumentation games are an important component of learning environments. Many learning environments involve students in authentic activities involving argumentation and decision making. For example, students might be called upon to apply mathematical skills and concepts to design a science station and to make mathematically based arguments for one design over another (Greeno & the MMAP Group, 1998). Argumentation is especially important in divergent problem solving (Van Bruggen, Boshuizen, & Kirschner, 2003) where individuals design and evaluate alternatives against constraints. Learning to make effective mathematical, scientific, historical, political, ethical, literary (etc.) arguments is part of mastering important social practices.

Furthermore, argumentation can, under certain circumstances, facilitate learning. Many (e.g., Andriessen, Baker, & Suthers, 2003) distinguish between *learning to argue* and *arguing to learn*. The former recognizes that learning to argue is intrinsically important, where the other idea is that argumentation can, under certain circumstances, facilitate deep, elaborate processing of information. This will only occur, of course, when the arguments made are themselves elaborate ones, and generating such arguments becomes a means to creating conceptual change or deeper conceptual understanding.

"Learning to argue" and "arguing to learn" are complementary ideas. In the late 1980s and 1990s, it became increasingly recognized by educational theorists that thinking is empty unless one has rich, disciplinary content to think about (Brown & Campione, 1990), and that "learning for understanding" is important to facilitate the long-run retention and transfer of content (Bransford, Brown, & Cocking, 2000). Argumentation became seen as a learning tool to have students reveal and reflect on prior conceptions, as well as reflecting an important disciplinary practice in its own right.

For example, Brown and Campione (1990) describe communities of learners where students became increasingly able to articulate warrants and provide evidence for arguments and causal explanations in environmental science; in physics, science educators wrote about guided methods for having students make and critique arguments about why books cannot pass through tables (Minstrell, 1982) or whether water would cool faster in a metal or Styrofoam cup (Slotta & Linn, 2009). Mathematics educators engaged students in argumentation to help them better understand procedures for mathematical algorithms (Lampert, Rittenhouse, & Crumbaugh, 1996). In history, scholars emphasized teaching argumentation as a disciplinary practice, including using multiple, primary sources and evaluating their objectivity (Wiley & Voss, 1999), as well as using argumentation to understand big ideas such as democracy. In English, teaching argumentation in the context of oral discussions (e.g., Nystrand & Gamoran, 1991) or persuasive writing (e.g., Harris, Graham, & Mason, 2002) was prominent. Concurrently, several cognitive and developmental psychologists, such as Voss, Kuhn, Perkins, Resnick, and various European researchers (e.g., Pontecorvo, 1993) examined psychological processes related to argumentation concerning social issues (e.g., the death penalty).

Since these beginnings, the study of argumentation has blossomed. In this chapter, it is not my intent to review the vast array of work in this area that has been produced over the last decade. Rather, I provide some recent examples of how argumentation has been incorporated into student-centered learning environments. First, however, I review some of the theoretical underpinnings of argumentation and learning.

Theoretical Underpinnings

Baker (cited in Andriessen, 2006) identified four causal mechanisms through which engaging in argumentation could produce stronger learning outcomes. First, argumentation makes knowledge explicit and visible (Bell & Linn, 2000). When students offer arguments in an oral discussion or in an essay, they reveal prior conceptions and misconceptions. Teachers can then take steps to address misconceptions, including allowing other students to make counterarguments. This leads into the second element postulated by Baker: argumentation can produce conceptual change. This itself is not a causal mechanism, but a set of possible mechanisms. Research suggests that argumentation can result in students considering a richer array of facets (Hunt & Minstrell, 1994), and variables in their thinking (Nussbaum, Sinatra, & Poliquin, 2008) can expose faults in students' own conceptions (Baker, 2003; Ravenscroft & McAlister, 2008), and can increase student understanding and commitment to alternative ideas (Asterhan & Schwarz, 2007; Yeh & She, 2010). The last mechanism assumes that students attend to conceptual conflicts, and that the better arguments win out over the weaker ones (both may require some teacher guidance).

Another mechanism identified by Baker is the co-elaboration of new knowledge. Elaboration is a psychological process that relates to depth of processing (Craik & Lockhart, 1972); when students identify multiple ways that two different items of information are related, the cuing of one item is more likely to activate the other. When students generate explanations for why one thing causes another (for example, why an arch can support more weight), they are elaborating on the relationship between "arch" and "support" and are more likely to recognize this relationship in other contexts. Such explanations may be generated during argumentation, for example two students arguing whether it is best to include a square or arched doorway in a model house. Each student may proffer explanations for their viewpoints. In addition to considering which explanation makes the most sense, the students might also consider empirical evidence produced from an experiment or simulation. These provide support or disconfirmation for arguments and a visual or kinesthetic memory trace, producing additional elaboration (and learning). Surprising experimental outcomes can also produce cognitive disequilibrium (triggering a need for conceptual change: see Chapter 4) and help resolve disagreements.

I have presented this example as if the two students were each advocating opposing ideas, but students can collaboratively explore the pros and cons of each idea. This does not mean the students never disagree, only that they are willing to be flexible and make concessions. This is known as *collaborative or collective argumentation* (Krummheuer, 1995) or *exploratory talk* (Mercer, 1994). Mercer and colleagues have conducted studies showing that exploratory talk, in comparison to *disputational talk* (in which the goal is to "win" a point), or *cumulative talk* (in which students build on one another's ideas but never disagree), results in better learning outcomes. Such considerations have led researchers such as Baker to stress co-elaboration, in which students elaborate on one another's ideas but also presumably critique them.

The final mechanism discussed by Baker is articulation. When engaging in argumentation, students need to be more articulate about their own questions and ideas. Gaps in their knowledge and chains of reasoning may become addressed. Students may need to organize their knowledge (and arguments) so the main ideas are explicit, and they may need to discuss and negotiate with one another about what they mean when referring to certain ideas, such as "heat" or "sound" (Baker, 2003).

We now come to a theoretical and practical difficulty. To be effective at argumentation and persuading others, students need to offer their ideas up for discussion, be articulate, think deeply and elaborate, provide evidence, be willing to disagree and evaluate various perspectives. These things will in turn promote learning, but there is no guarantee that students will have the skills or dispositions to do these things. Some students are frequently reticent or inarticulate, many are not particularly metacognitive (Vye *et al.*, 1998), most have difficulty coordinating theory and evidence (Kuhn, 1991), and many are reluctant to disagree with others for fear of losing face if they lose the argument (Lampert *et al.*, 1996). Some scaffolding of these behaviors may be necessary; how much is an empirical question and will vary among students and topic areas. The amount and nature of scaffolding needed is a key issue in the design of learning environments involving argumentation.

I have framed the above discussion relative to arguing to learn, but the same issues apply to learning to argue. In fact, the implication here is that one has to learn to argue to argue to learn. To some extent, the converse is also true, because one needs to acquire and use content knowledge to make effective arguments. The two goals are mutually necessary. "Learning to argue," however, also affords framing the activity in terms of mastering the social practices of a community, for example, learning to argue like a lawyer, engineer, mathematician, architect, or policy analyst. This provides students with additional motivation to learn to argue, from a sociocultural or situative perspective (Greeno & MMAP, 1998). In addition to identity development, argumentation can be intrinsically motivating to students by giving them choice and agency, arousing curiosity, and otherwise building intrinsic motivation to learn (Chinn, 2006). Engle and Conant (2002) proposed the idea of *productive disciplinary engagement*, where students engage (through discourse) in argumentation around the central themes and controversies in a discipline. For example, they analyzed how sixth-grade students, involved in an FCL (Brown & Campione, 1990) unit on endangered species, spent several months arguing whether killer whales were actually whales or dolphins ("one big ol' argument"). Students came to understand a lot about biological adaptation, as well as scientific argumentation. The time engaged with this issue also demonstrates the fun and motivating nature of argumentation.

The example, however, also raises another issue, that of time. Learning how to argue, using argumentation for conceptual change, investigating problems deeply, and creative problem solving all take time. More generally, students need time to learn about a topic and to think about the arguments from a discussion.

Some research by Howe (2010) suggests that the thinking conducted after an argumentative discussion creates conceptual change and deeper learning. The several rigorous studies of the relationship of argumentation and content learning that have been conducted have not found immediate advantages, compared with more traditional instruction, but have found delayed effects (Nussbaum, 2008), which is consistent with Howe's findings. It is the additional cognitive processing (elaboration and consolidation) occurring after argumentation that is often critical. This is not in itself an argument for using extended argument activities, but only for waiting to assess the results. But in combination with the other arguments expressed above, I do argue that learning environments should be designed to provide students with sufficient time to evaluate arguments and counterarguments (Nussbaum & Edwards, 2011), learn how to argue (Schwarz, Neuman, Gil, & Ilya, 2003), and develop disciplinary understanding (Engle & Conant, 2002).

In summary, I have considered several cognitive mechanisms for how argumentation can promote learning, supplemented with concepts related to situated social practice and disciplinary engagement. Argumentation is inherently both a cognitive and social activity; there are relationships and constraints related to content (these become the content of arguments and players argue what these are), and relationships and constraints related to social interaction (for example, how best to disagree with others). As suggested by various authors (Barron, 2003; Nussbaum, 1997), the problem space of those engaged in argumentation consists of both content and social constraints, and these must be coordinated in determining what to say, when, and how. These constraints define the "language game" in which participants become involved.

Examples of Argumentation in Student-Centered Learning Environments

In this section, I give several detailed examples of argumentation in student-centered learning environments, each involving different amounts and types of scaffolding and structure. The examples also vary in their use of technology, content domains, time devoted to argumentation, and whether evidence-based or practical arguments are stressed. Although not entirely exclusive, evidence-based arguments focus on "what is" and back up those claims with empirical evidence, whereas practical argumentation focuses on "what should we do?" and on designing and evaluating different courses of action. Along with each detailed example, I provide several minor examples demonstrating recurring themes related to the type of environment in question.

Argumentation Mapping

I begin with an example from Gürkan, Iandoli, Klein, and Zollo (2010) of how computer systems can be used to map the structure of arguments. Argumentation mapping provides users with categories of components that arguments should contain. These are known as *argument ontologies*. Maps also organize ideas visually.

Gürkan *et al.* report on how a Web 2.0 system, known as the *Deliberatorium,* was used by a large class of graduate students in industrial engineering at the University of Naples Federico II ($N = 160$) to create the largest argumentation map ever produced, to the authors' knowledge, consisting of about 1,900 posts! The map itself was akin to an organized list of posts in a threaded discussion. The system was inspired by discussion forums but users specifically have the capability to insert their notes anywhere in the map.

The platform was designed for use in virtual communities: open forums and blogs to carry out large-scale conversations about important social issues. Such open forums are often used to share ideas, but the signal-to-noise ratio is low, with many irrelevant and poorly written posts. The *Deliberatorium* platform was created to improve the quality of arguments in these virtual communities. Although not specifically designed for students, *Deliberatorium* could also be used with a class, as was the case in this study. Students learned not only about content (biofuels) but also about the argumentation practices used in virtual communities.

The platform's ontology was a combination of three formalisms: Issue-Based Information System (IBIS), Toulmin's ontology, and Walton's ontology. The IBIS ontology consists of questions, ideas, proposals, positive/negative arguments, questions, and decisions (Conklin, 2006). The Toulmin (1958) ontology consists of claims, grounds, and warrants. The Walton (1996) ontology consists of argumentation schemes, which are typical types of arguments, such as arguments from expert opinion or analogy; associated with each scheme are critical questions that should be asked about that type of argument (for example, how credible is an expert?). The Walton ontology is explained in more detail in Nussbaum (2011). In the *Deliberatorium* platform, users post notes, making decisions about what other notes to attach the note to. As illustrated in Figure 5.1, readers may comment on the note, choose an argumentation scheme and corresponding set of critical questions for any note, and then use these to "vote" on the quality of the argument (from poor to excellent).

To prevent the type of "edit wars" that occur in other virtual communities, the discussions are moderated. In the Gürkan *et al.* (2010) study, a team of about four students acted as the moderators. To be included in the final map, moderators had to certify that each note was on topic, correctly categorized, and posted in the right place. Moderators frequently had to change the headings and placement of notes, to ensure a logically organized map. They also made comments and suggestions to users. Out of a total of 5,003 notes posted, the moderators certified 1,119. This placed a heavy demand on the moderators' time, and the authors estimated that it would be more realistic to have 5–10 percent of the active users act as moderators.

Gürkan *et al.* report that:

> The level of direct debate was moderate. Users did attach many arguments to each other's posts (62% of all posts were arguments and 67% of these arguments were attached to posts authored by someone else) but the great majority of all arguments (78.3%) were pros rather than cons.
>
> (Gürkan *et al.*, 2010, p. 3694

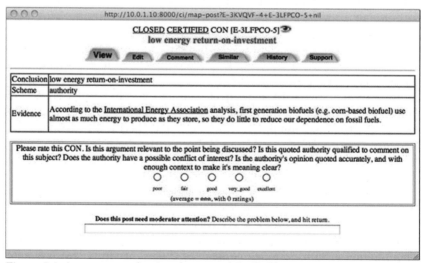

Figure 5.1 Argument evaluation form used in Deliberatorium.   From Gürkan, Iandoli, Klein, & Zollo (2010, p. 3690).   Copyright by Elsevier, used with permission

The authors surmised that students may have been reluctant to criticize one another's ideas. Other possible explanations for the dearth of debate could have been students' lack of conceptual mastery, so that while there may have been "fast content saturation" from students reading many notes, students may not have been able to explore subtopics in-depth. Also, the use of extrinsic awards for posting (e.g., points and small grants) may have reinforced quantity over quality. This study therefore demonstrates some of the challenges of creating argument maps, as well as some of the potential.

Related Efforts

The *Deliberatorium* falls into the general category of *Computer-Assisted Argument Mapping* (or CAAM). There are some other CAAM systems developed for small-scale use. For example, *Rationale* (Davies, 2009) creates hierarchical maps with relationships of support or objection (see Figure 5.2). *Rationale* is a diagramming tool that supports the construction, modification, and sharing of these diagrams (van Gelder, 2007) by organizing *infons* (the units of meaning in each box) into maps, with colors displaying some of the infons' attributes: green for supporting reasons, red for objections, and orange for rebuttals to objections. *Rationale* was

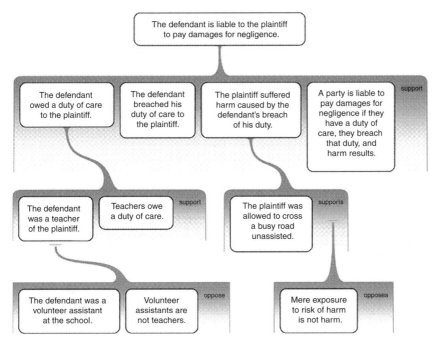

Figure 5.2 "Rationale" argumentation analysis map showing relationships of support and opposition. From van Gelder (2007, p. 4). Copyright by Tim van Gelder, used with permission

developed to help undergraduate students, working individually, to map the structure of written articles (e.g., in philosophy or economic history). Lots of individual practice (Rider & Thomason, 2008) has been found to increase scores on standardized tests of critical thinking (van Gelder, Bissett, & Gumming, 2004) by almost one standard deviation.

In relationship to scaffolding group discussion, *Compedium* users (Okada & Shum, 2008) create dialogue maps, such as the ones shown in Figure 5.3, based on the *IBIS* ontology (Rittel & Noble, 1989). *IBIS* was originally developed to facilitate problem-solving meetings in government and industry, where unaided discussions can be disjointed and repetitive (Conklin, 2006). Conklin explains that dialogue-mapping can make argumentation more systematic; for example, it makes clear where the disadvantages of an option have not been discussed. Okada (2008) has used *Compedium* in science classrooms (e.g., for writing essays on climate change), extending the ontology to include evidence nodes. Okada writes that the system is flexible, allowing the "freeform layout of nodes" but the flexibility has a downside in that maps can end up looking overly complex ("like spaghetti") if participants are not careful (Okada, 2008, p. 159).

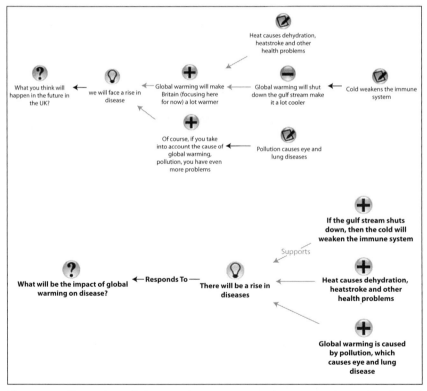

Figure 5.3 Illustration of Compendium argumentation maps. From Okada and Buckingham Shum (2008, p.305). Copyright by Routledge

Okada and Shum, who had students create maps in small groups, found that teacher coaching was needed to help students learn to make good maps.

The ability to create a good argument map represents a set of skills referred to as *cartography* (Okada, 2008). Cartographic skills are distinct from (but may support) the ability to write argument prose. Suthers (2008) has investigated the relationship of textual and mapping skills using the system *Belvedere*. The system's ontology consists of data and hypotheses, which are represented by nodes linked with green pluses (for support) and red minuses (for contradict), as shown in Figure 5.4. Some versions of *Belvedere* also allow pairs of students to chat with one another when constructing maps. Suthers (2008) found that integrating textual (chat) discourse and argument mapping in the same window was more effective than using each one separately (or together but in different windows). He has also found *Belvedere* to be more effective in helping students write integrative science essays when students worked in face-to-face groups than when working in an on-line chat mode, where

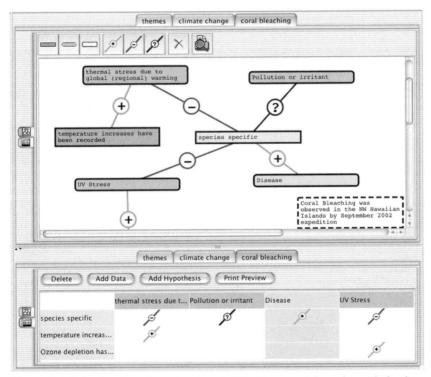

Figure 5.4 Belvedere interface (version 4.10). Retrieved from http://belvedere.sourceforge.net/. The interface supports evidence maps and matrix representations (both shown in figure) as well as concept maps. Copyright by Daniel Suthers, used with permission

it is harder to use some forms of communication (such as pointing) to form linkages between different parts of written documents (Suthers, Hundhausen, & Girardeau, 2003). (The interactive discourse of on-line users did, however, contain more of the epistemic distinctions supported by the software.)

Furthermore, combining *Belvedere* with argument rubrics, where students evaluated the quality of their scientific investigations (using web-based articles), was more effective in improving students' collective argumentation than using either one alone (Toth, Suthers, & Lesgold, 2002). Rubrics were especially effective in helping students attend to inconsistencies and discrepant events (Suthers, 2008).

Finally, the *Digalo* system (Schwarz & Glassner, 2007) is similar to the others but allows the teacher to decide what sort of ontology to use for particular mapping activities. *Digalo* allows for short textual notes to be placed inside each shape (see Figure 5.5). Schwarz and colleagues have used *Digalo* with secondary school students as a vehicle for teacher-moderated, synchronous discussions. *Digalo* is part of a larger computer system, Argunaut (Schwarz & Asterhan, 2011), that allows teachers to monitor and moderate several small-group discussions simultaneously

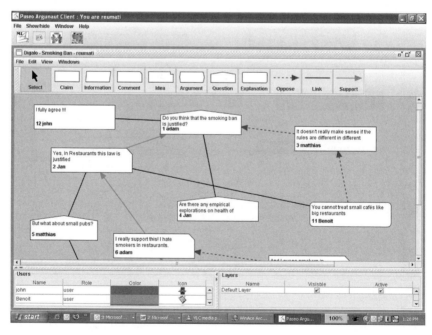

Figure 5.5 Example of a Digalo argumentation map. From Schwarz, B. B., & Asterhan, A. (2011). E-moderation of synchronous discussions in educational settings: A nascent practice. *The Journal of the Learning Sciences*, 20, 399. Copyright by Routledge, used with permission

by examining each group's developing map, as well as tabs showing individual participation levels, social networks (to identify any users who are being ignored), and the distribution of different ontological moves. Their research suggests that effective electronic moderators (*e-moderators*) balance their use of generic contributions (e.g., "Why do you think that?") with content-specific ones (e.g., paraphrasing and elaborating on a contribution; Schwarz & Asterhan, 2011), but the latter tend to stimulate more discussion (Asterhan & Schwarz, 2010).[1]

In general, when the pedagogical goal is consideration of more perspectives, this is easy to accomplish with a group-moderated discussion, rubrics, and simple mapping ontologies or with graphic organizers such as argumentation vee diagrams (see Nussbaum, Winsor, Aqui, & Poliquin, 2007). When the goal is to learn how to craft sophisticated arguments, sophisticated CAAM systems may be more appropriate, but only if used in conjunction with extensive coaching and feedback (provided by a teacher, moderator, intelligent tutoring system, or self- or peer-assessments with rubrics). When the goal is for students to learn content, for example complex relations between scientific concepts, the jury is still out. Some researchers have failed to find content learning effects (Schwarz *et al.*, 2003; Stegmann, Weinberger, & Fischer, 2007), whereas in other cases the evidence is anecdotal (Rider & Thomason, 2008; see Scheuer, Loll, Pinkwart, & McLaren, 2010, for a review). Van Amelsvoort, Andriessen, and Kanselaar (2007), on the other hand, found that students who constructed maps before an online chat with a partner and then revised their map, included more reasons in the final maps than those using text. The maps helped keep the discussions more focused. It is unclear if the effect was due to the premapping or postmapping activities (or both), but in either case maps did appear to contribute to some content learning. Schwarz, Schur, Pensso, and Tayer (2011) also documented conceptual change regarding the day/night cycle in some students after using *Digalo*, but this only occurred in conjunction with effective e-moderation on the part of teachers, a carefully designed discussion topic, and the use of graphical material.

It is certainly plausible that students learn content from using these systems, but questions remain as to how deep this learning is, how much the mapping features contribute to it (versus other aspects of the learning environment), and how well these systems can address complex, hard-to-teach concepts. Argumentation mapping imposes cognitive load on students (Kester & Pass, 2005), who have to learn cartographic skills on top of the content, and this may focus time and attention away from conceptual learning, in contrast to such practices as concept mapping (Cañas & Novak, 2008). Argumentation mapping may stimulate and organize student reasoning in some situations but overly constrain reasoning in other situations if the mapping task gets in the way of having a free-flowing discussion. Wegerif (2007) cautions that argumentation maps are not themselves dialogue but should be used to support dialogue and reflection (although one can also use maps to reflect on a dialogue; Enyedy & Hoadley, 2006). It is clear that argument-mapping environments must be carefully designed to be effective.

Collaborative Reasoning

My second major example concerns an instructional program known as *collaborative reasoning* (CR) developed by Anderson and colleagues (Waggoner, Chinn, Yi, & Anderson, 1995). The approach has been used with elementary students in the domain of literature. Typically students read a short story and then meet in small groups to discuss a question (e.g., moral dilemma) related to the text.

The aim is for students to have a free-flowing discussion where students collaboratively construct and critique arguments. The approach combines an aesthetic stance towards reading literature, where students savor the quality of the scenes and personalities (Rosenblatt, 1985) with a critical/analytic stance (Wade & Thompson, cited in Waggoner *et al.*, 1995). The teacher is present for the discussions, but he or she sits outside the group and only interjects when necessary. He or she will start off the discussion by posing a *central question* (Waggoner *et al.*, 1995). Students raise their hand to indicate which position they initially favor. Students then have a free-flowing discussion, using an *open-participation structure* where students speak without raising their hands or being called on. Students speak to one another, rather than the teacher.

More teacher involvement is needed in the initial couple of discussions while students are learning the discussion ground rules and norms, such as:

- think critically about ideas, not about people;
- try to understand both sides of an issue; and
- restate what someone has said if it is not clear (Waggoner *et al.*, 1995).

Anderson views the role of the teacher more as a coach than as a moderator, specifically coaching students on how to "play the game" of collaborative reasoning. Teachers prompt students for "a position, a reason, evidence, or evaluation" (p. 584), ask for clarification, challenge students with ideas they have not thought of, model behaviors such as providing counterarguments, and occasionally praise students for using argument terminology (Waggoner *et al.*, 1995).

In general, though, teachers need to get "out of the way" so students can have free-flowing discussions with an open-participation structure. When teachers contribute too much to a discussion, students begin to talk to the teacher rather than one another, and look for evaluative feedback from the teacher. It is easy for teachers and students to fall back into a discursive mode known as *Initiate–Respond–Evaluate* (IRE) (Mehan, 1972), where the teacher initiates a question, the student responds, and the teacher evaluates. This is the dominant "language game" in school. The aim of collaborative reasoning, on the other hand, is to have students engage in argumentative discourse where they take one another's perspectives and where other students, not the teacher, provide feedback to students on their ideas in the form of supportive or opposing arguments. It is also the intent that students learn to master the practice of engaging in collaborative discussion. They can only do this if they are allowed to "play the game" by engaging in discussion, with the teacher acting as a coach. For this reason, a long-term goal of collaborative reasoning is to foster student independence from teacher prompting. This can be accomplished by such teacher behaviors as "being silent" (not saying anything when the discussion falls silent), restating ideas instead of asking questions, and attaching names to ideas (for example, "What do people think about John's argument?") (Waggoner *et al.*, 1995, p. 585).

It is not the case, however, that students come into CR sessions with no prior practice in argumentation. Stein and Miller (1993) and Garvey and Shantz (1992) document how preschool children engaged in argumentation with their playmates and parents, as did Goodwin (1990) with a group of adolescent girls. So to some degree CR builds off students' informal argumentation skills, teaching them to apply these skills to academic contexts. Students in different cultures and subcultures may have somewhat different exposure to various types of argumentation, but most have had some exposure. Dong, Anderson, Kim, and Li (2008) document how students from Chinese schools learned to easily engage in CR even though this form of discourse is not common in Chinese schools. Chinese youngsters, nonetheless, may have engaged in collaborative discussions with friends in various social situations.

CR also builds on peer modeling; peers model for one another behaviors known as *argument stratagems*. A stratagem is a recurrent pattern of talk that reflects a reasoning strategy or plays a social function in the discourse (Anderson *et al.*, 2001). Anderson *et al.* (2001) identified a number of stratagems used by students during collaborative reasoning, such as: "In the [STORY] it said [EVIDENCE]", "If [ACTION] then [BAD CONSEQUENCE] so [NOT ACTION]," or "Hedge [PROPOSITION]" (e.g., "the action MIGHT do that but it might not"). They found that if one student used a stratagem, another might do so as well, appropriating the stratagem and using it to construct a different argument. Then another might copy that student, and so on, so the incidence of appropriation would increase exponentially over time, up to a certain point. Anderson *et al.* (2001) termed this the *snowball effect* (see also Nussbaum, 2003). The appropriation of stratagems is one way that students' argumentation skills can improve from engaging in CR. CR also builds students' skills and confidence for interacting dialogically with their classmates, for example, learning how to interject or disagree respectfully.

Here is an example of the snowballing of a stratagem, "I got something for you, [NAME]," which is a way of addressing/challenging a classmate's argument. In the following excerpt (from Anderson *et al.*, 2001, p. 17), the students are discussing the story, *Amy's Goose* (Holmes, 1977). Amy is a lonely farm girl who befriends an injured goose; the central question is whether Amy should keep the goose or let it go and fly south with its flock.

AURETHA: I got challenge for you, Kyle, um, if, he wouldn't able to feed himself, how come he was getting food, um, before he were there?

KEVIN: I got something for you, Auretha [Timothy sighs], if, he, if the goose, was still in the barn for a long time, then Amy let it go, then it would not get its food, because it hasn't been in a wild for a while.

TIMOTHY: I got something for you, Sylvia [Kevin giggles], but, he didn't, he didn't wanna go back there, they didn't want him because of the group.

...

AURETHA: I got something for Cassius, I disagree with Cassius and Kevin, um, you said if, if, he get, he might get sick, if (he get it all, that's it) every fall that, they'll come back, and maybe, he can go then, and sometimes, maybe, if Amy let him go to the lake in, lake in, and he could get water and he won't get sick.

AURETHA: I got a challenge for you, I am, because ... she's gonna be upset with herself, but ... if she let him go, she could find another pet somewhere, or ask her mother or father to go and get her one, another pet.[2]

It is often threatening to challenge another student and offer a different point of view because it can injure the *face* (social self-image; Goffman, 1963) of the other student or the challenging student if the other student argues back. The stratagem described above makes the discourse more playful and collaborative, as if one is sharing things, thus making it easier for students to proffer challenges.

Research indicates that CR enhances student participation, empathy, interest, vocabulary, use of evidence and the complexity of student reasoning (Clark *et al.*, 2003). In addition, a number of studies (Dong *et al.*, 2008; Reznitskaya, Anderson, & Kuo, 2007; Reznitskaya *et al.*, 2006) have documented how oral argumentation skills acquired through CR transfer to students' argumentative writing. This is both a group-to-individual and an oral-to-writing transfer effect. In writing individual essays on a novel topic, students who had participated in CR included more counterarguments and rebuttals than those who had not. Although quasi-experimental, the number of successful replications makes it less likely that the results are due to confounding factors. Anderson and colleagues posit that CR students have acquired or refined an *argument schema*, which is an abstract mental representation of the different parts of a complete and sound argument (Reznitskaya & Anderson, 2002). Engaging in written argumentation activates the schema, thus explaining the transfer effects.

One of my reasons for presenting CR as an example of an argument-based learning environment is that, unlike the other examples, CR involves entirely face-to-face discourse. However, Kim, Anderson, Nguyen-Jahiel, and Archodidou (2007) have implemented CR as part of a computer-supported collaborative learning (CSCL) environment. Specifically 10 groups of fourth- and fifth-graders (5–6 to a group) discussed several stories on-line, sometimes synchronously and sometimes asynchronously. The students in each group were from different schools, so the children mostly did not know one another. There was an adult moderator for each group. Kim *et al.* (2007) found high rates of participation and snowball effects for eight argument stratagems. Stratagems were rarely appropriated from the adult facilitator, perhaps because many students did not know him or her. Also, however, many of the facilitator's contributions were long and teacherly, and Kim *et al.* report that the more effective facilitators made short, active contributions (see also Asterhan & Schwarz, 2010). The quality of students' arguments were high, as Kim *et al.* report that "their messages displayed the full range of elements of argumentation, including explicitly formed arguments, appeals to evidence and other types of backing, counterarguments and rebuttals, and hypothetical reasoning" (p. 367).

These findings stand in sharp contrast to many CSCL studies finding that students often are reluctant to disagree and have trouble constructing complex arguments without substantial scaffolding. Nussbaum (2005) has shown, however, that often the difficulty is not that students in CSCL environments do not know how to make arguments, but rather that CSCL students do not know what sort of argument behaviors are expected and appropriate in the environment (see also Wegerif, 2007). It is important to note, however, that the CR students in the Kim *et al.* study were also participating concurrently in face-to-face CR sessions, so they had the benefit of the scaffolding provided there. Other useful CSCL strategies include providing students with a video-based worked example of the type of discussion expected (Rummel & Spada, 2005) or just telling them that they should produce counterarguments and rebuttals (Nussbaum, 2005).

However, there are other barriers to successful CSCL discussions besides knowledge of norms and expectations. For example, Nussbaum and Jacobson (2004) found that a lack of content knowledge makes students hesitant to disagree with one another. This was less of an issue in the Kim *et al.* study, which focused on children's literature. Also, as we have seen in the previous section, if students are asked to master a particular script, or categorize contributions into an ontology, or form an argumentation map, that requires another set of skills that can make CSCL discussions more difficult. The Kim *et al.* study shows, however, that technological scaffolds are not always necessary in on-line environments.

The CR findings stand in sharp contrast with those in science education. For example, in a recent volume edited by Erduran and Jiménez-Aleixandre (2008), many authors concluded that science students needed considerable scaffolding to (a) make scientific arguments that connect reasoning to evidence and (b) have productive discussions. There are several reasons why constructing arguments in the science domain could be more challenging than in children's literature. Students may lack or be less confident in their content knowledge. Scientific domains may be less meaningful or engaging to students unless the learning environment is well designed. The nature of evidence in science is typically more quantitative and the general concept of representative evidence (and the content of specific pieces of evidence) may be less well understood by students than the type of evidence used in CR (evidence from a story or personal experience). Finally, science students are typically expected to make their warrants explicit.

I am using *warrant* in the sense used by McNeill, Lizotte, Krajcik, and Marx (2006) of theoretical principles that explain why a piece of evidence supports or disconfirms a particular claim. Students typically need a lot of scaffolding to coordinate theories and evidence with their claims (Kuhn, 1991; McNeill *et al.*, 2006). Mastering and explaining scientific theories may be difficult for students without scaffolds such as Clark and Sampson's (2007) *Explanation Constructor,* where students can form arguments by picking from a menu of predefined principles, or computer simulations where students can see how and why a particular theory works (Jonassen, 2006). In contrast, Anderson, Chinn, and Chang (1997) report that CR students rarely express general theoretical principles unless one was surprising or implicated in a dispute (Anderson, Chinn, Waggoner, & Nguyen, 1998). This is consistent with Toulmin's (1958) assertion that in ordinary discourse, warrants are typically left implicit unless there is a need to express them. In general, it appears that the complexity of science concepts, and a lack of understanding of the nature of science (Kuhn, 1991), makes productive scientific argumentation harder for students. Science students need scaffolding and explicit teaching as to what arguments should look like in science.

Nevertheless, where possible, some free-flowing, dialogical discussions may flower in the science domain. Just as in CR, Jiménez-Aleixandre (2008) emphasizes the importance of building ground rules and norms of discussion in science classrooms. Engle and Conant (2002) documented the extended, free-flowing discussions in an FCL classroom, but this only followed from extensive norm building, and scaffolding content understanding with reciprocal teaching (which also builds discussion skills), jigsaw research groups, cross-talk between groups, occasional lectures and benchmark lessons (designed to foster conceptual understanding and change; Hunt & Minstrell, 1994). Adey and Shayer (1993) have developed a program known as *Thinking Science* which involves student discussion about scientific problems. The program has been found to foster students' scores on standardized tests in reading and mathematics when assessed 1–2 years following the intervention (see also Mercer, Dawes, Wegerif, & Sams, 2004, and Wegerif, Mercer, & Dawes, 1999, on exploratory talk in science and other domains). It could be that these programs develop students argumentation schemas in conjunction with metacognitive dispositions related to considering and testing alternative hypotheses. In general, engaging students in free-flowing, reflective dialogue is both engaging for them and potentially has far-reaching cognitive gains.

Argumentation and Game Playing

If argumentation is a type of language game, then it may make sense to embed it in a game-playing context. Ravenscroft and McAlister (2006) use the concept of *dialogic games*, where the focus is on making productive arguments as part of a language game. There can be different types of dialogic games with different rules; for example, tutoring sessions, debates, or creative brainstorming sessions. Each functions with a different set of rules defining legitimate or preferable moves for different situations. Ravenscroft and McAlister have designed two systems (*Academic Talk* and *InterLoc*). These systems provide users with several menus of *locution openers* that can be used to start a note (for example, "I disagree because," "Why do you say that?" "I think we need more evidence"). The system has different menus of openers, for example, menus such as question, challenges, reason, agree, and maintain. *InterLoc* also highlights locution options that might be productive in different stages of discourse. It combines synchronous chat with a map-like interface that allows thread development. Figure 5.6 presents a sample of dialogue from *InterLoc* (Ravenscroft & McAlister, 2006).

Their research shows that these systems can result in higher quality argumentation (Ravenscroft, McAlister, & Sagar, 2010); however, they also caution that high quality dialogue is not guaranteed. The systems should be embedded in carefully designed learning environments (Ravenscroft, 2007) which use engaging and meaningful content, a carefully designed central question, a means for practicing critical thinking skills, and thoughtful integration of discussions with other learning activities. Consideration should also be given as to how to integrate dialogue games with social media such as wikis, blogs, Facebook, and YouTube. The rationale is that this may enhance student engagement, and *InterLoc* has been developed so students can link to other web resources and use them as evidence in a dialogue game (Ravenscroft & McAlister, 2008).

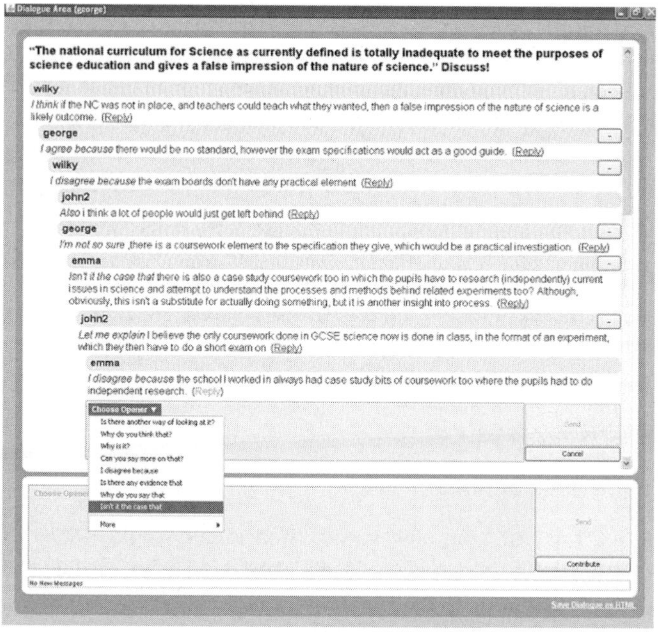

Figure 5.6 InterLoc interface and sample dialogue. From Ravenscroft (2010). Copyright by Andrew Ravenscroft, used with permission

Dialogue games can be embedded in larger, more complex game environments. Squire and Jan (2007) describe an augmented reality game in which students (in teams of three) learn about environmental science by investigating possible reasons for a death. Students play roles such as "government official" or "medical doctor," and use handheld computers to interview fictional characters in the field. For example, when they walk by a character such as the deceased's best friend, an electronic signal provides each student's handheld computer with interviews and documents containing both evidence and additional hypotheses to consider. There are *triggering events* in the game that encourage choice and discussion, such as students deciding as a group whom they should speak to next; making these choices requires students to engage in argumentation and to start exploring various hypotheses (e.g., suicide for insurance money, eating too much mercury-rich fish, or an interaction of factors). The game was found to be highly engaging, but especially younger students (elementary and middle-school) needed help considering multiple hypotheses simultaneously and coordinating various hypotheses with evidence. Also, the game was short (three to four hours), but could be inserted into a longer sequence of instruction involving various opportunities for argumentation and conceptual learning (Jan, 2010). Augmented reality games allow students to learn the *epistemic games* (forms of reasoning) engaged in by various communities (such as environmental specialists or government officials), which provides authenticity and enhances engagement, but should likely be used with other forms of conceptual and argumentation-related scaffolding. Wegerif (2007) argues that the main value of games (and argumentation scaffolds in general) is to induct students into a particular form of dialogue, and to open up a "dialogic space" in which learning and reflection can occur.

Conclusions

Argumentation is an important aspect of many student-centered learning environments. Argumentation is a valuable social practice for students to learn, and when used properly, can help enhance conceptual understanding by revealing and refuting student misconceptions. Students may need various amounts and kinds of scaffolding of their argumentation skills. Scaffolds come in various forms: CAAM and dialogue game systems, rubrics, worked examples, teacher and peer modeling, and facilitation by a discussion leader, especially in helping students balance and integrate reasons and evidence (Bell & Linn, 2000) or benefits and costs (Nussbaum & Edwards, 2011). Facilitators also play a key role in helping to establish norms and ground rules for discussion (Mercer, 1996), in clarifying and illustrating the type of discourse that is expected, in maintaining an environment where students can feel safe in sharing their ideas and disagreements, in managing collective argumentation maps, and in focusing and stimulating a discussion (Asterhan & Schwarz, 2010).

One key issue is in determining how much structure, scripting, and scaffolding students need. Unnecessary scaffolding can increase cognitive load (Kester & Pass, 2005), divert time away from developing conceptual understanding (Jan, 2010), and can get in the way of free-flowing discussion. Too little scaffolding can result in unfocused discussions, superficial argumentation, and little or no learning. Assessing students' argumentation and finding the right balance at appropriate points in a curriculum is one major instructional issue.

A second major issue is what sort of conceptual resources students need to engage in argumentation. On the one hand, argumentation is supposed to help them understand conceptual ideas better; on the other hand, students must have some grasp of the conceptual ideas to make effective arguments. There likely needs to be other conceptual scaffolds to bring students to the point where they have enough understanding to comprehend arguments and counterarguments but will still benefit from having their ideas challenged and understanding deepened. It might be profitable to view the use of argumentation as part of a "learning progression" (Berland & McNeill, 2010), to be used at points in a learning trajectory when it is profitable.

A third issue is how argumentation can be supported by other aspects of the learning environment. The topic and context must be meaningful and engaging. Using aspects of gaming or role playing can enhance motivation

(Gee, 2003). Designers should consider how much time to devote to argumentation in general and specific topics in particular, given the learning is often enhanced by the thinking students do after a discussion. Students might also need to consolidate their learning with additional discussion. Designers should also consider how much to vary the activity structure over time. Should there be an alternation between small-group and large-group discussion, or written and oral argumentation, or the use of structured and unstructured activities? Some variation may be highly desirable, as skills can be practiced in different contexts, variety may help maintain interest, and different activities have unique benefits for different students. On the other hand, too much variation can be detrimental if students have to constantly learn new tasks. Other factors to consider are the location where argumentation should be conducted (classroom, computer, or in the "field" with handheld devices). To what extent will social media and virtual communities be utilized? Will the learning community be defined with professional, civic, or online communities of practice? Will students generate their own arguments or will existing controversies and arguments in the relevant field of study be explored?

Finally, designers need to consider to what extent student arguments will be evaluated. Ideally, students will critique one another's arguments in the course of argumentation, but there may need to be other feedback mechanisms to deepen the nature and quality of student arguments. Students, at appropriate times, may also need to be fed arguments and counterarguments on which they can reflect (Nussbaum & Kardash, 2005).

Creating a learning environment that successfully supports student argumentation is a challenge but the payoff can be high in terms of student learning, engagement, and fostering higher levels of learning. Participants can be taught the rules of the "game" but they can also reflect on and discuss those rules (for example, there are communities of *InterLoc* users who discuss what ontologies might be useful to include in the system). In this way students can be empowered to create and participate meaningfully in the ever-evolving discursive forums of the 21st century.

Acknowledgments

The author would like to thank Dick Anderson, Kim Nguyen-Jahiel, Alexandra Okada, Ali Gürkan, Baruch Schwarz, Dan Suthers, and Andrew Ravenscroft for providing comments on sections of a previous draft of the chapter.

Notes

1 *Belvedere, Digalo,* and other systems can also be implemented with the LASAD system (Loll & Pinkwart, 2009). LASAD also allows instructors to author their own ontologies. LASAD, which at this writing is in the prototype stage,

reflects the "next generation" of CAAM system, offering more flexibility than previous systems.

2 From "The snowball phenomenon: Spread of ways of talking and ways of thinking across groups of children," by R. C. Anderson, K. Nguyen-Jahiel, B. McNurlen, A. Archodidou, S. Kim, A. Reznitskaya, M. Tillmans, & L. Gilbert, 2001, *Cognition and Instruction, 33,* pp. 17–18. Copyright 2001 by Lawrence Erlbaum and Associates, now Routledge. Used with permission.

References

Adey, P., & Shayer, M. (1993). An exploration of long-term far-transfer effects following an extended intervention program in the high school science curriculum. *Cognition and Instruction, 11,* 1–29.

Anderson, R. C., Chinn, C., & Chang, J. (1997). On the logical integrity of children's argument. *Cognition and Instruction, 15,* 135–167.

Anderson, R. C., Chinn, C., Waggoner, M., & Nguyen, K. (1998). Intellectually stimulating story discussions. In J. Osborn & F. Lehr (Eds.), *Literacy for all: Issues in teaching and learning* (pp. 170–186). New York: Guilford.

Anderson, R. C., Nguyen-Jahiel, K., McNurlen, B., Archodidou, A., Kim, S., Reznitskaya, A., Tillmans, M., & Gilbert, L. (2001). The snowball phenomenon: Spread of ways of talking and ways of thinking across groups of children. *Cognition and Instruction, 19,* 1–46.

Andriessen, J. (2006). *Arguing to learn.* In K. Sawyer (Ed.), *The Cambridge handbook of the learning sciences* (pp. 443–460). New York: Cambridge University Press.

Andriessen, J., Baker, M., & Suthers, D. (Eds.). (2003). *Arguing to learn: Confronting cognitions in computer-supported collaborative learning.* Boston: Kluwer.

Asterhan, C. S. C., & Schwarz, B. B. (2007). The effects of monological and dialogical argumentation on concept learning in evolutionary theory. *Journal of Educational Psychology, 99,* 626–639.

Asterhan, C. S. C., & Schwarz, B. B. (2010). Online moderation of synchronous e-argumentation. *International Journal of Computer-Supported Collaborative Learning, 5:* 259–282.

Baker, M. (2003). Computer-mediated argumentative interactions for the co-elaboration of scientific notions. In J. Andriessen, M. Baker, & D. Suthers (Eds.), *Arguing to learn*: *Confronting cognitions in computer-supported collaborative learning environments* (pp. 47–78). Dordrecht, The Netherlands: Kluwer.

Barron, B. (2003). When smart groups fail. *Journal of the Learning Sciences, 12,* 307–399.

Bell, P., & Linn, M. C. (2000). Scientific arguments as learning artifacts: Designing for learning from the web with KIE. *International Journal of Science Education, 22,* 797–817.

Berland, L. K., & McNeill, K. L. (2010). A learning progression for scientific argumentation: Understanding student work and designing supportive instructional contexts. *Science Education, 94,* 765–793.

Bransford, J. D., Brown, A. L., & Cocking, R. R. (Eds.) (2000). *How people learn: Brain, mind, experience, and school.* Washington DC: National Academy Press.

Brown, A. L., & Campione, J. C. (1990). Communities of learning and thinking, or a context by any other name. *Contributions to Human Development, 21,* 108–126.

Cañas, A. J., & Novak, J. D. (2008). Concept mapping using CmapTools to enhance meaningful learning. In A. Okada, S. B. Shum, & T. Sherborne (Eds.), *Knowledge cartography: Software tools and mapping techniques* (pp. 25–46). London: Springer.

Chinn, C. A. (2006). Learning to argue. In A. M. O'Donnell, C. E. Hmelo-Silver, & G. Erkens (Eds.), *Collaborative learning, reasoning, and technology* (pp. 355–383). Mahwah, NJ: Erlbaum.

Clark, A.-M., Anderson, R. C., Kuo, L.-J., Kim, I.-H., Archodidou, A., & Nguyen-Jaheil, K. (2003). Collaborative reasoning: Expanding ways for children to talk and think in school. *Educational Psychology Review, 115,* 181–198.

Clark, D. B., & Sampson, V. D. (2007). Personally-seeded discussions to scaffold online argumentation. *International Journal of Science Education, 29,* 253–277.

Conklin, J. (2006). *Dialogue mapping: Building shared understanding of wicked problems.* West Sussex, England: John Wiley & Sons.

Craik, F. I. M., & Lockhart, R. S. (1972). Levels of processing: A framework for memory research. *Journal of Verbal Learning and Verbal Behavior, 11,* 671–684.

Davies, W. M. (2009). Computer-assisted argument mapping: a *rationale* approach. *Higher Education.* Retrieved from: doi 10.1007/s10734-009-9226-9.

Dong, T., Anderson, R. C., Kim, I.-H., & Li, Y. (2008). Collaborative reasoning in China and Korea. *Reading Research Quarterly, 43,* 400–424.

Engle, R. A., & Conant, F. R. (2002). Guiding principles for fostering productive disciplinary engagement: Explaining an emergent argument in a community of learners classroom. *Cognition & Instruction, 20,* 399–483.

Enyedy, N., & Hoadley, C. M. (2006). From dialogue to monologue and back: Middle spaces in computer-mediated learning. *International Journal of Computer-Supported Collaborative Learning, 1,* 413–439.

Erduran, S., &. Jiménez-Aleixandre, M. P. (Eds.). (2008). *Argumentation in science education: Perspectives from classroom-based research.* Dordrecht, The Netherlands: Springer.

Garvey, C., & Shantz, C. (1992). Conflict talk: Approaches toward adversative discourse. In C. U. Shantz & W. W. Hartup (Eds.), *Conflict in child development* (pp. 93–121). New York: Cambridge University Press.

Gee, J. P. (2003). *What video games have to teach us about learning and literacy.* New York: Palgrave//Macmillan.

Goffman, E. (1963). *Interaction ritual.* New York: Anchor Books.

Goodwin, M. H. (1990). *He-said-she-said: Talk as social organization among Black children.* Bloomington: Indiana University Press.

Greeno, J. G., & the Middle-school Mathematics through Applications Project Group (1998). The situativity of knowing, learning, and research. *American Psychologist, 53,* 5–26.

Gürkan, A., Iandoli, L., Klein, M., & Zollo, G. (2010). Mediating debate through on-line large-scale argumentation: Evidence from the field. *Information Science, 180,* 3686–3702.

Harris, K., Graham, S., & Mason, L. (2002). POW plus TREE equals powerful opinion essays. *Teaching Exceptional Children, 34*(5), 74–77.

Holmes, E. T. (1977). *Amy's goose.* New York: Crowell.

Howe, C. (2010). Peer dialogue and cognitive development: A two-way relationship. In K. Littleton & C. Howe (Eds.), *Educational dialogues: Understanding and promoting productive interaction* (pp. 32–47). London: Routledge.

Hunt, E., & Minstrell, J. (1994). A cognitive approach to the teaching of physics. In K. McGilly (Ed.), *Classroom lessons: Integrating cognitive theory and classroom practice* (pp. 51–74). Cambridge, MA: Cambridge University Press.

Jan, M. (2010). Designing an augmented reality-game based curriculum for argumentation. (Doctoral dissertation, University of Wisconsin, Madison). *Dissertation Abstracts International, 70*(11-A), p. 4166.

Jiménez-Aleixandre, M. P. (2008). Designing argumentation learning environments. In S. Erduran & M. P. Jiménez-Aleixandre (Eds.), *Argumentation in science education: Perspectives from classroom-based research* (pp. 94–118). Dordrecht, The Netherlands: Springer.

Jonassen, D. H. (2006). *Modeling with technology: Mindtools for conceptual change.* Upper Saddle River, NJ: Pearson Merrill Prentice Hall.

Kester, L., & Pass, F. (2005). Instructional interventions to enhance collaboration in powerful learning environments. *Computers in Human Behavior, 21*, 689–696.

Kim, I.-H., Anderson, R. C., Nguyen-Jahiel, K., & Archodidou, A. (2007). Discourse patterns during children's collaborative online discussions. *Journal of the Learning Sciences, 16*, 333–370.

Krummheuer, G. (1995). The ethnography of argumentation. In P. Cobb & H. Baiersfeld (Eds.), *The emergence of mathematical meaning: Interaction in classroom cultures* (pp. 229–270). Hillsdale, NJ: Erlbaum.

Kuhn, D. (1991). *The skills of argument.* New York: Cambridge University Press.

Lampert, M. L., Rittenhouse, P., & Crumbaugh, C. (1996). Agreeing to disagree: Developing sociable mathematical discourse. In D. R. Olson & N. Torrance (Eds.), *Handbook of human development in education* (pp. 731–764). Cambridge, MA: Blackwell.

Loll, F., & Pinkwart, N. (2009). Collaboration support in argumentation systems of education via flexible architectures. In I. Aedo, N.-S. C. Kinshuk, D. Sampson, & L. Zaitseva (Eds.), *The Ninth IEEE International Conference on Advanced Learning Technologies* (pp. 707–708). Los Alamitos, CA: Conference Publishing Service.

McNeill, K. L., Lizotte, D. J., Krajcik, J., & Marx, R. W. (2006). Supporting students' construction of scientific explanation by fading scaffolds in instructional materials. *Journal of the Learning Sciences, 15*, 153–191.

Mehan, H. (1972). "What time is it, Denise?": Asking known information questions in classroom discourse. *Theory into Practice, 18*, 285–294.

Mercer, N. (1994). The quality of talk in children's joint activity at the computer. *Journal of Computer Assisted Learning, 10*, 24–32.

Mercer, N. (1996). The quality of talk in children's collaborative activity in the classroom. *Learning and Instruction, 6*, 359–377.

Mercer, N., Dawes, L., Wegerif, R., & Sams, C. (2004). Reasoning as a scientist: Ways of helping children to use language to learn science. *British Educational Research Journal, 30,* 359–377.

Minstrell, J. (1982). Explaining the "at-rest" condition of an object. *The Physics Teacher, 20,* 10–14.

Nussbaum, E. M. (1997). *The evolution of argumentation in an alternative learning environment.* Unpublished dissertation, Stanford University, Stanford, CA.

Nussbaum, E. M. (2003). Appropriate appropriation: Functionality of student arguments and support requests during small-group classroom discussions. *Journal of Literacy Research, 34,* 501–544.

Nussbaum, E. M. (2005). The effect of goal instructions and need for cognition on interactive argumentation. *Contemporary Educational Psychology, 30,* 286–313.

Nussbaum, E. M. (2008). Collaborative discourse, argumentation, and learning: Preface and literature review. *Contemporary Educational Psychology, 33,* 345–359.

Nussbaum, E. M. (2011). Argumentation, dialogue theory, and probability modeling: Alternative frameworks for argumentation research in education. *Educational Psychologist, 46,* 84–106.

Nussbaum, E. M., & Edwards, O. V. (2011). Argumentation, critical questions, and integrative stratagem: Enhancing young adolescents' reasoning about current events. *Journal of the Learning Sciences, 20,* 443–488.

Nussbaum, E. M., & Jacobson, T. E. (2004). *Reasons that students avoid intellectual arguments.* Poster session presented at the annual meeting of the American Psychological Association, Honolulu, HI.

Nussbaum, E. M., & Kardash, C. M. (2005). The effect of goal instructions and text on the generation of counterarguments during writing. *Journal of Educational Psychology, 97,* 157–169.

Nussbaum, E. M., Sinatra, G. M., & Poliquin, A. M. (2008). The role of epistemic beliefs and scientific argumentation in science learning. *International Journal of Science Education, 30,* 1977–1999.

Nussbaum, E. M., Winsor, D. L., Aqui, Y. M., & Poliquin, A. M. (2007). Putting the pieces together: Online argumentation vee diagrams enhance thinking during discussions. *International Journal of Computer-Supported Collaborative Learning, 2,* 479–500.

Nystrand, M. & Gamoran, A. (1991). Instructional discourse, student engagement, and literature achievement. *Research in the Teaching of English, 25,* 261–290.

Okada, A. (2008). Scaffolding school pupils' scientific argumentation with evidence-based dialogue maps. In A. Okada, S. B. Shum, & T. Sherborne (Eds.), *Knowledge cartography: Software tools and mapping techniques* (pp. 131–162). London: Springer.

Okada, A., & Buckingham Shum, S. (2008). Evidence-based dialogue maps as a research tool to investigate the quality of school pupils' scientific argumentation. *International Journal of Research & Method in Education, 31,* 291–315.

Pontecorvo, C. (Ed.). (1993). Discourse and shared reasoning [Special issue]. *Cognition & Instruction, 11*(3–4).

Ravenscroft, A. (2007). Promoting thinking and conceptual change with digital dialogue games. *Journal of Computer Assisted Learning, 23,* 453–465.

Ravenscroft, A. (2010). Dialogue and Connectivism: A new approach to understanding and promoting dialogue-rich networked learning, Invited Article for *International Review of Open and Distance Learning* (IRODL), Special Edition: Connectivism: Design and delivery of social networked learning. (Eds.) George Siemens and Gráinne Conole.

Ravenscroft, A., & McAlister, S. (2006). Digital games and learning in cyberspace: A dialogical approach. *E-Learning, 3*(1), 37–50.

Ravenscroft, A., & McAlister, S. (2008). Investigating and promoting educational argumentation: Towards new digital practices. *International Journal of Research & Methods in Education, 31*, 317–335.

Ravenscroft, A., McAlister, S., & Sagar, M. (2010). Digital dialogue games and InterLoc: A deep learning design for collaborative argumentation on the Web. In N. Pinkwart and B. M. McLaren (Eds.), *Educational technologies for teaching argumentation skills*, Bentham Science E-Books.

Reznitskaya, A., & Anderson, R. C. (2002). The argumentation schema and learning to reason. In C. C. Block and M. Pressley (Eds.), *Comprehension instruction: Research-based best practices* (pp. 319–334). New York: Guilford.

Reznitskaya, A., Anderson, R. C., & Kuo, L.-J. (2007). Teaching and learning argumentation. *The Elementary School Journal, 107*, 449–472.

Reznitskaya, A., Anderson, R. C., McNurlen, B., Ngyuen-Jahiel, K., Archodidou, A., & Kim, S. (2006). Influence of oral discussion on written argument. *Discourse Processes, 32* (2/3), 155–175.

Rider, Y., & Thomason, N. (2008). Cognitive and pedagogical benefits of argument mapping: LAMP guides the way to better thinking. In A. Okada, S. B. Shum, & T. Sherborne (Eds.), *Knowledge cartography: Software tools and mapping techniques* (pp. 113–130). London: Springer.

Rittel, H., & Noble, D. (1989). Issue-based information systems for design. Working Paper 492, Berkeley, CA: Institute of Urban and Regional Development, University of California.

Rosenblatt, L. M. (1985). Viewpoints: transaction versus interaction: A terminological rescue operation. *Research in the Teaching of English, 19*, 96–107.

Rummel, N., & Spada, H. (2005). Learning to collaborate: An instructional approach to promoting collaborative problem solving in computer-mediated settings. *Journal of the Learning Sciences, 14*, 201–241.

Scheuer, O., Loll, F., Pinkwart, N., & McLaren, B. M. (2010). Computer-supported argumentation: A review of the state of the art. *International Journal of Computer-Supported Collaborative Learning, 5*, 43–102.

Schwarz, B., & Glassner, A. (2007). The role of floor control and of ontology in argumentative activities with discussion-based tools. *International Journal of Computer-Supported Collaborative Reasoning, 2*, 449–478.

Schwarz, B., Neuman, Y., Gil, J., & Ilya, M. (2003). Construction of collective and individual knowledge in argumentative activity. *Journal of the Learning Sciences, 12*, 219–256.

Schwarz, B. B. & Asterhan, C. S. (2011). E-moderation of synchronous discussions in educational settings: A nascent practice. *Journal of the Learning Sciences, 20*, 365–442.

Schwarz, B. B., Schur, Y., Pensso, H., & Tayer, N. (2011). Perspective taking and synchronous argumentation for learning the day/night cycle. *International Journal of Computer-Supported Collaborative Learning, 6*, 113–138.

Slotta, J. D., & Linn, M. C. (2009). *WISE science: Web-based inquiry in the classroom.* New York: Teachers College.

Squire, K. D., & Jan, M. (2007). Mad City Mystery: Developing scientific argumentation skills with a place-based augmented reality game on handheld computers. *Journal of Science Education and Technology, 16,* 5–29.

Stegmann, K., Weinberger, A., & Fischer, F. (2007). Facilitating argumentative knowledge construction with computer-supported collaboration scripts. *International Journal of Computer-Supported Collaborative Learning, 2,* 421–447.

Stein, N. L., & Miller, C. A. (1993). The development of memory and reasoning skill in argumentative contexts: Evaluating, explaining, and generating evidence. In R. Glaser (Ed.), *Advances in instructional psychology* (Vol. 4, pp. 285–335). Hillsdale, NJ: Erlbaum.

Suthers, D. D. (2008). Empirical studies of the value of conceptually explicit notations in collaborative learning. In A. Okada, S. B. Shum, & T. Sherborne (Eds.), *Knowledge cartography: Software tools and mapping techniques* (pp. 1–23). London: Springer.

Suthers, D. D., Hundhausen, C. D., & Girardeau, L. E. (2003). Comparing the roles of representations in face-to-face and online computer supported collaborative learning. *Computers and Education, 41,* 335–351.

Toth, E. E., Suthers, D. D., & Lesgold, A. M. (2002). "Mapping to Know": The effects of representational guidance and reflective assessment on scientific inquiry. *Science Education, 86,* 264–286.

Toulmin, S. (1958). *The uses of argument.* New York: Cambridge University Press.

Van Amelsvoort, M., Andriessen, J., & Kanselaar, G. (2007). Representational tools in computer-supported collaborative argumentation-based learning: How dyads work with constructed and inspected argumentative diagrams. *Journal of the Learning Sciences, 16,* 485–521.

Van Bruggen, J. M., Boshuizen, H. P., & Kirschner, P. A. (2003). A cognitive framework for cooperative problem solving with argument visualization. In P. A. Kirschner, S. J. Buckingham Shum, & C. S. Carr (Eds.), *Visualizing argumentation: Software tools for collaborative and educational sense-making* (pp. 25–48). New York: Springer.

van Gelder, T. (2007). The rationale for rationale. *Law, Probability and Risk, 6,* 23–42.

van Gelder, T., Bissett, M., & Gumming, G. (2004). Cultivating expertise in informal reasoning. *Canadian Journal of Experimental Psychology, 58,* 142–152.

Vye, N. J., Schwartz, D. L., Bransford, J. D., Barron, B. J., Zech, L., and the Cognition and Technology Group at Vanderbilt (1998). SMART Environments that support monitoring, reflection, and revision. In D. J. Hacker, J. Dunlosky, & A. C. Graesser (Eds.), *Metacognition in educational theory and practice* (pp. 305–346). Mahwah, NJ: Erlbaum.

Waggoner, M., Chinn, C., Yi, H., & Anderson, R. C. (1995). Collaborative reasoning about stories. *Language Arts, 72,* 582–589.

Walton, D. N. (1996). *Argumentation schemes for presumptive reasoning.* Mahwah, NJ: Erlbaum.

Wegerif, R. (2007). *Dialogic education and technology: Expanding the space of learning.* New York: Springer.

Wegerif, R., Mercer, N., & Dawes, L. (1999). From social interaction to individual reasoning: An empirical investigation of a possible socio-cultural model of cognitive development. *Learning and Instruction, 9*, 493–516.

Wiley, J., & Voss, J. F. (1999). Constructing arguments from multiple sources: Tasks that promote understanding and not just memory for text. *Journal of Educational Psychology, 91*, 301–311.

Wittgenstein, L. (2009). *Philosophical investigations* (4th edn, G. E. M. Anscombe, P. M. S. Hacker, & J. Schulte, Trans.). West Sussex, UK: Blackwell.

Yeh, K.-H., & She, H.-C. (2010). On-line synchronous scientific argumentation learning: Nurturing students' argumentation ability and conceptual change in science context. *Computers & Education, 55*, 586–602.

6   Theory and Practice of Case-Based Learning Aids

Janet L. Kolodner, Brian Dorn, Jakita Owensby Thomas and Mark Guzdial

Introduction

A case-based learning aid is a support that helps learners interpret, reflect on, and apply experiences—their own or those of someone else—in such a way that valuable learning takes place. Case-based learning aids have cases at their core. The creation and importance of case-based learning aids arose out of research and practice in two disciplines—work in computer science on case-based reasoning and work in education on constructivist approaches to learning.

Case-based reasoning (CBR), inspired by people, was developed as a model for creating intelligent systems—computer systems that could reason by reference to their previous experiences. Such systems, it was conjectured, had the potential to behave more like real experts than could traditional expert systems. Reasoning based on experience would allow intelligent systems to be more flexible and less brittle than rule-based systems, and, with learning from experience built into their architectures, they would become more capable over time (Hammond, 1989; Kolodner & Simpson, 1989; Schank, 1982). Many experimental automated case-based reasoners have been created (see the lists in, e.g., Kolodner, 1993) and, indeed, CBR has proven to be quite a useful technology. More interesting to education, however, are the implications case-based reasoning holds as a model of cognition—implications about what it means to be a learner and implications about learning and education.

Case-based reasoning, as a cognitive model, values the concrete over the abstract (Kolodner, 1993). While most traditional theories of cognition emphasize how general-purpose abstract operators are formed and applied, case-based reasoning makes concrete cases, representing experience, primary. CBR suggests that we think in terms of cases—interpretations of our experiences that we apply to new situations.

Consider, for example, an architect designing an office building. She knows that many modern office buildings have atriums. Should this new building have an atrium? To answer that, she first looks at the reasons for including atriums in those buildings. In some, it was to provide light to inside offices; in others to provide a friendly informal space to meet.

Are those goals in the new design? They are, but she wonders whether the noise of a central meeting space might be problematic. She examines those buildings again, looking at the effects of the atriums on use of the offices. Indeed, some did cause too much noise, but others were quite successful. Why did some succeed and some fail? The architect looks to see the reasons for failures. Will they be present in the new building? If so, is there a way to avoid the failure by doing it another way (perhaps suggested by one of the successful atria), or should an atrium not be used?

Cases are used in this example to identify potential problems, to suggest ideas about solutions, and to suggest explanations. All of the cases used are cases of others—records of designed buildings, including the reasoning involved in getting to those designs and the outcomes of the decisions that were made. But the example is typical of the way people use cases from day to day—their own experiences and those of others. For example, a child who throws a ball in the air expects it to come down because that's what she's always seen before. A caterer remembers other meals she's planned when planning a new event; some suggest dishes to serve, and others warn of pitfalls.

Given what we know about effective ways of using cases to reason, case-based reasoning makes three types of suggestions with respect to educational practice:

- **Engineering sequencing in the learning environment**: Learning from experience is not a one-shot deal. Ideas extracted from one's experiences need to be debugged and tried out again and again. The sequencing of activities and facilitation of discussion in a learning environment can be engineered to increase the frequency of accessing cases in one's memory and ultimately the educational impact of learners' experiences.
- **The need for supports for reflection**: Interpreting one's experiences so that they can be easily remembered and effectively used later is a requirement of case-based reasoning. People engage in such reflection when they are interested enough to do it, and, depending on how much they know and how interested they are, they can do a better or not as good a job after such reflection. Helping learners have reason to want to interpret their experiences and providing prompts and other guidance for learners can promote more productive reflection.
- **Use of case libraries as a resource**: The development and deployment of collections of cases and experiences may act as external memory for a learner, and writing up personal experiences as cases may lead learners to reflect appropriately on their experiences and turn them into useful cases in their own memories.

In this chapter, we first review CBR as a model of cognition and describe its core components. We then discuss CBR's implications for promoting learning both with and without technology, followed by a description of two examples of how CBR has shaped the design of large-scale learning environments. Finally, we review a number of examples from the research literature demonstrating various aspects of designing software applying the lessons of CBR to promote learning.

Case-Based Reasoning as a Model of Cognition

Case-based reasoning is a model of cognition that explicitly integrates memory, learning, and reasoning. A reasoner, it says, is a being in the world that has goals. It seeks to navigate its world in such a way that its goals are successfully achieved. It has experiences, some of them successful and some not as successful, some pleasant and some not so pleasant, that allow it to learn about its environment and ways of using that environment to achieve its goals. As it has experiences, it seeks to learn the skills and concepts that will allow it to achieve its goals more productively in the future. It is engaged, therefore, in recording its experiences, interpreting its experiences to derive lessons useful to its future, anticipating when those lessons might be useful, and labeling its experiences appropriately so that it will be able to recognize the applicability of an experience in a later situation. A case-based reasoner is also engaged in noticing the similarities and differences between situations and experiences so that it can draw conclusions about its world and notice the subtle differences that suggest when each of the lessons it has learned is most appropriately applicable. Essential to its learning is failure—it needs to attempt to apply what it thinks is applicable and fail at that in order to know to focus its attention on subtleties of which it had not previously been aware.

Cases, in a case-based reasoner, are *interpretations of experiences*. Cases have several sub-components, just as stories do: their setting, the actors and their goals, a sequence of events, results, and explanations linking results to goals and the means of achieving them. The better the interpretations of each of these pieces, and the better the explanations linking them to each other, the more useful a case will be when it is remembered later. For example, if we know that a plan carried out in a case failed, we can wonder whether it might fail again in a new similar situation, but we cannot make predictions. If, on the other hand, we know what caused the failure, we can check to see if the conditions that led to failure are present in the new situation. If they are, failure can be predicted; if not, the old plan might be reused.

The explanations that tie pieces of a case together allow us to derive lessons that can be learned from the case—its *lessons learned*. For example, if I served fish to vegetarians at a dinner party, and they did not eat it, I might explain the failure as being due to my not having inquired about whether any of my guests were vegetarians or had special eating requirements. The lesson learned is that I should make those inquiries whenever I invite guests for dinner. Upon recall of a case, the lessons an individual has derived from it are available for application to the new situation, as are the explanations from which those lessons were derived. Lessons in a case can identify why things went wrong and why things worked, and they can help learners make predictions about the results of an experience given certain criteria and constraints. For maximum usefulness, cases should be interpreted with the goal of deriving lessons that might be useful in the future.

Cases reside in an individual's memory, and the set of cases in an individual's memory is referred to as his or her *case library* or library of cases. Cases in an individual's case library might be derived from his or her own experiences or from the experiences of others. For example, one might read about someone else's experience and remember its lessons to apply in the future. In general, one's own cases will be more embellished, but the cases of others play a very important role in learning and reasoning, filling in where one's own experience is deficient.

A library is only as good as the indexes and indexing scheme available for locating things in it. So too with an individual's case library. People can find the right cases in their memories if they "*indexed*" them well when they entered the cases into the library, and if the indexing scheme is well enough defined that they can recreate an index for an appropriate case when trying to locate something in memory. The most effective case-based reasoners interpret their experiences as they are having them to identify what they are learning from the situation and to anticipate when those lessons might be useful.

A good indexing scheme for a case-based reasoner allows the reasoner to see a past situation as being relevant to the current one. Thus, a case's indexes should allow an individual to find it at times when it might be productive to apply. Good indexes are critical for *transfer*, the ability to apply knowledge or skills derived in one kind of situation to a situation that might be quite a bit different.

The best indexing results from anticipating the circumstances when a lesson learned from a case might be useful and marking the case so that it will be recalled in such circumstances. For example, if I index the case where vegetarians did not eat the fish as "serving fish as the main course of a dinner party," I will be reminded of that case each time I plan to serve fish as the main course at a dinner party. Remembering the case would remind me to apply the lesson it teaches: ask guests if they have any special eating requirements. Or, I might index the case more generally under "having a dinner party," allowing me to be reminded that I ought to ask guests for their dietary constraints even before I begin planning dinner.

It is important to keep in mind, though, that it is almost always impossible to identify every lesson an experience might teach and every situation in which it might be applicable. It is common to have an experience that one doesn't completely understand or appreciate until much later—sometimes because one lacks the knowledge necessary to interpret the situation, sometimes because one lacks the experience to know whether a result is positive or negative, sometimes for other reasons. A person might recognize that his or her understanding is incomplete at the time of experience, or he or she may only come to realize that his or her understanding was incomplete when attempting to use the case later and finding that its application led to poor results. Either way, indexing will be incomplete.

But incomplete indexing does not have to mean that cases are inaccessible if the reasoner engages in situation assessment at the time he/she/it is trying to address a new situation. *Situation assessment* is a process of analyzing a new situation so as to understand it better. One attempts to infer unknown details of a new situation or to look at the situation from several different perspectives. This interpretation process allows the reasoner to construct a hypothetical but better description of a new situation, allowing potentially useful cases to be recalled. One way to look at situation assessment is as a process of imagining: If I'd encountered a situation like this in the past, what would it have looked like, and how would it have been described?

Neither does a poor index at the time one encounters or experiences a situation mean that the situation can never be described well as a case or be well indexed. Situation assessment allows a reasoner to remember a case that was not well indexed. If, after a case is recalled and used, the reasoner is better able to interpret it, he/she/it might extract new lessons from the case or identify something critical about it and re-interpret the case, updating the indexes associated with the case at that time.

A variety of experimental case-based reasoners serve as the basis for CBR's cognitive model. More detail about CBR and early case-based reasoners can be found in Kolodner (1993), more detail about CBR as a cognitive model from Kolodner (1993, 1997), and more detail about CBR's implications for learning and education from Kolodner (1997), Kolodner *et al.* (1998, 2003a, 2003b), and Schank (1999).

CBR's Implications for Supporting Learning

CBR's implications for supporting learning are in line with those made by constructivist approaches to learning and the constructionist approach to education. All focus on promoting the kinds of thinking that will allow learners to construct productive mental models from concrete experiences. One constructivist approach, called *constructionism* (Papert, 1991) suggests that experiences involving the active construction of an artifact are particularly good for promoting such knowledge development.

Similarly, CBR suggests that the best environments for deep learning will be those where learners are having hands-on experiences where they actively construct artifacts and actively construct mental models at the same time. In addition, case-based reasoning suggests five important facilitators for learning effectively from such experiences:

- having the kinds of experiences that afford learning what needs to be learned;
- interpreting those experiences so as to recognize what can be learned from them (drawing connections between their parts so as to transform them into useful cases and extracting lessons that might be applied elsewhere);
- anticipating their usefulness so as to be able to develop indexes for these cases that will allow their applicability to be recognized in the future;
- experiencing failure, especially failure of one's expectations, explaining those failures, and trying again (iteration); and
- learning to use cases effectively to reason.

With respect to what the right kinds of experiences are, CBR suggests that they are experiences that afford concrete, authentic, and timely feedback, so that learners have the opportunity to confront their conceptions and identify what they still need to learn, that learners have the opportunity to iteratively move toward better development of the skills and concepts they are learning so as to experience them in a range of situations and under a variety of conditions, and that they are experiences that allow cases to be compared and contrasted.

Drawing on CBR's cognitive model, we can derive a number of specific suggestions about constructing effective learning environments:

- CBR's focus on the role of failure in promoting learning suggests the importance of acquiring feedback on decisions made, in order to be able to identify holes in one's knowledge and to generate goals for additional learning. CBR's approach emphasizes the need for learners to actually carry out and test their ideas, not only think about them.
- CBR's focus on explanation suggests that the learners should be pushed to both predict and explain, and they should be helped to do both successfully. One cannot recognize a need to explain without first seeing a difference between what was expected and what happened. This means that making predictions is important so that learners recognize gaps in what they know.
- CBR's focus on indexing as the key to reuse suggests that in addition to having experiences, students should reflect on and assess those experiences to extract both what might be learned from them and the circumstances under which those lessons might be appropriately applied.

- CBR's focus on iterative refinement suggests that learners should, necessarily, try out their ideas in a variety of situations and to cycle through application of what they are learning, interpretation of feedback, and explanation and revision of conceptions several times.
- CBR's focus on the role previous experience plays in reasoning suggests that learners should be encouraged to reuse their own previous experiences as they solve "school" problems. Further, they might be helped to solve more complex problems by having easy access to the cases (experiences) of others.

These suggestions have informed the creation of two different approaches to sequencing learning activities—Goal-Based Scenarios (Schank *et al.*, 1993/94) and Learning by Design (Kolodner *et al.*, 1998, 2003a, 2003b). Further, they imply two roles that computers might play in learning environments more generally:

- Software can support reflection, especially that involved in explaining experiences, interpreting them to make them accessible and easily applicable, and anticipating the applicability of lessons that can be learned from them.
- Software interfaces can provide case libraries to serve as a resource as learners engage in problem solving, explanation, or other reasoning. Learners might create their own case libraries for others to use as a way of encouraging them to interpret their own experiences more completely.

Using CBR's Ideas to Engineer Sequencing in the Learning Environment

Learning from experience is not a one-shot deal. Ideas extracted from one's experiences need to be debugged and tried out again and again. The sequencing of activities and facilitation of discussion in a learning environment can be engineered to increase the frequency of accessing cases in one's memory and ultimately the educational impact of learners' experiences. Here we briefly discuss two approaches to engineering the learning environment that derive from case-based reasoning—Goal-Based Scenarios (GBS) and Learning by Design (LBD).

Goal-Based Scenarios

During the 1990s, Roger Schank applied the lessons of CBR to the development of a new kind of computational learning environment, a Goal-Based Scenario (GBS) (Schank, Fano, Bell, & Jona, 1994). A goal-based scenario places learners in a situation where they have to achieve some interesting goal that also requires them to meet certain curricular objectives. In one goal-based scenario, for example, high-school students play the role of advisors to the President in dealing with a hostage situation in a foreign land (Bareiss & Beckwith, 1993). They are introduced to several hostage-taking events in history and matters of foreign policy. They learn history because they need the history to successfully achieve the challenge set for them. In another scenario, museum visitors play the role of a genetic counselor (Bell & Bareiss, 1993), learning genetics concepts in the context of providing advice to a mock couple trying to make family planning decisions. In another, adult learners act as salespeople in a simulation and learn tricks of the trade for selling ads (Kass *et al.*, 1993). The trick, of course, is to design challenges that both engage targeted learners and focus them on the intended content and skills.

Such scenarios were not atypical then in computer games, and they are not atypical now. However, goal-based scenarios were designed specifically to aid learning, and they include in them whatever resources are needed to aid learning as learners engage in the GBS. One type of resource typical in a GBS is a library of videos in which experts describe their stories, strategies, and perspectives in ways that might help the learner with his or her task. When learners reach an impasse, they ask a question of the video library, and an appropriate video is retrieved and shown. Sometimes a video's story will suggest a topic they should learn more about or a skill they need to learn; other times it will tell how an expert dealt with some difficult issue the student is addressing. Based on suggestions made by the case library, learners move forward with their task. Learners engaged in a well-designed goal-based scenario take on goals that lead them to want to know new concepts and learn new skills; the case library in a well-designed GBS has plenty of advice for helping them and makes it easy to find appropriate videos, and its story line gives learners plenty of opportunities to apply the recorded experiences of others. In such a system, when learners fail at a task or are surprised, they ask for cases (videos) that can help them explain and recover from their failures.

Case libraries used in a goal-based scenario need to index material based both on its content and on the context in which a retrieved video will be used. What task is the learner working on? What is his/her solution in progress? What difficulty is the learner having? When building a case library to be used as part of a goal-based scenario, case indexes should be chosen by anticipating the situations in which a learner will want to hear a story. By focusing indexing on the learner's goals, such case libraries can act as powerful supports for learning.

Details on the design of goal-based scenarios can be found in several articles and chapters (Bareiss & Osgood, 1993; Ferguson, Bareiss, Birnbaum, & Osgood, 1992; Schank, Berman, & Macpherson, 1999). Most critical is that the design of a GBS requires anticipating a learner's goals and subgoals while working on a challenge. This, in turn, requires anticipating the tasks learners will carry out, the avenues of thought and strategies they will pursue, and the kinds of choices they will make. The designer of a GBS can then anticipate the kinds of impasses they will encounter and, therefore, the kinds of stories the case library should include and the ways those stories ought to be indexed.

Learning by Design

While the GBS approach focuses on designing computer programs that help a learner achieve an exciting challenge, Learning by Design (LBD) (Kolodner, 1997; Kolodner *et al.*, 1998, 2003a, 2003b) focuses on using CBR's model to suggest how to orchestrate a classroom environment. In addition to suggesting ways of integrating the computer into the classroom, LBD is explicit about teacher roles and the sequencing of individual, small-group, and whole-class activities.

LBD curriculum units ask middle-school students (ages 12–14) to achieve design challenges while learning science concepts and skills. Design challenges provide opportunities for engaging in and learning complex cognitive, social, practical, and communication skills. For example, students design and build parachutes to learn about air resistance and gravity, miniature vehicles and their propulsion systems to learn about Newtonian mechanics, and ways of managing the erosion on barrier islands to learn about erosion, water currents, and the relationship between people and the environment. Construction and trial of real devices gives students the motivation to want to learn, the opportunity to discover what they need to learn, the opportunity to experience uses of science, and the opportunity to test their conceptions and discover the gaps in their knowledge. The teacher helps students reflect on their experiences in ways that help them extract, articulate, and keep track of the content and skills they are learning.

Case-based reasoning implies that learning requires impasses and expectation failures to show us what we don't know, to focus us on what we need to learn, and to motivate us to want to learn. This suggests an iterative approach to learning from experience: try to solve a problem or achieve a challenge, use the impasses and failures of expectation to show what needs to be learned, investigate to learn more, and try again. Based on these suggestions from CBR, Learning by Design's curriculum units are centered on the design and construction of working devices or working models that illustrate physical phenomena or that measure phenomena. Working with such tangible devices highlights learner misconceptions (e.g., a vehicle may fail to move as expected) and prompts redesign.

CBR also implies that learning from experience requires reflecting on one's experiences in order to derive well-articulated cases and insert them appropriately into one's memory. LBD includes in its environment a system of classroom activities that promotes such derivations. "Messing about" is guided play done in small groups that promotes making connections between a design challenge and what students already know. This is followed by "whiteboarding," a whole-class activity in which learners collectively articulate what they discovered and then generate ideas about how to proceed. Multiple presentation venues ("poster sessions", "pin-up sessions", and "gallery walks") provide opportunities for students to present and critique their investigation procedures, data interpretations, and solutions in progress. All three types of presentations require students to articulate what they are doing well enough for others to understand; they also provide students with ideas to build on in moving forward and a venue for getting feedback on their communicative effectiveness, for getting advice and suggestions, and for gaining knowledge from the vicarious experiences of others.

Using guidelines from case-based reasoning, LBD provides (i) libraries of cases for students to use as resources; (ii) paper-and-pencil and software tools that allow students to keep track of their design experiences; (iii) a system of classroom activities that help students make contact with their own previous experience and bring it to bear, help them anticipate what they need to learn more about, and help them share their ideas with each other; (iv) software tools that prompt students to explain their design decisions and design experiences to each other and get feedback from their peers; (v) software tools that prompt students to extract and articulate the content and skills they are learning from their experiences and write them up .as stories to share with other students; (vi) software tools that help students read the cases written by experts and extract from them the science and advice that can help them with their design challenge; and (vii) teacher guidelines for facilitating reflective discussions and other activities in ways that help students turn their experiences into cases—stored in their memories in ways that allow them to remember and apply them in later situations (e.g., helping them identify what they learned, how they learned it, under what conditions it might be applicable, and when such conditions might come up in the future). The LBD tools act as resources helping students create cases for others to use, helping students keep track of what they have been doing, and helping students reflect on their experiences in order to turn them into cases in their own memories.

Learning by Design's framework and units have been incorporated into a comprehensive three-year middle school science curriculum called Project-Based Inquiry Science (Kolodner *et al.*, 2008, 2010).

CBR-Informed Software to Support Learning

As mentioned in the discussion of both GBS and LBD, software can help learners process their own experiences to build cases in their minds, and software can supply learners with external cases from which they can reason. A range of case-based learning aids have been designed with each of these functionalities in mind. Case-based learning aids support the learner as a case processor by taking on various responsibilities (e.g., interpretation, indexing) with the hope that, as the learner interacts with the learning aid more and more, he or she will gradually assume responsibility for these tasks. Here we present two primary categories of case-based learning aids: those that aid reflection (including case authoring tools) and case libraries as resources.

CBR's primary contribution to the use of software to support learning is its claims about the kinds of reflection that are productive for helping learners understand their experiences and describe them in ways that will allow them to be able to access and use them productively later (Kolodner, Hmelo, & Narayanan, 1996). According to CBR, learning from and reusing experiences requires (a) interpreting an experience to connect its pieces together and extract what might be learned from it, (b) creating indexes, and (c) creating and evaluating solutions.

CBR-inspired support for reflection encourages learners to think about (i) the kinds of issues they've considered in solving a problem, developing a skill, or achieving a design challenge; (ii) the kinds of solutions they constructed; and (iii) the future situations in which the solutions might be used again, focusing particularly on how the lessons learned from an experience might be utilized in new ways. There are several challenges to creating good CBR-informed supports for reflection:

- **Motivating reflection**: Reflection is hard to do and offers few extrinsic rewards. Motivating good reflection is a real challenge.
- **Encouraging quality reflection**: Reflection is hard to do, but easy to "fake," that is, it is easy to generate text that sounds reflective but really isn't (Ng & Bereiter, 1995). Encouraging learners to reflect about things that can lead to better learning is hard to prompt and structure.
- **Generating feedback**: Computer-based supports for reflection can rarely respond intelligently about a learner's reflection. In several of the tools listed, collaborative discussion areas are used to generate feedback on the learners' reflective statements; this kind of feedback is dependent on the quality of the discussants and may or may not result in additional reflection.
- **Not overdoing it**: Periodic reflection while attempting to solve a problem or understand a situation is productive, as is summative reflection when one is finished. It is easy to identify times when reflection would be productive, but it is also easy to overdo it—to try to force reflection at times when it interferes with other reasoning or so often that it becomes a hated activity. It is important to find some happy medium— promoting reflection at productive times without damaging a train of thought.

A particular approach to promoting reflection on one's experiences is the activity of authoring cases for a case library. Learners authoring cases explicitly have to deal with issues of identifying appropriate ways to index the case, identifying strategies and process elements, and decomposing the case for others to use. By making these activities explicit in formal learning activities, instruction can encourage learners to take on a goal that will help them generate transferable knowledge (Ram & Leake, 1995). The activity of authoring a case can be motivating for students, as they are creating a public artifact whose purpose is to help future learners or practitioners. This is the same kind of motivating activity that Harel and other constructionists suggest using to promote learning (Harel & Papert, 1990; Papert, 1991). Cognitively, the need to explain to others in a way that will allow them to understand requires sorting out the complexities of a situation, making connections between its parts, and organizing what one has to say into coherent and memorable chunks—the same sorts of reflection needed to interpret one's experiences in ways that permit accessing them and using them productively in later situations.

CBR also suggests providing learners with case libraries to support their learning. A case library may offer two potential opportunities: the opportunity to learn from the experiences of others, and the opportunity to learn by sharing one's own experiences. Case libraries can provide learners with a variety of valuable information:

- **Advice in the form of stories**: Stories about success are valuable for the advice they give about how to proceed or what strategies to use. Stories about failure provide advice about what to avoid or issues to focus on. Stories can also provide the basis for predicting what might happen if an individual tries out his or her solution. While stories might be presented in a variety of media, the important thing is that their lessons learned are drawn out and made clear. As mentioned earlier, it is also important that stories be indexed in ways that anticipate their use. The library's stories should be organized so that the user can easily find the stories that address his or her questions (Kolodner, 1993).
- **Vicarious experience using a concept or skill**: Learning a concept or skill well requires several encounters (Redmond, 1992); this is necessary to observe its varied uses, the other concepts or skills to which it relates, and to debug its applicability and refine its definition. But there usually is not time in school for students to actively experience the full range of applicability of a concept. Sharing experiences with other students or looking at the ways experts have applied concepts and skills can fill those gaps. Case libraries and other CBR-inspired environments can present numerous examples of related solutions from which someone can learn without having to experience every case first-hand.

- **The lay of the domain and guidance on what to focus on**: An on-line case library's indexing system, if it is available for examination, can serve as an advanced organizer for the student or even scaffolding for how the student might think about her own cases (Spiro, Feltovich, Jacobson, & Coulson, 1991). For example, the system of indexes in ARCHIE-2 (a case library that aided architectural students) helped students develop an understanding of the issues that needed to be addressed in designing libraries: the kinds of spaces libraries have and the perspectives different kinds of patrons might take on how well a library functions. In this role, the case library's indexing system provides a view of the domain's major concepts, their relationships, and guidance on what to focus on when designing or solving problems.
- **Strategies and procedures**: Sometimes what is most valuable about a story is not the solution itself but the strategies employed or even just the starting point. For novices in a domain, the biggest problem is sometimes how to start (Guzdial, 1991)—what is the first thing to do or to try or to explore? In many models of design, simply the definition of the problem is the most challenging aspect (Schon, 1982). Cases that describe somebody's problem-solving or design process can show how others have defined problems and proceeded through to a solution.
- **How to use cases**: Learning about others' experiences in such a way that learners can reuse the lessons learned in novel situations is a complex meta-cognitive activity (Silver, Branca, & Adams, 1980). Cases that are about applying someone else's case can help students understand how experts reuse cases. Case libraries that prompt for the kinds of analysis that is necessary in deciding whether a case is relevant and how to adapt it for reuse can help learners develop case-based reasoning skills.

The context in which case libraries are used is critical to their effectiveness. Case libraries have proven most useful as *a resource that provides information as needed* as learners are engaged in constructive learning activities. In a project-based learning situation, a case library may provide guidance for getting started, for moving forward, and so on—if its cases answer the project-related issues that arise as learners are working on a project. For cases to be a useful resource to learners, they must be engaged in an activity where their impasses might be answered by cases in the case library. If learners are facing challenges that arise naturally in problem solving (e.g., "How do I model a situation like this?" or "What's a good starting point for this kind of problem?"), then a case library of relevant situations and problems can help them address those impasses.

Supports for Reflection and Interpretation of One's Experiences

Reflective Learner

Students in undergraduate project-based design courses face a huge number of challenges as part of their learning. They have to do design at the same time as they are learning about design, using theory and engineering principles that they may have just learned a term before (Turns, Guzdial, Mistree, Allen, & Rosen, 1995a). Often, they are working in groups, so they also have to deal with collaboration issues (Turns *et al.*, 1995b).

Turns conducted ethnographic studies of students in engineering design courses and discovered that students often did not know what they were supposed to be learning, why they were engaging in the activities they were, and worse yet, how to reflect upon their activities in order to learn from them (Turns, Newstetter, Allen, & Mistree, 1997). Accordingly she built a support for learning that directly addressed the issue of reflection.

Her tool, the REFLECTIVE LEARNER, aided students in producing "learning essays" about their experiences. The requirement for the students to write learning essays already existed in the engineering design class that she chose to study. However, the unsupported learning essays were not particularly satisfying to the teacher or students. Students still seemed confused about why they were doing what they were being asked to do.

The REFLECTIVE LEARNER provided scaffolding in the form of prompts to help students write learning essays in a more effective manner. Its prompts were directly informed by CBR's suggestions about the reflection needed to be able to learn from and reuse one's experiences. It asked students:

- To identify and describe a problem that they had encountered when undertaking the current phase of their design project;
- To describe their solution to the problem;
- To say what they had learned from the experience; and
- To anticipate the kinds of situations where a similar solution might be useful.

The tool itself was very simple, as seen in Figure 6.1. Qualitative evaluation suggested that students found this activity useful and that it helped them to understand why they were doing what they were doing.

Supporting Student Sharing in Smile

One of Learning by Design's hallmarks is the use of presentation sessions that promote reflection on and sharing of experiences. Poster sessions, gallery walks, and pin-up sessions were designed for that purpose. However, learners preparing for those sessions work in small groups without a teacher available. A case authoring tool-suite called SMILE (Kolodner & Nagel, 1999) provides scaffolding to help learners articulate their experiences

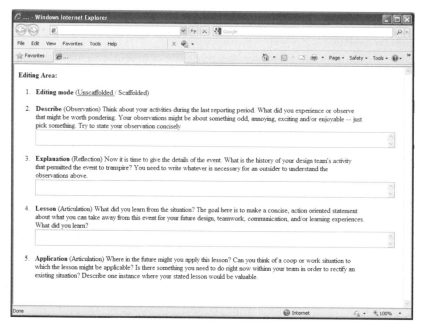

Figure 6.1 REFLECTIVE LEARNER prompts

well so that sharing them with others is easy. SMILE provides prompts that are specific to the kind of experience being reflected on and the kind of presentation that needs to be made. Figures 6.2 and 6.3 illustrate two of these tools; the left-hand side of the screen always provides structure for the task students are working on, while the right side holds hints and examples, or, as in Figures 6.2 and 6.3, might be overlaid with a task-specific template to help with the reflection needed to complete the task.

The Pin-Up tool (Figure 6.2) helps students use the results of their investigations to come up with the best solution to a project challenge. Students formulate Design Decisions and justify them with evidence— from experiments just performed, rules of thumb extracted, and scientific principles. The template helps them line up their design decisions with their justifications.

The Gallery Walk tool (Figure 6.3) scaffolds students as they reflect on their design experiences and plan presentations of their solutions-in-progress for their peers. Their first time through, students have constructed a solution based on design decisions reported in their Pin-Up presentation. But those solutions rarely work exactly as they had expected. After trying out those ideas, this tool helps them look back on the decisions they made and articulate what happened differently than they had imagined. It then prompts them to explain, if they can, why their solution behaved differently than they had predicted. By revisiting the

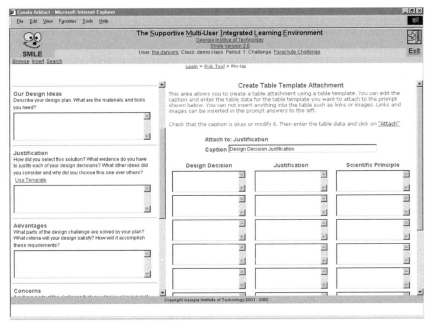

Figure 6.2 The Pin-Up tool in SMILE

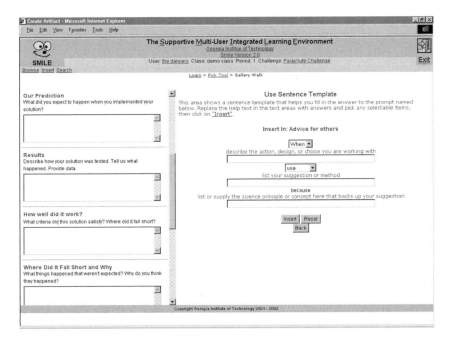

Figure 6.3 The Gallery Walk tool in SMILE

Gallery Walk tool after each of their design/test iterations, they produce a document that chronicles all of the decisions that were made and why those decisions were made. This set of decisions can enable them to reflect on their experience holistically, and it can also serve as a case to be examined by future students addressing the same challenge.

SMILE's suite of case-authoring tools also includes tools specialized for reporting on experiences carrying out investigations, for interpreting case studies, and for summarizing and presenting their project history. Each is configured similarly to the two tools discussed above.

Whichever the tool they are using, after authoring their entry, students' published artifacts are available through SMILE's Library. Looking at another team's or person's entry will open two side-by-side windows: the presentation on the left and a comment window on the right. This anchored collaboration (Guzdial *et al.*, 1997) ties each student presentation to its own threaded discussion space. Other students may add a new comment or question for case authors (i.e., form a new thread) or insert a comment into an existing discussion.

SMILE derives from earlier special-purpose case authoring tools (e.g., DESIGN DISCUSSION AREA [Kolodner & Nagel, 1999] and JAVACAP [Shabo *et al.*, 1997]). Several lessons about the benefits of case authoring tools were learned from pilot studies (Kolodner, Owensby, & Guzdial, 2004): (i) writing up their experiences as cases can help middle-school students reflect in the specific ways that allow them to learn from their experiences; (ii) with scaffolding like that in SMILE, students need less help from the teacher in extracting what they have learned from their experiences and in writing up detailed reports of what they have experienced and learned; (iii) writing up their science experiences as cases before discussing those experiences in class raises the level of discussion in the classroom.

Lessons were learned as well about designing scaffolding to achieve these goals (Kolodner, Owensby & Guzdial, 2004):

- **Scaffolding the remembering and articulation of an experience**: To identify which tools are needed in a case-authoring tool suite, the reasoning tasks students will engage in during lab or project work should be identified, and a tool with scaffolding specific to the needs of each task should be created. Creating such a systematic suite of tools, each specific to a task, supplies scaffolding for each task and also allows learners to grasp and manage the whole combination of tasks they need to undertake to complete a project.
- **Supporting collaborative discussions about experiences across groups**: An important role of case authoring is to support collaboration across groups in a class. Good collaboration across groups depends on each group being able to articulate their ideas to others well. To support cross-group collaboration, scaffolding should therefore be designed to support the articulation of ideas that must be shared across groups.

- **The pragmatics of designing scaffolding systems:** To help learners report on their experiences and pull out what they have learned, four interconnected kinds of scaffolding are needed in each tool: questions that structure the task into pieces of manageable size, hints about what is expected in answer to each question, examples as models of the way to answer each question, and templates for those responses that themselves have a regular structure.

Case Libraries as Resources

The second type of software support case-based reasoning suggests is case libraries as resources. Case libraries are very important resources, providing examples of successful and unsuccessful attempts at problem solving and providing models of case application. However, applying cases to new situations is not always easy. Sometimes learners have difficulty recognizing that a case can be applied to a new situation; other times, students have difficulty figuring out how to adapt the case to meet their needs. Some case libraries, like ARCHIE-2, STABLE, and SCRIPTABLE, supply cases and focus on ways to structure them so that learners can easily understand them. Other case library tools, such as the CASE APPLICATION SUITE (part of SMILE), also try to help students with case application—applying a case from a library to a new situation.

Archie-2

ARCHIE-2 (Zimring, Do, Domeshek, & Kolodner, 1995) was created as a case-based design aid for professional architects. Its cases describe public buildings, focusing on libraries and courthouses (see Figure 6.4). The intent was that as a designer was working on the design of a public building, he or she would consult ARCHIE-2 periodically for advice. To get started, the architect would use ARCHIE-2 much as architects use file cabinets, architectural journals, and the library—to find projects similar in intent to the new one and to see how others had handled the issues. An architect designing courthouses would browse the courthouses; one designing libraries would browse the libraries. Later, while addressing a particular issue (e.g., placement of the children's section in a library, lighting reading areas, access to management), the architect would go back to ARCHIE-2 again, this time focusing on that particular issue. It was used extensively in architecture studios at Georgia Tech (Zimring *et al.*, 1995).

Stable

STABLE (SmallTalk Apprenticeship-Based Learning Environment) is a descendent of ARCHIE-2 designed to help students learn the skills involved in doing object-oriented design and programming. STABLE

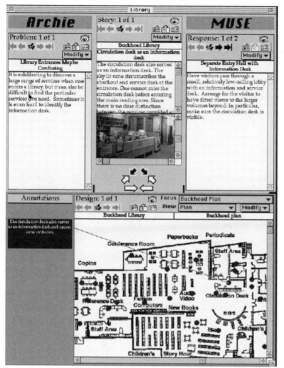

Figure 6.4 ARCHIE-2

used a Web-based collection of cases made from previous students' work. Since STABLE's intent was to support skill learning, it was based on theories of apprenticeship learning (Collins, Brown, & Newman, 1989). In apprenticeship learning, a student attempts problems under the supervision and coaching of a master in the domain. The master uses a variety of methods to help the student learn, often referred to as *scaffolding.*

STABLE was designed to provide a large amount of information but scaffolded in such a way that students were encouraged to think for themselves and only request the information they needed (see Figure 6.5).

- Each step of a design process was provided at three or more levels of detail, where the initial visit to a step was at the least amount of detail.
- Strategy information ("Why was this step done now or in this way?") was available, but not initially presented.
- Potential problems and solutions were presented, but mostly as links to previous steps. For example, a given step might say "A problem like this might occur" and "If it does, the cause probably occurred during this step" with a hyperlink provided to the previous step.

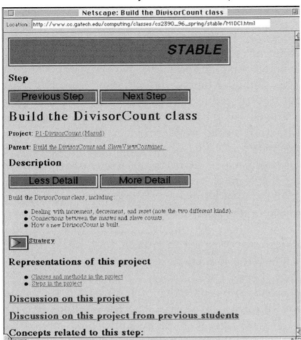

Figure 6.5 A STABLE Step Page. Note the ability to increase or decrease the amount of detail on the Step, as well as the link to Strategy information

- Each step was linked to expert's observations on the case (e.g., "This is an example of a part–whole object relationship"), and the observations were also linked to other steps, in order to provide more concrete examples of an abstract observation.

Evaluation of STABLE suggested that it was successful in improving student performance and learning (Guzdial & Kehoe, 1998). Students were able to solve more complicated problems earlier in the term, and students were able to solve design problems on a final exam better than students in previous years.

Surprisingly, though, students expressed several complaints about STABLE. STABLE was designed to offer various levels of details *about a case*. However, it was not designed to offer much in the way of support for *comparing cases*, except through experts' observations. The lesson learned from STABLE was that a case library to support students engaged in design activities can facilitate student learning, be successful in supporting design, and be placed in a curricular setting which creates the relevant context that Schank (1982) identified as critical for successful learning from cases. However, STABLE also showed that what students see as "relevant" is important to determine, and it may not always be evident without careful examination of student practices (with and without the designed tool).

ScriptABLE

Sharing many similarities with the STABLE system, SCRIPTABLE is a Web-based case library aimed at supporting professional graphic and web designers as they learn about computer programming (JavaScript) in their work environment. This setting is quite a bit different from the other learning environments explored in this chapter. Here, the learners employ largely informal educational practices. For example, they search for example code on the Internet related to the problems they are currently working on, and they acquire knowledge about programming concepts in a piecemeal fashion (Dorn & Guzdial, 2010). SCRIPTABLE was designed to leverage the importance that examples play in such users' existing learning practices, while also conveying additional instruction about fundamental computing concepts like iteration, selection, and recursion. Such concepts can often be overlooked when learning is not guided by a teacher.

SCRIPTABLE is a case library of example projects (i.e., cases) that are consistent with the kinds of programming activities in which web and graphic designers engage. Figure 6.6 illustrates a portion of one project page contained in the system. Inspired by Clancy and Linn's (1995) work on teaching computing through case studies, the presentation of each project is structured to provide learners with a goal-oriented context for the problem being solved, the relevant index terms (called tags), which link a project to others in the system, possible test cases for the program being written, and discussion of the iterative development process that led from a naïve solution to a fully-functional one.

The development process is presented in a narrative form that comprises the majority of each project page. The narrative first presents a straightforward solution to the problem being addressed, demonstrates its partially correct behavior, but then shows how the solution fails for a particular test case. Failure then serves as the impetus within the narrative to present a new computing concept, which is described within the context of the project being solved. Thus conceptual knowledge is always motivated by the demands of a particular project. This iterative structure is designed as a template to guide learners' problem solving.

The SCRIPTABLE case library includes a hyperlinked indexing system that cross references each project along several dimensions: program syntax, computing concepts, and task- or goal-oriented concerns. This allows a learner to quickly move between related projects to compare and contrast their circumstances and solutions. The interface also provides search capabilities.

Early evaluation of SCRIPTABLE suggests that case-based learning aids like this can indeed be effective at promoting conceptual knowledge development for independent learners engaged in problem-solving tasks related to the content of the case library (Dorn, 2010). Results showed detectable differences in the quality of conceptual answers when learners were asked to explain how they would solve particular problems with a

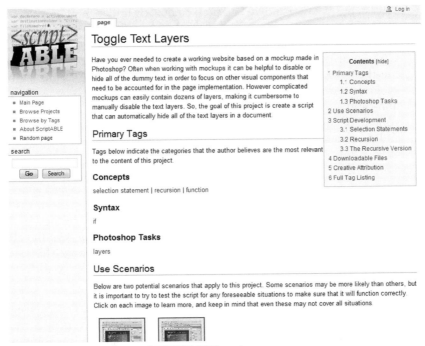

Figure 6.6 Excerpt from a SCRIPTABLE project page

given program. Those who had access to SCRIPTABLE while completing a series of problems showed greater increases in the technical correctness and use of normative vocabulary in their responses than those who used an impoverished version of the system.

Based on observations and user feedback, we can draw out several specific recommendations for the design of case libraries to be used as reference material:

- Providing explicit connections between project-related concerns and conceptual information within the case itself allows learners to identify why something should be learned. This is especially important when a case library is intended to be used by learners without other curricular supports.
- Even when the distance between the context of the case and the context of the problem being solved by the learner is small, it can be very difficult for a learner to recognize that a particular case is relevant.
- Consistency and organization of the written case is important to build credibility and increase comfort for users. Users frequently commented how the consistent format was a positive change from the resources they typically encounter on the Web at large. More importantly,

consistent structure allowed learners to quickly understand how cases are written and to be able to predict what content is present and where it might be found, allowing for more efficient interactions.

- Case libraries need to contain a reasonably large collection of cases for them to be perceived as useful in practical applications of a general nature. When the goal is to develop resources to be used by non-captive audiences (like groups of users on the Internet), both volume of content (so that the case library will be useful) and quality and consistency of that content are important.

Some of these findings echo results and observations from ARCHIE-2 and STABLE. The exploration of a learner's notions of what is and is not relevant continues to be an open research question in the context of case libraries. The relationships between case library size and its usefulness and usability are important, but it is unlikely that there is a one-size-fits-all solution to the challenge of content creation and curation in a case library.

Case Application Suite

As noted above, case application can be difficult for novices. Discovering that a case is relevant is a challenge in and of itself, but even then the productive application of a prior case requires several capabilities (Owensby & Kolodner, 2002):

- An understanding of both the new situation and old ones well enough to recognize similarities between cases that might be applicable and the situation students have been presented with that they wish to apply the case to;
- The ability to recognize what is known that might be applicable;
- An available library of applicable cases that makes the job of remembering the right cases at the right times easier.

The CASE APPLICATION SUITE (CAS), implemented within SMILE, is a collection of tools designed to help novices apply cases while working on projects. Its scaffolding aims to provide support to small groups as they engage in case interpretation and application, especially helping them to articulate and record their interpretations and reasoning. Hints, examples, and templates are designed to help students articulate appropriate content.

A big issue that had to be addressed was how to help students apply an old situation to a new one. The idea of a "design rule of thumb" as a representation of a lesson learned (Ryan, Camp & Crismond, 2001) became the vehicle for case application. Rules of thumb were already being used in Learning by Design's physical science units to help students connect their design experiences to the science they are learning (e.g., to make a car go farther, make sure the wheels don't rub on the chassis because this adds friction). The CASE APPLICATION SUITE uses rules of thumb similarly to help students connect the expert cases they are reading to the challenges they are trying to solve. The application process revolves around pulling out lessons learned from cases as rules of thumb, analyzing their applicability and applying them to a challenge, and then predicting the effects of that solution and assessing how well it meets the challenge. A template helps students articulate their rules of thumb. The intention is to scaffold students so that they can create detailed rules of thumb and use scientific principles to justify the lessons learned.

One component of CAS (Figure 6.7) scaffolds the examination and understanding of an expert case, focusing on sequencing, general understanding, highlighting alternative solutions, the science used, and the rules of thumb that can be derived. The case being interpreted is on the left, questions that help learners organize what they are reading are in the middle, and hints about how to respond to those questions are given in the right-hand pane.

Other tools in CAS system help students analyze their rules of thumb in light of the challenge to determine if those rules of thumb can be applied. Students are prompted to analyze a rule of thumb's applicability with respect to their design goals, issues and sub-issues, and criteria/constraints. When using this tool, the students think about whether their solution can be improved using this rule of thumb and decide whether they should

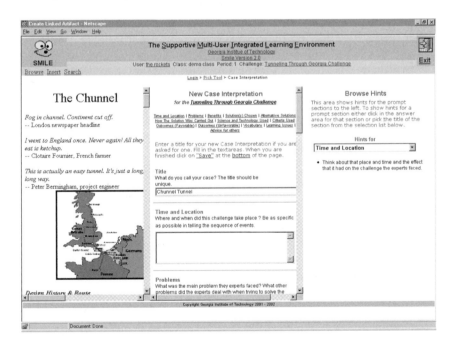

Figure 6.7 Case application suite

apply it. Once students come to a solution, the results of applying a case or rule of thumb must be assessed.

Evaluation efforts show that, in general, the tools in CAS were easily usable; students using the tools were able to extract rules of thumb far better than those who did not use CAS (even later, when the tool was not available to them); when a teacher had not modeled case interpretation well for students before using the tool, they were still able to interpret a case well; and when the teacher did model case interpretation well, those students using the tool wrote more cogent summaries of their cases than those who did not use the tool.

Concluding Thoughts

Case-based reasoning makes a variety of suggestions about how to promote better learning.

- CBR suggests ways of making learning from hands-on activities more effective: (i) by making sure students have the opportunity to iteratively apply what they are learning—getting real feedback about what they've done so far, being helped to explain what happened if it was not what was expected, and having an opportunity to try again and again until they are successful and come to a full understanding of what they are learning; (ii) by making sure to include in classroom activities the kinds of discussions and reflective activities that ask students to reflect on their experiences, extract what they are doing and learning, and articulate those lessons learned for themselves or others; and (iii) by making sure students anticipate the kinds of future situations in which they will be able to apply what they are learning.
- CBR suggests resources that might be useful during learning—well-indexed libraries of well-structured expert cases and well-indexed libraries that hold the ideas and lessons learned by peers.
- CBR suggests activities that can enhance learning in any setting—writing cases to share with others and reading the cases of experts and preparing them for other students to learn from.
- CBR suggests ways of managing a student-centered problem-based, project-based, or design-based classroom so that students help each other move forward at about the same pace—gallery walks for sharing ideas keep everyone at about the same pace; archives of on-line cases allow those who can move forward at a faster pace to gain from the experiences of those who came before.
- CBR suggests ways of creating useful case libraries without an undue amount of up-front work by the teacher—seed a case library with several cases that model what's expected, and then have students each year add to that case library for students in the years to come.

A simple list. But we hope the discussions of the different systems and what makes them effective will help readers to understand that a great deal of planning and thought is needed to integrate these kinds of activities into classrooms and software in ways that work. We hope too that those discussions provide some guidelines on how to get started.

Acknowledgments

The writing of this chapter was supported by grants from the National Science Foundation and the National Physical Science Consortium. Research of the authors reported in the chapter was supported by grants from NSF, the National Physical Science Consortium, the McDonnell Foundation, the Woodruff Foundation, Georgia Tech's EduTech Institute, and DARPA. Any opinions, findings, and conclusions or recommendations expressed in this material are those of the authors and do not necessarily reflect the views of the aforementioned funding agencies.

References

Bareiss, R., & Beckwith, R. (1993). Advise the President: A hypermedia system for teaching contemporary American history. Paper presented at the annual meeting of the American Educational Research Association.

Bareiss, R., & Osgood, R. (1993). Applying AI models to the design of exploratory hypermedia systems. *Proceedings of the ACM Conference on Hypertext* (pp. 94–105).

Bell, B. L., & Bareiss, R. (1993). Sickle cell counselor: Using goal-based scenarios to motivate the exploration of knowledge in a museum context. *Proceedings of the World Conference on AI in Education* (pp 153–160).

Clancy, M. J., & Linn, M. (1995). *Designing Pascal solutions: A case study approach*. New York: W. H. Freeman.

Collins, A., Brown, J. S., & Newman, S. E. (1989). Cognitive apprenticeship: Teaching the craft of reading, writing, and mathematics. In L. B. Resnick (Ed.), *Knowing, Learning, and Instruction: Essays in Honor of Robert Glaser* (pp. 453–494). Hillsdale, NJ: Lawrence Erlbaum and Associates.

Dorn, B. (2010). *A case-based approach for supporting the informal computing education of end-user programmers*. Unpublished PhD Thesis, School of Interactive Computing, Georgia Institute of Technology.

Dorn, B., & Guzdial, M. (2010). Learning on the job: Characterizing the programming knowledge and learning strategies of web designers. In *CHI'2010: Proceedings of the 28th International Conference on Human Factors in Computing Systems* (pp. 703–712).

Ferguson, W., Bareiss, R., Birnbaum, L., & Osgood, R. (1992). ASK systems: An approach to the realization of story-based teachers. *Journal of the Learning Sciences, 2* (1), 95–134.

Guzdial, M. J. (1991). The need for education and technology: Examples from the GPCeditor, *Proceedings of the National Educational Computing Conference* (pp. 16–23). Phoenix, AZ.

Guzdial, M., & Kehoe, C. (1998). Apprenticeship-based learning environments: A principled approach to providing software-realized scaffolding through hypermedia. *Journal of Interactive Learning Research*, 9(3/4).

Guzdial, M., Hmelo, C., Hubscher, R., Nagel, K., Newstetter, W., Puntembakar, S., Shabo, A., Turns, J., and Kolodner, J.L. (1997). Integrating and guiding collaboration: Lessons learned in computer-supported collaboration learning research at Georgia Tech. *Proceedings of the International Conference on Computer Support for Collaborative Learning (CSCL'97)* (pp. 91-100).

Hammond, K. J. (1989) *Case-based planning: Viewing planning as a memory task.* Boston: Academic Press.

Harel, I., & Papert, S. (1990). Software design as a learning environment. *Interactive Learning Environments*, 1 (1), 1–32.

Kass, A., Burke, R., Blevis, E., & Williamson, M. (1993). Constructing learning environments for complex social skills. *Journal of the Learning Sciences*, 3, 387–427.

Kolodner, J. (1993). *Case based reasoning.* San Mateo, CA: Morgan Kaufmann.

Kolodner, J. L. (1997). Educational implications of analogy: A view from case-based reasoning. *American Psychologist.*

Kolodner, J. L., & Nagel, K. (1999). The design discussion area: A collaborative learning tool in support of learning from problem-solving and design activities, *Proceedings of CSCL '99*. Palo Alto, CA, pp. 300–307.

Kolodner, J. L., & Simpson, R. L. (1989). The MEDIATOR: Analysis of an early case-based problem solver. *Cognitive Science* 13(4): 507–549.

Kolodner, J. L., Crismond, D., Fasse, B., Gray, J., Holbrook, J., & Puntembakar, S. (2003a). Problem-based learning meets case-based reasoning in the middle-school science classroom: Putting learning-by-design™ into practice. *Journal of the Learning Sciences*, 12(4).

Kolodner, J. L., Crismond, D., Gray, J., Holbrook, J., & Puntambekar, S. (1998). Learning by design from theory to practice. In A. Bruckman, M. Guzdial, J. Kolodner, & A. Ram (Eds.), *Proceedings of International Conference of the Learning Sciences 1998 (ICLS-98)* (pp. 16–22). Atlanta, GA.

Kolodner, J., Gray, J., & Fasse, B. (2003b). Promoting transfer through case-based reasoning: Rituals and practices in learning by design classrooms. *Cognitive Science Quarterly*, Vol. 3.

Kolodner, J. L., Hmelo, C. E., & Narayanan, N. H. (1996). Problem-based learning meets case-based reasoning. In Edelson, D. & Domeshek, E., *Proceedings of the International Conference of the Learning Sciences 1996 (ICLS-96)*. Charlottesville, VA: AACE, pp. 188–195.

Kolodner, J. L., Krajcik, J., Edelson, D., Reiser, B., & Starr, M. (2010). *Project-based inquiry science* (13 volumes). Armonk, NY: It's About Time.

Kolodner, J. L., Owensby, J. N.. & Guzdial, M. (2004). Case-based learning aids. In D. H. Jonassen (Ed.), *Handbook of research for education communications and technology, 2nd Edn.* Mahwah, NJ: Lawrence Erlbaum Associates.

Kolodner, J. L., Starr, M. L., Edelson, D., Hug, B., Kanter, D., Krajcik, J., Lancaster, J. A., Laster, T. A., Leimberer, J., Reiser, B. J., Ryan, M. T., Schneider, R., Sutherland, L. M., & Zahm, B. (2008). Implementing what we know about learning in a middle-school curriculum for widespread dissemination: The project-based inquiry science (PBIS) story. In *Proceedings of the 8th*

International Conference on the Learning Sciences—Volume 3 (ICLS'08), International Society of the Learning Sciences, pp. 274–281.

Ng, E., & Bereiter, C. (1995). Three levels of goal orientation in learning. In A. Ram & D. B. Leake (Eds.), *Goal-driven learning* (pp. 354–370). Cambridge, MA: MIT Press.

Owensby, J., & Kolodner, J. L. (2002). Case application suite: Promoting collaborative case application in learning by design™ classrooms. *Proceedings of the International Conference on Computer Support for Collaborative Learning, CSCL-2002*, pp. 505–506.

Papert, S. (1991). Situating constructionism. In I. Harel & S. Papert (Eds.), *Constructionism* (pp. 1–11). Norwood, NJ: Ablex.

Ram, A., & Leake, D. B. (1995). Learning, goals, and learning goals. In A. Ram & D. B. Leake (Eds.), *Goal-driven learning* (pp. 1–37). Cambridge, MA: MIT Press.

Redmond, M. (1992). *Learning by observing and understanding expert problem solving*. Unpublished PhD Thesis, College of Computing, Georgia Institute of Technology.

Ryan, M., Camp, P., & Crismond, D. (2001). Design rules of thumb—Connecting science and design. Presented at AERA 2001, Seattle, WA. http://www.cc.gatech.edu/projects/lbd/pubtopic.html#designrules.

Schank, R. C. (1982). *Dynamic memory*. Cambridge: Cambridge University Press.

Schank, R. C. (1999). *Dynamic memory revisited*. Cambridge: Cambridge University Press.

Schank, R. C., Berman, T. R., & Macpherson, K. A. (1999). Learning by doing. In C. Reigeluth (Ed.), *Instructional design theories and models* (pp. 161–181). Mahwah, NJ: Lawrence Erlbaum Associates.

Schank, R. C., Fano, A., Bell, B., & Jona, M. (1993/1994). The design of goal-based scenarios. *Journal of the Learning Sciences*, 3 (4), 305–346.

Schon, D. A. (1982). *The reflective practitioner: How professionals think in action*. New York: Basic Books.

Shabo, A., Nagel, K., Guzdial, M., & Kolodner, J. (1997). JavaCAP: A collaborative case authoring program on the WWW. In R. Hall, N. Miyake, & N. Enyedy (Eds.), *Proceedings of Computer-Supported Collaborative Learning '97 (CSCL-97)* (pp. 241–249). Toronto, Ontario.

Silver, E. A., Branca, N. A., & Adams, V. M. (1980). Metacognition: The missing link in problem solving? In R. Karplus (Ed.), *Proceedings of the Fourth International Conference for the Psychology of Mathematics Education* (pp. 213–222). Berkeley, CA: University of California.

Spiro, R. J., Feltovich, P. J., Jacobson, M. J., & Coulson, R. L. (1991). Cognitive flexibility, constructivism, and hypertext: Random access instruction for advanced knowledge acquisition in ill-structured domains. *Educational Technology*, 31 (5), 24–33.

Turns, J., Guzdial, M., Mistree, F., Allen, J. K., & Rosen, D. (1995a). I wish I had understood this at the beginning: Dilemmas in research, teaching, and the introduction of technology in engineering design courses, *Proceedings of the Frontiers in Education Conference*. Atlanta, GA.

Turns, J., Mistree, F., Rosen, D., Allen, J., Guzdial, M., & Carlson, D. (1995b). A collaborative multimedia design learning simulator. Paper presented at the ED-

Media 95: World Conference on Educational Multimedia and HyperMedia, Graz, Austria, June 17–21.

Turns, J. A., Newstetter, W., Allen, J. K., & Mistree, F. (1997). The reflective learner: Supporting the writing of learning essays that support the learning of engineering design through experience, *Proceedings of the 1997 American Society of Engineering Educators Conference*. Milwaukee, WI.

Zimring, C. M., Do, E., Domeshek, E., & Kolodner, J. (1995). Supporting case-study use in design education: A computational case-based design aid for architecture. In J. P. Mohsen (Ed.), *Computing in engineering: Proceedings of the second congress*. New York: American Society of Civil Engineers.

7 Metacognition and Self-Regulated Learning in Student-Centered Learning Environments

Roger Azevedo, Reza F. Behnagh, Melissa Duffy, Jason M. Harley, and Gregory Trevors

The ubiquity and widespread use of Student-Centered Learning Environments (SCLEs) poses numerous challenges for learners. Learning with these non-linear, multi-representational, open-ended learning environments typically involves the use of numerous self-regulatory processes such as planning, reflection, and metacognitive monitoring and regulation (Azevedo, 2005, 2007, 2008, 2009; Greene & Azevedo, 2009, 2010; Moos & Azevedo, 2008; Veenman, 2007; White & Frederiksen, 2005; Zimmerman, 2008). Unfortunately, learners do not always monitor and regulate these processes during learning with SCLEs, which limits these environments' potential and effectiveness as educational tools to enhance learning about complex and challenging topics and domains.

Metacognition and self-regulation comprise a set of key processes that are critical for learning about conceptually-rich domains with SCLEs such as open-ended hypermedia environments, multi-agent tutoring systems, serious games, and other hybrid systems. We emphasize that learning with SCLEs involves a complex set of interactions between cognitive, metacognitive, motivational, and affective processes (Aleven, Roll, McLaren, & Koedinger, 2010; Azevedo, Moos, Johnson, & Chauncey, 2010; Biswas, Jeong, Kinnebrew, Sulcer, & Roscoe, 2010; Graesser & McNamara, 2010; White, Frederiksen, & Collins, 2009; Winne & Nesbit, 2009). Current interdisciplinary research provides evidence that learners of all ages struggle when learning about these conceptually rich domains with SCLEs. To briefly summarize, this research indicates that learning with SCLEs is particularly difficult because it requires students to monitor and regulate several aspects of their learning. For example, regulating one's learning involves analyzing the learning context, setting and managing meaningful learning goals, determining which learning and problem-solving strategies to use, assessing whether the strategies are effective in meeting the learning goals, monitoring and making accurate judgments regarding one's emerging understanding of the topic and contextual factors, and determining whether there are aspects of the learning context that could be used to facilitate learning. During self-regulated learning (SRL), students need to deploy several metacognitive processes to determine whether they understand what they are learning, and perhaps modify their plans, goals, strategies, and efforts in relation to dynamically changing contextual conditions. In addition, students must also monitor, modify, and adapt to fluctuations in their motivational and affective states, and determine how much social support (if any) may be needed to perform the task. Also, depending on the learning context, instructional goals, perceived task performance, and progress made towards achieving the learning goal(s), they may need to modify certain aspects of their cognition, metacognition, motivation, and affect. As such, we argue that metacognition and self-regulation play a critical role in learning with SCLEs.

In this chapter, we provide an overview of SRL with SCLEs, describe assumptions and commonalities across several leading models, describe the assumptions and components of a leading information-processing model of SRL, provide examples and definitions of key specific metacognitive monitoring processes and regulatory skills used when learning with SCLEs, provide specific examples of how models of metacognition and SRL have been embodied in four contemporary SCLEs, and provide implications for the future of SCLEs that focus on metacognition and SRL.

Self-Regulated Learning in Student-Centered Learning Environments

The complex nature of metacognitive and self-regulatory processes can be exemplified by providing an example of learning with a multi-agent, adaptive, hypermedia learning environment such as MetaTutor. Typically, a student is asked to learn about the human circulatory system for two hours with the system. The environment contains several dozen illustrations and hundreds of paragraphs containing thousands of words with corresponding static diagrams. Each of these representations of information is organized in some fashion, similar to sections and sub-sections of book chapters, thus allowing students to navigate freely throughout the environment. Imagine a self-regulated student who analyzes the learning situation, sets meaningful learning goals, and determines which strategies to use based on the task conditions. The student may also generate motivational beliefs based on prior experience with the topic and learning environment, success with similar tasks, contextual constraints (e.g., provision of scaffolding and feedback by an artificial pedagogical agent), and contextual demands (e.g., a time limit for completion of the task). During the course of learning, the student may assess whether particular strategies are effective in meeting his learning sub-goals, evaluate his emerging understanding of the topic, and make the necessary adjustments regarding his knowledge, behavior, effort, and other aspects of the learning context. Ideally, the self-regulated learner will make adaptive adjustments, based on continuous metacognitive monitoring and control related to the standards for the particular learning task and these adjustments will facilitate decisions regarding when, how, and what to regulate (Pintrich, 2000; Schunk, 2001; Winne & Hadwin, 1998, 2008; Winne & Nesbit, 2009; Zimmerman, 2008; Zimmerman & Schunk, 2011). Depending on the task with the learning environment and sometime after the learning session, the learner may make several cognitive, motivational, and behavioral attributions that affect subsequent learning (Pintrich, 2000; Schunk, 2001). This scenario represents an idealistic approach to self-regulating one's learning with an SCLE. Unfortunately, the typical learner does not engage in these complex adaptive cognitive and metacognitive processes during learning with SCLEs (see Azevedo & Witherspoon, 2009; Biswas *et al.*, 2010). As such, the educational potential of these environments is severely limited.

Overview of SRL Models

Self-regulated learning (SRL) theories attempt to model how cognitive, metacognitive, motivational, and emotional processes and contextual factors influence the learning process (Pintrich, 2000; Winne, 2001; Winne & Hadwin, 1998, 2008; Zimmerman, 2000, 2008). Although there are important differences between various theoretical definitions, self-regulated learners are generally characterized as active and efficient at managing their own learning through monitoring and strategy use (Boekaerts, Pintrich, & Zeidner, 2000; Butler & Winne, 1995; Efklides, 2011; Greene & Azevedo, 2007; Pintrich, 2000; Winne, 2001; Winne & Hadwin, 1998, 2008; Zimmerman, 2001). Students are self-regulated to the degree that they are metacognitively, motivationally, and behaviorally active participants in their learning (Zimmerman, 1986).

SRL has also been described as a constructive process wherein learners set goals on the basis of both their past experiences and their current learning environments (Pintrich, 2000). These goals become the criteria toward which regulation aims. In essence, SRL mediates the relations between learner characteristics, context, and performance (Pintrich, 2004). Pintrich (2000) organized SRL research using a taxonomy focusing on the phases and areas of self-regulation. These phases include task identification and planning, monitoring and control of learning strategies, and reaction and reflection. The various areas in which self-regulation can occur fall into four broad categories: cognition, motivation, behavior, and context. By crossing phases and areas, Pintrich presented a four-by-four grid wherein various research findings and theoretical constructs can be categorized. For example, feeling of knowing (FOK) is a monitoring process within the area of cognition, whereas changing or re-negotiating a task with a pedagogical agent, teacher, or peer presents the enactment of a context-control strategy.

Pintrich's (2000) taxonomy helps researchers organize the many lines of current SRL research and gives some general information regarding how they might relate. This is particularly relevant for understanding the nature of SRL during learning with SCLEs. Different models of SRL focus on specific cells or groups of cells within Pintrich's (2000) taxonomy. For example, Winne and Hadwin's (1998, 2008) model of SRL, based on the Information Processing Theory (IPT), complements the work of Pintrich and others by more specifically outlining the cognitive processes that occur during learning, as well as re-conceptualizing some of the phases (Winne, 2001). This affords a different perspective on SRL. However, given the number of SRL models currently in existence, the question is how these contributions aid in understanding learning with SCLEs. More specifically, this chapter addresses how these processes influence students' learning with SCLEs and how they can be designed to support and foster students' SRL processes.

Theoretical Framework: Information-Processing Theory of SRL

Self-regulated learning (SRL) involves actively constructing an understanding of a topic or domain by using strategies and goals; monitoring and regulating certain aspects of cognition, behavior, and motivation; and modifying behavior to achieve the desired goal(s) (see Boekaerts *et al.*, 2000; Pintrich, 2000; Zimmerman & Schunk, 2001). Though this definition of SRL is commonly used, the field of SRL consists of various theoretical perspectives that make different assumptions and focus on different constructs, processes, and phases (see Azevedo *et al.*, 2010; Dunlosky & Lipko, 2007; Metcalfe & Dunlosky, 2009; Pintrich, Wolters, & Baxter, 2000; Schunk, 2005; Winne & Hadwin, 2008; Zimmerman, 2008). We further specify SRL as a concept superordinate to metacognition that incorporates both metacognitive monitoring (i.e., knowledge of cognition or metacognitive knowledge) and metacognitive control (involving the skills associated with the regulation of metacognition), as well as processes related to manipulating contextual conditions and planning for future activities within a learning episode. SRL is based on the assumption that learners exercise agency by consciously monitoring and intervening in their learning.

Most of the contemporary research on SRL with SCLEs (e.g., see special issues by Azevedo, 2005; Clarebout, Horz, & Elen, 2009; Greene & Azevedo, 2010; Zumbach & Bannert, 2006) have drawn on Winne and colleagues' (Butler & Winne, 1995; Winne, 2001; Winne & Hadwin, 1998, 2008) Information Processing Theory (IPT) of SRL. This IPT theory suggests a four-phase model of SRL. The goal of this section is to explicate the basics of the model so as to emphasize the linear, recursive, and adaptive nature of SRL (see Greene & Azevedo, 2007, for a recent review).

Winne and Hadwin (1998, 2008) propose that learning occurs in four basic phases: (1) task definition, (2) goal-setting and planning, (3) studying tactics, and (4) adaptations to metacognition. Winne and

Hadwin's SRL model differs from the majority of other SRL models in that they hypothesize that information processing occurs within each phase. Using the acronym COPES, they describe each of the four phases in terms of the interactions between a learner's conditions, operations, products, evaluations, and standards. All of the terms except operations are kinds of information used or generated during learning. It is within this cognitive architecture, comprised of COPES, that the work of each phase is completed. Thus, their model complements other SRL models by introducing a more complex description of the processes underlying each phase. It should be noted that Winne and Hadwin's model is similar to other models which focus on the underlying cognitive and metacognitive processes, accuracy of metacognitive judgments, and control processes used to achieve particular learning goals (see Hacker, Dunlosky, & Graesser, 2009).

Cognitive and task conditions are the resources available to the person and the constraints inherent to the task or environment. Cognitive conditions include beliefs, dispositions and styles, motivation, domain knowledge, knowledge of the current task, and knowledge of study tactics and strategies. Task conditions are external to the person, and include resources, instructional cues, time, and the local context. Thus, in Winne and Hadwin's model, motivation and context are subsumed in conditions. Conditions influence both standards as well as the actual operations a person performs. The conditions represent both the characteristics of the learner and the context that set the stage for initially deciding how to proceed with a task (e.g., generate a plan, activate relevant prior domain knowledge) and how external task conditions may influence a learner's ability to monitor and regulate their learning given particular task conditions such as the amount of time to solve a set of problems and the level of accessibility to relevant instructional resources needed to complete the task.

Standards are multi-faceted criteria that the learner believes are the optimal end state of whatever phase is currently running, and they include both metrics and beliefs. For example, in the task definition phase, a learner might examine a list of learning goals set by an artificial pedagogical agent for a learning task and develop task standards including what needs to be learned (metrics). The learner may also develop beliefs about the act of studying itself, such as the depth of understanding required, or how difficult the task will be. The model uses a bar graph to illustrate how a learner actively determines criteria for "success" in terms of each aspect of the learning task, where each bar represents a different standard with varying qualities or degrees. The overall profile of these standards from phase one constitutes the learner's goal. These standards or goals are used to determine the success of any operations the learner might perform within each phase. One of the most challenging aspects of understanding the role of standards is that they are internally represented in a learner's cognitive system and are rarely accessible to the learning environment during learning.

Operations are the information manipulation processes that students use during learning, which include searching, monitoring, assembling, rehearsing, and translating. These processes are also known as SMART processes (Winne, 2001). These SMART processes are cognitive in nature, rather than metacognitive and as such they only result in cognitive products, or information for each phase. For example, the product of phase one is a definition of the task; whereas the product of phase three might be the ability to recall a specific piece of information for a test. These products are then compared with the standards by way of monitoring. Through *monitoring*, a learner compares products with standards to determine if their objectives for a given phase have been met, or if further work remains to be done. These comparisons are called cognitive evaluations, and they become important when, for example, a student detects a poor fit between products and standards and as a result, enacts control over the learning operations to refine the product, revise the conditions and standards, or both. This is the object-level focus of monitoring. However, this monitoring also includes a meta-level information, or metacognitive, focus. For example, a learner may believe that a particular learning task is easy, and thus translate this belief into a standard in phase two. However, in iterating through phase three, perhaps the learning product is consistently evaluated as unacceptable in terms of object-level standards. This may initiate metacognitive monitoring that determines that this meta-level information, in this case regarding the actual difficulty of this task, does not match the previously set standard that the task is easy. At this point, a metacognitive control strategy might be initiated to modify (or to update) that particular standard (e.g., "this task is difficult") which might, in turn, affect other standards created during phase two; goal setting. These changes to goals from phase two may include a review of past material or the learning of a new strategy. Thus, the model is a "recursive, weakly sequenced system" (Winne & Hadwin, 1998) where the monitoring of products and standards within one phase can lead to updates of products from previous phases. The inclusion of monitoring and control in the cognitive architecture allows these processes to influence each phase of SRL.

Overall, while there is no typical cycle, most learning involves recycling through the cognitive architecture until a clear definition of the task has been created (phase one), followed by the production of learning goals and the best plan to meet them (phase two), which leads to the enactment of strategies to begin learning (phase three). The products of learning, for example, an understanding of pulmonary circulation, are compared against standards including the overall accuracy of the product, the learner's beliefs about what needs to be learned, and other factors like efficacy and time constraints. If the product does not adequately fit the standard, then further learning operations are initiated, perhaps with changes to conditions such as setting aside more time for studying. Finally, after the main processes of learning have occurred, learners may decide to further alter their beliefs, motivation, and strategies that make up SRL (i.e., phase four of the model). These changes can include the addition or deletion of conditions or operations, as well as minor (tuning) and major (restructuring) changes to the ways conditions cue operations (Winne, 2001). The output, or performance, is the result of recursive processes that cascade back and forth, altering conditions, standards, operations, and products as needed.

Lastly, Winne and Nesbit (2009) state that certain hypotheses can be postulated when adopting a model of SRL. First, before committing to a goal, a learner must recognize the features of the learning environment that affect the odds of success. Second, if such features are recognized, then they need to be interpreted, a choice must be made (e.g., set a goal), and the learner needs to select amongst a set of learning strategies that may lead to successful learning. If these first conditions are satisfied, the learner must have the capability to apply these learning strategies. If these three conditions are met, then the learner must be motivated to put forth the effort required to apply the selected learning strategies. In sum, this model provides a macro-level model and elegantly accounts for the linear, recursive, and adaptive nature of SRL with SCLEs.

Micro-Level Model of SRL as an Event

Azevedo, Greene, Moos, and colleagues, following Winne's model, have provided a detailed analysis of the cognitive and metacognitive processes used by learners of all ages when using several SCLEs including hypermedia, simulations, intelligent tutoring systems, and multi-agent learning environments (see Azevedo, Greene, & Moos, 2007; Azevedo, Moos, Greene, Winters, & Cromley, 2008; Azevedo, Cromley, Moos, Greene, & Winters, 2011; Azevedo & Witherspoon, 2009; Greene & Azevedo, 2007, 2009, 2010). Their analyses of SRL processes during learning with SCLEs are of particular relevance since they treat SRL as an event. Their analyses of hundreds of concurrent think-aloud protocols and other process data (e.g., log-files) provide detailed evidence of the micro-level processes that can augment Winne and Hadwin's (1998, 2008) model. In general, these processes include planning, monitoring, strategy use, handling of task difficulty and demands, and interest activities. In this section, we describe definitions and examples of metacognitive processes typically used with SCLEs and then present how their monitoring processes and corresponding judgments are addressed by regulatory processes.

Monitoring Processes during Learning with SCLEs

In this section, we present several monitoring processes, which we have identified in our studies on SRL with hypermedia. Although many of these processes are likely context-independent, applicable to learning with various SCLEs, some are most appropriately applied to learning with hypermedia, in situations where learners have control over which content and in which modality, they access at any given moment. As previously mentioned, Winne and colleagues' model provides a macro-level framework for the cyclical and iterative phases of SRL. The data presented in this section provide the micro-level details that can interface Winne's model. In particular, we present the eight metacognitive monitoring processes we have identified as essential to promoting students' SRL with hypermedia. Some of these monitoring processes include valence, positive (+) or negative (–), which indicates the learners' evaluation of the content, their understanding, progress, or familiarity with the material. For example, a learner might state that the current content is either appropriate (content evaluation +) or inappropriate (content evaluation –), given their learning goals and according to which valence is associated with the evaluation (and accuracy of the metacognitive judgment). They may also make choices about how and which metacognitive regulatory process to choose in order to address the result of the metacognitive judgment (e.g., set a new goal, summarize the content).

Feeling of knowing (FOK) is when the learner is aware of having (+) or not having (–) read, heard, or inspected something in the past and having (+) or not having (–) some familiarity with the material. For example, a learner may be familiar with a particular static external representation of the circulatory system showing oxygenated and deoxygenated blood paths. *Judgment of learning* (JOL) is when a learner becomes aware that he does (+) or does not (–) know or understand something he read, inspected, or heard. For example, a learner states that he does not understand the explanation of the concept of homeostasis verbally described to him by a pedagogical agent. Another important monitoring process is *monitoring use of strategies* (MUS). In MUS, the learner acknowledges that a particular learning strategy he has employed was either useful (+) or not useful (–). An example of a learner monitoring use of strategies is: "Yeah, drawing it really helps me understand how blood flows throughout the heart." *Self-test* (ST) is when a learner poses a question to himself to assess his understanding of the content and determine whether to proceed with additional content or to re-adjust his use of strategies. An example of a learner self-testing is: "Ok, how do lower-level organisms support a pond's ecosystem?" In *monitoring progress toward goals* (MPTG), learners assess whether previously set goals have been met (+) or not met (–), given time constraints. This monitoring process includes a learner comparing the goals set for the learning task with those that he/she has already accomplished and those that still need to be addressed in the remainder of the session, but rarely occurs during a learning session. A related metacognitive process is *time monitoring* (TM) which involves the learner becoming aware of the remaining time which was allotted for the learning task. An example of a learner monitoring his time is: "I still have 30 minutes, that's plenty of time." *Content evaluation* (CE) is when the learner monitors the appropriateness (+) or inappropriateness (–) of the current learning content (e.g., text, diagram, animation or any other type of static and dynamic external representation of information), given their pre-existing overall learning goal and sub-goals. An example of a learner evaluating the content is: "This section, which includes a description of the cycles of blood flow through the heart and lungs and a labeled diagram of the heart is important and helpful for me to understand the different components of the heart." Finally, *evaluation of adequacy of content* (EAC) is similar to CE, in that learners are monitoring the learning content, given their learning goals, but in this process, learners evaluate learning content they have not yet navigated toward. An example of a learner evaluating the adequacy of content is: "Do they have a picture of the blood flow through the heart?" In sum, these are just a few of the relevant metacognitive monitoring processes used by students during learning with SCLEs. It should be highlighted, based on our previous discussions of models of SRL, that these as well as other metacognitive processes play a role in facilitating and supporting students' SRL with SCLEs.

Self-Regulation Based on Metacognitive Monitoring Processes

In this section, we describe the learner's application of these eight monitoring processes within the context of self-regulation with hypermedia. The processes described in this section are based on empirical findings (e.g., Azevedo *et al.*, 2010). For each monitoring process, we provide the aspects of the learning environment that are evaluated by learners and illustrate them using examples of task and cognitive conditions, which may lead to the various monitoring processes, as well as examples of appropriate control mechanisms which might be deployed following the evaluations. Feeling of knowing (FOK) is used when the learner is monitoring the correspondence between his or her own pre-existing domain knowledge and the current content. The learner's domain knowledge and the learning resources are the aspects of the learning situation being monitored when a learner engages in FOK. If a learner recognizes a mismatch between his pre-existing domain knowledge and the learning resources, more effort should be expended in order to align the domain knowledge and the learning resources. Following more effortful use of the learning material, a learner is more likely to experience/generate more positive FOKs. However, if a learner experiences familiarity with some piece of material, a good self-regulator will attempt to integrate the new information with existing knowledge by employing knowledge elaboration (KE). Often, a learner will erroneously sense a positive FOK toward material, and quickly move on to other material, with several misconceptions still intact. In contrast to FOK, judgment of learning (JOL) is used when the learner is monitoring the correspondence between his own emerging understanding of the domain and the learning resources. Similar to FOK, when engaging in JOL, a learner is monitoring his domain knowledge and the learning resources. If a learner recognizes that his emerging understanding of the material is not congruent with the material (i.e., the learner is confused by the material), more effort should be applied to learn the material. A common strategy deployed after a negative JOL is re-reading previously encountered material. In order to capitalize on re-reading, a good self-regulator should pay particular attention to elements in a passage, animation, or illustration that confused him. When a learner expresses a positive JOL, he might self-test to confirm that the knowledge is as accurate as the evaluation suggests. As with FOK, learners often over-estimate their emerging understanding and progress too quickly to other material. When monitoring use of strategies (MUS), a learner is monitoring the efficacy of recently used learning strategies, given his expectations for learning results. MUS encompasses a learner's monitoring of learning strategies, expectations of results, and domain knowledge. By noting the learning strategies used during a learning task and the resulting change in domain knowledge, learners can compare their emergent knowledge with their learning expectations and engage in SRL to make changes to the strategies employed accordingly. For example, many learners will begin a learning episode by taking copious amounts of notes, then realize that the learning outcomes from this strategy are not as high as they would have expected. Good self-regulators will then make alterations to their strategy of note-taking such as employing more efficient methods (making bullet points, outlines, or drawings), or even abandon this strategy for another, more successful strategy (e.g., summarizing). However, if a learner realizes that a particular strategy has been especially helpful to his learning, he should continue to employ this strategy during the learning session. Learners self-test (ST) to monitor their emerging understanding of the content and the aspects of the learning situation being monitored are their domain knowledge and their expectations of the content. While tackling difficult material, learners should occasionally assess their level of understanding of the material by engaging in self-testing. If the results of this self-test are positive, the learner can progress to new material, but if the learner recognizes, through this self-test, that his emergent understanding of the current material is not congruent with what is stated in the material, he should revisit the content to better comprehend it. When monitoring progress toward goals (MPTG), a learner is monitoring the fit between his learning results and previously set learning goals for the session. The aspects of the learning situation which are monitored during MPTG are the learner's domain knowledge, his expectations of results, and the learning goals. Closely related to time monitoring, MPTG is an essential monitoring activity that learners should use to stay "on-track" to their completion of the learning task. A learner may be able to generate several critical sub-goals for his learning task, but if he does not monitor the completion or incompletion of these sub-goals, the sub-goal generation SRL strategy will be inadequate. When a learner monitors the progress toward his goals and realizes that he has only accomplished one out of three of his sub-goals in 80 percent of the time devoted to the learning task, a good self-regulator will revisit the remaining sub-goals and decide which is most important to pursue next. In time monitoring, the learner is monitoring the task condition of time, with respect to his pre-existing learning goals. These learning goals can be either the global learning goal defined before engaging in the learning task, or sub-goals created by the learner during the learning episode. If the learner recognizes that very little time remains and few of the learning goals have been accomplished, he should make adaptations to the manner in which the material is being tackled. For example, if a learner has been reading a very long passage for several minutes and realizes that he has not accomplished the learning goals, a good self-regulator will begin scanning the remaining material related to the goals he has not yet reached.

When learners engage in content evaluation, they are monitoring the appropriateness or inappropriateness of the learning material that they are currently reading, hearing, or viewing with regard to the overall learning goal or sub-goal(s) they are currently pursuing. In contrast to content evaluation, evaluation of adequacy of content relates to the learner's assessment of the appropriateness of available learning content, rather than content currently being inspected. The aspects of the learning situations monitored in both of these processes are the learning resources and the learning goals. The learner should remain aware of whether learning goals and learning resources are complementary. If a learner evaluates a particular piece of material as particularly appropriate given his learning goal, he should direct more cognitive resources toward this material (or navigate toward this material), and persist in reading or inspecting the content in order to achieve this goal. Conversely, if a particular piece of content is evaluated as inappropriate with respect to a learning goal, a good self-regulator will navigate away from (or not at all toward) this content to seek more appropriate material. In sum, these monitoring processes and corresponding regulatory processes are based on studies examining the role of self-regulatory processes deployed by learners during learning with open-ended hypermedia learning environments. They also play a critical role during learning with other SCLEs described in the next section.

Examples of SRL in Several SCLEs

In this section, we exemplify how SRL has been embodied in several contemporary SCLEs designed to detect, track, support and foster students' metacognitive monitoring and control processes during learning. The aim is to illustrate how different researchers have conceptualized assumptions and models in the architecture of their SCLEs. The examples include Azevedo and colleagues' MetaTutor, a multi-agent, adaptive hypermedia learning environment; Biswas and colleagues' Betty's Brain, an agent-based environment for teaching middle-school students about ecology; White and Frederiken's multi-agent ThinkerTools environment for inquiry learning; and Lester and colleagues' Crystal Island, a narrative-based and inquiry-oriented serious game learning environment for science.

MetaTutor

MetaTutor is a multi-agent, adaptive hypermedia learning environment, which presents challenging human biology science content. The primary goal underlying this environment is investigating how SCLEs can adaptively scaffold SRL and metacognition within the context of learning about complex biological content. MetaTutor is grounded in a theory of SRL that views learning as an "active, constructive process whereby learners set goals for their learning and then attempt to monitor, regulate, and control" their cognitive and metacognitive processes in the service of those goals (Pintrich, 2000, p. 453). More specifically, MetaTutor adopts Winne and Hadwin's IPT model and is based on several theoretical assumptions of SRL that emphasize the role of cognitive, metacognitive (conceptualized as being subsumed under SRL, cf. Veenman, 2007), motivational, and affective processes. Moreover, learners must regulate their cognitive and metacognitive processes in order to integrate multiple informational representations available from the system (Azevedo, 2008, 2009; Azevedo *et al.*, 2011; Mayer, 2005). While all students have the potential to regulate, few students do so effectively, possibly due to inefficient or lacking cognitive or metacognitive strategies, knowledge, or control (Dunlosky & Bjork, 2008; Pressley & Hilden, 2006; Veenman, 2007).

Embedded in MetaTutor are a multitude of features that embody and foster SRL. Four pedagogical agents guide students through the two-hour learning session and prompt students to engage in planning, monitoring, and strategic learning behaviors. The system uses natural language processing to allow learners to express metacognitive monitoring and control processes. For example, learners can type that they do not understand a paragraph and can also use the interface to summarize a static illustration related to the circulatory system. In addition, the agents can provide feedback and engage in a tutorial dialogue in an attempt to

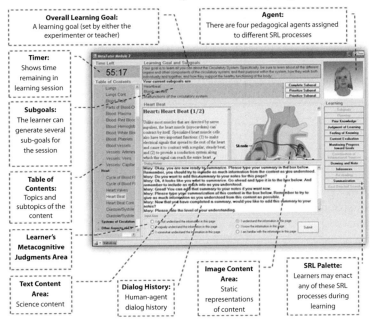

Figure 7.1 Screenshot and brief descriptions of MetaTutor learning environment

scaffold students' selection of appropriate learning sub-goals, accuracy of metacognitive judgments, and use of particular learning strategies. Additionally, the system collects information from user interactions with the system to provide adaptive feedback on the deployment of their SRL behaviors. For example, students can be prompted to self-assess their understanding (i.e., system-initiated JOL) and are then administered a brief quiz. Results from the self-assessment and quiz allow pedagogical agents to provide adaptive feedback according to the calibration between students' confidence of comprehension and their actual quiz performance.

The design layout also supports SRL processes. As depicted on the right in Figure 7.1, an embedded palette provides the opportunity for learners to initiate an interaction with the system according to the SRL process selected (e.g., take notes). Overall, and in line with its theoretical foundations, MetaTutor supports and fosters a variety of SRL processes including: prior knowledge activation, goal setting, evaluation of learning strategies, integrating information across representations, content evaluation, summarization, note-taking, and drawing. Importantly, it also scaffolds specific metacognitive processes such as judgments of learning, feelings of knowing, and monitoring progress towards goals.

Some aspects of the espoused theoretical models of SRL are yet to be implemented. Initially, the theoretical and empirical foci were on cognitive, metacognitive, and behavioral learning processes. Thus, this SCLE does not extensively incorporate the motivational and affective dimensions of SRL into its design. Moving forward, the varieties and regulation of learners' affective processes, the affective qualities of human-agent interaction, and how the system and learners' self-regulation influence the activation, awareness, and protection of motivation will be areas of interest with important implications for SRL theory and instructional design.

Betty's Brain

Betty's Brain (Biswas, Leelawong, Schwartz, & Vye, 2005; Biswas *et al.*, 2010; Leelawong & Biswas, 2008) is an agent-based learning environment developed to help students learn about complex topics in middle-school science classrooms. Learning takes place by students performing a knowledge construction task in which they teach a virtual agent, called Betty, using a visual representation called a causal map. The causal map includes concepts and causal links between pairs of concepts in the relevant science domain, like ecology and thermoregulation. Students can access the science content, which is available in hypertext, to identify the relationships between the concepts during their learning task. They can also ask Betty questions about the cause-and-effect relationships they just created in the causal map to see if she understands what she has been taught, to which Betty responds by explaining her chain of reasoning using text and animation schemes. Betty's understanding can also be checked by asking her to take quizzes, which are administered by the Mentor Agent, Mr. Davis, in the learning environment. Mr. Davis grades Betty's responses based on the hidden "expert" concept map implemented into the system, which is not visible for the student or Betty (Biswas *et al.*, 2010). In the event that Betty makes a mistake, students can browse the hypertext content or get hints from Mr. Davis, to teach Betty the correct causal relationship (see Figure 7.2).

According to Kinnebrew, Biswas, and Sulcer (2010), one of the goals of the Betty's Brain project was to find out the degree to which the agents' metacognitive and SRL prompts could help improve student learning. They also developed methods to identify and interpret students' learning strategies based on the trace of students' interactions with the system. Moreover, Biswas and his research team sought to determine students' acceptance of the strategies recommended by the agents, and how the feedback provided by the agents influenced their learning activities.

Betty's Brain utilizes learning-by-teaching and social constructive learning frameworks (Schunk, 2005; Zimmerman & Schunk, 2001) and helps students learn science and mathematics topics in a self-directed and open-ended setting (Kinnebrew *et al.*, 2010). In the learning-by-teaching method, students take the role of teaching a virtual student, Betty, which is believed to lead to the development of sophisticated metacognitive strategies in students. Kinnebrew *et al.* (2010) also indicate

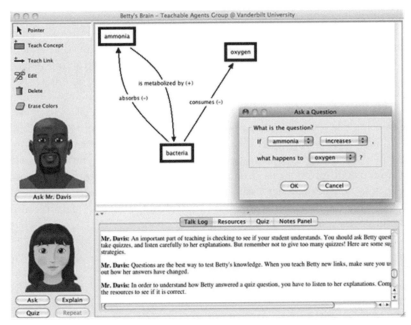

Figure 7.2 Betty's Brain system with the query window (Kinnebrew, Biswas, Sulcer, & Taylor, in press)

that this approach is a less threatening way for students to assess their own understanding. The theory underlying the design of Betty's Brain is the model of self-regulation proposed by Pintrich (2002), where he differentiates between two major aspects of metacognition for learners: metacognitive knowledge and metacognitive control. Kinnebrew *et al.* (2010) further explain their adoption of Pintrich's (2002) model by classifying the knowledge construction strategies into information seeking and information structuring, and the monitoring strategies into checking (querying or quizzing to test the correctness of one's causal map) and probing (asking for explanations and identifying errors). They also believe that Betty's Brain supports five types of activities: reading (the hypermedia content), editing (teaching concepts to Betty), querying (asking Betty questions), explaining (prompting Betty to explain her reasoning), and quizzing (having Betty take quizzes). Two interactive factors of the Betty's Brain environment are believed to support students' self-regulation of learning: the visual shared representation used to teach Betty and the shared responsibility, which refers to the joint responsibility of teaching and learning between the student and Betty (Biswas, Roscoe, Jeong & Sulcer, 2009).

According to Biswas and Sulcer (2010), the detailed log file data collected by the Betty's Brain learning environment, which includes quizzes, the resources visited, queries made, or explanations asked, contain a lot of irrelevant data, which are hard to interpret for pedagogical purposes and for deciding on the type of feedback that the agent should give students to assist them in scaffolding their learning. They also argue that screen recording videos contain a great deal of irrelevant and distracting detail, which makes the analysis difficult. They attribute the problem to the fact that Betty's Brain is an open-ended learning environment, in which students have many different ways to solve the learning task. However, detailed log file data have the potential to provide interesting trace data regarding students' metacognitive calibration during the learning session, and can also be used to investigate how students set goals, monitor their learning, use different strategies, and remedy their lack of understanding. These data sources further assist researchers, designers, and teachers in better understanding when and how to scaffold students' learning and provide timely and appropriate feedback.

ThinkerTools

The ThinkerTools Research Group has developed a suite of SCLEs that aim to promote collaborative inquiry and SRL by scaffolding these processes through student–agent interactions. The multi-agent systems developed by this group include SCI-WISE (Shimoda, White, & Frederiksen, 2002; White, Shimoda, & Frederiksen, 1999), Web of Inquiry, and Inquiry Island (White & Frederiksen, 2005; White et al., 2002, 2009). These systems are successors to the original ThinkerTools Force and Motion software (White, 1993), which aimed to help improve young students' understanding of Newtonian physics principles using interactive simulations and reflective learning.

ThinkerTools uses collaborative inquiry as a platform for SRL and metacognitive development. According to the inquiry cycle, groups of students are guided through the process of question and hypothesis development, experimentation, modeling, application, and evaluation, which then leads back to the generation of new questions in a cyclical manner (White & Frederiksen, 1998, 2005). To effectively support this type of learning, White et al. (2009) argue that metacognitive skills are critical. Given their emphasis on promoting the *forethought, performance*, and *self-reflection* phases of SRL in collaborative environments (White & Frederiksen, 2005), the design of ThinkerTools is grounded in a social-cognitive model of SRL (e.g., Schunk & Zimmerman, 1998; Zimmerman & Schunk, 2001). Several features embedded in these systems serve to support this SRL framework.

To begin with, the intelligent agents within these systems are designed to provide explicit models of cognitive, metacognitive, and social processes. A team of agents, referred to as software advisors, are available to offer students advice and strategies that prompt them to engage in SRL processes such as planning, monitoring, reflecting, and revising

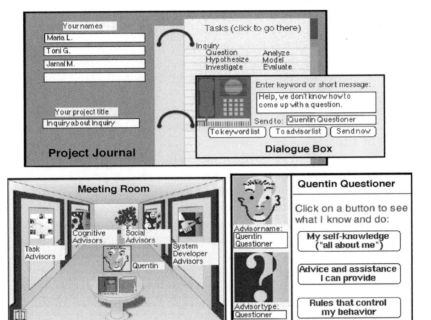

Figure 7.3 SCI-WISE interface: screenshots of the project journal, meeting room, and software advisor (White, Shimoda, & Frederiksen, 1999)

throughout each stage of inquiry (White *et al.*, 2009). Additional features of these programs include goal sliders, project journals, progress reports and research notebooks, which allow students to track and assess their progress and task products, such as models or questions they have created (Shimoda *et al.*, 2002; White & Frederiksen, 2005).

In the more recent developments, such as Inquiry Island and SCI-WISE (see Figure 7.3), students can improve agent interactions by modifying advice settings, such as the content and timing of the advice that they receive (Shimoda *et al.*, 2002; White & Frederiksen, 2005). The Inquiry Island curriculum has also extended its pedagogical approach by providing opportunities for students to adopt advisor responsibilities through role-play (beyond the use of the system)—a process that encourages students to internalize the self-regulatory skills modeled by the agents. Combined, these features allow students to build and modify their own models of SRL and apply them to new contexts (White & Frederiksen, 2005).

Empirical findings suggest that these inquiry-based systems serve as effective metacognitive tools. For instance, results from an inquiry test revealed that fifth-grade students who used Inquiry Island demonstrated significantly higher scores than a comparison group that did not participate (White & Frederiksen, 2005). Moreover, in terms of SRL, those who used Inquiry Island and engaged in subsequent role-play activities showed significant improvements in metacognitive knowledge compared with those who did not participate. This finding, along with analyses of student dialogues, interview responses, and answers to test questions suggest that when ThinkerTools programs are coupled with role-playing activities, students demonstrate improved understanding of the purpose and applications of metacognition and SRL (White & Frederiksen, 2005; White *et al.*, 2009).

ThinkerTools learning outcomes have typically been assessed using data from interviews, observations, metacognitive knowledge tests, and analysis of artifacts, such as research projects. While this provides useful information, these types of SCLEs could also benefit from finer grained analysis by incorporating trace methodologies to capture SRL processes as they unfold over time (admittedly, this becomes more challenging in collaborative environments). This could include assessing micro-level metacognitive and SRL processes, such as judgments of learning and feelings of knowing. Furthermore, affective and motivational dimensions of SRL do not appear to be directly integrated into agents' metacognitive expertise. Still, the ThinkerTools curriculum represents an important shift toward authentic learning environments by providing students with opportunities to internalize SRL processes through system modifications and role-play. Such an approach is unique from other SCLEs in that it provides students with more autonomy to design and apply their personal model of SRL.

Crystal Island

Crystal Island is an innovative SCLE that deploys a rich, narrative-centered, inquiry-based approach to teaching eighth-grade microbiology (McQuiggan, Rowe, Lee, & Lester, 2008; Nietfeld, Hoffman, McQuiggan, & Lester, 2008). An additional distinguishing feature of Crystal Island is its game-like environment, which benefits both from the developed storyline and the use of Valve Software's Source™ engine; the same engine used by the Half Life 2 game. Narrative-centered learning environments (NLEs) combine story contexts and pedagogical support strategies, including the use of artificial intelligence (AI) techniques, to deliver engaging, educational experiences where both the narrative and educational content is tailored to students' actions, metacognitive and affective states, and abilities (McQuiggan *et al.*, 2008) (see Figure 7.4).

Crystal Island has been used to investigate the roles and interactions of a variety of processes and phenomena in a narrative-centered learning environment, including inquiry-based learning, human–computer interaction, affect, engagement, presence, perception of control and a number of metacognitive and SRL elements and strategies (see McQuiggan *et al.* 2008; McQuiggan, Goth, Ha, Rowe & Lester, 2007a; McQuiggan, Hoffman, Nietfeld, Robinson, & Lester, 2008a; McQuiggan, Lee, & Lester, 2007; Mott & Lester, 2006; Nietfeld *et al.* 2008; Robinson, McQuiggan, & Lester, 2010).

Figure 7.4 Crystal Island narrative-centered learning environment (Rowe, Shores, Mott, & Lester, 2010)

Crystal Islands' ability to foster SRL (Butler & Winne, 1995; Greene & Azevedo, 2007; Pintrich, 2000; Winne & Hadwin, 1998; Zimmerman, 2000) has been investigated by looking at goal orientations (Elliot & Dweck, 1988; Elliot & McGregor, 2001), situational interest (Schraw & Lehman, 2001) and metacognitive and SRL strategies such as note-taking and metacognitive monitoring (Butler & Winne, 1995; Winne, 2001). The majority of this research comes from recent studies, such as McQuiggan *et al.* (2008b), which examined several types of note-taking and their relationship with outcome and post-test measures. They found that students who took in-game, hypothesis-type notes (containing a possible solution to the problem in the Crystal Island storyline) performed significantly better on post-test measures than students who did not. Furthermore, hypothesis-type notes were significantly and positively correlated with students' self-efficacy scores from Bandura's Self-Efficacy for SRL scale (2006). Another SRL strategy Crystal Island deployed was metacognitive monitoring, where participants were prompted at 90-second intervals to evaluate their progress towards accomplishing their goals. Nietfeld and colleagues (2008) found that students' evaluations were highly correlated with their performance, including score, actions and goals completed and negatively correlated with number of guesses. Goals were generated by the game, the most superordinate of which was to identify the source of an outbreak on the island. Nietfeld *et al.* (2008) found that presenting the goal of the game as learning-oriented rather than performance-oriented led learners to report significantly higher levels of interest towards the game.

These initial results highlight Crystal Island's capacity as an environment designed to foster SRL and metacognitive skills and processes through various aspects of its narrative and game-like architecture. Future directions for Crystal Island may include expanding the scope of the SRL and metacognitive processes and strategies measured and evaluated as well as moving from measuring to scaffolding students' SRL and metacognitive skill development. One approach to doing this, which would be in line with Crystal Island's narrative-based approach, would be to have the non-playable characters (NPCs) act as in-game SRL and metacognitive tutors. In this capacity, these agents would try to help the students' avatar solve the problem "they" collectively face by equipping him/her with cognitive and metacognitive problem-solving skills. For example, a brief tutorial of effective note-taking could be provided at the beginning of the game and followed up throughout the serious game with NPCs prompting note-taking as well as evaluating the quality of the notes (e.g., verbatim, summary, unrelated). NPCs could also evaluate the effectiveness of students' confidence ratings in the monitoring task as well as prompt them to monitor their feeling of knowing, use of strategies (e.g., note-taking, summarization, help seeking), and progress towards sub-goals. Other elements of SRL and metacognition, such as planning, sub-goal setting, and prior-knowledge activation could also be integrated in the form of NPC plot-relevant dialogue. Indeed, Crystal Island has demonstrated that it is a unique and promising potential test bed for SRL and metacognitive theory and research.

Conclusions and Future Implications

This chapter has highlighted the importance of metacognition and SRL when using SCLEs for learning complex and challenging topics and domains. We continue to advocate that these processes are key to learning and that SCLEs need to be able to detect, track, model, support, and foster these processes during learning episodes. It would be unwise to expect that all SCLEs have these capabilities for several reasons. However, it is important to highlight that SCLEs need to be designed based on sound assumptions, frameworks, models, and theories of metacognition and SRL. A principled, theoretically-based foundation is the key to the design of these systems in order for them to support and foster students' SRL. We have provided an overview of the SRL assumptions commonly accepted by researchers from various theoretical orientations, provided an in-depth description of Winne and Hadwin's model, described specific key metacognitive monitoring and self-regulatory processes related to learning with several SCLEs, and exemplified the embodiment of metacognition and SRL by providing examples of four contemporary SCLEs.

Future work in the area of SRL and SCLEs needs to address several outstanding issues. First, issues related to the *learning context* need to be clearly described and accounted for by the learner and the learning environment. In this category, several variables of interest need to be addressed:

1   The learning goal(s) (e.g., provision of a challenging learning goal(s), self- or other-generated goal(s)).
2   The accessibility of instructional resources (e.g., accessibility of these resources to facilitate goal attainment, engaging in help-seeking behavior and scaffolding while consulting resources).
3   Dynamic interactions between the learner and other external/in-system regulating agents (e.g., pedagogic agents' role(s), levels of interaction, scaffolding, feedback, embodiment of modeling and scaffolding, and fading metaphor behaviors).
4   The role of assessment in enhancing performance, learning, understanding, and problem solving (e.g., the type of assessment, the timing of assessment, whether it is metacognitive knowledge and regulatory skills, or conditional knowledge for the use of SRL skills).

The second set of issues is related to the *learners' cognitive and metacognitive SRL knowledge and skills*. Several issues need to be addressed, including:

1   What self-regulatory strategies are students knowledgeable about? How much practice have they had in successfully using them?
2   How familiar are students with the tasks they are being asked to complete? Are they familiar with the various aspects of the context and learning system they are being asked to use?
3   What are students' levels of prior knowledge? What impact will it have on a learner's ability to self-regulate?
4   Do students have the necessary declarative, procedural, and conditional knowledge essential to regulate their learning? Will the learning system offer opportunities for learning about these complex processes? Will the environment provide opportunities for students to practice and receive feedback about these opportunities?
5   What are students' self-efficacy, interest, task-value, and goal orientations, which may influence their ability to self-regulate?
6   Are students able to monitor and regulate their emotional states during learning?

The third set of issues is related to the *characteristics and features of the SCLE*. Several issues need to be addressed, including:

1   Instructional goal(s) and the structure of the system (e.g., using open-ended hypermedia to acquire a mental model of a science topic, engaging in a tutorial dialogue to refine a misconception, or using inquiry strategies to understand a particular scientific phenomenon).

2 What is the role of multiple representations (e.g., what kinds of external representations are afforded by the environment)? How many types of representations exist? Are they associated with each other (to facilitate integration) or are they embedded in some random fashion (potentially causing extraneous cognitive load)? Are the representations static (e.g., diagrams), dynamic (e.g., animations), or both? Are students allowed to construct their own representations? If so, are they used (by the system or some other external regulating agent) to assess emerging understanding? Or, are they just artifacts that may show the evolution of students' understanding, problem solving, learning, etc.? Or is the purpose for learners to off-load their representations to increase working memory?).

3 What are the types of interactivity between the learner and SCLE (and other contextually embedded external agents)? Are there different levels of learner control? Is the system purely learner-controlled and therefore relies on the learner's ability to self-regulate or is the system adaptive in externally regulating and supporting students' SRL through the use of complex AI algorithms that provide SRL scaffolding and feedback?

4 What types of scaffolding exist (e.g., what is the role of external regulating agents? Do they provide cognitive and metacognitive strategies? Do they play different roles (e.g., scaffolding, modeling, etc.)? Is their role to monitor or model students' emerging understanding, and does it facilitate knowledge acquisition, provide meaningful feedback, successfully scaffold learning, etc.? Are these scaffolding strategies what we would expect from artificial pedagogical agents? Do the levels of scaffolding remain constant during learning, fade over time, or fluctuate during learning? When do these agents intervene? How do they demonstrate their interventions (e.g., verbal, conversation, gesturing, facial moves, dialogue system)?

In sum, there are endless possibilities for the future design of SCLEs that embody metacognition and SRL.

References

Aleven, V., Roll, I., McLaren, B., & Koedinger, K. (2010). Automated, unobtrusive, action-by-action assessment of self-regulation during learning with an intelligent tutoring system. *Educational Psychologist, 45*(4), 224–233.

Azevedo, R. (2005). Computers as metacognitive tools for enhancing learning. *Educational Psychologist, 40*(4), 193–197.

Azevedo, R. (2007). Understanding the complex nature of self-regulated learning processes in learning with computer-based learning environments: An introduction. *Metacognition & Learning, 2*(2/3), 57–65.

Azevedo, R. (2008). The role of self-regulation in learning about science with hypermedia. In D. Robinson & G. Schraw (Eds.), *Recent innovations in educational technology that facilitate student learning* (pp. 127–156). Charlotte, NC: Information Age Publishing.

Azevedo, R. (2009). Theoretical, methodological, and analytical challenges in the research on metacognition and self-regulation: A commentary. *Metacognition & Learning, 4*, 87–95.

Azevedo, R., & Witherspoon, A. M. (2009). Self-regulated learning with hypermedia. In D. J. Hacker, J. Dunlosky, & A. C. Graesser (Eds.), *Handbook of metacognition in education* (pp. 319–339). Mahwah, NJ: Routledge.

Azevedo, R., Greene, J. A., & Moos, D. C. (2007). The effect of a human agent's external regulation upon college students' hypermedia learning. *Metacognition and Learning, 2* (2–3), 67–87.

Azevedo, R., Johnson, A., Chauncey, A., & Burkett, C. (2010). Self-regulated learning with MetaTutor: Advancing the science of learning with MetaCognitive tools. In M. Khine & I. Saleh (Eds.), *New science of learning: Computers, cognition, and collaboration in education* (pp. 225–247). Amsterdam: Springer.

Azevedo, R., Johnson, A. M., Chauncey, A., & Graesser, A. (2011). Use of hypermedia to assess and convey self-regulated learning. In B. Zimmerman & D. Schunk (Eds.), *Handbook of self-regualtion of learning and performance* (pp. 102–121). New York: Routledge.

Azevedo, R., Moos, D. C., Johnson, A. M., & Chauncey, A. D. (2010). Measuring cognitive and metacognitive regulatory processes during hypermedia learning: Issues and challenges. *Educational Psychologist, 45*, 210–223.

Azevedo, R., Cromley, J. G., Moos, D. C., Greene, J. A., & Winters, F. J. (2011). Adaptive content and process scaffolding: A key to facilitating students' learning with hypermedia. *Psychological Test and Assessment Modeling, 53* (1), 106-140.

Azevedo, R., Moos, D. C., Greene, J. A., Winters, F. I., & Cromley, J. G. (2008). Why is externally-facilitated regulated learning more effective than self-regulated learning with hypermedia? *Educational Technology Research and Development, 56*(1), 45–72.

Bandura, A. (2006). Guide for constructing self-efficacy scales. In F. Pajares & T. Urdan (Eds.), *Self-efficacy beliefs of adolescents* (pp. 307–337). Greenwich: Information Age Publishing.

Biswas, G., & Sulcer, B. (2010). Visual exploratory data analysis methods to characterize student progress in intelligent learning environments. In *2010 International Conference on Technology for Education* (T4E), pp. 114–121, Mumbai, India.

Biswas, G., Leelawong, K., Schwartz, D., & Vye, N. (2005). Learning by teaching: A new agent paradigm for educational software. *Applied Artificial Intelligence, 19* (3), 363–392.

Biswas, G., Roscoe, R., Jeong, H., & Sulcer, B. (2009). Promoting self-regulated learning skills in agent-based learning environments. *Proceedings of the 17th International Conference on Computers in Education*. Hong Kong: Asia-Pacific Society for Computers in Education.

Biswas, G., Jeong, H., Kinnebrew, J., Sulcer, B., & Roscoe, R. (2010). Measuring self-regulated learning skills through social interactions in a teachable agent environment. *Research and Practice in Technology-Enhanced Learning, 5*(2), 123–152.

Boekaerts, M., Pintrich, P., & Zeidner, M. (2000). *Handbook of self-regulation*. San Diego, CA: Academic Press.

Butler, D., & Winne, P. (1995). Feedback and self-regulated learning: A theoretical synthesis. *Review of Educational Research, 65*(3), 245–281.

Clarebout, G., Horz, H., & Elen, J. (2009). The use of support devices in electronic learning environments. *Computers in Human Behavior, 25*(4), 793–794.

Dunlosky, J., & Bjork, R. (Eds.). (2008). *Handbook of metamemory and memory.* New York: Taylor & Francis.

Dunlosky, J., & Lipko, A. R. (2007). Metacomprehension: A brief history and how to improve its accuracy. Current Directions in Psychological Science, 16(4), 228–232.

Efklides, A. (2011). Interactions of metacognition with motivation and affect in self-regulated learning: The MASRL model. *Educational Psychologist, 46,* 6–25.

Elliot, A., & McGregor, H. A. (2001). A 2 × 2 achievement goal framework. *Journal of Personality and Social Psychology, 80,* 501–519.

Elliot, E. S. & Dweck, C. S. (1988). Goals: An approach to motivation and achievement. *Journal of Personality and Social Psychology, 54*(1).

Graesser, A. C., & McNamara, D. S. (2010). Self-regulated learning in learning environments with pedagogical agents that interact in natural language. *Educational Psychologist, 45,* 234–244.

Greene, J. A., & Azevedo, R. (2007). A theoretical review of Winne and Hadwin's model of self-regulated learning: New perspectives and directions. *Review of Educational Research, 77,* 334–372.

Greene, J. A., & Azevedo, R. (2009). A macro-level analysis of SRL processes and their relations to the acquisition of sophisticated mental models. *Contemporary Educational Psychology, 34,* 18–29.

Greene, J. A. & Azevedo, R. (2010). The measurement of learners' self-regulated cognitive and metacognitive processes while using computer-based learning environments. *Educational Psychologist, 45*(4), 203–209.

Hacker, D., Dunlosky, J., & Graesser, A. (Eds.). (2009). *Handbook of metacognition in education.* Mahwah, NJ: Erlbaum.

Kinnebrew, J., Biswas, G., & Sulcer, B. (2010). Measuring self-regulated learning skills through social interactions in a teachable agent environment. *AAAI Fall Symposium on Cognitive and Metacognitive Educational Systems (MCES),* Arlington, VA.

Kinnebrew, J., Biswas, G., Sulcer, B., & Taylor, R. (in press). Investigating self-regulated learning in teachable agent environments. In R. Azevedo & V. Aleven (Eds.), *International Handbook of Metacognition and Learning Technologies.* Amsterdam, The Netherlands: Springer.

Leelawong, K., & Biswas, G. (2008). Designing learning by teaching agents: The Betty's Brain system. *International Journal of Artificial Intelligence in Education, 18* (3), 181–208.

Mayer, R. E. (2005). Cognitive theory of multimedia learning. In R. E. Mayer (Ed.), *The Cambridge handbook of multimedia learning* (pp. 31–48). New York: Cambridge University Press.

McQuiggan, S., Lee., S., & Lester, J. (2007). Early prediction of student frustration. In Paiva, A., Prada, R., & Picard, R. (Eds.), *Affective computing and intelligent interaction* (pp. 698–709). Berlin, Germany: Springer.

McQuiggan, S., Rowe, J., Lee, S., & Lester, J. (2008). Story-based learning: The impact of narrative on learning experiences and outcomes. In Woolf, B.,

Aïmeur, E., Nkambou, R., & Lajoie, S. (Eds.), *Intelligent tutoring systems* (pp. 530–539). Berlin, Germany: Springer.

McQuiggan, S., Goth, J., Ha, E., Rowe, J., & Lester, J. (2008a). Student note-taking in narrative-centered learning environments: Individual differences and learning effects. In Woolf, B., Aïmeur, E., Nkambou, R., & Lajoie, S. (Eds.), *Intelligent tutoring systems* (pp. 510–519). Berlin, Germany: Springer.

McQuiggan, S., Hoffman, K. L., Nietfeld, J. L., Robinson, J. L., & Lester, J. (2008b). Examining self-regulated learning in a narrative-centered learning environment: An inductive approach to modeling metacognitive monitoring. In *Proceedings of the ITS'08 Workshop on Metacognition and Self-Regulated Learning in Educational Technologies,* Montreal, Canada.

Metcalfe, J., & Dunlosky, J. (2009). *Metacognition: A textbook for cognitive, educational, life span & applied psychology*, Thousand Oaks, CA: Sage.

Moos, D. C. & Azevedo, R. (2008). Exploring the fluctuation of motivation and use of self regulatory processes during learning with hypermedia. *Instructional Science, 36* (3), 203–231.

Mott, B. & Lester, J. (2006). Narrative-centered tutorial planning for inquiry-based learning environments. *Proceedings of the Intelligent Tutoring Systems Conference* (pp. 675–684). In M. Ikeda, K. Ashley & T. W. Chan (Eds.), Berlin, Germany: Springer.

Nietfeld, J., Hoffman, K., McQuiggan, S., and Lester, J. (2008). Self-regulated learning in a narrative-centered learning environment. *Proceedings of the World Conference on Educational Multimedia, Hypermedia, and Telecommunications.* Vienna, Austria.

Paris, S. G., & Paris, A. H. (2001). Classroom applications of research on self-regulated learning. *Educational Psychologist, 36*(2), 89–101.

Pintrich, P. R. (2000). The role of goal orientation in self-regulated learning. In M. Boekaerts, P. Pintrich & M. Zeidner (Eds.), *Handbook of self-regulation* (pp. 451– 502). San Diego, CA: Academic Press.

Pintrich, P. R. (2002). The role of metacognitive knowledge in learning, teaching, and assessing. *Theory in Practice, 41*(4), 219–225.

Pintrich, P. R. (2004). A conceptual framework for assessing motivation and self-regulated learning in college students, *Educational Psychology Review, 16*(4), 385–407.

Pintrich, P. R., Wolters, C., & Baxter, G. (2000). Assessing metacognition and self-regulated learning. In G. Schraw & J. Impara (Eds.), *Issues in the measurement of metacognition* (pp. 43–97).

Pressley, M., & Hilden, K. (2006). Cognitive strategies. In D. Kuhn & R. S. Siegler (Eds.), *Handbook of child psychology: Volume 2: Cognition, perception, and language* (6th edn., pp. 511–556). Hoboken, NJ: Wiley.

Robinson, J., McQuiggan, S. & Lester, J. (2010). Developing empirically based student personality profiles for affective feedback models. In V. Aleven, J. Kay, & J. Mostow (Eds.), *Intelligent tutoring systems* (pp. 285–295). Berlin, Germany: Springer.

Rowe, J., Shores, L., Mott, B., & Lester, J. (2010). Integrating learning and engagement in narrative-centered learning environments. *Intelligent Tutoring Systems, Lecture Notes in Computer Science, 6095,* 166–177.

Schraw, G., & Lehman, S. (2001). Situational interest. A review of the literature and directions for future research. *Educational Psychology Review, 13*(1), 23–52.

Schunk, D. (2001). Social cognitive theory of self-regulated learning. In B. Zimmerman & D. Schunk (Eds.), *Self-regulated learning and academic achievement: Theoretical perspectives* (pp. 125–152). Mahwah, NJ: Erlbaum.

Schunk, D. (2005). Self-regulated learning: The educational legacy of Paul R. Pintrich. *Educational Psychologist, 40*, 85–94.

Schunk, D., & Zimmerman, B. (Eds.). (1998). *Self-regulated learning: From teaching to self-reflective practice.* New York: Guilford.

Shimoda, T., White, B., & Frederiksen, J. (2002). Student goal orientation in learning inquiry skills with modifiable software advisors. *Science Education, 86*, 244–263.

Veenman, M. (2007). The assessment and instruction of self-regulation in computer-based environments: A discussion. *Metacognition and Learning, 2*, 177–183.

White, B. Y. (1993). Causal models, conceptual change and science education. *Cognition and Instruction, 10*, 1–100.

White, B. Y., & Frederiksen, J. R. (1998). Inquiry, Modeling, and metacognition: Making science accessible to all students. *Cognition and Instruction, 16*, 3–118.

White, B. Y., & Frederiksen, J. R. (2005). A theoretical framework and approach for fostering metacognitive development. *Educational Psychologist, 40*, 211–233.

White, B. Y., Frederiksen, J. R., & Collins, J. (2009). The interplay of scientific inquiry and metacognition. In D. J. Hacker, J. Dunlosky, and A. C. Graesser (Eds.), *Handbook of metacognition* (pp. 175–205). New York: Routledge.

White, B., Frederiksen, J., Frederiksen, T., Eslinger, E., Loper, S., & Collins, A. (2002). Inquiry Island: Affordances of a multi-agent environment for scientific inquiry and reflective learning. In P. Bell, R. Stevens, & T. Satwicz (Eds.), *Proceedings of the Fifth International Conference of the Learning Sciences* (ICLS). Mahwah, NJ: Erlbaum.

White, B. Y., Shimoda, T. A., & Frederiksen, J. R. (1999). Enabling students to construct theories of collaborative inquiry and reflective learning: Computer support for metacognitive development. *International Journal of Artificial Intelligence in Education, 10*, 151–182.

Winne, P. H. (2001). Self-regulated learning viewed from models of information processing. In B. Zimmerman & D. Schunk (Eds.), *Self-regulated learning and academic achievement: Theoretical perspectives* (pp. 153–189). Mahwah, NJ: Erlbaum.

Winne, P., & Hadwin, A. (1998). Studying as self-regulated learning. In D. Hacker, J. Dunlosky, & A. Graesser (Eds.), *Metacognition in educational theory and practice* (pp. 227–304). Mahwah, NJ: Erlbaum.

Winne, P., & Hadwin, A. (2008). The weave of motivation and self-regulated learning. In D. Schunk & B. Zimmerman (Eds.), *Motivation and self-regulated learning: Theory, research, and applications* (pp. 297–314). Mahwah, NJ: Erlbaum.

Winne, P. H., & Nesbit, J. C. (2009). Supporting self-regulated learning with cognitive tools. In D. J. Hacker, J. Dunlosky, & A. C. Graesser (Eds.), *Handbook of metacognition in education.* Mahwah, NJ: Erlbaum.

Zimmerman, B. (1986). Becoming a self-regulated learner: Which are the key sub-processes? *Contemporary Educational Psychology, 11*, 307–313.

Zimmerman, B. (2000). Attaining self-regulation: A social cognitive perspective. In M. Boekaert, P. R. Pintrich, and M. Zeidner (Eds.), *Handbook of self-regulated learning* (pp. 13–39). San Diego, CA: Academic Press.

Zimmerman, B. (2001). Theories of self-regulated learning and academic achievement: An overview and analysis. In B. Zimmerman & D. Schunk (Eds.), *Self-regulated learning and academic achievement: Theoretical perspectives* (pp. 1–37). Mahwah, NJ: Erlbaum.

Zimmerman, B. (2008). Investigating self-regulation and motivation: Historical background, methodological developments, and future prospects. *American Educational Research Journal, 45*(1), 166–183.

Zimmerman, B. J., & Schunk, D. H. (Eds.). (2001). *Self-regulated learning and academic achievement: theoretical perspectives.* New York: Erlbaum.

Zimmerman, B. J., & Schunk, D. H. (Eds.). (2011). *Handbook of self-regualtion of learning and performance.* New York: Routledge.

Zumbach, J., & Bannert, M. (2006). Analyzing (self-)monitoring in computer assisted learning. *Journal of Educational Computing Research, 35*(4), 315–317.

8 Embodied Cognition and Learning Environment Design

John B. Black, Ayelet Segal,
Jonathan Vitale and Cameron L. Fadjo

Much learning that takes place through formal learning environments is of a fragile, shallow variety where students forget what they have learned soon after the end of the learning events (and the testing at the end) and does not get applied when relevant situations arise that are removed from the learning setting in time, space and conceptual context. The learning never seems to become a part of the way the student thinks about and interacts with the everyday world. Recent basic cognitive research in embodied or perceptually-grounded cognition provides a new perspective on what it means for learning to become more a part of the way students understand and interact with the world; further it provides guidance for the design of learning environments that integrate the learning with experiences that make it more meaningful and usable (Dewey, 1938).

Embodied Cognition

There are a variety of perspectives on embodied cognition (e.g., Damasio, 1994; Semin & Smith, 2008; Varela, Thompson, & Rosch, 1991) with more linguistic approaches focusing on the grounding of semantics in bodily metaphors (e.g., Gibbs, 2005; Johnson, 1987; Lakoff & Johnson, 1999) and more cognitive psychological ones focusing on evidence for modal (sensory) representations and mental simulations (e.g., Barsalou, 1999; Glenberg, 1997; Pecher & Zwaan, 2005). The embodied or perceptually-grounded cognition perspective we will focus on here says that a full understanding of something involves being able to create a mental perceptual simulation of it when retrieving the information or reasoning about it (Barsalou, 2008, 2010; Black, 2010). Both behavioral and neuroimaging results have shown that many psychological phenomena that were thought to be purely symbolic show perceptual effects. For example, property verification (e.g., retrieving the fact that a horse has a mane) was thought to involve a search from a concept node (horse) to a property node (mane) in a symbolic propositional network and thus the time to answer and errors was determined by how many network links needed to be searched and how many other distracting links were present. However, embodied cognition research shows that perceptual variables like size (e.g., bigger properties are retrieved faster) affect verification times and errors (Solomon & Barsalou, 2004). Also, neuroimaging results (e.g., fMRI) show that perceptual areas of the brain (involving shape, color, size, sound and touch) also become active during this task, not just the symbolic areas (e.g., Martin, 2007). Thus, if one is familiar with horses and manes then doing even this simple property verification involves a perceptual simulation.

Even text comprehension shows spatial (perceptual) effects. For example a switch in point of view in a narrative creates longer reading times and more memory errors because the reader has to switch the spatial perspective from which they are viewing the narrative scene in their imagination. For example:

John was working in the front yard then he went inside.

This is read faster than with a one-word change that switches the point of view:

John was working in the front yard then he came inside.

(Black, Turner, & Bower, 1979).

Thus, when reading even this brief sentence the reader is forming a rough spatial layout of the scene being described and imaging an actor moving around it – i.e., this is a simple perceptual simulation.

Glenberg, Gutierrez, Levin, Japuntich, and Kaschak (2004) show how to teach reading comprehension using a grounded cognition approach. These studies found that having 2nd grade students act out stories about farms using toy farmers, workers, animals and objects increased their understanding and memory of the story they read. Further, if they also imagined these actions for another related story after acting it out with the toys, they seemed to acquire the skill of forming the imaginary world of the story (Black, 2007) when reading other stories, and this increased their understanding and memory of these stories. Thus, this grounded cognition approach increased the students' reading comprehension. These studies also seem to indicate that there are three steps involved in a grounded cognition approach to learning something:

1   Have an embodied experience
2   Learn to imagine that embodied experience
3   Imagine the experience when learning from symbolic materials.

An Embodied Learning Environment Example in Physics

An example of using an embodied cognition approach to designing a learning environment and the learning advantages of doing so is provided by the graphic computer simulations with movement and animation that Han and Black (2011) used in perceptually enhancing the learning experience. In learning a mental model for a system, students need to learn and understand the component functional relations that describe how a system entity changes as a function of changes in another system entity. Chan and Black (2006) found that graphic computer simulations involving movement and animation were a good way to learn these functional relations between system entities. Han and Black (2011) have enhanced the movement part of these interactive graphic simulations by adding force feedback to the movement using simulations like that shown in Figure 8.1. Here the student moves the gears shown in the middle by moving the joystick shown in the lower left, and the bar graphics show the input and output force levels for the two gears. Allowing the student to directly manipulate the gears enhances the students' learning, and enriching the movement experience by adding force feedback increases the students' performance even more. Thus the richer the perceptual experience, and therefore the mental perceptual simulation acquired, the better the student learning and understanding.

The following sections provide more detailed examples of using embodied cognition to design learning environments that improve student learning and understanding. The first uses the gestural-touch interface provided by the iPad to provide the embodiment needed to improve young students' number sense and addition performance. The second looks at students learning geometry embodied in an agent spatially navigating an obstacle course in a game. The third looks at student learning by embodying

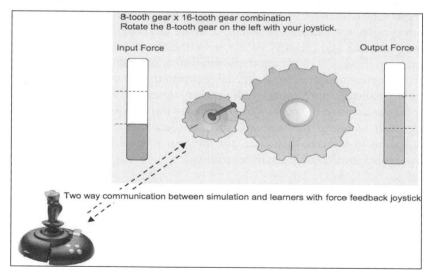

Figure 8.1 Gear graphic simulation with movement (joystick and gears) and animation with force feedback (joystick)

their understanding of agent-based movements, decisions, and behaviors during the construction of a video game and robot programming.

Gestural Interfaces and Learning Environments

Gestural interfaces are also known as natural user interfaces and include two types: touch interfaces and free-form interfaces. Touch use interfaces (TUIs) require the user to touch the device directly and could be based on a point of single touch (i.e., SMART Board) or multi-touch (i.e., SMARTtable/iPhone/iPad/Surface). Free-form gestural interfaces do not require the user to touch or handle the device directly (e.g., Microsoft Kinect). The mechanics of touch screens and gestural controllers have at least three general parts: a sensor, a comparator, and an actuator. Saffer (2009) defines gesture for a gestural interface as any physical movement that a digital system can sense and respond to without the aid of a traditional pointing device, such as a mouse or stylus. A wave, a head nod, a touch, a toe tap, or even a raised eyebrow can be a gesture. These technologies suggest new opportunities to include touch and physical movement, which can benefit learning, in contrast to the less direct, somewhat passive mode of interaction suggested by a mouse and keyboard. Embodied interaction involving digital devices is based on the theory and body of research of grounded cognition and embodiment. The following sub-sections review evidence from studies on embodiment, physical manipulation, embodied interaction, and spontaneous gestures that support the theory of how gestural interfaces can promote thinking and learning. These are followed by a study conducted by Segal, Black, and Tversky (2010) about the topic.

Action Compatibility Effect

Bodily rooted knowledge involves processes of perception that fundamentally affect conceptual thinking (Barsalou, 2008). Barsalou and colleagues (2003), who have conducted extensive research in the field of grounded cognition and embodiment, found that there is a compatibility effect between one's physical state and one's mental state. This means that an interface that is designed to take advantage of embodied metaphors results in more effective performance. For example, they found that participants who were asked to indicate liking something by pulling a lever towards them showed a faster response time than those who were asked to indicate liking by pushing the lever away. These findings have implications for the design of learning environments.

Physical Manipulation and Learning

Some educational approaches, such as the Montessori (1949/1972) educational philosophy, suggest that physical movement and touch enhance learning. When children learn with their hands, they build brain connections and knowledge through this movement. Schwartz and Martin (2006) found that when children use compatible actions to map their ideas in a learning task, they are better able to transfer learning to new domains. For example, children who had only a beginner's knowledge of division were given a bag containing candy and asked to share it with four friends. One group of children were asked to organize piles of candy into various groups (i.e., four equal groups). The other group solved the problem using a graphical representation (i.e., drawing pictures of the candy to be shared). Children who learned through complementary actions were in a better position to solve problems of division in arithmetic. Physical manipulation with real objects has also been proven effective with children as young as preschool- and kindergarten-age (Siegler & Ramani, 2009). In this study, using linear number board games, children who played a simple numerical board game for four 15-minute sessions improved their numerical estimation proficiency and knowledge of numerical magnitude.

Embodied Interaction and Learning

Embodied interaction involves more of our senses and in particular includes touch and physical movement, which are believed to help in the retention of the knowledge that is being acquired. In a study about including the haptic channel in a learning process with kinematics displays, Chan and Black (2006) found that the immediate sensorimotor feedback received through the hands can be transferred to working memory for further processing. This allowed better learning for the students who were in the direct manipulation animation condition, essentially enabling the learners to actively engage and participate in the meaning-making journey. In a study that incorporates the haptic channel as force feedback to learn how gears operate, Han and Black (2011) found that using three sensory modalities, and incorporating tactile feedback, helped participants efficiently learn how simple machines work. Furthermore, the haptic simulation group outperformed the other group not only in the immediate post-test, but also in the near transfer test, meaning that effectiveness of these embodied experiences with haptic simulation was maintained during reading instructional text.

Do Spontaneous Gestures Reflect Thought?

According to theories of embodied cognition (Barsalou, 1999; Glenberg, 1997), concepts are primarily sensorimotor; thus, when speakers activate concepts in order to express meaning, they are presumably activating perceptual and motor information, just as comprehenders do when they activate meaning from language input. In theory, then, language producers must start with sensorimotor representations of meaning, just as language comprehenders end there. Hostetter and Alibali (2008) claim that these sensorimotor representations that underlie speaking are the basis for speech-accompanying gestures.

There is a growing body of research regarding spontaneous gestures and their effect on communication, working memory, information processing, learning, mental modeling, and reflection of thought. Goldin-Meadow (2009) found that gesture plays a role in changing the child's knowledge; indirectly through its effects on the child's communicative environment, and directly through its effects on the child's cognitive state. Because gestures reflect thought and are an early marker of change, it may be possible to use them diagnostically, which may prove useful in learning and development. In a study on how gestures could promote math learning, it was found that requiring children to produce a particular set of gestures while learning the new concept of grouping strategy helped them better retain the knowledge they had gained during the math lesson, and helped them to solve more problems.

Schwartz and Black (1996) argued that spontaneous hand gestures are "physically instantiated mental models." In a study about solving interlocking gear problems, they found that participants gestured the movement of the gears with their hands to help them imagine the correct direction of the gears, gradually learning to abstract the symbolic rule for that. In a study about mental representations and gestures, Alibali *et al.* (1999) found that spontaneous gestures reveal important information about people's mental representations of math-based problems. They based their hypothesis on a former body of research that showed that gestures provide a window into knowledge that is not readily expressed in speech. For example, it may be difficult to describe an irregular shape in speech but easy to depict the shape with a gesture. The authors hypothesized that such mental models might naturally lead to the production of spontaneous gestures, which iconically represent perceptual properties of the models.

Gestural Interfaces and Spontaneous Gestures

If spontaneous gestures reflect thought, could it be that choosing well-designed gestures (for gestural interface) could affect the spatial mental models of subjects? Hostetter and Alibali's (2008) theory of Gestures as Simulated Action (GSA) suggests that gestures emerge from perceptual and motor simulations that underlie embodied language and mental imagery. They provide evidence that gestures stem from spatial representations and mental images, and propose the gestures-as-simulated-action framework to explain how gestures might arise from an embodied cognitive system. If gestures are simulated actions that result from spatial representation and mental imagery, it is very likely that asking users to perform one gesture versus another could affect users' mental operations to solve the problem in different ways.

Spontaneous gestures are being adopted by gestural interface designers in order to incorporate more natural and intuitive interactions. There are four types of spontaneous gestures: deictic, iconic (show relations), metaphoric (more abstract), and beat (discourse). Deictic gesture, such as pointing, is typically used for gestural interfaces. Iconic and metaphoric types of gesture are also very common to adopt for gestural interfaces, and usually indicate a more complex interaction. Using a familiar gesture (from everyday language) to interact with interfaces could ease the cognitive load of the user. It creates a more transparent interface and natural interaction with the computer.

Congruent Gestures Promote Performance

Segal, Black, and Tversky (2010) explored the compatibility of gestures designed for gestural interfaces with the digital representation of the mathematical concepts of counting, addition, and number-line estimation. By simulating the mental operations needed to solve the problem with the correct gestures, learners constructed better spatial mental models of these mathematical procedures. When mapping gestures to the learned concept, one enhances the simulation for the mental operations, which needs to be constructed to solve a problem. The embodied metaphor, the gesture, represents the operation that needs to be mapped to the mental operations.

Can action support cognition? From a grounded cognition perspective, the use of gestural interfaces (such as multi-touch like the iPad) versus traditional interfaces (such as monitor–mouse) should yield better learning with computers. This question is addressed by observing children's performance in arithmetic and numerical estimation. Arithmetic is a discrete task, and should be supported by discrete rather than continuous actions. Estimation is a continuous task, and should be supported by continuous rather than discrete actions. Children either used a gestural interface or a traditional interface. The actions either mapped congruently to the cognition or not. If action supports cognition, performance should be better with a gestural interface when the actions map conceptually to the desired cognition, Gestural Conceptual Mapping.

Direct Manipulation: Gestural Conceptual Mapping

Marshall (2007) states that there is a gap in the existing research on tangible interfaces and learning. He claims that there is no research on how users abstract the underlying rules or laws of a domain, and how different levels of representation become integrated within the design. The gap, theoretically speaking, is about how the structure of the learning domain can be represented by the interface. The following case study explores the gap and defines it as Gestural Conceptual Mapping. The term

Gestural Conceptual Mapping is used to convey the mapping between the representations of the physical embodied metaphor (the gesture), and the digital representation of the learned domain. This term is one of three properties of direct manipulation. It is a new term that Segal, Black, and Tversky (2010) define, explore, and focus on, in the design and use of gestures within interfaces to promote thinking and support better learning.

Segal, Black, and Tversky (2010) explored the compatibility of the learned concept "visualization" (digital representation) with the physical representation of the gesture, and with the internal representation of the learned concept. Using a specific gesture to illustrate the learned concept helps the student construct a better mental model of the learned concept. For example, tapping with a finger on a virtual block or clicking with a mouse on a virtual block to count and add up are gestures that are congruent with the discrete representation of counting. In contrast, sliding the finger vertically over a series of blocks or dragging a mouse on a series of blocks to count them are continuous movements that are not congruent with the discrete procedure of counting. In other words, both the digital representation of the content and the gestures need to be compatible with the learned concept. Therefore, there must be compatibility between the external representation of the content and the internal representation that the user constructs. This compatibility supports the user's mental imaging and allows for the construction of better mental models. In order to achieve this compatibility, designers should find the compatible embodied metaphor that would best illustrate the learned concept. The embodied metaphor is the type of gesture chosen by the designer to manipulate the educational content on the screen.

Direct Manipulation: Haptic Channel, Sensorimotor Input

Direct manipulation has been defined by Shneiderman (1983) as the ability to manipulate digital objects on a screen without the use of command-line commands (i.e., dragging a file to a trash can instead of typing "del"). Direct manipulation in the Human Computer Interaction field has been consistently changing over the past few years. This is a result of a boom in the development of new technologies and innovative interfaces, which have taken direct manipulation to another level. This is especially true for touch screen and free-form gestural interfaces that do not require external control devices (i.e., mouse) to manipulate objects on the screen. Instead, they utilize the user's own body to manipulate objects on a screen, changing the level of direct manipulation.

Research has shown that physical manipulation could enhance the processing of abstract content and the comprehension of learned concepts. Based on this body of research, Segal, Black, and Tversky (2010) showed that gestural interfaces that incorporate the haptic aspect of touching the interface and manipulating the objects by using sensorimotor input could benefit users' comprehension of learned concepts. They hypothesized that by touching the objects on a screen directly with a finger/fingers, participants help themselves process abstract content and build internal representations that are more accurate. Touching the objects on a screen directly, with our body, rather than having a control device such as a mouse or even a stylus, could enhance the haptic channel experience and make the learning experience more direct and integrated with the content. It is a more concrete experience that could support young children's internal representations of learned concepts, as indicated in the study described next.

Congruent Gestural Interface Experiment

Participants

The researcher recruited 107 subjects (60 boys and 47 girls) from 1st and 2nd grade. Children were recruited from two after-school programs in public schools in a low Social Economic Status (SES) area of New York City.

Materials

Two learning tasks with virtual manipulatives were given to participants to examine the effect of high direct manipulation provided by gestural interfaces versus traditional interfaces. Two educational applications were developed to allow interaction and learning with two math concepts. The learned concepts explored were 1) discrete-change problems that focus on change over a series of steps, such as counting blocks, versus 2) continuous-change problems that focus on change over a single, non-partitioned event, such as number-line estimation. For the discrete-change problem, the tasks were counting and addition; for the continuous-change problem, the task was number estimation on a number line. The gestural interface was a 10-inch multi-touch iPad device by Apple, and the traditional interface was a Macintosh Macbook Pro laptop by Apple, which requires the use of a mouse. Software developed by the experimenter recorded the child's answers. In order to accurately record all children's strategies, the experimenter marked the strategies chosen by the child on a check box strategies list.

Variables and Design

This was a 2 by 2 between subjects design. The children were randomly assigned to one of four conditions. These conditions were: 1) the haptic, gestural conceptual mapping condition; 2) the haptic non-gestural conceptual mapping condition; 3) the non-haptic gestural conceptual mapping condition; and 4) the non-haptic, non-gestural conceptual mapping condition. The direct manipulation was examined in both tasks and included two direct manipulation properties:

1   Gestural Conceptual Mapping: mapping the gesture to the learned concept. This refers to the mapping between the information carried in the physical and digital aspects of the system, using congruent gestures versus non-congruent gestures to support cognition.
2   Haptic channel: adding the haptic channel to perform these tasks, such as physical manipulation of the interface. This integrates the level of sensorimotor input (mouse versus touch).

Counting and Addition Task: Discrete Procedure

Children were required to solve 10 addition problems by working on a virtual manipulatives interface that showed virtual blocks arranged in side-by-side piles of two 10-block towers. The answers to the problems ranged from 1 to 20, e.g., $6 + 7 = ?$ $2 + 9 = ?$ (see Figure 8.2). The computer narrated the questions so children did not need to recognize the symbols.

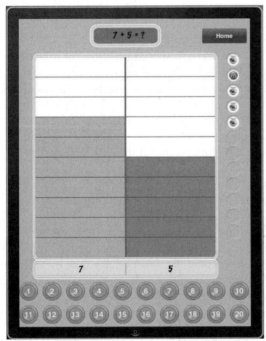

Figure 8.2 Counting and addition task interface

Haptic Channel Variable: Counting and Addition Task

The first variable compared use of the haptic channel (e.g., tapping with a finger on a multi-touch screen [iPad] to fill in digital blocks in a bar chart, performing addition) with use of the non-haptic channel (e.g., filling in the digital blocks by clicking them with a mouse via a traditional interface) (see Figure 8.2).

Gestural Conceptual Mapping Variable: Counting and Addition Task

The second variable compared the use of Gestural Conceptual Mapping to the use of Non-Gestural Conceptual Mapping, both on the multi-touch screen (iPad). This explored the representation of the gesture to support the mental model of discrete counting. In one condition, children tapped with their finger on each digital block in a bar chart to highlight the block's color, then performed addition of both columns. This is a gesture that is conceptually mapped to the discrete concept of counting. In the other condition, children tapped on the numbers under each column of blocks (not on each block) and this automatically highlighted the colors of the blocks, which is not conceptually mapped to the discrete concept of counting (see Figure 8.2).

Number-Line Estimation Task: Continuous Procedure

The second task of the number-line estimation was chosen to benefit the procedure of a continuous concept, such as magnitude of number line. Number-line estimation requires translating a number into a spatial position on a number line, or translating a spatial position on a number line into a number. As noted in Siegler and Booth's (2005) review of the estimation literature, numerical estimation is a process of translating between alternative quantitative representations, at least one of which is inexact and at least one of which is numerical. Number-line estimates correlate substantially with other measures of numerical magnitude knowledge, such as magnitude comparison and numerical categorization (Laski & Siegler, 2007).

In the present study, children were required to estimate 23 numbers (1–100) on a virtual number line (see Figure 8.3). The computer narrated the questions so children did not need to recognize the symbols. Prior to the task, the experimenter asked the child to show her if there was zero on the number line, and if there was the number 100, to make sure the child recognized the numbers. The experimenter explained the task by saying, "A number line is a line with numbers across it. The numbers on the line go from the smallest number to the largest number, and the numbers go in order, so each number has its very own spot on the number line." After each answer, the child received an animated feedback with the numbers appearing on the number line from left to right, up to the correct value.

Haptic Channel Variable: Number-Line Estimation Task

The first variable compared use of the haptic channel to use of the non-haptic channel in a continuous number-line task. In the haptic channel condition, using a multi-touch screen (iPad), the child slid his or her finger horizontally on the number line to estimate numbers; in the non-haptic channel condition, using a traditional (mouse) interface, the child dragged the mouse horizontally on the number line to estimate numbers.

Gestural Conceptual Mapping Variable: Number-Line Estimation Task

The second variable compared use of gestural conceptual mapping with use of non-gestural conceptual mapping, both on the multi-touch screen (iPad). The number-line estimation task explored the compatibility of the gesture with the mental model of a continuous concept. In one condition, the child tapped on the screen to estimate numbers on the number line (discrete gesture); in the other, the child slid his or her finger horizontally (continuous gesture) to reach the number (see Figure 8.3). The sliding gesture, in that case, is mapped conceptually to the concept of continuous magnitude of a number line. It simulates the mental operation of increasing something (i.e., a number-line bar) continuously.

Children in the Haptic, Gestural Conceptual Mapping condition group had the best performance across both tasks. Thus the children who moved their finger across the iPad screen to indicate numerical magnitudes and tapped on stacked blocks to indicate addition performed the best. They had the fewest errors on both numerical estimation and addition problems. Children who were in the Haptic Channel (iPad touch) condition used an

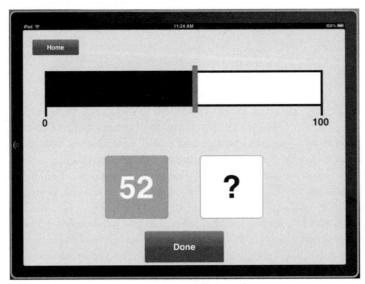

Figure 8.3 Number-line estimation task interface

advanced strategy significantly more times to solve the addition task. This means that the touch screen provided a better virtual environment for advanced strategies. This advanced strategy is the "count on" strategy. Children in the Haptic Channel (touch) condition outperformed the children in the non-Haptic Channel (mouse click) group in the use of this strategy. The children in the Haptic Channel condition, both in the TC (Touch, Conceptual condition) and TNC (Touch, non-Conceptual condition) used the advanced strategy "count on" significantly more times than the children in the non-Haptic Channel (mouse) condition.

These findings suggest evidence for the importance of designing gestures congruent with the learned concept. This means that actions affect performance and that congruent gestures are important for cognition and learning, especially when combined with the haptic channel (touch condition), but not only then. Congruent gestures are also effective in the non-haptic condition (mouse condition) facilitating better performance. The best performance was found when the touch screen and the congruent gestures were combined. The findings also suggest that the haptic channel allows better use of strategies (i.e., children constructed better mental models), providing evidence that touch-based interfaces could benefit thinking and learning.

Embodied Cognition, Gaming and Robotics

Learning Geometry with an Agent Spatial Navigation Game

The number-line estimation example described in the preceding section demonstrates how embodied interaction affects conceptual representation for basic mathematical principles. The perceptual-motor basis of early cognitive development is a prominent feature in Piaget's theory (e.g., Piaget, 1954). But, the embodied perspective further asserts that "abstract" thought, associated with higher levels of development, also shares a perceptual-motor basis. In the case of geometry, where researchers have frequently posited series of stages or levels to account for increasing abstraction (e.g., Piaget & Inhelder, 1967; Piaget, Inhelder, & Szeminska, 1960; van Hiele, 1986), the embodied perspective entails that performance across tasks, both simple and complex, is based on physical interaction with the environment and the corresponding mental representations formed through those interactions. How then does embodied cognition explain behaviors that appear to reflect abstract, symbolic thought?

First, we must understand the source of geometric knowledge. Clearly those processes engaged in number-line estimation are relevant in geometry. Furthermore, Spelke, Lee, and Izard (2010) claim that the innate human navigational and object perception abilities represent core systems, upon which Euclidean geometry may emerge. Object perception is particularly relevant as young children may be introduced to geometric figures just as they might be introduced to any other object (e.g., physical objects and their corresponding names). This can be seen in young children who base their source of reasoning in identification and sorting tasks on a shape's "holistic" appearance (Clements, Swaminathan, Hannibal, & Sarama, 1999). The challenge with this approach is that children are often exposed to a limited number of exemplar figures, generating a sparse mapping between shape names and associated figures. For example, Clements *et al.* (1999) found an inverse U-pattern in triangle identification such that only very young children and older children correctly identified non-prototypical, scalene triangles as triangles. In this case, repeated exposure to prototypical, equilateral triangles produced a misconception about the meaning of the word "triangle".

A clear remedy for this type of misconception is to provide children with a wider range of curricular materials. Yet, geometric thinking requires more than just a large visual vocabulary of shapes. A child's success distinguishing a trapezoid from a parallelogram, for example, does not entail that he or she understands the defining features of the shapes or how they relate to each other. Rather, children – and adults – are likely to attend to perceptually salient, but formally irrelevant features of shapes.

For example, in a classic demonstration by Mach (1886/1959), adults may be prompted to perceive a shape as either a square or diamond, depending on its orientation. Similarly, in a study analyzing the perceptual similarity of four-sided figures participants' judgments appeared to be based on factors of "dispersion" (regularity), "elongation", and "jaggedness" (Behrman & Brown, 1968). Likewise, Shepard and Chipman (1970) found similar dimensions in participants' categorizations of US state shapes. While these features are clearly relevant to the perception of commonplace objects (e.g., jagged objects can cut), they are only partially related to formal geometric properties of objects (e.g., acute angles). By applying terms like "slanty", "pointy", and "skinny", young children's verbal reasoning about shapes often reflects these informal characteristics (Clements *et al.*, 1999).

How, then, may children's conception of shapes be guided towards more formal elements of geometry? Direct verbal instruction of shape definitions is a common, if unsatisfactory, method (Clements & Battista, 1992). A child may remember, for example, that a parallelogram has parallel sides. But, would he or she be able to recognize parallel lines in another figure, like a square oriented as a "diamond"? Rather, the child must develop a spatial understanding of geometric properties (such as parallel lines) that is independent of any specific figure. From this perspective, a mature mental representation integrates, or blends, both a general sense of what a shape looks like and independent spatial representations for its properties (Lakoff & Nuñez, 2000). Developing this kind of complex representation requires both tools to ground individual mathematical concepts in spatially-meaningful representations and an environment to facilitate their integration.

To implement this framework we developed a digital learning environment, in the form of a game, in which children construct polygons to serve as a path for an agent navigating an obstacle course. The obstacle course includes both "dangers", i.e., grid squares through which the path may not pass, and "goals", i.e., squares through which the path must pass. The layout of the obstacle course promotes the construction of a specific geometric shape, like a square. This may be achieved by placing danger objects that either circumscribe or inscribe the intended path, or (more directly) by placing goal objects along the intended path.

The child proceeds by first viewing the obstacle course, attempting to imagine a potential path, and then constructing the path from memory on an empty grid. The child constructs the polygonal path by iteratively plotting sides and angles through direct manipulation with the mouse. Upon closing the figure, the child may then drag-and-drop vertex points to achieve greater precision (see Figure 8.4).

By providing a variety of obstacle courses, the child may be exposed to a wide range of geometric shapes that he or she has constructed. Yet, as described above, exposure is insufficient to promote higher-level thinking. Rather children must understand the properties which determine polygon class – e.g., congruency, parallelism, and right angle. To provide a spatial-grounding for these concepts we depicted each with a "hand metaphor", inspired by previous work demonstrating that children may spontaneously use their hands to model geometric properties, like right angles (Clements & Burns, 2000).

During a "property validation" phase (see Figure 8.5) the child is instructed to verify that a given number of sides or angles meet a specific property criterion, while a pair of virtual hands modeled the process. For parallelism two hands move in parallel at the same slope as a chosen side and are matched for slope against the second chosen side. For congruency two hands mark the length of one chosen side and are matched against the length of the second chosen side. For right angles two perpendicular hands are matched against the internal angle at the chosen vertex. If the polygon does not meet the property criteria, the child returns to the adjustment phase. If the polygon successfully meets the property criteria, the child proceeds to testing on the obstacle course.

We tested this design with an afterschool class of 20 fourth grade students from a low income population. Ten children were randomly assigned to the experimental condition in which they performed a series of shape construction tasks with the software described above. For comparison, the other ten children were assigned to a control group, in which the property validation phase was removed, but all other aspects of the task remained the same. Therefore, these children were not exposed to the "hand metaphors" and received no feedback about the validity

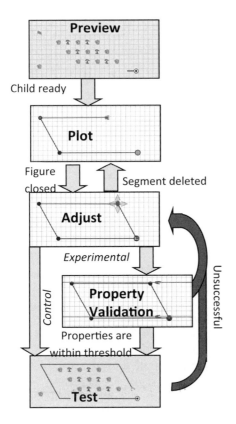

Figure 8.4 Polygon construction game flow, with cropped screenshots from a parallelogram task. Light gray arrows demonstrate progress in the intended direction. Dark gray arrows demonstrate mistake-based reversals

of their figures based on class-defining properties. In both conditions all children proceeded through a series of 22 construction tasks, in three units focusing on parallel lines (trapezoids and parallelograms), congruent adjacent sides (kites and rhombi), and right angles (rectangles and squares).

Following each unit the child was assessed with a shape identification task, targeting trapezoids, parallelograms, rhombi, isosceles trapezoids and triangles (mixed), rectangles, and right trapezoids and triangles (mixed). For each class, a single prototypical shape was constructed (e.g., a 2 × 1 rectangle oriented with its longer side parallel to the ground). This prototype was then altered on dimensions that changed its shape identity (e.g., a nearly rectangular parallelogram), and dimensions that did not change its shape identity (e.g., elongating or rotating the rectangle). In

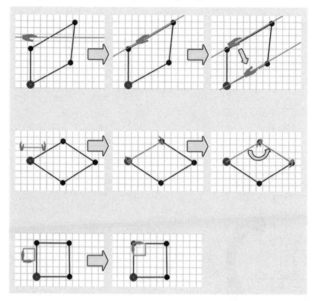

Figure 8.5 Visual depictions in property validation phase. Displays validation of parallel sides, congruent sides, and right angles (from top to bottom)

each trial the child was shown four shapes, and asked to identify the two valid shapes.

The results show that the median number of trials in which the child selected both correct shapes was greater for children in the experimental than in the control condition, for each shape type. On the other hand, the children in the control group were more likely to choose only one correct shape. Therefore, children in the control group were drawn towards the shapes that were visually similar to prototypes, yet class invalid (e.g., the nearly rectangular parallelogram), while children in the experimental group were more likely to overlook these irrelevant perceptual features in favor of class-defining properties (e.g., the two shapes with right angles).

From an outside perspective the difference in the two conditions might imply greater abstract reasoning by those in the experimental condition, and more reliance on perception by those in the control condition. This difference could be interpreted as evidence for a general concrete-to-abstract shift in development, typical of stage-based theories. However, as details of the intervention reveal, better performance in the experimental condition was promoted through embodied interaction. Rather than abandoning concrete representations the children reorganized their representations to integrate (or blend) more normatively meaningful, yet perceptually accessible components. We suggest that the development of higher-level mathematical skills, in general, reflects this reorganization of embodied representations. While some proportion of mathematical activity may simply be rote symbol manipulation, to understand how, when, and why to apply these procedures, mathematical concepts must be grounded in a deeper understanding.

Learning Through Embodying in Video Game and Robot Programming

Recent research we have done seems to indicate that learning of abstract computational concepts can be improved when embodied instruction is grounded in familiar actions and scenarios (Fadjo & Black, 2011). In this research, we were interested in whether middle school subjects who learned abstract computational constructs through physical and imagined grounded embodiment would implement more mathematical and computational constructs in the individual video-game artifacts than those who learned the same constructs without the aid of physical embodiment. From a cognitive perspective, we were primarily interested in whether providing the formal instruction of abstract concepts through action and perception, both high-level cognitive constructs, would have a positive effect on the structures used to define the artifacts. To explore a grounded approach to the instruction of computational and mathematical thinking, we devised a curriculum where subjects received explicit instruction on Code Literacy (Fadjo, Black, Chang, & Lee, 2011; Fadjo, Black, Chang, & Hong, 2010), which would then provide a sufficient foundation upon which to explore Direct Embodiment (Fadjo *et al.*, 2009, 2010) during Imaginary World (Black, 2007) construction.

For the most recent experiment we explored the effects of Instructional Embodiment on mathematical and computational thinking in video-game design. Instructional Embodiment is the use of action and perception for the development of understanding and comprehension of concepts (abstract or concrete) through direct, surrogate, augmented, or imagined embodiment within a formal instructional setting. Unlike other pedagogical frameworks where an instructor may solely model, or embody, the concepts or principles she or he wishes to teach, Instructional Embodiment is the use of embodiment as an engaging activity for the student that may be modeled by the teacher, but is fundamentally designed to engage the student in a sequence or system of movement, imagination, and exploration. Seminal work by Seymour Papert and colleagues during the late 1960s to mid-1980s addressed a similar principle wherein the student used "feel" and aesthetics with motion and augmented supports, such as an anthropomorphized robot, to learn (and "do") geometry through Logo (Papert, 1976, 1980; Minksy, 1970). Indeed, Papert promulgated the theory that in order to understand geometry one must "do" geometry, or mathematics for that matter, and in doing so one is thinking as a mathematician would think. Similarly, we defined a framework of Instructional Embodiments that can be used in the classroom setting.

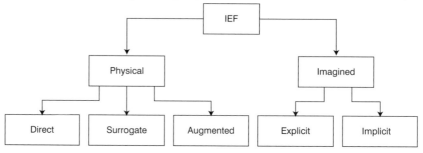

Figure 8.6 Instructional Embodiment Framework (IEF)

The Instructional Embodiment Framework (IEF – see Figure 8.6) is composed of two main categories, physical and imagined embodiment. A physical Instructional Embodiment may be Direct, Surrogate, or Augmented. Direct Embodiment (DE) is when the learner physically enacts a scenario using his or her body to enact statements or sequences. Surrogate Embodiment (SE) is physical embodiment that is controlled by the learner whereby the manipulation of an external "surrogate" represents the individual. Augmented Embodiment (AE) is the use of a representational system, such as an avatar, in conjunction with an augmented feedback system (such as Microsoft's Kinect and display system) to embed the embodied learner within an augmented representational system. Recent technological advances have made it possible to capture the entire human figure and embed him or her within a virtual space where the learner is not removed from reality (as was and is often characterized by virtual reality systems), but, rather, instantiated through a representational avatar who, in turn, becomes the augment of the learner during an instructional phase.

In addition to the physical Instructional Embodiments within IEF, an individual also embodies action and perception through imagination. Imagined Embodiment is characterized as the mental simulation of physically embodied action that is either Explicit (EI) or Implicit (II). Glenberg and colleagues' work on physical and imagined simulation showed that, while physical manipulation increases free-recall facilitation, it was physical manipulation in concert with imagined manipulation that led to the significant learning-strategy maintenance of indexing novel terminology (Glenberg *et al.*, 2004). We believe that embodied cognition in a learning environment must first be physically enacted (either through Direct, Surrogate, or Augmented Embodiment) as a full perceptual experience, then the learning activity is maintained through imagined embodiment (typically as Explicit Imagined Embodiment, EI) before finally resulting in tasks where transfer of learned content can occur. We also believe that cognition must be grounded, but not necessarily situated, within various contexts in order to be effective within an embodied learning environment design.

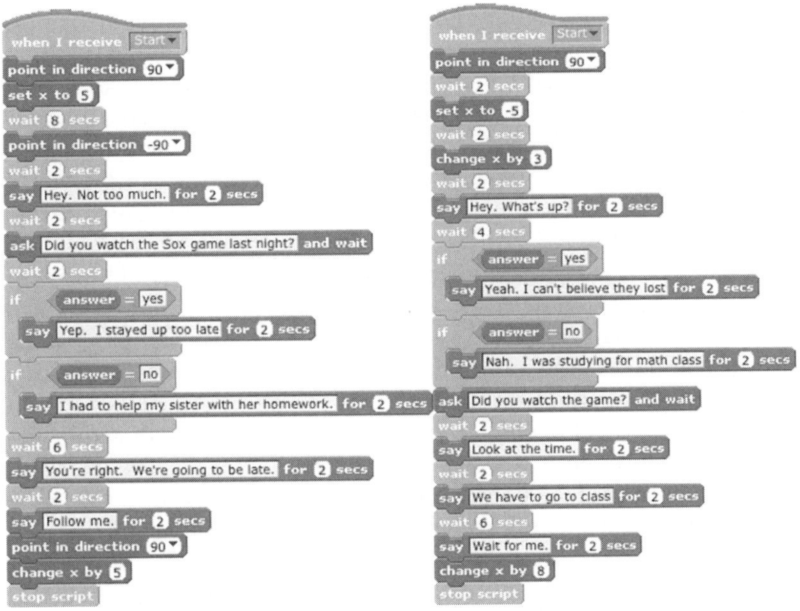

Figure 8.7 Embodiment scripts

Grounding cognition involves both environment and body as "external informational structures that complement internal representations" (Barsalou, 2010, p. 716). In the context of an embodied approach to learning environments, grounding cognition involves contextualizing and situating action within the goal structures outlined. With regard to the study we conducted on grounded embodied learning environments for computational and mathematical thinking in video-game design, the scenarios that define the situations and environment are critical and, as we found from the results, essential to representing cognition in embodied instruction.

For the content we used local sports teams, popular musical artists, playing video games, and homework completion topics to ground the instruction in contexts familiar with our target population of suburban middle school students from the northeast. The basic structure of the pre-defined scripts used to ground the embodied actions are shown in Figure 8.7. Each script was matched for length, structure, and sequence. In particular, following an "hour-glass"-like shape, every scenario began with movement and a socially-guided prompt in the form of a question. Next, the learners, reading the scripts in parallel as to embody a dialogue, had to evaluate a Simple or Complex Conditional Statement (Fadjo *et al.*, 2008). Based on the outcome, the sequence would continue with more dialogue and conclude with movement synonymous with the termination of a typical conversation. This grounded embodied learning environment characterizes the foundation upon which the mathematical and computational thinking concepts were taught and reinforced.

Within this comprehensive three-week curricular intervention at a suburban public middle school in New Hampshire, we compared numerous measures and outcomes from the artifacts students created and the surveys they completed to evaluate what effect embodiment and Imaginary World Construction (IWC) had on their computational and mathematical thinking. We had a Direct Embodiment with Explicit Imagined Embodiment condition (DE-EI), a Non-Physical Embodiment with Explicit Imagined Embodiment condition (X-EI), a Continued Imaginary World Construction (IWC-C), and a Different Imaginary World Construction (IWC-D) condition. In the Imaginary World Construction conditions the students either continued the scenario previously defined during the Code Literacy instructional session (IWC-C) or developed a completely new scenario (IWC-D) within the same constraints offered to the continued group.

With the grounded embodied conditions, we found that not only did those who engaged in Direct Embodiment and Explicit Imagined Embodiment (DE-EI) during instruction utilize significantly more mathematical structures in their artifacts, but that those who engaged in DE-EI also wrote significantly more code structures within their video game/story artifact. Thus, the mere fact that students physically enacted pre-defined code structures for five minutes at the beginning of class resulted in artifacts that were mathematically more complex, had significantly more code structures (and often utilized more complex code structures), and showed more evidence of computational thinking (in particular, decomposition of pre-defined exemplars into individual artifacts). We believe that this grounded embodied learning environment design can extend beyond the language with which computational thinking is historically taught (namely, computer programming languages such as *Scratch*, the block-based programming language used in this experiment; Resnick, 2009) to other domains and topics such as word problems, geometric patterning, or probability thinking where abstract concepts are fundamentally challenging for the instructor to teach and the student to learn in formal classroom settings.

In the Imaginary Worlds Construction conditions, we found a strong correlation between the option to construct an Imaginary World that was presented distinctly different than the initial video game world to all students (IWC-D) and the self-reported satisfaction of doing the task. Coupling the ability to construct an Imaginary World that is individually meaningful with a grounded embodied approach to learning abstract computational and mathematical concepts is evidence that a Constructionist (Papert, 1980, 1991; Harel & Papert, 1991; Harel, 1991; Harel Caperton, 2010) learning environment where grounded (Barsalou, 2008, 2010) embodied cognition (Glenberg *et al.*, 2004, 2009) is coupled with Imaginary World Construction (Fadjo & Black, 2011) that is constrained, but individually meaningful leads to significant gains in mathematical and computational thinking.

Similarly, Lu, Black, Kang, and Huang (2011) found that using direct physical embodiment (having students act out with their own bodies before programming) together with robot programming Surrogate Embodiment led to the best learning of physics concepts. In this study, having the students embody their understanding of physical science concepts (force and motion) by building and programming robot surrogates (using LEGO Mindstorms NXT robots) increased their understanding and learning. Further, having the students directly physically embody the physics concepts by acting out the situations first with their own bodies and then programming their robots to do the same thing led to much greater learning and understanding. Thus, having students directly experience something then imagine these experiences and embody their understanding in robot surrogates led to the best learning and understanding of all. This combination (experience, imagination, Surrogate Embodiment) also led to large increases in students' interest in physics topics and their confidence that they had understood them.

Conclusions

We have provided a variety of examples of how one can design learning environments using an embodied or perceptually-grounded cognition approach, and how this kind of design can lead to greater student learning, understanding and performance in addition to increasing student interest in what they are learning and confidence that they have mastered it. Specifically, in the studies summarized here we have a number of results that yield more effective learning, understanding and motivation when designing embodied learning environments:

1   The richer the perceptual environment using multiple sensory modalities (e.g., using visuals, voiceovers, and movement) during initial learning, the better the student learning, understanding and motivation.
2   Utilizing movements (e.g., gestures) that are conceptually congruent with the knowledge being learned increases student performance, learning, understanding and motivation.
3   Having students directly experience a phenomenon through activities like acting it out by moving their own bodies, then learning about it in a more general way increases student learning, understanding and motivation.
4   Having students embody their understanding in surrogates then observe the surrogate behavior through activities like programming video-game-like virtual environments with avatar surrogates and programming robot surrogates like the LEGO NXT ones, increases student learning, understanding and motivation.

Recent inexpensive technology developments provide tools that make implementing theses embodied learning environments easier, e.g., touch-gesture interfaces like the iPhone and iPad, simple programming tools like the *Scratch* programming environment and simple robot kits and programming like the NXT LEGO robots. We think that this approach provides a way to design learning environments that produce learning that becomes more a part of the way students think about and interact with the world, and thus will lead to greater transfer of learning beyond classroom settings. Fortunately, current technology developments are providing more and better ways to produce these embodied learning environments integrated with the real world. For example, our group is currently working on a new generation of embodied computer simulations using the Microsoft *Kinect* general gestural and speech interface.

References

Alibali, M. W., Bassok, M., Olseth Solomon, K., Syc, S. E., & Goldin-Meadow, S. (1999). Illuminating mental representations through speech and gesture. *Psychological Science, 10*(4), 327–333.

Barsalou, L. W. (1999). Perceptual symbol systems. *Behavioral and Brain Sciences,* 22, 577–660.

Barsalou, L. W. (2008). Grounded cognition. *Annual Review of Psychology,* 59, 617–645.

Barsalou, L. W. (2010). Grounded cognition: Past, present, and future. *Topics in Cognitive Science,* 2, 716–724.

Barsalou, L. W., Niedenthal, P. M., Barbey, A. K., & Ruppert, J. A. (2003). Social embodiment. In B. H. Ross (Ed.), *The psychology of learning and motivation.* San Diego, CA: Academic Press.

Behrman, B. W., & Brown, D. R. (1968). Multidimensional scaling of forms: A psychological analysis. *Perception & Psychophysics,* 4, 19–25.

Black, J. B. (2007). Imaginary worlds. In M. A. Gluck, J. R. Anderson, & S. M. Kosslyn (Eds.), *Memory and mind.* Mahwah, NJ: Lawrence Erlbaum Associates.

Black, J. B. (2010). An embodied/grounded cognition perspective on educational technology. In M. S. Khine & I. Saleh (Eds.), *New science of learning: Cognition, computers and collaboration in education.* New York: Springer.

Black, J. B., Turner, T. J., & Bower, G. H. (1979). Point of view in narrative comprehension, memory and production. *Journal of Verbal Learning and Verbal Behavior,* 18, 187–198.

Chan, M. S., & Black, J. B. (2006). Direct-manipulation animation: Incorporating the haptic channel in the learning process to support middle school students in science learning and mental model acquisition. *Proceedings of the International Conference of the Learning Sciences.* Mahwah, NJ: LEA.

Clements, D. H., & Battista, M. T. (1992). Geometry and spatial reasoning. In *Handbook of research on mathematics teaching and learning.* New York: Macmillan.

Clements, D. H., & Burns, B. A. (2000). Students' development of strategies for turn and angle measure. *Educational Studies in Mathematics,* 41, 31–45.

Clements, D. H., Swaminathan, S., Hannibal, M. A., & Sarama, J. (1999). Young children's concept of shape. *Journal for Research in Mathematics Education*, 30, 192–212.

Damasio, A. (1994). *Decartes' error: Emotion, reason, and the human brain*. New York: Penguin Books.

Dewey, J. (1938). *Experience and education*. New York: Touchstone.

Fadjo, C. L., & Black, J. B. (2011). A grounded embodied approach to the instruction of computational thinking. *Proceedings of the Association of Computing Machinery Special Interest Group on Computer Science Education (ACM SIGCSE)*, Dallas, TX.

Fadjo, C. L., Black, J. B., Chang, C., & Hong, J. (2010). Using embodied cognition in the instruction of abstract programming concepts. *Proceedings of the Annual Meeting of the Cognitive Science Society*, Portland, OR.

Fadjo, C. L., Black, J. B., Chang, C., & Lee, J. (2011). *Instructional embodiment: Incorporating embodied cognition in the learning of abstract computer programming concepts*. Paper presented at the annual conference of the American Educational Research Association, New Orleans, LA.

Fadjo, C. L., Lu, M. T., & Black, J. B. (2009). Instructional embodiment and video game programming in an after school program. *Proceedings of Educational Multimedia, Hypermedia, and Telecommunications,* Association for the Advancement of Computing in Education, Charlottesville, VA.

Fadjo, C. L., Shin, J., Lu, P., Chan, M., & Black, J. B. (2008). Embodied cognition and video game programming. *Proceedings of Educational Multimedia, Hypermedia, and Telecommunications*, Association for the Advancement of Computing in Education, Charlottesville, VA.

Gibbs, R. W. J. (2005). *Embodiment and cognitive science*. New York: Cambridge University Press.

Glenberg, A. M. (1997). What memory is for. *Behavioral and Brain Sciences*, 20, 1–55.

Glenberg, A. M., Gutierrez, T., Levin, J. R., Japuntich, S., & Kaschak, M. P. (2004). Activity and imagined activity can enhance young children's reading comprehension. *Journal of Educational Psychology*, 96, 424–436.

Glenberg, A. M., Goldberg, A., & Zhu, X. (2009). Improving early reading comprehension using embodied CAI. *Instructional Science*, 39, 27–39.

Goldin-Meadow, S. (2009). How gesture promotes learning throughout childhood. *Child Development Perspectives*, 3, 106–111.

Han, I., & Black, J. (2011). Incorporating haptic feedback in simulations for learning physics. *Computers and Education*, 57, 2281–2290.

Harel, I. (1991). *Children designers: Interdisciplinary constructions for learning and knowing*. Westport, CT: Greenwood Publishing Group.

Harel, I., & Papert, S. (1991). *Constructionism*. Norwood, NJ: Ablex.

Harel Caperton, I. (2010). *Constructionism 2.0*. New York: World Wide Workshop Foundation.

Hostetter, A. B., & Alibali, M. W. (2008). Visible embodiment: Gestures as simulated action. *Psychonomic Bulletin and Review*, 15, 495–514.

Johnson, M. (1987). *The body on the mind: The bodily basis of meaning, imagination, and reason*. Chicago, IL: University of Chicago Press.

Lakoff, G. & Johnson, M. (1999). *Philosophy in the flesh: The embodied mind and its challenges to Western thought*. New York: Basic Books.

Lakoff, G., & Nuñez, R. E. (2000). *Where mathematics comes from: How the embodied mind brings mathematics into being.* New York: Basic Books.

Laski, E. V., & Siegler, R. S. (2007). Is 27 a big number? Correlational and causal connections among numerical categorization, number line estimation, and numerical magnitude comparison. *Child Development,* 76, 1723–1743.

Lu, C., Black, J., Kang, S., & Huang, S. (2011). The Effects of LEGO robotics and embodiment in elementary science learning. *Proceedings of 33rd Annual Conference of the Cognitive Science.* Austin, TX: Cognitive Science Society.

Mach, E. (1886/1959). *The analysis of sensations and the relation of the physical to the psychical.* New York: Dover.

Marshall, P. (2007). Do tangible interfaces enhance learning? Learning through physical interaction. Paper presented at *TEI'07 (Tangible, Embedded and Embodied Interaction)* conference. Baton Rouge, LA.

Martin, A. (2007). The representation of object concepts in the brain. *Annual Review of Psychology,* 58, 25–45.

Minsky, M. (1970). Form and content in computer science. *Journal of the Association for Computing Machinery,* 17, 265-274.

Montessori, M. (1972). *Discovery of the child.* Location: Ballantine Books (original work published 1949).

Papert, S. (1976). *An Evaluative Study of Modern Technology in Education.* Artificial Intelligence Memoranda 371, Massachusetts Institute of Technology. Artificial Intelligence Laboratory.

Papert, S. (1980). *Mindstorms. Children, computers and powerful ideas.* New York: Basic Books.

Papert, S. (1991). Situating constructionism. In I. Harel & S. Papert (Eds.), *Constructionism: Research reports and essays, 1985–1990.* Norwood, NJ: Ablex.

Pecher, D., & Zwaan, R. A. (2005). *Grounding cognition: The role of perception and action in memory.* New York: Cambridge University Press.

Piaget, J. (1954). The construction of reality in the child. New York: Basic.

Piaget, J., & Inhelder, B. (1967). *The child's conception of space.* (F. J. Langdon, & J. L. Lunzer, Trans.) New York: W. W. Norton.

Piaget, J., Inhelder, B., & Szeminska, A. (1960). *The child's conception of geometry.* New York: Basic Books.

Resnick, M. (2009). Scratch: Programming for all. *Communications of the Association for Computing Machinery,* 11, 60–67.

Saffer, D. (2009). *Designing gestural interfaces,* New York: O'Reilly Publishing.

Schwartz, D. L., & Black, J. B. (1996). Shuttling between depictive models and abstract rules: Induction and fallback. *Cognitive Science,* 20, 457–497.

Schwartz, D. L., & Martin, T. (2006). Distributed learning and mutual adaptation. *Pragmatics and Cognition,* 14, 313–332.

Segal, A., Black, J., & Tversky, B. (2010). Do gestural interfaces promote thinking? Congruent gestures promote performance in math. Paper presented at 51st Annual meeting of Psychonomic Society Conference. St. Louis, Missouri.

Semin, G. R., & Smith, E. R. (2008). *Embodied grounding: Social, cognitive, affect, and neuroscientific approaches.* New York: Cambridge University Press.

Shepard, R. N., & Chipman, S. (1970). Second-order isomorphism of internal representation: Shapes of states. *Cognitive Psychology,* 1, 1–17.

Shneiderman, B. (1983). Direct manipulation: A step beyond programming languages. *IEEE Computer*, 16, 57–69.

Siegler, R. S., & Booth, J. L. (2005). Development of numerical estimation: A review. In J. I. D. Campbell (Ed.), *Handbook of mathematical cognition*. Boca Raton, FL: CRC Press.

Siegler, R. S., & Ramani, G. B. (2009). Playing linear number board games – but not circular ones – improves low-income preschoolers' numerical understanding. *Journal of Educational Psychology*, 101, 545–560.

Solomon, K., & Barsalou, L. (2004). Perceptual simulation in property verification. *Memory and Cognition*, 32, 244–259.

Spelke, E., Lee, S. A., & Izard, V. (2010). Beyond core knowledge: Natural geometry. *Cognitive Science*, 34, 863–884.

van Hiele, P. M. (1986). *Structure and insight: A theory of mathematics education*. Orlando, FL: Academic Press.

Varela, F. J., Thompson, E., & Rosch, E. (1991). *The embodied mind: Cognitive science and human experience*. Cambridge, MA: MIT Press.

9 Everyday Expertise

Learning Within and Across Formal and Informal Settings

Heather Toomey Zimmerman and Philip Bell

The everyday expertise framework is a perspective on learning and design that takes into account how people accomplish thinking and doing in their daily lives with the things and other people around them. In this way, the everyday expertise theoretical framework allows for learning to have multiple dimensions—individual, social, and cultural—which results in a broad consideration of how people learn within and across learning environments. Because the everyday expertise perspective incorporates values, emotions, knowledge, social practices, and other competencies, these holistic aspects of learning are leveraged when designing new educational environments.

With colleagues (Bell, Bricker, Lee, Reeve, & Zimmerman, 2006; Bell, Bricker, Reeve, Zimmerman, & Tzou, in press), we developed the everyday expertise framework in order to analyze the holistic, multidimensional influences on various learning processes to understand learning in a cross-setting ethnography. Our research group has applied the everyday expertise framework to support our research and design in a variety of contexts. For example, we have applied this framework to understand everyday expertise in argumentation (Bricker, 2008), health (Reeve, 2010; Reeve & Bell, 2009), engineering (Bricker & Bell, 2009), and home-based science practices (Zimmerman, 2008; Zimmerman, in press). Additionally, group members have used this framework in other studies to connect learning from home to school and back again (Tzou & Bell, 2010; Tzou, Zimmerman, & Bell, 2007) and to understand learning in museum contexts (Zimmerman, Reeve, & Bell, 2010).

In this chapter, we first discuss everyday expertise as conceptualized by members of our research group, and then we present ways that the everyday expertise perspective has been used for the design of learning environments. While we have used the everyday expertise framework in informal and formal settings, as well as to connect across settings, the focus of this chapter is on the use of the everyday expertise framework to support research and development of learning in informal environments and to connect informal spaces to other informal or formal learning environments.

The Need for a New Framework

A national consensus panel suggested new directions for the study of informal learning environments (Bell, Lewenstein, Shouse, & Feder, 2009) when they asked researchers to consider how people learn both within single settings (such as homes, workplaces, schools, and museums) and across multiple settings. In this way, the cumulative effects of learning experiences would be reflected and documented more holistically in designed environments. This initiative requires studying the same people as they interact across different learning environments in order to better understand the learning processes and tools that they use to study the interactions, intersections, and incongruencies of people's learning experiences. For example, in the life of a teenager, one would study the cumulative and competing effects of her experiences in school, while playing videogames, during soccer practices, in hobbies, during science summer camp, and in her summer job. And, once researchers better understand learning across settings, then they can begin to create designs for educational interventions that connect learning experiences.

This call was motivated by research findings that conclude that learners do not act with equal competency in all the settings that they participate in, even if the content is the same from a researcher's perspective. Most often, this differential performance shows that learners competent in informal and everyday settings (like personal hobby pursuits, museums and other informal institutions, or out-of-school time programs) may falter in more formalized learning settings, such as school. For example, in studies of street sellers in Brazil (Saxe, 1998), children could complete complex mathematics to earn profits for themselves and their family. However, when faced with the same math problem in school, the Brazilian children struggled to not only feel competent in solving the problem but also in doing the arithmetic. A study of adolescent male basketball players in a US high school (Nasir & Hand, 2008) had similar findings: young men developed strong mathematics skills in basketball but struggled in their mathematics classrooms. These studies, and more like them (e.g., Bell, Bricker, Lee, Reeve, & Zimmerman, 2006; Goldman, 2006), suggest that what people can accomplish cognitively is only one element needed to understand learning performances. The social and physical aspects of the setting and the cultural resources used in the learning activity must be considered alongside the individual's cognition. Consequently, we developed the everyday expertise framework to meet the need for a multidimensional view of learning that considers the cognitive, social, and cultural (which includes physical) influences on people across, as well as within, learning environments.

The everyday expertise framework builds from social theories of development: sociocultural views (Vygotsky, 1978; Rogoff, 2003), ecological models of psychology (Bronfenbrenner, 1979), and distributed perspectives on thinking and doing (Pea, 1993; Hutchins, 1995). From sociocultural theory, we adopt the idea that cultural tools mediate learners' experiences, and novice learners often have a more experienced guide assisting in the learning environment. (Modern technological sociocultural theorists can consider the social guide to be not only a person but also a computer-generated character or text.) Using ecological psychology theories, we add the idea that learners are part of communities at various levels and that within each community, different learning experiences are available to them. From distributed perspectives, we incorporate the idea that to understand learning and doing in an environment, one needs to look beyond just the cognition that occurs within one's head. The role of the environment in learning, as well as how an individual makes use of his or her environment during the thinking process, must be recognized and appreciated. The result of bringing these theories together is that to account for learning and to more effectively research and design learning settings, one must understand the interweaving of the individual, social, and cultural aspects that shape one's learning processes.

The Everyday Expertise Framework for Understanding Learning Environments

In the everyday expertise framework, when an individual is engaged in an activity, their affective and epistemic resources are considered along with influences from social interactions (family, classrooms, and peer groups) and larger societal influences (cultural and material/physical resources). Here, we will describe the three analytical planes of the everyday expertise framework, but it should be noted that these planes are not hierarchical levels. Instead, we see the individual, social, and cultural aspects of the everyday expertise framework as interweaving and interacting elements in learning environments. We first describe each plane in the everyday expertise framework, and then we describe how these planes work together to mutually influence each other and learners.

Three Interconnected Levels of the Everyday Expertise Framework

Individual Aspects

The individual plane of the everyday expertise framework considers the array of resources that an individual uses to make sense of his or her world. It includes knowledge and conceptual elements people have developed over time (see diSessa, 2002, for discussion of science-related knowledge), the way people understand the nature of knowledge (Hammer, Elby, Scherr, & Redish, 2005), and the interests and emotional states held by an individual (Hidi & Renninger, 2006; Renninger, 2009).

Cultural Aspects

The cultural plane of the everyday expertise framework is where people's everyday practices depend upon cultural tools (Wertsch, 1998) in their physical environment. Cultural tools include languages, technologies, dispositions, styles of talking, and physical artifacts. Worldviews, stereotypes and other conceptual elements that broadly permeate societal groups are also considered as cultural tools. All these cultural tools—whether conceptual or material—are available uniquely at distinct temporal moments. Individuals uptake these tools differently to create unique cultural toolkits from available cultural resources (see the description of Swidler's, 1986, cultural toolkit and the concept of Funds of Knowledge; González, Moll, & Amanti, 2005). The everyday expertise framework considers culture and cultural toolkits broadly, to include practices from participation in ethnic or social class groups, to cultures of disciplines like science (Aikenhead, 1996) to family's or small group's subcultures or ideocultures (see Fine, 1983).

Social Aspects

Informal learning environments have long been considered social learning environments (e.g., Ash, 2003; Crowley & Jacobs, 2002; Falk & Dierking, 2000). Social aspects of learning in the everyday expertise framework do include interactions with people; however, social is conceptualized much more broadly than the standard definition of "more than one person interacting." In the everyday expertise framework's social plane, social means a person and his or her social settings are an interconnected unit. This connection of the learner and the specific cultural learning environment is called situated activity. Building from socio cultural historical activity systems (Cole & Engeström, 1993; Vygotsky, 1978), situated activity is a mid-level construct between cultural groups and individuals (Goodwin, 1990). In situated activity, the learner is considered as he or she engages in social practices with conceptual, social and material cultural tools within and across cultural communities. In this way, a situated activity can be a social activity even if only one person is directly present because situated activity presumes that others are asynchronously involved. Reading a book in a library study carrel, for example, involves not only the reader, but also the author and the publisher. A young college student reading this book in a library involves social norms such that in a library she reads silently and does not write inside the book. This individual may turn on the light in her carrel because a grandparent had said that reading in the dark is bad for her eyes. Solitary reading as a situated activity then includes a wide variety of social influences. As a consequence of this broad conceptualization, within situated activity, one can study how individuals engage in cultural work in social practices with the physical artifacts and other people within and across multiple environments.

Bringing the Three Planes Together

The everyday expertise framework, as its origins in the introductory section above suggest, is fundamentally a social theory of learning because the three analytical planes described above are linked. For example, individual knowledge resources are considered, but they are considered in tandem with the cultural origins of this individual knowledge that was gained in contextual, situated activities. The planes then not only mutually inform each other but they also mutually constitute each other because individuals change as they participate in social practices using cultural tools in situated activities and the individuals adapt, resist, and change these tools and practices, which can result in changes in the situated activities and the cultural tools. Culture then does not predestine individuals, but instead culture provides resources (i.e., cultural tools) that individuals can use, while also providing individuals the agency they need to resist and change culture (Wertsch, 1998). Given these interconnections between planes, when using the everyday expertise framework one can focus more on one plane than the others, but a researcher or designer using this perspective must keep in mind that cultural tools, social practices within situated activity systems, and individual attributes are all linked in learning environments.

A benefit of using the everyday expertise framework—with its three analytical planes—is that researchers avoid essentializing learners by presuming individuals have stereotypical traits because of their membership in ethnic or cultural groups (Nasir, Rosebery, Warren, & Lee, 2006). Essentializing means assuming that characteristics, traits and practices apply uniformly to individuals within a cultural group, without acknowledging the variation within groups of people. For example, one may presume that all members of the science cultural group are "geeks" or that all people of certain ethnicity are good at a specific sport. When applying everyday expertise, one would instead look at individuals to understand which competencies have been adopted within their situated activities. Also, the specific details of the situated activity systems may be different for members of the same cultural group since individuals hold divergent goals, motives, and desired outcomes. Through looking at the use of tools and practices of individuals in their situated activities, researchers avoid the assumption of homogeneity—with the result of more scientifically accurate research findings and more well-designed learning environments.

The Everyday Expertise Framework in Practice: Two Examples

To better elucidate the usefulness of the everyday expertise framework when studying informal learning environments, we provide two examples of how researchers used the framework to understand what was supportive or non-supportive for learners in specific designed spaces. The first example is from a research study of learning within a science center. The second research project looks at youth on a fieldtrip from an environmental youth program from a community center and from a girls' school. In these examples, the everyday expertise framework is used to accomplish different kinds of analyses of the learning environment. In the study of the science center, the authors used the everyday expertise framework to understand the ways families used individual, social, and cultural knowledge resources. In the environmental education program study, the authors used the everyday expertise model to understand issues of equity and access for youth of color.

Everyday Expertise and Families in Science Centers

In a study of museum-going families in a large science center, Zimmerman, Reeve, and Bell (2010) used the everyday expertise framework to understand how families made sense of the biological content present in the museum. In this study, the authors sought to understand the museum visits from the perspectives of the families, and accordingly, they used ethnographic and discourse analysis methods including pre- and post-visit interviews, video recordings of museum visits, and coding and analysis of the families' conversations. Using the everyday expertise framework to understand the science center was key, given the complexity of the learning environment and the differential experiences visitors had with the science center. For example, visitors could start their learning experience from multiple entrances, go to various exhibitions, and interact with different components within each exhibition. In addition, with approximately one million visitors per year, the people within this museum learning environment had a wide range of prior knowledge and experiences from diverse social interactions and from a myriad of cultural experiences.

To get a sense of how people were using the learning environment to support their sense-making practices, Zimmerman and colleagues mapped what families said and did during their visits. Within each map, all three planes of the everyday expertise framework were highlighted— individual's contribution, social interactions, and cultural tool use. Figure 9.1 is an example of one of these learning environment use maps from one family's visit to a science center. Figure 9.1 is from a family of three—Ned, Laura, and their mother (all pseudonyms)—who liked to collect bugs and learn about insects. The thick-lined rectangles with rounded corners are the museum's exhibitions that this family stopped in, and the thin-lined rectangles with angular corners are data segments representing what this family said and did at each exhibition.

From Figure 9.1, one can see how individual, social, and cultural influences led to the children's incredible knowledge of insects that mediated the learning experience in the museum. Ned's values and future

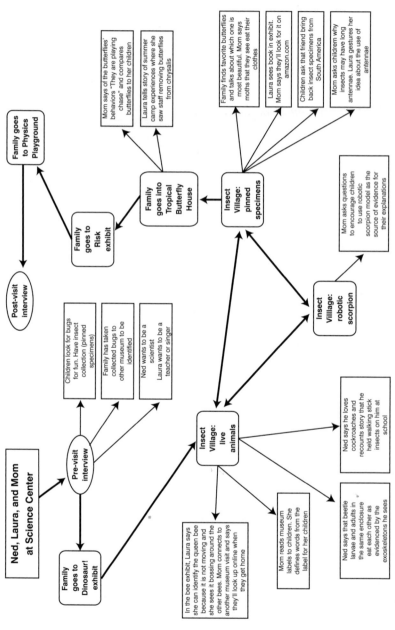

Figure 9.1 A learning environment map made using the everyday expertise framework. From Zimmerman, Reve, & Bell (2010, Figure 1, p. 490). Copyright: Wiley-Blackwell

goals to have a career in science led to his interest in insects. Laura's experience in summer camp led to her developing knowledge of butterflies that the other family members did not have. The family's shared social dialogue within the museum allowed for much biological learning. Within the museum conversations, the family referenced experiences from regularly occurring activities including evening time spent as a family in the out-of-doors looking for insects and hobby time spent on their insect collection. The parents arranged for the children to have interactions with the cultural tools of science, including visits to institutions like museums and having access to books and online resources.

The use of the everyday expertise framework also allows one to see the role that the science center played in their learning by observing and documenting the family's use of signage and interactive exhibit components. For example, across the biological talk, Zimmerman, Reeve, and Bell found nearly 5 percent of the science statements came from a family member that read out loud from the museum signage. With this knowledge in hand about reading texts aloud, the authors were able to make design implications on exhibit signage with the everyday expertise framework. For example, through examining families' dialogue and interactions with the cultural tools provided by the museum, some youth in the study had more expertise in certain museum-based science content than their parents. As in the example of Ned and Laura, these children had learned relevant science content from museum summer camps, school, hobbies, and visits to other museums. Yet, the signage of the museum was often placed at a reading height for the adults (the taller visitors) that the children could not easily read. This finding about the value of placing more complex exhibit information at lower heights for children to read was afforded by the use of the everyday expertise framework.

Everyday Expertise and Adolescent Youth in Environmental Education Programs

In a cross-setting ethnography, Tzou, Scalone, and Bell (2010) used the everyday expertise framework to understand how narratives position youth in certain ways in environmental learning environments. Using Bruner's (1987) definition of narrative cognition, Tzou and colleagues defined narratives as social accounts that are inseparable from the learning environment's place-based aspects. Using this definition, narratives within that learning environment could include stories about specific people or stereotypes about cultural groups. Consequently, the narratives within the learning environment were considered at the multiple levels of the everyday expertise framework. Employing the everyday expertise framework added the ability to focus on issues of social justice by understanding how individual, social, and cultural aspects influence the access that youth have to meaningful learning within environmental education programs.

The study revealed that narratives about place were constructed within environmental education institutions in ways that either limited or opened certain learning pathways for youth. Through an analysis of youth from resource-rich and resource-impoverished communities, researchers found that the messages given to all youth did not reflect the lived reality of the resource-impoverished youth. For example, Tzou and colleagues found that the environmental education messages to "drive less and walk more" did not match up to the safety concern that some youth felt in their neighborhood where a recent drive-by shooting had occurred.

Tzou, Scalone, and Bell also found that the environmental education institution held cultural narratives about Mexican ethnic identity and Spanish language that led to stereotyping of certain youth. The environmental education institution positioned the adolescents in such a way that their social learning experience became less about ecology and more of a manual labor work experience, namely, the hauling of the compost on a farm. Figure 9.2 shows the relationship between the cultural narratives (and stereotypes) and the social interactions within the activity system (i.e., hauling of the compost), which influenced the individual (youth) in the learning environment. Individuals are not seen as passive receivers of social and cultural influences in the everyday expertise framework. Rather, individuals have agency, which results in the individual, social, and cultural aspects mutually constituting each other. The youth from this study were seen to develop their own narratives about race and environmental education, and these new narratives may influence their future participation in activity systems and their use of cultural tools.

The Everyday Expertise Framework in Design: Considering Learning Within and Across Settings

Not only can everyday expertise be used to understand learning within or across certain spaces, but it can also help designers to develop learning environments that connect youth, backgrounds, and values to the goals of formal and informal institutions. Two examples are provided where the design teams thought through individual, social, and cultural aspects of learning—with the goal of making instruction relevant to youth by connecting learning from one setting to learning in a new environment. Both examples use digital technology devices to support learners.

Micros and Me—Connecting Home and School with Digital Photography

The first example, *Micros and Me* (Tzou, Bricker, & Bell, 2007), is a fifth grade school curriculum in biology. While the curriculum includes multiple ways to make science relevant to youth's lives, only one aspect

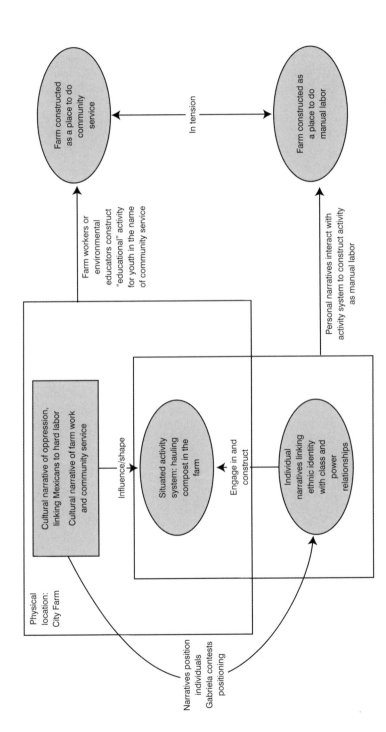

Figure 9.2 The everyday expertise framework used to understand the role of narratives in an environmental education learning environment. From Tzou, Scalone, & Bell (2010, Figure 2, p. 115). Copyright: Taylor & Francis

is highlighted here. This example (Tzou & Bell, 2010) shows the use of digital photography and self-documentation to connect learners' home and community experiences to school-based biology lessons. Tzou and Bell applied the everyday expertise framework to develop a means for teachers to tap into individual, social, and cultural aspects of youth's knowledge without essentializing youth to predetermined ethnic group membership traits.

Micros and Me (Tzou, Bricker, & Bell, 2007), a seven-week educational curriculum for elementary students, has two goals. First, the designers intended to make the biological sciences more personally relevant to fifth grade youth's lives—inside and outside of school. Second, the team aspired to have learners participate in authentic scientific practices so youth could gain access to the cultural tools of science. Micros and Me accomplishes this connection through focusing on learners' cultural understanding about health to connect microbiology (authentic science practices) and health (everyday and scientific practices).

Researchers Tzou and Bell used the everyday expertise framework to design and study the implementations of Micros and Me in an urban elementary school in the Pacific Northwest. The example here is on a specific element of the curriculum where students were given a digital camera to borrow and asked to take photographs of things they use at home to keep their bodies healthy (Tzou & Bell, 2010). This project was a self-documentation task (Clark-Ibañez, 2004) and aimed to elicit elements of individual youth and families' cultural toolkits for items they use to keep healthy. In this way, Tzou and Bell leveraged most from the cultural toolkit level of analysis, while considering the individual knowledge of learners and the situated activity systems that the individual participated in to gain the knowledge of health.

While working in the classroom with fifth grade students, a teacher Ms. E employed the Micros and Me curriculum. She gave her students digital cameras to take photos of things in their lives that were involved in keeping them healthy. The fifth grade students also filled out a journal to say what the image was, where it came from, and how it worked to keep them healthy. These pictures and journal entries were then placed by the researchers in a worksheet that was formatted like a comic strip. The idea of the comic strip worksheet was to connect the individual knowledge, the cultural toolkit item, and the situated activity knowledge together for individual students to share with the other class members. See Figure 9.3 for an example of the everyday expertise comic worksheet that ties the individual, social, and cultural planes together.

Tzou, Bricker, and Bell (2007) encouraged teachers using the curriculum to consider these images as from situated activities that may differ, even among members of the same ethnic group. Teachers adapted this suggestion in ways that made sense to the youth in their classrooms. For example, when Ms. E used these worksheets in classroom discussions,

Figure 9.3 An everyday expertise comic strip about a youth's ideas about health. Copyright Carrie T. Tzou, used with permission

she asked individuals who identified the same object for keeping healthy, "Do you use it as well? Do you use it for the same thing?" (Tzou & Bell, 2010) to avoid essentializing.

Tree Investigators—Connecting Home and Outdoor Education in Museums

In the second example, *Tree Investigators* (Land *et al.*, 2011), researchers developed an augmented learning program for an outdoor learning environment, the Arboretum at Penn State. The project built on youth's competencies and interests with mobile learning devices and connected their interests and experiences to the scientific cultural practices of observation and classification. Zimmerman and Land applied the everyday expertise framework to create a new situated activity in an informal institution that leveraged cultural tools from home and school activities, so the youth could enjoy shared success with biological knowledge and science practices.

This design-based research project, from the Augmented Learning Research Group, is another example that used the three-pronged approach of the everyday expertise model to design a program for youth. This project, Tree Investigators (co-directed by Susan M. Land and Heather Toomey Zimmerman), has graduate students and faculty working with informal learning environments to develop programs for youth as they move across learning environments through the use of small mobile learning devices (like smart phones, iPods™, iPads™, and wireless-enabled tablets). Members of the group develop educational technologies to support informal educational programming related to environmental education issues relevant to youth in rural communities. The group has adopted mobile computing devices to support learning across multiple settings, based on research on the use of these technologies both within and outside of formal classrooms (Bell *et al.*, 2009; Pea & Maldonado, 2006; Roschelle, 2002; Wagner, 2008; Zimmerman, Kanter *et al.*, 2010). One strategy for mobile computing is augmented reality, which brings new content to add to one physical space with scenarios, animations, game-play, or textual information (Rogers *et al.*, 2004) from another space. This augmentation provides learners additional resources to engage with in their physical space. With augmented reality environments, the technology only adds information; it is not a stand-alone program. In this way, augmented learning has a strong reliance on place-sensitive aspects from the original learning setting. The blend of the technology augmentations and key elements from the outdoor learning space changes the situated activity by combining aspects from two settings (technological and physical) into one.

The Tree Investigators project described here involves developing an augmented learning project, that uses Microsoft™ Tag Reader to bring specific web-based content to an iPod or iPad via an app (an app is an application for a mobile device). The Tree Investigators app is designed for elementary aged youth in various social group configurations—with their school classroom on a fieldtrip, in youth-based organizations on the weekends, for summer camps, or with their families. The Tree Investigators app allows youth to explore trees on site at the Arboretum, and when the children use the camera on an iPad or iPod to snap a picture of a "tag" made with Microsoft™ Tag Reader, additional photographs and textual information (written at a reading level of elementary aged students) appear on their touch screen as a customized website. See Figure 9.4 for a student using Tree Investigators.

This project used the everyday expertise framework to ensure the situated activity of learning at the Arboretum was tailored to the youth's interests and their shared (and divergent) experiences in school and the community to gain access to the cultural tools of science. For example, while generic websites (like Wikipedia) or specific nature organizations have websites and books with similar scientific content to the Tree Investigators app, multiple benefits are afforded to the learners from the development team's consideration of individual, social, and cultural aspects

Figure 9.4 A fourth grade girl uses an iPod™ with a digital camera to scan a tag to access relevant content at the Arboretum at Penn State. Copyright Susan M. Land, used with permission

during the Arboretum learning experience. For example, the text is tailored to the youth's age level and school requirements. Also, because the tags are strategically available on site, the research team provides place-specific information that uses both common social experiences that the youth have in school, while it also leverages scientific cultural practices. The youth, for example, are directed to compare and contrast relevant features of two species that grow next to each other (i.e., compare an oak's branching structure with a maple's branching structure) in order to expand their classification skills. Sizes of the trees and other features are compared with buildings the youth can see from the Arboretum or that are prominent in the community. The cultural tools that the current generation of youth value (like iPods and iPads) are leveraged so that youth are provided access to these scientific cultural tools, and so they may use these tools to practice observing and classifying natural phenomena in an outdoor learning setting.

From the everyday expertise framework, the developers attempted to have youth work in small group of familiar peers or family members, so that the experience leveraged school- and home-based existing situated activities to create a new situated activity at the Arboretum. The goal of the new situated activity was supported by research from informal learning institutions (Allen & Gutwill, 2009; Gutwill & Allen, 2010) that found that people learned more in a science center when they engaged in a social group to interact with the museum content in ways that supported inquiry practices. The new outdoor education situated activity included elements of asking and answering questions, careful observing of nature phenomena, and sharing findings with other members of the group. The text of the Tree Investigator app was designed so that the text asked questions and encouraged users to work together to share aloud observations of the plants on site at the Arboretum. This app then allowed for a social learning experience that helped youth develop scientific understandings of trees in their local community.

Conclusion

The everyday expertise perspective on learning and design allows for learning to have multiple dimensions—individual, social, and cultural—which results in a full consideration on how people learn within and across learning environments. By using the everyday expertise framework to study designed spaces or to create new learning environments, developers can create an end product that is a culturally relevant and individually consequential learning space.

Acknowledgements

The everyday expertise framework was developed by members of the Everyday Science & Technology Group as part of the Learning in Informal and Formal Environments (LIFE) Center, http://www.life-slc.org/. Research team members Leah A. Bricker, Suzanne Reeve, Tiffany R. Lee, and Carrie T. Tzou were intellectual partners in this effort with the authors of this chapter. The Everyday Science & Technology Group thanks the National Science Foundation for their support and for the opportunity to develop the framework described here (award # SBE – 0354453).

The Tree Investigator Project described here is a collaboration between Susan M. Land, Heather Toomey Zimmerman, Brian J. Selley, Joshua Burch, Michele Crowl, Lucy Richardson McClain, Michael Mohney, and Tutaleni Asino. It was funded in part by the Penn State Educational Technology Service unit and Penn State College of Education.

All opinions expressed are strictly those of the authors.

References

Aikenhead, G. S. (1996). Science education: Border crossing into the subculture of science. *Studies in Science Education.* 27, 1–52.

Allen, S., & Gutwill, J. P. (2009). Creating a program to deepen family inquiry at interactive science exhibits. *Curator: The Museum Journal.* 52 (3), 289–306.

Ash, D. (2003). Dialogic inquiry in life science conversations of family groups in a museum. *Journal of Research in Science Teaching,* 40(2), 138–162. doi: 10.1002/tea.10069.

Bell, P., Bricker, L., Lee, T. R., Reeve, S., & Zimmerman, H. T. (2006). Understanding the cultural foundations of children's biological knowledge: Insights from everyday cognition. *Proceedings of the International Conference of the Learning Sciences 2006.*

Bell, P., Bricker, L. A., Reeve, S., Zimmerman, H. T., & Tzou, C. (in press). Discovering and supporting successful learning pathways of youth in and out of school: Accounting for the development of everyday expertise across settings. In B. Bevan, P. Bell, & R. Stevens (Eds.), *Learning about Out of School Time (LOST) Learning Opportunities*: Springer.

Bell, P., Lewenstein, B., Shouse, A. W., & Feder, M. A., (Eds.) (2009). *Learning science in informal environments: People, places, and pursuits.* Washington DC: National Academies Press.

Bricker, L. A. (2008). *A sociocultural historical examination of youth argumentation across the settings of their lives: Implications for science education.* Seattle, WA: University of Washington. (Doctoral dissertation).

Bricker, L. A., & Bell, P. (2009, April). Frame and positioning dynamics with youth learning and expertise development across settings and time scales. Paper presented at the annual meeting of the American Educational Research Association (AERA), San Diego, CA.

Bronfenbrenner, U. (1979). *The ecology of human development: Experiments by nature and design.* Cambridge, MA: Harvard University Press.

Bruner, J. (1987). *Actual minds, possible worlds.* Cambridge, MA: Harvard University Press.

Clark-Ibañez, M. (2004). Framing the social world with photo-elicitation interviews. *American Behavioral Scientist, 47*(12), 1507–1527. doi: 10.1177/0002764204266236.

Cole, M., & Engeström, Y. (1993). A cultural-historical approach to distributed cognition. In G. Salomon (Ed.), *Distributed cognitions: Psychological and educational considerations* (pp. 1–46). Cambridge: Cambridge University Press.

Crowley, K., & Jacobs, M. (2002). Building islands of expertise in everyday family activity. In G. Leinhardt, K. Crowley, & K. Knutson (Eds.), *Learning conversations in museums* (pp. 333–356). London: Lawrence Erlbaum Associates.

diSessa, A. (2002). Why "conceptual ecology" is a good idea. In M. Limón & L. Mason (Eds.), *Reconsidering conceptual change: Issues in theory and practice* (pp. 29–60). Dordrecht: Kluwer.

Falk, J. H., & Dierking, L. D. (2000). *Learning from museums: Visitor experiences and the making of meaning.* Walnut Creek, CA: Alta Mira Press.

Fine, G. A. (1983). *Shared fantasy: Role playing games as social worlds.* Chicago: University of Chicago Press.

Goldman, S. (2006). A new angle on families: Connecting the mathematics of life with school mathematics. In Z. Bekerman, N. C. Burbules, & D. Silberman-Keller (Eds.), *Learning in Places: The Informal Education Reader* (pp. 55–76). New York: Peter Lang Publishing.

Gonzâlez, N., Moll, L. C., & Amanti, C. (2005). *Theorizing education practice: Funds of knowledge in households.* Mahwah, NJ: LEA.

Goodwin, M. H. (1990). *He-said-she-said: Talk as social organization among black children.* Bloomington: Indiana University Press.

Gutwill, J. P., & Allen, S. (2010). Facilitating family group inquiry at science museum exhibits. *Science Education. 94*(4), 710–742.

Hammer, D., Elby, A., Scherr, R. E., & Redish, E. F. (2005). Resources, framing, and transfer. In J. Mestre (Ed.), *Transfer of learning: Research and perspectives.* Greenwich, CT: Information Age Publishing.

Hidi, S., & Renninger, K. A. (2006). The four-phase model of interest development. *Educational Psychologist, 41*(2), 111–127. doi: 10.1207/s15326985ep4102_4.

Hutchins, E. (1995). *Cognition in the wild.* Cambridge: MIT Press.

Nasir, N., & Hand, V. (2008). From the court to the classroom: Opportunities for engagement, learning, and identity in basketball and classroom mathematics. *Journal of the Learning Sciences,* 17(2), 143–179. doi:10.1080/10508400801986108.

Nasir, N. S., Rosebery, A. S., Warren, B., & Lee, C. D. (2006). Learning as a cultural process: Achieving equity through diversity. In R. K. Sawyer (Ed.), *The Cambridge handbook of the learning sciences* (pp. 489–504). New York: Cambridge University Press.

Pea, R. (1993). Practices of distributed intelligence and designs for education. In G. Salomon (Ed.), *Distributed cognitions: Psychological and educational considerations* (pp. 47–87). Cambridge: Cambridge University Press.

Pea, R. & Maldonado, C. (2006). WILD for learning: Interacting through new computing devices anytime, anywhere. In K. Sawyer (Ed.), *The Cambridge Handbook of the Learning Sciences* (p. 427–441). Cambridge, MA: Cambridge University Press.

Reeve, S. (2010). *Health beliefs and practices of young people in a multicultural community: Findings from a child-centered ethnography.* Seattle, WA: University of Washington (Doctoral dissertation).

Reeve, S., & Bell, P. (2009). Children's self-documentation and understanding of the concepts "healthy" and "unhealthy." *International Journal of Science Education, 31*(14), 1953–1974.

Renninger, K. A. (2009). Interest and identity development in instruction: An inductive model. *Educational Psychologist, 44*(2), 105–118. doi: 10.1080/00461520902832392.

Rogers, Y., Price, S., Fitzpatrick, G., Fleck, R., Harris, E., Smith, H., Randell, C., Muller, H., O'Malley, C., Stanton, D., Thompson, M., & Weal, M. (2004). Ambient wood: designing new forms of digital augmentation for learning outdoors. *Proceedings of the 2004 Conference on Interaction Design and Children: Building a Community* (pp. 3–10). Maryland.

Rogoff, B. (2003). *The cultural nature of human development.* New York: Oxford University Press.

Roschelle, J. (2002). Unlocking the learning value of wireless mobile devices. *Journal of Computer Assisted Learning. 19*(3), 260–272.

Saxe, G. B. (1998). The mathematics of child street vendors. *Child Development, 59*(5), 1415–1425.

Swidler, A. (1986). Culture in action: Symbols and strategies. *American Sociological Review, 51*(2), 273–286.

Tzou, C., & Bell, P. (2010). Micros and Me: Leveraging home and community practices in formal science instruction. In K. Gomez, L. Lyons & J. Radinsky (Eds.), *Learning in the Disciplines: Proceedings of the 9th International*

Conference of the Learning Sciences Volume 1 (pp. 1127–1134). Chicago, IL: International Society of the Learning Sciences.

Tzou, C., Bricker, L. A., & Bell, P. (2007). Micros and Me: A fifth-grade science exploration into personally and culturally consequential microbiology. Seattle, WA: Everyday Science & Technology Group, University of Washington.

Tzou, C., Scalone, G., & Bell, P. (2010). The role of environmental narratives and social positioning in how place gets constructed for and by youth. *Equity & Excellence in Education*, 43(1), 105–119. doi: 10.1080/10665680903489338.

Tzou, C. T., Zimmerman, H. T., & Bell, P. (2007). Bringing students' activity structures into the classroom: Curriculum design implications from an ethnographic study of fifth graders' images of science. In P. Bell (chair). *Understanding the nature of science is not enough: The cultural nature of elementary school children's images of science.* Symposium conducted at the annual meeting of the National Association for Research in Science Teaching, New Orleans, LA.

Vygotsky, L. S. (1978). Tools and symbols in child development. In M. Cole, V. John-Steiner, S. Scribner & E. Souberman (Eds.), *Mind in society* (pp. 19–30). Cambridge, MA: Harvard University Press.

Wagner, E. D. (2008). Realizing the promises of mobile learning. *Journal of Computing in Higher Education, 20*, 4–14.

Wertsch, J. (1998). *Mind as action.* New York: Oxford University Press.

Zimmerman, H. T. (2008). *Everyday science & science every day: Science-related talk & activities across settings.* Seattle, WA: University of Washington (Doctoral dissertation).

Zimmerman, H. T. (in press). Participating in science at home: The roles of recognition work and agency in science learning. *Journal of Research in Science Teaching.*

Zimmerman, H. T., & Land, S. M. (2011). Tree Investigators: An augmented learning research and design project. White Paper prepared for the 2011 Association for Educational Communications and Technology conference Mobile Computing: Perspectives on Design, Learning, and Development. Available at www.personal.psu.edu/haz2/Heather_Zimmerman/Publications. html.

Zimmerman, H. T., Kanter, D. E., Ellenbogen, K., Lyons, L., Zuiker, S. J., Satwicz, T., Martell, S. T., Hsi, S., & Smith, B. K. (2010). Technologies and tools to support informal science learning. *Proceedings of the Ninth International Conference for the Learning Sciences – ICLS 2010. Volume 2;* pp. 260–266.

Zimmerman, H. T., Reeve, S., & Bell, P. (2010). Family sense-making practices in science center conversations. *Science Education, 94*, 478–505. doi: 10.1002/sce.20374.

10 Activity Theory in the Learning Technologies

Benjamin DeVane and Kurt D. Squire

Activity theory is a social psychological framework that grew out of two theoretical pillars of Soviet psychological thought in the 1920s and 1930s: Vygotskian cultural-historical psychology and praxis-focused Marxist materialism. Activity theory, also sometimes called Cultural Historical Activity Theory (or CHAT) seeks to create an account of human cognition in which people, their intentions, tools, culture, and encompassing social structures are all considered as inherently inseparable components of human activity which constitute thought. Within educational technology and the learning sciences, hereafter referred to as the "learning technologies," CHAT is used in many ways. Most often, learning technologists have used third-generation CHAT (identified with the Scandanavian school) as a guiding theoretical framework to understand how technologies are adopted, adapted, and configured through use in complex social situations.

Thus, this chapter provides a brief historical account of how CHAT originated and was taken up by learning technologists, and then we use brief examples from our own work to illustrate its application. We argue that within learning technologies, CHAT has been primarily used as an analytic tool for understanding human activity in a manner that honors human agency (consistent with constructivism) that accounts for how people think *with* tools (such as models, simulations or games), and examines learning within social and cultural contexts (such as schools or gaming guilds). A key feature of CHAT, we argue, is that it treats people working with these tools within social contexts for particular purposes (individual and collective) as the minimally meaningful unit of analysis. In other words, we cannot understand cognition (and hence learning) without considering these components of human activity that comprise it. Admittedly, this chapter is not a thorough review of the nuances of CHAT, nor does it explore more cutting-edge developments within the community of scholars, practitioners, and theoreticians pushing the paradigm forward. We have made many simplifications to CHAT in an effort to make it readable (relying heavily on Cole, 1996, and Engeström, 2001) and hope that those interested in this intellectual tradition will pursue it further.

For general readers of this volume, we hope to convey an appreciation for what kinds of problems CHAT might illuminate, the theoretical traditions underlying it, and some of its limitations.

We begin by providing a historical overview of the evolution of CHAT from first- and second-generation activity theory. This overview is strongly indebted to a number of rich, existing histories of the evolution of CHAT, notably those provided by Engeström (2001), Cole (1996) and Nardi (1996b), and traces the evolution of CHAT over three-quarters of a century. We continue by laying out the basic characteristics of CHAT as a framework, outlining what we see as the most salient features, characteristics and caveats of the model. Finally, we describe many examples of the use of CHAT in the learning technologies, and detail the implications of CHAT for the design and analysis of learning technologies.

First Generation CHAT: Origins in Vygotskian Social Psychology

Engeström (2001), among others, notes that CHAT is rooted in Vygotskian social psychology, which might be loosely described as the psychological tradition that treats human activity as socially, culturally and historically situated. First, Vygotsky (1978) famously argued that human thought was not simply a matter of a response in reaction to a stimulus, but that thinking is inherently *mediated* by abstract symbols and physical objects, like language, tools, numbers and signs. To use a mundane example, the existence of an axe deeply alters our experience of trees, as we can cut them and use them for various purposes (or study their inner rings). Similarly, cultural tools such as language color our experience; consider the equally mundane example of the watch:

> They (children) name things, denoting them with expressions established earlier in human history, and thus assign things to certain categories and acquire knowledge. Once a child calls something a "watch" (chasy), he immediately incorporates it into a system of things related to time (chas); once he calls a moving object a "steamship" (parovoz), he automatically isolates its defining properties – motion (vozit') by means of "steam" (par). Language, which mediates human perception, results in extremely complex operations: the analysis and synthesis of incoming information, the perceptual ordering of the world, and the encoding of impressions into systems. Thus words – the basic linguistic units – carry not only meaning but also the fundamental units of consciousness reflecting the external world.
>
> (Luria, 1976, p. 9)

In this way, *mediation*, the idea that tools (physical and cultural) mediate our experience and understanding of phenomena, was a primary

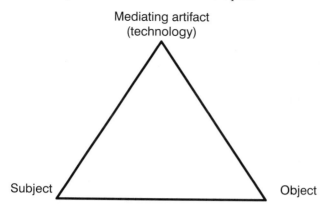

Figure 10.1 Vygotsky – tools as mediational means

contribution of Vygotsky to understandings of human thought and cognition (see Figure 10.1). These mediated abstractions, which are inherent in "higher-order" mental processes, Vygotsky argued, serve to allow for greater freedom in thought and expression. Vygotsky emphasized this point in his examination of the fundamental psychological differences between primates and young children:

> One important manifestation of this greater flexibility is that the child is able to ignore the direct line between actor and goal. Instead, he engages in a number of preliminary acts, using what we speak of as instrumental, or mediated (indirect), methods. In the process of solving a task the child is able to include stimuli that do not lie within the immediate visual field. Using words (one class of such stimuli) to create a specific plan, the child achieves a much broader range of activity, applying as tools not only those objects that lie near at hand, but searching for and preparing such stimuli as can be useful in the solution of the task, and planning future actions.
>
> (Vygotsky, 1978, p. 26)

Objects in the world fundamentally mediate – that is influence and shape – how people think and act. These objects, which include both physical tools like a measuring cup and sign-representations like symbolic variables in elementary algebra, are often integrated into a person's internal patterns of thought. A child learning how to subtract fractions, for instance, initially relies upon external representations like groups of blocks, but soon internalizes those representations and is able to perform such operations in her or his head.

CHAT (particularly as described later by Leontiev, 1978) emphasizes how objects and language are tied to broader collective action; indeed, particular notions of time (and watches) are tied to broader socio-cultural institutions that created the notion of a "second" and manufactured watches and steamships. In a related manner, Vygotsky argued that human thought is fundamentally a social phenomenon that achieves structure in children through the internalization of social norms and cultural practices. This social view of cognition was encapsulated by a famous Vygotskian formulation:

> Any function in the child's cultural development appears twice, or on two planes. First it appears on the social plane, and then on the psychological plane. First it appears between people as an interpsychological category, and then within the child as an intrapsychological category.
>
> (Vygotsky, 1981, p. 163)

Thus, Vygotsky points to social *interaction* between humans as the location of learning, rather than the lone, isolated individual. Learning, from this perspective is usually studied in "natural" situations, such as parent–child interactions rather than "constructed" environments, such as schools (acknowledging that parent–child interactions are also constructed). An important, related concept in Vygotsky's cultural-historical psychology is the notion of the *zone of proximal development* (or ZPD), which is,

> The difference between the actual developmental level as determined by independent problem solving and the level of potential development as determined through problem solving under ... guidance or collaboration with more capable peers.
>
> (Vygotsky, 1981, p. 86)

Restated, ZPD is the theoretical range of what a performer can do with competent peers and assistance, as compared with what can be accomplished on one's own. A classic example of the ZPD is considering how parents engage in joint activity with children that are on the upward edge of their competence (including conversation). Parents quite naturally adjust tasks, guidance, and feedback so that children are constantly achieving success, and gradually learning to function independently (Conner, Knight & Cross, 1997; Gauvain, 2001).

Second-Generation CHAT

The "second generation" of work in CHAT was in fact the period in which activity theory became distinct from traditional cultural-historical psychology. The Kharkov school of Russian psychology, a group of Vygotsky's students led after his passing by A. N. Leontiev, began to revise the extant understandings of Vygotskyan psychology with an eye toward a) understanding human thought in *practice*; and b) producing a more *materialist* account of human thought (Leontiev, 1978). Leontiev, like Vygotsky, considered himself a Marxist, and accordingly wanted to produce a framework for understanding cognition that accorded with Marx's emphasis on both the objective, material nature of the world and the way in which human thought is fundamentally linked to human *practice* (see Marx & Engels, 1998). Note that for Engeström (and indeed most activity theorists) second wave activity theory is an extension of Vygotsky's work (and perhaps an acknowledgment of themes that existed). Leontiev, in this way, sought to produce a material psychological account that understood human thought as a "social object" that is fundamentally part of the subjective practice of human activity.

Thought and cognition, in Leontiev's understanding, should be understood as a part of social life – as a part of the means of production and systems of social relations on one hand, and the intentions of individuals in certain social conditions on the other (Leontiev, 1978). Many contemporary frameworks like behaviorial and Pavlovian psychology understood mental processes only in terms of an immediate mental stimulus and an immediate response, ignoring the role that the social world and social history played in structuring thought. Activity theory, as Leontiev understood it, presented an alternative to the stimulus-response model. Leontiev argued that activity facilitated a dialogue between interior mental processes and the real, external social world, a theory he clearly and forcefully articulated in a short paper called "Activity and Consciousness":

> Thus in dealing with the problem of how consciousness is determined we are confronted with the following alternative, either to accept the view implied in the "axiom of immediacy", i.e., proceed from the "object-subject" pattern (or the "stimulus-response" pattern, which is the same thing), or to proceed from a pattern which includes a third, connecting link – the activity of the subject (and, correspondingly, its means and mode of appearance), a link which mediates their interconnections, that is to say, to proceed from the "subject-activity-object" pattern.
>
> In the most general form this alternative may be presented as follows. Either we take the stand that consciousness is directly determined by surrounding things and phenomena, or we postulate that consciousness is determined by being, which, in the words of Marx, is nothing else but the process of the actual life of people.
>
> (Leontiev, 1977, pp. 2–3)

Leontiev, then, understood thought and cognition as mediated not just by signs and objects, but also by the larger structures of activity in which they are embedded. Activity in such a framework should be the primary focus when studying human thought and cognition.

Yrjö Engeström (1987) articulated the clearest distinction between classic Vygotskian psychology, which emphasizes the way semiotic and cultural systems mediate human *action*, and Leontiev's second-generation CHAT, which is focused on the meditational effects of the systemic organization of human *activity*. CHAT is marked by an explicit emphasis on how collective activity – including the social institutions that co-constitute actions – characterizes experience (and hence thought and learning). Engeström writes,

> The second generation of activity theory derived its inspiration largely from Leont'ev's work. In his famous example of "primeval collective hunt" Leont'ev (1981, pp. 210–213) explicated the crucial difference between an individual action and a collective activity. The distinction between activity, action and operation became the basis of Leont'ev's three-level model of activity. The uppermost level of collective activity is driven by an object-related motive; the middle level of individual (or group) action is driven by a conscious goal; and the bottom level of automatic operations is driven by the conditions and tools of the action at hand. However, Leont'ev never graphically expanded Vygotsky's original model into a model of a collective activity system.
>
> (Engeström, 1987, p. 78)

Engeström's now famous graphic depiction of second-generation activity theory expands the unit of analysis to include collective motivated activity toward an object (or goal), which makes room for understanding how social groups (collective action) mediate activity.

Engeström's graphic depiction of Leontiev's theory (Figure 10.2) has become so synonymous with CHAT more generally (perhaps because it provides a useful graphic organizer for crystallizing multi-layered, complex phenomena) that it is worth explicating further. A key addition to understanding how it builds on Vygotsky's socio-cultural model of learning is how it transforms the notion of *object*. The object in CHAT is profoundly historically and culturally situated. Rather than describing the chopping of trees in abstract terms, activity theorists are very interested in human collective action in particular cultural and historical terms (the C and H in CHAT). For an activity theorist, how and why forests are being cleared are crucially important for understanding it as goal-directed action, and thus, a meaningful unit of analysis might be logging practices in Eastern Tennessee in the mid-19th century. This object (transforming the landscape) would be understood in terms of particular subjects

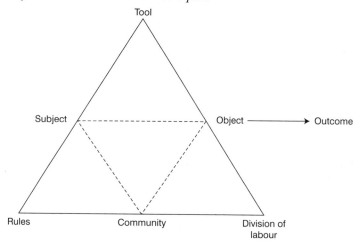

Figure 10.2. Engeström's (1987) diagram of second-generation CHAT

(logging companies and loggers, more about contradictions between such groups in third-generation CHAT), tools they employ, and the broader social context.

This social context, or notion of the collective and how it mediates activity is a second profound evolution in second-generation CHAT. The social layer of mediation tries to capture: 1) how social structures – including formal and informal rules (logging regulations or local customs about trees) mediate activity, and 2) how divisions of labor mediate activity. In the case of logging, today we primarily have lumberjacks and truck drivers, but mid-19th-century American logging might have included increased specialization such as whistle punks, buckers, and fallers. In both cases, one might also include various industrialists, bankers, lobbyists, and so on who mediate activity. The result of this collective activity is a transformation of the object, which leads to *outcomes* (wood, deforested land, perhaps profit).

One of the strengths of CHAT is how it enables researchers to look for *contradictions* in an activity system that will drive its evolution. To extend our logging example, one might imagine how new transportation devices such as gas-powered vehicles transformed logging, enabling loggers to access new lands. One can use this notion of contradictions to examine how new tools (like chainsaws, steam engines and gas-powered vehicles) transform formal and informal rules (such as leading to legislative restrictions on how areas are clear cut or how industrial waste is disposed of) and new divisions of labor as new technologies make old jobs like muleskinners obsolete.

How and why logging has anything to do with learning may seem opaque, but consider how such an analysis might be turned toward a classroom or school. An analyst might examine a high school in Madison, WI, and see that the object is to transform subjects (students) to becoming adults prepared to enter the workforce, college, and participate in a democratic republic. The *outcomes* might be graduation rates (or perhaps even learning). *Tools* (textbooks, chalkboards, tables, desks, paper, pencils) might be employed to facilitate this transformation. *Formal and informal rules* (attendance and grading policies, as well as informal rules such as ways of denoting respect toward teachers) mediate these outcomes, as do *divisions of labor* (teachers, administrators, school boards, students).

These components of an activity system are all dependent upon the hierarchical structure of activity that Leontiev described. Any activity system, in other words, is composed of three different levels of scales of activity-related processes: activity, actions and operations (Leontiev, 1978). These three levels of a system can be described thus:

> Activities are oriented to motives, that is, the objects that are impelling by themselves. Each motive is an object, material or ideal, that satisfies a need. Actions are the processes functionally subordinated to activities; they are directed at specific conscious goals. According to activity theory, the dissociation between objects that motivate human activity and the goals to which this activity is immediately directed is of fundamental significance. Actions are realized through operations that are determined by the actual conditions of activity.
>
> (Kaptelinin, 1996, p. 55)

CHAT attempts to capture how these components and levels of an activity system all evolve in coordination with one another, driven by systems' inherent need to resolve *contradictions*. Thus, one can see how CHAT provides one set of analytic tools for understanding how the American High School has largely been so resilient (see Tyack, 1974), despite attempts to introduce new tools (televisions, computers) or divisions of labor (reading specialists, class sizes) without fundamentally rethinking the activity system.

Third-Generation CHAT

Attempting to apply a CHAT analysis to a school reveals a limitation of second-generation CHAT: from whose perspective is the system being analyzed, how are boundaries around activity systems conceptualized, and how do we reconcile these without reifying problematic power relations? Returning to the example of school, who defines the object of the activity system? How do students conceptualize the object? How do teachers or parents, and how do we reconcile how one group might state the goals of a system (participate in a democratic republic) with what *actually* occurs? These questions lie at the heart of the field of inquiry known as third-generation CHAT, which is the generation in which the use of the term CHAT first emerged (see Engeström, 1987; Kuutti, 1996; Kaptelinin, 1996; Nardi, 1996b; Cole & Engeström, 2007). Engeström (1987) describes the contradictions *between* constituents in an activity system as secondary contradictions (as opposed to the primary contradictions between the components of an activity system). Because the determination of whose voices are heard in an analysis has deep ethical and cultural implications, the third generation of CHAT is focused on developing "conceptual tools to understand dialogue, multiple perspectives, and networks of interacting activity systems" (Engeström, 2001, p. 135).

A second, related important characteristic of third-generation CHAT is a deeper move toward the social and cultural. Rather than talk about "a high school in Madison, WI", third-generation CHAT has begun to describe a particular high school (such as Madison High East) at a particular time (say the spring of 2011) with a specific set of social norms and cultural practices. Grounding an analysis in particular time, place and socio-cultural context enables CHAT researchers to make much more specific claims about constituent groups, and even for constituent groups to co-define them themselves. This approach, which we call the *deep historical approach* is typified by Engeström and Middleton's (1998) work examining health facilities or office environments, Brown and Cole's (2002) work with the 5th Dimension in libraries and schools, or even Etienne Wenger's analogous work with communities of practice among claims workers (Wenger, 1999), which is not strictly activity theory but shares deep affinities with the core approach. Researchers conducting such studies employ ethnographic data collection methods such as interviewing and observations, as well as historical methods of document gathering and analysis to understand the particulars of an activity system from multiple perspectives.

CHAT: Characteristics and Caveats

This third generation of activity theory has been the generation in which most work employing learning technologies has been done, and will subsequently be the basis for the remainder of the chapter. As Engeström describes, the bulk of this work has applied the CHAT framework through empirical studies, using it to illuminate findings about human activity systems, and adjusting the underlying theory accordingly. Before turning to such an analysis, we highlight five characteristics of CHAT as a theoretical foundation of learning environments to guide the reader. CHAT is unusual in that it is not a learning theory (per se), not an instructional theory, and certainly not an instructional-design theory. Rather, researchers employing CHAT use it as a tool for understanding learning, refining instruction, and suggesting directions for instructional design. We return to these in the conclusions, but present them here so as to circumvent any potential misunderstandings.

1. *CHAT is an analytic tool, not a prescriptive theory that prescribes particular forms of instruction.* As an outgrowth of Vygotskian social psychology, CHAT makes particular claims about learning, namely that we learn through social interaction, and thus learning is most powerful when people are engaged in joint activities with peers (especially when using a variety of tools and resources while engaged in activities of ever-increasing complexity). For this reason, many CHAT researchers are not especially interested in school-based learning. Schools traditionally sequester learning (students working independently), and operate according to a logic of *content* flowing from increasing layers of authority (federal government à state standards à textbooks à teachers) to students, who then re-present the information back up a chain of increasing authority culminating in validated tests (see Lemke, 1990; Leander & Lovvorn, 2006). Indeed, CHAT can be used to illuminate issues in such systems, such as that learning technologies like constructionist tools that require individual autonomy and value creative expression will be rejected from the system because they contradict the object of the system (and everything else in it, see Barab *et al.*, 2002; Collins & Halverson, 2009). Thus, CHAT does not necessarily prescribe how to design instruction, but is an analytic framework that can be applied to workplaces, schools, digital gaming communities, and so on.

2. *CHAT does not prescribe any particular research method, although as a theoretical tradition, CHAT's methods are often deeply cultural and historical.* CHAT is a theoretical framework, or a set of assumptions that a researcher makes that points his or her analytic lens toward a particular phenomenon (such as the contradictions in an activity system) and away from others (such as the mental inner workings of a student). CHAT does not, in and of itself prescribe any particular research method or methodology, and researchers such as Michael Cole, Jay Lemke, Yrjö Engeström, Bonnie Nardi, Sasha Barab, and ourselves have employed a variety of research techniques within CHAT studies. However, because CHAT involves understanding the interplay among subjects, tools, communities and the objects they transform, CHAT analyses typically employ cultural methods such as ethnography (participant observation, interviews, interaction analysis) and historical analysis (oral histories, document analysis, archival analysis).

Many affiliated scholars are hostile to the notion of prescribing or standardizing methods for CHAT-based research, because of their deep belief that research methods need to emerge from the context being studied. Drawing on Hegel's work on the phenomenology of mind, Engeström argues that "the substantive theory and the methods of study are genetically intertwined, not separate. Methods should be developed or 'derived' from the substance, as one enters and penetrates deeper into the object of study" (Engeström, 1993, p. 99). In other words CHAT scholars commonly hold that there are no "silver bullet" methods that can be applied to any context, but rather that the methods used have to suit both the question being asked and the context in which it is asked. As such, there are many methods like ethnography and formative experiments that are commonly used in CHAT research, but none that are formally prescribed or recognized (Kaptelinin & Nardi, 1997). CHAT is not, however, a methodological free-for-all, as there are shared methodological beliefs in most CHAT research. For example, Nardi (1996b) describes some of the key methodological implications of CHAT for the study of human–computer interaction:

- A research time frame long enough to understand users' objects, including, where appropriate, changes in objects over time and their relation to the objects of others in the setting studied.
- Attention to broad patterns of activity rather than narrow episodic fragments that fail to reveal the overall direction and import of an activity.
- The use of a varied set of data collection techniques including interviews, observations, video, and historical materials, without undue reliance on any one method (such as video).
- A commitment to understanding things from the users' points of view, as in, for example, Holland and Reeves (this volume). (Excerpt from Nardi, 1996b)

As such, although CHAT endorses a methodological pluralism, as a theory it has methodological commitments that are shared across the field of researchers. These methodological commitments grow out of CHAT's emphasis on the systematic nature of activity, historicity, multi-vocality, and dialogic processes (Engeström, 2001).

3. *CHAT, as a research approach, is a structured and ideationally-driven approach in the sense that researchers use theoretical assumptions to understand human activity.* CHAT shares affinity with critical design ethnography (Barab *et al.* 2004), both of which bring strong theoretical frameworks to inquiry and use them to illuminate issues, in direct contrast to approaches like grounded theory, which seek to *remove* pre-existing models and find theory "in the data" (cf. Glaser & Strauss, 1967). Activity theory is strongly driven by the existing theoretical constructs and models that are used to describe systems of activity, actions and operations (Bakhurst, 2009; Engeström, 2001). Engeström (2001) for example, prescribes a fairly specific approach to understanding activity and expansive learning (see Figure 10.3), detailing a matrix for analyzing learning that touches on different precepts in activity theory.

Engeström here prescribes a framework for analyzing learning and activity, instructing researchers to focus on activity systems as a unit of

	Activity system as unit of analysis	Multi-voicedness	Historicity	Contradictions	Expansive cycles
Who are learning?					
Why do they learn?					
What do they learn?					
How do they learn?					

Figure 10.3 Matrix for the analysis of expansive learning (Engeström, 2001)

analysis, the multivoicedness and historicity of those activity systems, the contradictions embedded within them that exist in a dialectic relationship, and the cycles of expansive and transformative learning that take place. In such a way, Engeström, like most third-generation CHAT theorists, has a strong theoretical model that he brings to analysis, unlike methodologies that strive to avoid generalizable theories and models (e.g. Garfinkel, 1967; Glaser & Strauss, 1967).

Engeström's emphasis on the importance of general theoretical models is almost universal in the CHAT literature. Time and again, CHAT scholarship emphasizes the importance of building general analytic tools and models of activity to use in different settings, while acknowledging the importance of context to adjusting those tools and models. In a paper introducing CHAT to scholars in computer-supported collaborative work (CSCW) and human–computer interaction (HCI), for example, Kuutti and Arvonen (1992) provide a strongly prescriptive model for understanding the relationship between actors (e.g. software users) and information technology "support systems" (see Figure 10.4). This typology of the relationships between actors and support systems is characteristic of the strong emphasis on hypothesis and shared theoretical frameworks in CHAT. In these respects, CHAT is closely related to positivist positions in the social sciences, as its research questions are driven by theory, and seek to improve upon theory, although positivists may or may not acknowledge their ideologies and governing assumptions.

Role of a person towards the support system in an activity

Area of support	Pre-determined	Active	Expansive
Instrument	Routine automation	Tool	Automation or tool construction
Rules	Control	Shared meanings	Rule construction, negotiation
Divsion of labour	Fixed, 'forced coordination'	Mutual coordination	Organizing work
Subject 'thinking'	Triggering of a predetermined action	Searching information	Learning, understanding
Object	Data	Shared material	Object construction
Community	Fixed hierarchy/ network (invisible)	Malleable visible network	Community construction

Figure 10.4 The range of relationships between an actor and a support system in an activity (Kuutti & Arvonen, 1992, p. 236)

4. *Underlying CHAT is an interactionist epistemology, meaning that for CHAT researchers, learning and knowledge are inseparable from context.* For a CHAT researcher, the minimal meaningful unit of analysis is a person engaged in an activity with tools and resources in some social context. With roots in Vygotsky, knowing is, for CHAT researchers, *action* (to quote Wertsch, 1998), meaning that knowledge arises through an interaction among tools, resources, people, and extant social structures (including everything from language to cultural models to overt rules). Building on the work of Hutchins (1995), and Pea (1993), for CHAT theorists and researchers, knowledge is stretched across material tools (such as notes) and conversations (which trigger different situations and ways of being). CHAT researchers generally reject the symbolic, information-processing model of the mind, which assumes that information can be "stored" free from language, culture, or situation, and can be "recalled" reliably independently of situation. More often, CHAT researchers embrace metaphors of the mind as a rhizome (see Cunningham, 1998), semiotics as a neural network (see Gee, 1992), or as simulator grounded in embodied experiences (Barsalou, 1999; Gee, 1992; Glenberg & Robertson, 2000). Regardless of which metaphor one employs, many CHAT researchers come from the non-symbolic processing tradition, maintaining that knowing is action, manifests itself

through social activity, and is co-comprised of tools, language and social interactions.

5. *Finally, embedded within CHAT is a* conflict-driven theory of change *in which evolution occurs through* contradictions *embedded in a system.* CHAT is grounded in the intellectual tradition of dialectical materialism, with its notions of change driven by contradictions owing much to the German philosophers Hegel and Marx. One of the core principles of CHAT is the "central role of contradictions as sources of change and development", which are defined as "historically accumulating structural tensions within and between activity systems" (Engeström, 2001, p. 137). While contradictions lead to conflicts and perturbations within activity systems, they also lead to innovation in and transformation of the activity system. To be sure, it is beyond the scope of this introduction to provide a thorough accounting for the nature of contradictions in CHAT or to trace the notion of contradictions through Hegelian and Marxist philosophical thought. However, we argue that central to CHAT is this notion that through tracing contradictions, one can trace the evolution of historical systems and identify ways in which they are coming-to-be. We find this notion of contradictions to be quite useful irrespective of CHAT or Marxist thought more generally; however, researchers should be aware that this approach differs from the utopian or other theories of social change.

CHAT in Learning Technologies

Vygotsky was responding to behaviorism and the traditional psychoanalysis / introspection, both of which treated the individual (or arguably the person plus stimulus) as the meaningful unit of analysis, but in the late 1980s, Vygotsky's social psychology gained renewed attention for its capacity to respond to new critiques of cognitive science's view of the mind. The symbolic processing model, which largely dominated the first 30 years of cognitive psychology, treated knowing as a process of information inputs (through the senses), information processing (in the brain), information storage (knowing is a function of memory), and then information retrieval and recall (see Derry & Steinkuehler, 2006; Gardner, 1987). Several inter-related changes in understandings of the mind led to this so-called "social turn", including the realization that the senses actively construct information (see Gibson, 1979); that knowledge is profoundly embodied, tied to our senses and experiences (see Glenberg & Robertson, 2000); that knowledge is constructed individually and uniquely through experience (von Glasersfeld, 1996); that knowledge is co-constituted by tools (material and cultural, see Gee, 1992; Pea, 1991); that knowledge is created through social processes (particularly communities that legitimize ways of knowing; Scardamalia & Bereiter, 1994); and that knowledge is reconstituted through social practices that are tied to broader social, cultural, historical (and thus inherently political) concerns (Lave & Wenger, 1991). In short, old models viewed the mind as a digital computer, and a wave of cognitive science research demonstrated the shortcomings of this view.

As cognitive scientists (and later learning technologists) adopted what might be broadly described as a *socially-situated* view of cognition, Vygotsky's socio-cultural psychology provided an intellectual tradition in which learning is studied not only through laboratory experiments, but also through investigating learning in complex, everyday environments (see Anderson, Reder & Simon, 1996; Derry & Steinkuehler, 2006; DeVane *et al.*, 2009; Gee, 2000/2004; Greeno, 1997; Hutchins, 1995; Kirshner & Whitson, 1997; Moss, Pullin, Gee, Haertel, & Young, 2005; Wertsch, 1998). As Cole (1996) described, this movement toward Vygotsky's cultural psychology sought to return culture back to the center of the study of human cognition, as it was for Vygotsky (and perhaps Dewey). A host of groundbreaking studies typifying this approach emerged from this period such as Walkerdine's (1990) study of Mexican chiclet salespeople, Goody *et al.*'s (1977) study of learning through apprenticeship among Vai tailors, or Lave's (1988) study of weight watchers' participants. Lave and Wenger's (1991) *Legitimate Peripheral Participation* synthesized these studies and described learning through the metaphor of participation (as opposed to acquisition), arguing that in much of human activity, learning occurs through social processes in which newcomers become increasingly central to legitimate social practices.

Within this context, CHAT gained popularity as a framework for conceptualizing learning in such spaces. Michael Cole's 5th Dimension project, an after-school technology-enhanced learning environment, is one of the most influential examples of a Vygotskian-inspired learning design in which CHAT was used to iteratively understand and refine the program (see Cole, 2006). In the 5th Dimension, children voluntarily attend after-school computer clubs designed to support literacy development (defined broadly). The 5th Dimension is a network of activities ranging from digital games to reading stories, tied together through a fantastic maze that embeds curricular goals within it. By design, 5th Dimension is decentralized, non-linear, designed to appeal to broad tastes, and meant to facilitate learning through interaction. Also by design, 5th Dimension sites pull in community members (particularly pre-service teachers) to serve as peers and mentors for children.

5th Dimension: CHAT-Based Design

The 5th Dimension (5thD) is one of the most thoroughly researched learning technology interventions to date, with perhaps over 100 publications on it performed with a variety of approaches (see Cole, 2006; Mayer, Schustack & Blanton, 1999). Many insights were gained from this body of research, but one of the most important from a CHAT perspective was the limitations of a particular intervention (such as 5thD) to create its own unique activity system. As one of the local enactors of 5thD described,

> The original 5thD was developed by adults who had a strong theory about learning and development, strong culturally-based views of what children should learn, and well established patterns of interacting with children and with other adults. Other adults in other environments have different views, different goals, different theories. At the (local) YMCA it seems important to the adults (parents, directors, counselors) that children learn manners, deference, obedience. It is important that they use tools and other equipment "the right way".
> (Brown & Cole, 2002, no page)

This analysis is a classic kind of CHAT analysis; one group of subjects (Cole and colleagues who designed 5thD) envisioned learners and mentors working together with adults in joint activity in open-ended tasks that honored their interest. In contrast, local subjects enacting the program held a model of childhood in which children need to be inculcated with values (the object of the activity system). Understanding these contradictions among different subjects and objects enabled researchers to understand how the program should evolve.

A finding from these 5thD enactments is that an intervention alone does not constitute its own new activity system (or at least 5thD did not). Rather educational interventions (from Read 180 to Digital Games) are more akin to tools that subjects appropriate in their effort to transform objects. Note, however that the arrows between components in activity systems go both ways, suggesting that tools can under certain conditions create contradictions that push activity systems toward new objects. Elsewhere, we have argued that mobile phones may be one such tool (particularly if students come with them to school, see Squire & Dikkers, in review). However, the idea of creating entirely new activity systems within broader nested systems (such as after school clubs) has proven to be thus far unattainable (cf. Squire *et al.*, 2003). Rather, through cycles of design – research – redesign that identify contradictions and introduce changes that might resolve them (ranging from tools to new divisions of labor), learning technologists might be able to better understand activity systems and how to design new ones more in accordance with their goals.

CHAT as a Framework when Redesigning a University Course

Barab and colleagues (2002) used CHAT in a similar vein to examine students' learning in the Virtual Solar System (VSS) Project. VSS investigated what happened when instructors, researchers, and learning scientists collaboratively redesigned a lecture-based university course, *Introduction to the Solar System*, to emphasize learning astronomy through developing 3D models. Researchers observed and video-recorded students throughout the duration of the course, enabling researchers to make more robust claims about the inter-relationship between *individual actions* and *collective activity* over longer timescales. For example, using micro-level analyses, researchers demonstrated how concepts such as scaling, which was an object of early activity, was produced and then mobilized as a tool. Theoretically, this study contributed an understanding of the *fractal* nature of actions and activities within activity systems, suggesting how educational researchers can connect individual and group action to collective activity to show how understandings emerge in situ and then are mobilized as tools for future action.

Yet, as in Cole's 5thD work, the analytic power of CHAT may be in its capacity to illuminate *contradictions* that drove change in the system. Early in the course, a contradiction between learning to build 3D models vs. learning astronomy arose as a primary contradiction within the *object* of the activity system. Students and instructors alike wanted activity to focus on transforming participants' understandings of astronomy, but the opacity of the 3D modeling tools made *learning to build 3D models* the object driving activity. When presented with this analysis, instructors created new initial assignments (formal rules) that introduced the tool more gradually, which enabled the system to evolve toward *learning astronomy*. Other contradictions were noted in *divisions of labor*. Students were required to work in groups, but the instructor and university grade individually (with grades being consequential toward other activities). Further, resources such as the instructor that were not directly useful for transforming the *object* (whether it be learning the tool or building models) were rejected for tools that did. For example, the instructor delivered many thoughtful mini-lectures on the history of astronomy, which, while researchers found them quite fascinating, students who were consumed with building models rejected as less useful.

It is worth pausing to ask what analytic power CHAT might purchase a researcher that simple case studies do not. After all, if a complex 3D modeling tool is introduced into an astronomy course, is it not commonsensical that problems would arise? Is it not understood that grading systems need to be designed to balance learning, group dynamics, and broader concerns?

Indeed, CHAT is not the only method that could detect such patterns nor suggest solutions to them, but (part of) its analytic power is in providing a ready framework for detecting, describing, anticipating, and considering the ramifications of them. In the case of the complex 3D modeling tool, CHAT encouraged researchers to frame the problem *not* simply as a matter of the tool being too *complex*, but as a mismatch among current assignments, rules, and tools. Perhaps more importantly, it asks researchers and instructors to *embrace* such contradictions as the drivers of change in a system. Rather than "throw out" the program because

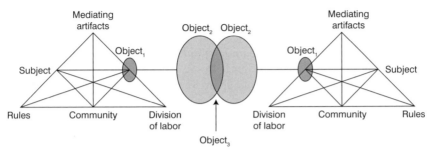

Figure 10.5 Activity systems in dialogue (Engeström, 2001)

of conflicts, or even look for simple answers, it requires researchers to step back and examine the system as a whole, which includes considering the object of the system as it was designed and as it was experienced for various subject groups. CHAT provides researchers – particularly design researchers – with an analytic lens for stepping back and examining their designed educational interventions as a whole to understand their quality and to suggest modifications. Critically, it requires researchers to examine not only their own goals as subjects in the system, but also different constituent groups, including different groups of students, administrators, teachers, and so on. Engeström (2001) seeks to capture this idea in Figure 10.5, a depiction that shows how CHAT researchers must examine how at least two different subject groups experience activity systems.

After the first full iteration of the Virtual Solar System Project, Barab and colleagues note several driving contradictions (see Figure 10.5) that characterize the course, and once again highlight the difficulty of introducing novel technologies with different embedded values into an activity system *even when the entire course was redesigned with the new pedagogy in mind*. Truly embracing a modeling-based curriculum meant several changes. The first was setting expectations of students-as-subjects. Most students entered the course expecting to be relatively passive recipients of information and expecting to transform their transcripts to have more credits that meet the university science requirements. Many students had some curiosity or interest in science, but even then, they were not expecting to be involved in an active model building community in which they learned in a self-directed manner through building and testing understandings. Similarly, this shift toward a modeling-based community drastically changed aspects of course participation that instructors had not intended. For example, Barab and colleagues found that whichever participant created the group inscriptions that specified how their model would be built generated the deepest understandings, because other participants were relegated to roles in which they implemented findings. Barab concludes by questioning the possibility of transforming such introductory classes given their function of generating revenue and sorting students within the broader university system.

CHAT Applied to Digital Media

Within the nascent field of digital media and learning, the role of CHAT is adapting, as researchers seek to understand how digitally-mediated affinity spaces function, and then design learning environments based on them. Within this paradigm (see Steinkuehler, Squire & Barab, 2011), the idea is that digital affinity spaces, such as video game communities are important sites of learning because 1) learning is interest (or passion) driven (Gee, 2003); 2) learning is driven by closed and open problem solving rather than memorization (Gee, 2005; Steinkuehler, 2006); 3) learners interact with peers of different ages and ability levels, enabling the broadening of weak social ties (Steinkuehler, 2005); 4) learners marshal a variety of tools in the service of game play (Steinkuehler & Duncan, 2009); and 5) learning is supported through robust networks of just-in-time learning (DeVane *et al.*, 2010). Although few researchers have formally applied third-generation CHAT as Engeström or Barab might, games researchers such as Gee, Steinkuehler, or Squire have used case study or discourse methods to employ socio-cultural similar analyses.

As an example of what such a research paradigm might look like, consider Apolyton University, an online community of digital game players nested within the Apolyton.net community. This brief description draws from more in depth, previously published research articles (Squire & Giovanetto, 2008; Squire, 2011). Apolyton University is an online informal "university" started by players of the game *Civilization III* in the early 2000s. *Civilization III* (or *Civ3*) is a popular digital turn-based strategy game in which players lead a civilization for 6,000 years by gathering resources, building cities, and negotiating with other computer-controlled players. The University formed when Theseus, a veteran player, wanted to sharpen his skills, find a community to learn with and from, and prepare for an upcoming expansion pack which would enable online collaborative and competitive play.

The core community came from the Apolyton.net site. They had previously participated in a "best of the best" activity in which players used stock editing tools to "rewrite" the rules so as to produce the most playable, accurate, well-balanced game possible. In short, they were unsatisfied with the stock game as it came "out-of-the-box" and wanted to fix it. The fact that *Civ3* ships with an editor that enables players to rewrite its rules made this possible.

Within a few weeks, the community grew to a few hundred player-students. Players designed courses around themes, such as "Give Peace a Chance," the course that requires players to win without waging war. In each course, players downloaded a common saved game file (created with the editor), took notes on their play, took screenshots illustrating their play, and posted these notes and screenshots in the form of During-Action-Reports. Most reports followed a format of posting a short narrative to recap the action, posing a question to the community of players related to what they were working on, and reporting the basic descriptive statistics from their game (rate of population and economic growth, and so on).

Soon, dozens of courses emerged. The University formed its own curricular committee to establish core courses and identify what needed to be learned. Soren Johnson of Firaxis games, who was the lead programmer on *Civ3* joined and posed new challenges to the community, such as reverse engineering the algorithm behind barbarian uprisings. They even went so far as to elect a Dean.

After about 18 months, interest in the University waned. In part, the community had exhausted *Civ3*'s possibilities. There was, in one participant's words, not much else to learn. But also, the community dispersed in part because they were recruited to help build *Civ4*, the sequel to *Civ3*. Soren Johnson, now the lead designer of *Civ4* was so impressed with Apolyton that he recruited about 100 "beta testers" to create their own "best of the best" activity in which they would improve *Civ4* just as they had *Civ3*. Eventually several players were hired to work full time at Firaxis.

If we apply a cursory CHAT analysis, we might consider students such as Theseus as *subjects* who participated in this activity so as to transform themselves into more adept Civ players in order to experience pleasure, be challenged, develop skills, and perhaps expand their social networks (see Figure 10.5). They employed a variety of *tools* to do so, including the game and its editor, but also a variety of modeling tools developed by the community, such as the Civ3MultiTool (developed by Gramphos) which enables players to edit saved games, fan-generated tutorials which explain how to edit the game's rules or graphics, and fan-generated art packs (created with a variety of tools such as PhotoShop). The community also developed *conceptual tools*, such as REXing, or Alex's Archer Rush, which were known strategies developed by the community and employed in various situations. The community created a glossary to explain knowledge learned in the community that had been codified into new terminology. These physical and conceptual tools were *outcomes* of the activity system that were continuously fed back into the system.

The community, although emergent, generated *formal* and *informal* *rules* to mediate participation. They created formal processes for proposing and approving courses, although they remained quite open, in that *anyone* could propose or participate in a course. Informal rules emerged governing how participants interacted. Most posts were responded to within 2–5 hours. Informal rules governing behavior, such as a reluctance to discuss current events or politics, emerged as well, as this International community of players held divergent views toward current events such as the Iraq War. As a result, players tended to discuss the game as a game within Apolyton without using it as a tool to talk through current events (although many were eager to do so in private). Using the game to talk about history was more common, although many players drew sharp distinctions between historically accurate scenarios (which many of them built) and the entertainment play at Apolyton. Even within this voluntary, ad hoc organization, labor was divided among Committees and Deans helped tend to the overall health of the community, tending to requests for content, tools, or new experiences. In the course of our year-long study, 174 players participated in the University.

Through this brief account, we get a snapshot of Apolyton University as an activity system. Contradictions drove activity in the space – players' desire to improve their skills and improve the game led to the creation of new mods and new structures, until players felt as if they were complete. At the end, as players themselves transformed, many entered new activity systems, namely beta testing the game design, and in the case of some, securing new employment as full-time game-designers. As learning technologists, we were intrigued by the rapidity with which new knowledge and *tools* were generated and fed back into the system (as well as into other game communities) and the degree to which players transformed themselves as *objects*. In comparison to school, the enterprise appeared quite *generative* in that the system generated new outcomes that fed back into other systems. This generativity was born out of a dialectical relationship between the community of users on the Apolyton forums, the tools (message board systems, game modding tools, game system, etc.) that were used to support the activity of the community, the object of the community's activity, and the acts undertaken by the individual subjects within that community. Outside the immediate scope of the activity system, this generativity was also born out of the dialogue that this activity system entered into with a number of other activity systems. Learning and activity in Apolyton resulted from the activity of a community working with a specific set of tools toward agreed-upon ends.

Conclusion: Using CHAT to Design Learning Technologies

At the most basic level, CHAT forwards that "an activity is a form of doing directed toward an object and activities are distinguished from one another by their objects" (Kuutti, 1996, p. 26). Activity, in other words, consists of a person or persons doing something toward some end. Learning, accordingly, is strongly linked to this doing, the end to be accomplished in the doing, the tools used in the doing, and the social system in which the doing takes place. Learning technologies, according to CHAT, are not a medium that unproblematically transmits knowledge to a user, but rather a tool that structures and mediates the learning accomplished through activity. CHAT views learning technologies not as "teaching machines" but as a "support system" for learning through doing (see Kuutti & Arvonen, 1992). Learning is not only accomplished by observing, but also by doing, and learning technologies serve to support and structure that doing.

From its inception in the activity theory of Leontiev and the Kharkov school, CHAT has always sought to understand human thought not just as an abstract and symbolic phenomenon, but also as a thing that takes place – that is practiced – in the real everyday world. Its study of cognition in the world – in classrooms, in workplaces, in hospitals – leads it to understand both the importance of tools to learning activities and the importance of activity systems in shaping how tools and technologies help people learn. Neither learning nor learning technologies were understood as abstract and self-contained, but rather as phenomena with rich cultural histories of use that are embedded in larger social systems and undertaken/used by persons with different intentions and goals. Activity theory, in short, embraces understanding the complex and messy reality of learning with tools and technologies, rather than an idealized and formulaic abstraction that occurs in a laboratory.

Perhaps the most important benefit of activity theory is not that it situates learning technologies in ecologies of activity, but rather that it gives teachers, designers and scholars a systematic way to understand learning technologies as they function in the complexity and untidiness of the real world. Many an educator or instructional designer has come to the conclusion that the success of learning technologies depends on how they are actually used in a learning context, but it is often difficult to imagine what conclusions to draw from this understanding. What does it mean for the design of a learning technology that its success depends upon how, where and why it is used? Who cares if learning with technology is a messy real-world process if such a realization does not help its users learn? Activity theory answers these questions by providing learning technologists with a structure for understanding how learning with technology occurs with activity – its utility lies in its ability to provide a formal grammar for understanding the "buzzing, blooming confusion" (James, 1981, p. 462) of learning in the real world.

References

Anderson, J. R., Reder, L. M., & Simon, H. A. (1996). Situated learning and education. *Educational Researcher, 25*(4), 5.

Bakhurst, D. (2009). Reflections on activity theory. *Educational Review, 61*(2), 197–210.

Barab, S., Thomas, M., Dodge, T., Squire, K., & Newell, M. (2004). Critical Design Ethnography: Designing for Change. Anthropology & Education Quarterly, 35(2), 254–268.

Barab, S. A., Barnett, M., Yamagata-Lynch, L., Squire, K., & Keating, T. (2002). Using activity theory to understand the systemic tensions characterizing a technology-rich introductory astronomy course. *Mind, Culture, and Activity, 9*(2), 76–107.

Barsalou, L. (1999). Perceptual symbol systems. *Behavioral and Brain Sciences*, 22(04), 577–660.

Brown, K., & Cole, M. (2002). Cultural historical activity theory and the expansion of opportunities for learning after school. In G. Wells & G. Claxton (Eds.), *Learning for life in the 21st century: Sociocultural perspectives on the future of education* (pp. 225–238). New York: Blackwell.

Cole, M. (1996). *Cultural Psychology: A Once and Future Discipline*. Cambridge: Harvard University Press.

Cole, M. (2006). *The Fifth Dimension: An after-school program built on diversity*. New York: Russell Sage Foundation.

Cole, M., & Engeström, Y. (2007). Cultural-historical approaches to designing for development. *The Cambridge handbook of sociocultural psychology*, 484–507.

Collins, A., & Halverson, R. (2009). *Rethinking education in the age of technology: The digital revolution and schooling in America*. New York: Teacher's College Press.

Conner, D. B., Knight, D. K., & Cross, D. R. (1997). Mothers' and fathers' scaffolding of their 2-year-olds during problem-solving and literacy interactions. *British Journal of Developmental Psychology*, 15(3), 323–338.

Cunningham, D. J. (1998). Cognition as semiosis. *Theory & Psychology*, 8(6), 827

Derry, S. J., & Steinkuehler, C. A. (2006). Cognitive and situative theories of learning and instruction. *Encyclopedia of Cognitive Science*. New York: John Wiley & Sons.

Dewey, J. (1938). *Logic: The Theory of Inquiry*. New York: Henry Holt and Company.

DeVane, B., Durga, S., & Squire, K. (2009). Competition as a driver for learning. *International Journal of Learning and Media*, 1(2). Retrieved from http://dx.doi.org/10.1162/ijlm.2009.0018

DeVane, B., Durga, S., & Squire, K. (2010). "Economists who think like ecologists": Reframing systems thinking in games for learning. *E-Learning and Digital Media*, 7(1), 3–20.

Engeström, Y. (1987). *Learning by expanding: An activity-theoretical approach to developmental research*. Orienta-Konsultit Oy.

Engeström, Y. (1993). Developmental studies of work as a testbench of activity theory: The case of primary care medical practice. *Understanding Practice: Perspectives on activity and context*, 64–103.

Engeström, Y. (1999). Activity theory and individual and social transformation. In Y. Engeström, R. Punamäki-Gitai, R. Miettinen, & R. Punamäki (Eds.), *Perspectives on activity theory* (pp. 19–38). Cambridge: Cambridge University Press.

Engeström, Y. (2001). Expansive learning at work: Toward an activity theoretical reconceptualization. *Journal of Education and Work*, 14(1), 133–156.

Engeström, Y., & Middleton, D. (Eds.). (1998). *Cognition and communication at work*. New York: Cambridge University Press.

Gardner, H. (1987). *The mind's new science: A history of the cognitive revolution*. New York: Basic Books.

Garfinkel, H. (1967). *Studies in ethnomethodology*. Englewood Cliffs, NJ: Prentice-Hall.

Gauvain, M. (2001). *The social context of cognitive development*. New York: Guilford Press.

Gee, J. (1992). *The social mind: Language, ideology, and social practice.* New York: Bergin & Garvey.

Gee, J. (2000). The new literacy studies and the "social turn". In D. Barton, M. Hamilton, & J. Ivanic (Eds.), *Situated literacies: Reading and writing in context* (pp. 180–196). New York: Routledge.

Gee, J. P. (2003). *What video games have to teach us about learning and literacy.* New York: Palgrave Macmillan. Retrieved from http://www.amazon.com/Video-Games-Teach-Learning-Literacy/dp/1403961697.

Gee, J. (2005). Semiotic social spaces and affinity spaces. In D. Barton & K. Tusting (Eds.), *Beyond communities of practice: language power and social context* (pp. 214-232). Cambridge: Cambridge University Press.

Gibson, J. J. (1979). *The ecological approach to perception.* Boston: Houghton Mifflin.

Glaser, B., & Strauss, A. (1967). *The discovery of grounded theory: Strategies for qualitative research.* Chicago: Aldine.

Glenberg, A., & Robertson, D. (2000). Symbol grounding and meaning: A comparison of high-dimensional and embodied theories of meaning. *Journal of Memory and Language, 43*(3), 379–401.

Goody, J., Cole, M., & Scribner, S. (1977). Writing and formal operations: A case study among the Vai. *Africa: Journal of the International African Institute, 47*(3), 289–304.

Greeno, J. (1997). On claims that answer the wrong questions. *Educational Researcher, 26*(1), 5.

Hutchins, E. (1995). *Cognition in the wild.* Cambridge, MA: MIT Press.

James, W. (1981). *Principles of psychology.* Cambridge, MA: Harvard University Press.

Kaptelinin, V. (1996). Activity theory: implications for human–computer interaction. In B. A. Nardi (Ed.), *Context and consciousness: Activity theory and human–computer interaction* (pp. 103–116). Cambridge, MA: MIT Press.

Kaptelinin, V., & Nardi, B. A. (1997). Activity theory: Basic concepts and applications (pp. 158–159). Presented at the CHI'97 extended abstracts on Human factors in computing systems: looking to the future, ACM.

Kirshner, D., & Whitson, J. A. (1997). *Situated cognition: Social, semiotic, and psychological perspectives.* Mahwah, NJ: Lawrence Erlbaum.

Kozulin, A. (1986). Vygotsky in context. In A. Kozulin (Trans.), *Thought and language.* Cambridge, MA: MIT Press.

Kuutti, K. (1996). Activity theory as a potential framework for human–computer interaction research. In B. A. Nardi (Ed.), *Context and consciousness: Activity theory and human–computer interaction* (pp. 17–44).

Kuutti, K., & Arvonen, T. (1992). Identifying potential CSCW applications by means of activity theory concepts: A case example (pp. 233–240). *Proceedings of the 1992 ACM conference on Computer-supported Cooperative Work*, ACM.

Lave, J. (1988). *Cognition in practice: Mind, mathematics and culture in everyday life.* Cambridge: Cambridge University Press.

Lave, J., & Wenger, E. (1991). *Situated learning: Legitimate peripheral participation.* Cambridge: Cambridge University Press.

Leander, K. M., & Lovvorn, J. F. (2006). Literacy networks: Following the circulation of texts, bodies, and objects in the schooling and online gaming of one youth. *Cognition and Instruction, 24*(3), 291–340.

Lemke, J. (1990). *Talking science: Language, learning, and values*. Westport, CT: Ablex.

Leont'ev, A. N. (1981). *Problems of the development of the mind*. Moscow: Progress.

Leontiev, A. (1977). Activity and consciousness: Philosophy in the USSR, problems of dialectical materialism. In N. Schmolze & A. Blunden (Trans.), Moscow: Progress Publishers.

Leontiev, A. (1978). *Activity, consciousness, and personality* (M. Hall, Trans.), Englewood Cliffs, NJ: Prentice-Hall.

Luria, A. R. (1976). *Cognitive development, its cultural and social foundations*. Cambridge, MA: Harvard University Press.

Marx, K., & Engels, F. (1998). *The German ideology: including theses on Feuerbach and introduction to the critique of political economy*. Prometheus Books.

Mayer, R. E., Schustack, M. W., & Blanton, W. E. (1999). What do children learn from using computers in an informal, collaborative setting? *Educational Technology, 39*, 27–31.

Mead, G. H. (1934). *Mind, self and society*. Chicago: University of Chicago Press.

Moss, P. A., Pullin, D., Gee, J. P., & Haertel, E. H. (2005). The idea of testing: Psychometric and sociocultural perspectives. *Measurement: Interdisciplinary Research & Perspective, 3*(2), 63–83.

Nardi, B. (1996a). Studying context: A comparison of activity theory, situated action models, and distributed cognition. *Context and consciousness: Activity theory and human–computer interaction* (pp. 69–102). Cambridge, MA: MIT Press.

Nardi, B. A. (1996b). *Context and consciousness: activity theory and human–computer interaction*. Cambridge, MA: MIT Press.

Pea, R. (1993). Practices of distributed intelligence and designs for education. In G. Salomon (Ed.), *Distributed cognitions: Psychological and educational considerations* (pp. 47–87). Cambridge, UK: Cambridge University Press.

Peirce, C. S. (1998). Ed. N. Houser and C. J. W. Kloesel. Bloomington: Indiana University Press.

Scardamalia, M., & Bereiter, C. (1994). Computer support for knowledge-building communities. *Journal of the Learning Sciences, 3*(3), 265–283.

Squire, K. (2011). *Video games and learning: teaching and participatory culture in the digital age*. New York: Teachers College Press.

Squire, K., & Dikkers, S. (in review) *Amplifications of Learning: Use of Mobile Media Devices Among Youth*. Convergence.

Squire, K., & Giovanetto, L. (2008). The Higher Education of Gaming. *E-Learning, 5*(1), 2–28.

Squire, K. D., MaKinster, J. G., Barnett, M., Luehmann, A. L., & Barab, S. L. (2003). Designed curriculum and local culture: Acknowledging the primacy of classroom culture. *Science Education, 87*(4), 468–489.

Steinkuehler, C. A. (2006). Massively multiplayer online video gaming as participation in a discourse. *Mind, Culture, and Activity, 13*(1), 38–52.

Steinkuehler, C. A. , & Duncan, S. (2009). Informal scientific reasoning in online virtual worlds. *Journal of Science Education & Technology, 530*–543.

Tyack, D. B. (1974). *The one best system: A history of American urban education*. Cambridge, MA: Harvard University Press.

Van der Veer, R., & Valsineer, J. (1993). *Understanding Vygotsky: A quest for synthesis*. New York: Wiley-Blackwell.

Von Glasersfeld, E. (1996). *Radical constructivism: A way of knowing and learning*. New York: Routledge.

Vygotsky, L. S. (1978). *Mind in Society: Development of Higher Psychological Processes* (14th ed.). Cambridge, MA: Harvard University Press.

Vygotsky, L. S. (1979). The development of higher forms of attention in childhood. *Journal of Russian and East European Psychology*, *18*(1), 67–115.

Vygotsky, L. S. (1981). The development of higher forms of attention in childhood. In J. V. Wertsch (Ed.), *The Concept of Activity in Soviet Psychology*. Armonk, NY: Sharpe.

Walkerdine, V. (1990). Difference, cognition, and mathematics education. *For the Learning of Mathematics*, *10*(3), 51–56.

Wenger, E. (1999). *Communities of practice: Learning, meaning, and identity*. Cambridge: Cambridge University Press.

Wertsch, J. V. (1998). *Mind as action*. New York: Oxford University Press.

11 Learning Communities

Theoretical Foundations for Making Connections

Janette R. Hill

Unique as snowflakes, learning communities are formed in countless ways.
(Frazier, 2006, p. 21)

Introduction

Interest in creating a community to help facilitate and support learning has been a long-term interest for many educators seeking ways to enhance the learning experience for their students. This interest has ranged across time and disciplines, from business and industry (Lave & Wenger, 1991), to multiculturalism in educational settings (Nieto, 1999), as well as across technologies that enable communities to form in face-to-face environments (see, for example, Greyling & Wentzel, 2007), and online contexts (see, for example, Tu, Blocher, & Roberts, 2008). The concept has received particular attention in educational circles, especially with the growth in online learning. Palloff and Pratt (2004) were among the first authors to write about creating a community in online learning environments with interest continuing to grow with the growth of social networking tools in the last decade (see, for example, Burgess, 2009).

While creating learning communities remains an on-going interest for many, the formation of the communities remains an on-going challenge. Jonassen (1995) indicated that creating a learning community was one of the primary pedagogical challenges facing any educational setting. This challenge has been echoed more recently, particularly for creating learning environments online (Tu, Blocher, & Roberts, 2008; Burgess, 2009). Another challenge can be found in defining *community* and *learning community*. In the next section, I set a foundation for the rest of the chapter by providing operational definitions.

Defining Community and Learning Community

Communities and *learning communities* have been defined in a variety of ways. On a very fundamental level, *community* may refer to a physical or virtual space; it can also refer to a social group (e.g., club, organization).

An early definition was provided by Manning, Curtis, and McMillen (1996): a community "can tap levels of emotion and energy that otherwise remain dormant" (p. 3). As stated by Komito (1998), "community is rarely defined other than in a sort of 'we all sort of know what one is' way" (p. 97). Komito then goes on to provide a definition of community: "A community is not fixed in form or function, but is a mixed bag of possible options whose meanings and concreteness are always being negotiated by individuals, in the context of changing external constraints" (p. 105).

Learning community also has several definitions. Komito's definition is used as a frame to provide a foundation for an early definition: a *learning community* is a culture of learning in which everyone is involved in the collective and individual effort to understand (Bielaczyc & Collins, 1999). More recently, Yang, Yeh, and Wong (2010), proposed a definition originally offered by Wenger and colleagues: "Wenger, McDermott and Snyder (2002) define a learning community as 'groups of people who share a concern, a set of problems or a passion about a topic, and who deepen their knowledge and expertise in these areas by interacting on an ongoing process' (p. 4)" (pp. 287–288). Underlying both definitions is a sense of a group of people working together to facilitate the learning process.

Another distinction can be made regarding learning communities: how are they formed? Hannafin *et al.* (2003) make a distinction between directed, negotiated, and informal learning environments within the context of distance education. According to Hannafin *et al.*:

> [in] directed distance learning environments (DDLEs), an authority establishes learning goals and means in accordance with the norms and practices of a specific discipline or community. Consistent with objectivist epistemology, the expert or instructor supplies particular instructional and evaluation strategies to ensure student acquisition of specific knowledge or skills. In a negotiated distance learning environment (NDLE), learning goals and means are jointly determined, balancing individual priorities with those established by the authority. Informal distance learning environments (IDLEs) include the greatest degree of learner autonomy. Learners identify personal learning goals, personal learning processes and strategies, and assume responsibility for assessing their own learning.
>
> (Hannafin *et al.*, 2003, p. 246–7)

Similar distinctions can be made in the types of learning communities that are formed. For example, a learning community that is initiated and facilitated by an expert or instructor may be considered directed or bounded (Wilson *et al.*, 2004). Efforts to form a learning community in a formal learning environment like a classroom or training setting is one example of a directed learning community.

Learning communities can also be negotiated. Looking again at a formal learning environment, perhaps the community is initiated by an instructor but the learners are actively engaged in setting norms and expectations for the learning community. Finally, informal or spontaneous (Wilson *et al.*, 2004) learning communities may evolve and grow. Many have argued that as much as 80 percent of our learning occurs informally and given technological trends, this is perhaps more readily apparent than ever. Most recently, we have seen exponential growth in the establishment of informal learning communities enabled by Web 2.0/social networking technologies. According to the Nielsen Company (NielsenWire, 2011), use of social networking technologies grew by 82 percent between 2008 and 2009 and this growth is only expected to increase in the coming decade, bringing with it continued interest in how learning communities form, function and grow.

It is clear that many have been working on creating an understanding of *communities* and *learning communities* for some time. Despite this effort, along with hundreds of years of experience in the classroom, how best to engage community building is not readily apparent. Arguments related to learning communities range from their importance for learning and a sense of belonging (see, for example, Moore & Kearsley, 1996; Palloff & Pratt, 1999), while others argue that learning communities may never occur (Cook, 1995). Indeed, while advocating for the value of a learning community, even I have raised the question of whether a community is needed for the learning process to occur (Hill, 2002). Regardless of whether there is full support or skepticism, exploring how to utilize specific theories and/or strategies and techniques for creating a learning community is important if we are to see continued growth in this potentially impactful learning strategy.

Examples of Learning Communities

Learning communities are found in a variety of contexts, formal to informal, and in a variety of disciplines. Before examining some of the key theoretical constructs underlying learning communities, I present a few examples, ranging from well-established to emerging learning communities.

Perhaps one of the most well-known formal learning communities is found in the *Knowledge Forum*. Early work that led to the *Knowledge Forum* started in the 1990s when Scardamalia and Bereiter proposed the idea of "knowledge building communities" (Scardamalia & Bereiter, 1991). The *Knowledge Forum*, used in classrooms in the K-12 environment as well as in higher education, emphasizes collective building upon and extending ideas as learners come together in community. Learners use Web-based tools to post ideas and notes related to the topic under discussion. The learners can comment and elaborate on the ideas shared as well as reorganize their own ideas as well as those of others to generate a variety of perspectives (Scardamalia & Bereiter, 2006). *Knowledge Forum* enables learners to facilitate their own understanding and knowledge building as well as make contributions to the understanding and knowledge of the larger learning community.

Learning communities have also been established within the context of courses without the structure of an environment like the *Knowledge Forum*. Hudson, Hudson, and Steel (2006) presented information on the establishment of an international online learning community in their digital media course. Based in a master's program situated within a partnership between universities in the Netherlands and the UK, a primary goal was to foster group collaboration in international teams. To help facilitate this, students collaborated on a group project with the teams representing students from both universities. Students were engaged in a variety of activities in a face-to-face context as well as online. The students used a variety of tools to engage in the learning process with their international group members and to facilitate the building of a learning community including video conferencing, online chat and email. While issues related to language, culture and identity were found in the completed research related to the community, Hudson *et al.*'s work serves as an example of how a learning community can be established without building an elaborate learning environment.

Informal learning communities continue to grow in number and popularity. Informal learning communities have been developed to support communities as diverse as teacher professional development (Lock, 2006), newcomers in the workplace (Blaaka & Cathrine, 2006), and distributed automobile sales and service personnel (Land *et al.*, 2009). One of the most promising developments has come in the continued expansion of Web 2.0 technologies. Brown and Adler (2008) describe several Web 2.0 technologies, providing examples of how learning communities form as a result of the use of some of the tools. They also describe the opportunities these informal learning environments afford: "Whereas traditional schools offer a finite number of courses of study, the 'catalog' of subjects that can be learned online is almost unlimited. There are already several thousand sets of course materials and modules online, and more are being added regularly. Furthermore, for any topic that a student is passionate about, there is likely to be an online niche community of practice of others who share that passion" (p. 12).

One example that exemplifies what is discussed in the Brown and Adler (2008) article is *Inside Teaching*, a site "designed to support a community of learning, which includes teachers, professional developers, and other educators interested in learning and in teaching" (see http://gallery. carnegiefoundation.org/insideteaching/). Sponsored by the Carnegie Foundation for the Advancement of Teaching, *Inside Teaching* provides educators the ability to

Visit collections of multimedia records of teaching practice. Learn from others' perspectives on using records of practice for teacher learning. Contribute your own teaching and learning experiences and browse materials and resources that reflect the larger context of the work featured here. This site itself is an environment of learning, a "living archive" that relies upon the contributions of visitors in order to grow and to thrive.

By participating in *Inside Teaching* educators not only extend their own practice and knowledge base, they also actively contribute to and extend the knowledge base and practices of others.

Theoretical Foundations of Learning Communities

Many have worked in the area of theory building, explicit or related to learning communities. Some theories are particular theories for building a specific kind of community (e.g., community of practice). Yet others build off more foundational theories, like social presence building out of theories specifically related to distance education. Most if not all of the theories build out of a social constructivist perspective on how learning occurs. In the following, I explore some of these theories and how they help inform the creation of learning communities, including social constructivist theory, social interdependence, social presence, and self-directed learning. Naturally, there are other theories that are relevant to learning communities, including activity theory and communities of practice. As both of these are talked about at length in other chapters in this book, they will not be discussed here.

Social Constructivist Theory

Social constructivist theory builds on the foundations of constructivism, extending into how interaction with others impacts and influences the learning process. Vygotsky (1978) is perhaps the most well-known theorist influencing social constructivist theory as well as the thinking about learning communities. Specifically, Vygotsky's work with the zone of proximal development and scaffolding are important considerations.

The *zone of proximal development* or ZPD relates to an individual's ability to do work on his or her own or with assistance. According to Vygotsky (1978), the ZPD is "the distance between the actual developmental level as determined by independent problem solving and the level of potential development as determined through problem solving under adult guidance, or in collaboration with more capable peers" (p. 86). *Scaffolding* is a term closely associated with ZPD as it relates to the support given to assist learners as they engage in a task. Support is reduced over time as learners become more skilled in a task and can work more independently.

A social constructivist perspective emphasizes the interdependence of the individual learner and the context in which s/he is learning. ZPD and scaffolding are important considerations for learning communities as interaction amongst and between learners is what enables community to form within a particular context. For example, a novice in a learning community may pose a challenge to the group in order to help find a solution. Initially, a novice is at one end of the ZPD continuum; significant scaffolding may be provided by more knowledgeable colleagues and experts in order to find a solution. Over time, the novice would become more of an expert, moving along the ZPD continuum and then she eventually would need no scaffolding for problem solving.

Coyle (2007) recently explored the role social context plays as learners develop learning strategies. His study specifically looked at how a learning community could assist foreign language learners with developing strategies for learning a language. Results indicated that a combined approach mindful of the learning context (the social) and the individual has powerful potential for learning.

In addition to the larger theoretical foundation of social constructivism, there are many "smaller" theories that provide insight into how learning communities form, grow and perform. One theory that has received recent attention with the growth of online communities is social presence. This theory is explored in the next section.

Social Presence

Connections between members are building blocks for the formation and growth of a learning community. Social presence theory explores how these connections occur in a community. Short, Williams, and Christie (1976) defined social presence as "the degree of awareness of another person in an interaction and the consequent appreciation of an interpersonal relationship" (p. 66). More recently, Tu (2002) defined it as "a measure of the feeling of community that a learner experiences in an online environment" (p. 131).

The degree of perceived social presence may influence the functioning of a learning community (Gunawardena & Zittle, 1997; Tu, 2004). Tu and McIsaac (2002) explored the relationship of social presence and interaction in online courses. The study results involving 51 students in an online course indicated that social presence influences interaction. Tu and McIsaac stressed that frequency of participation does not represent high social presence. Instead, the results of their study indicated that three dimensions impact social presence: social context, online communication and interactivity. Finding ways to enhance these, among other strategies, can impact social presence.

Greyling and Wentzel (2007) explored social presence in the context of a large, technology-assisted course with 3,000 students. In addition to the face-to-face meetings, the instructor created an online environment where students posted ideas about the topic (economics). The online environment also had a social space for sharing information not necessarily related to class. As stated in the article: "Creating a social presence had more positive effects than I expected. My original intention had been simply to create a separate space to reduce the non-academic messages that cluttered the discussion board. The result was that more students participated or read the discussions and started to associate the positive feelings created by the social space with the subject of Economics" (p. 664). The researchers go on to indicate that the increased social presence appeared to form a foundation for learning and teaching in the course.

Establishing a sense of social presence may not "just happen." Finding ways to facilitate this "sense of connection" may play a key role in the effectiveness of a learning community. Social interdependence theory can provide some insights into how this might occur.

Social Interdependence

A key characteristic of a learning community is that the community members not only collaborate but they also cooperate together in a variety of ways. Social interdependence is a foundational theory in cooperative learning. It has a long, rich history, starting with Koffka and Lewin at the turn of the 20th century with Johnson and Johnson extending the theory in the later part of the century (Johnson, Johnson, & Holubec, 2009). According to Johnson and Johnson (2009), "*Social interdependence* exists when the outcomes of individuals are affected by their own and others' actions" (p. 366). Johnson and Johnson go on to explain that "There are two types of social interdependence: positive (when the actions of individuals promote the achievement of joint goals) and negative (when the actions of individuals obstruct the achievement of each other's goals)" (p. 366).

In a learning community, facilitating positive social interdependence is important for the individual as well as for the overall community. Hudson, Hudson, and Steel (2006) explored the explicit facilitation of interdependence in their study of an international online learning community. Within this context, they specifically designed "well-orchestrated interdependence. By this we mean collaboration based upon genuine interdependence involving a shared sense of purpose, a division of labour and joint activity that is open to examination, elaboration and change by all within the peer group" (p. 735). The results of their study indicate that the learning community raised several issues at the individual and group level, including language, culture and identity. The researchers also highlighted the importance of assessment, noting an emphasis on the assessment *for* learning rather than assessment *of* learning. When working from a frame of social interdependence, many aspects of the learning context are influenced at multiple levels.

Social interdependence theory helps to explain how members of a learning community may develop more effective and more meaningful environments for interaction. The larger context in which the learning community is formed is also important to consider. Situated learning theory can provide insights into this area.

Situated Learning

From a situated learning perspective, meaning does not exist independent of context, but rather context shapes and defines meaning (Brown, Collins, & Duguid, 1989). More specifically, learning is situated in a specific social context (Brown, Collins, & Duguid, 1989; Wenger, 1998) and cognition is distributed across individuals, tools, and artifacts (Pea, 1993, 2004; Salomon, 1993). Within a learning community, knowledge and learning occur in convergence through interactive communication and facilitated collaboration. There is no separation of knowing from that which is known from a situated learning perspective. Practice, meaning, and identity are interwoven, and at the same time constituted and constructed within a specific context (Barab & Kirschner, 2001; Kirshner & Whitson, 1997). In situated contexts, learning occurs as a learner recognizes the practical utility of knowledge as well as the need to use it for more cognitive purposes in an effort to analyze, interpret, and solve real-world problems (Hannafin, Hill, Land, & Lee, in press).

Espinoza (2009) used a lens of *situated learning* in her study exploring students, work in electronics workshops as well as with their own projects. Espinoza interviewed and observed students as they completed their tasks. Her study indicated that students constructed their knowledge during action as well as through problem-solving, asking questions and getting answers. Interactions included student–student as well as student–teacher in a more knowledgeable peer orientation. Finding ways to support and enable interactions is a key characteristic of a learning community.

From the larger context of situated learning we narrow down to the individual – a critical component of the learning community. Two primary theories will be explored in the next section: self-directed learning and self-regulation theory.

Self-Directed Learning and Self-Regulation Theory

As indicated throughout this chapter, learning is "strongly influenced by setting, social interaction, and individual beliefs, knowledge, and attitudes" (Dierking, 1991, p. 4). This is particularly important to keep in mind while turning attention to the individual within the learning community. While there is often a focus on the collective that is the learning community, individuals are the foundation that enable the community to form. Two theories can help guide our understanding of how to support learners within the context of a learning community: self-regulated and self-directed learning.

Self-regulation encompasses a variety of individual characteristics, including self-efficacy, motivation, and metacognitive skills. Each characteristic has been studied to various extents (see, for example, Lim & Kim, 2003; Oliver & Shaw, 2003; Song & Hill, 2009), with the majority of the studies indicating that all of the components play an important role in students' learning experience. An individual's self-efficacy may influence the nature and quality of cognitive engagement. The higher the self-efficacy, the better an individual is able to engage within a social context such as in a learning community (Pajares, 1996). Motivation to be a part of the community is also an important consideration. Members of a learning community need to be motivated to fully participate in the community, perhaps overcoming challenges like procrastination (see, for example, Elvers, Polzella, & Graetz, 2003) as well as taking advantage of the communication affordances of the larger community to participate in meaningful interaction (King, 2002). Finally, members of a learning community need to have an awareness of what they know and don't know – making judgments on various aspects in their learning process (Petrides, 2002) to benefit from and contribute to the learning community.

Self-directed learning is a closely related theory that has implications for individuals interacting and learning within a learning community. Historically, self-directed learning has been explored from two perspectives: process (e.g., Mocker & Spear, 1982), and personal attribute (e.g., Garrison, 1997). Self-directed learning research waned in the broader educational research arena in the late 1990s, but with the increasing trend of online learning in higher education (The Sloan Consortium, 2004), self-directed learning research saw a resurgence as we moved into the 21st century (e.g., Hartley & Bendixen, 2001; Whipp & Chiarelli, 2004; Robertson, 2011), with some scholars noting a need for exploring self-directed learning within a particular context, like learning communities.

Robertson (2011) explored the use of a particular technology to assist with self-directed learning with a blended online learning community: blogs. In her study involving 113 computer science students, blogs were used to enable students to extend their face-to-face interactions with the larger learning community in their class. Results indicated that students did enhance their self-directed learning skills and also helped to support each other in the learning community.

Issues and Challenges Associated with Building a Learning Community

Developing a learning community, face-to-face or online, is not an easy undertaking. It takes time and attention from all involved in the learning community. It also takes interaction, which has been widely studied particularly in the context of online learning communities. Indeed, interaction is considered a key element in a learning experience (Garrison & Cleveland-Innes, 2005). For a participant in a learning community, interactions may occur with other participants, more knowledgeable others or experts, and/or the content (Garrison & Cleveland-Innes, 2005; Moore, 1989). Facilitating interactions is key within a learning community.

Building a sense of presence is another important consideration (Tu, 2004). Several researchers have posed various forms of presence, from social presence (see, for example, Tu & McIsaac, 2002) to learning presence (see, for example, Shea & Bidjerano, 2010). Garrison and colleagues proposed a larger framework that incorporated several forms of presence. The Community of Inquiry Framework includes social, cognitive and teaching presence (see, for example, Garrison & Arbaugh, 2007; Garrison, Anderson, & Archer, 2010). Although the framework was originally designed to help guide an online educational experience, the key features of the framework – supporting discourse, selecting content, and setting climate – are key elements for learning communities. Enabling and supporting the social, cognitive and teaching presence within the learning community can be challenging.

The purpose of a learning community is an issue worthy of consideration. A learning community may emerge, somewhat like a grassroots movement. There may not be an explicit purpose at the beginning; instead, the need and/or desire for a learning community may grow over time. A learning community may also be intentionally formed; further, the type of community may be an important consideration. For example, a facilitator may hope to facilitate a community of inquiry as proposed by Garrison and colleagues. There may also be a desire to facilitate a community of practice for a particular purpose. According to Wenger (2006), communities of practice "are groups of people who share a concern or a passion for something they do and learn how to do it better as they interact regularly" (p. 1). Wenger goes on to state that not every community is a community of practice. Along those same lines, I argue that not every learning community is a community of practice. Providing time to consider the purpose of the learning community is important.

Another challenge facing the creation of learning communities are some of our inherent assumptions. For example, given the dearth of studies exploring learning communities in physical learning environments, it appears that we assume to some extent that communities form in a face-to-face classroom, if not readily at least more readily than in online learning environments. While some (with me among them) may argue that this is an erroneous assumption, I also believe that a form of community does emerge from the day-to-day and/or week-to-week interactions that occur in a traditional face-to-face learning environment. Our social nature as human beings enables these connections to occur, and indeed for some almost demands it.

While there may be somewhat of an assumption that a learning community will form in a face-to-face learning environment, significant challenges do exist (e.g., limited one-on-one interaction). Indeed, the same challenges faced in learning communities in a face-to-face learning environment also appear in an online learning environment. However, there are additional issues that arise due to the nature and types of interactions (or lack thereof) in an online environment, including technological challenges as well as challenges associated with time (e.g., synchronous and asynchronous communication). Thankfully, strategies and techniques for creating learning communities have been recommended by previous research, which can guide others in their efforts.

Creating Learning Communities: Strategies and Techniques

As indicated earlier in the chapter, a learning community does not "just happen;" it takes planning, continuous care and maintenance throughout the life cycle of the community (Hill, Raven, & Han, 2007). Previous research (Hill, 2002) has indicated that challenges occur in three areas: learning community environment, time, and technology. Each area will be used to provide a context for recommendations for building an effective and rewarding community.

Learning Community Environment

There are several key elements to consider within the context of the environment for the learning community. Building on sociocultural theory, it is important to provide a context in which the learners feel "safe" to interact and share. This enables the community to establish shared goals and values (Guldberg & Pilkington, 2006). Having a safe environment also establishes a context in which the learners can grow, perhaps even taking risks because they know they are supported (Allan & Lewis, 2006). Having a safe environment may also allow learners to be present as a "real person" (Greyling & Wentzel, 2007), helping to further facilitate social presence for the individual as well as the larger community.

From a social interdependence perspective, it is important to establish common ground (Johnson & Johnson, 2009) from which the learners participate. This may include such things as setting ground rules for interaction. Providing a grounded environment will enable learners to build an understanding of their role in the community – and may also enable exploration of different roles. Further, it will nurture the establishment of relationships (Lock, 2006), providing a "foundation for the exchange of beliefs, values, knowledge, and skills" (Bird & Sultmann, 2010, p. 143).

Creating an authentic, real-world situation within the learning community is an important consideration from a situated learning perspective. Yang, Yeh, and Wong (2010) illustrated this in their study in which learners adopted real-world roles of writers, editors and commentators. Students read and edited the texts of their peers, evaluated the corrections from the peer editors and then revised the texts based on the feedback. The results of the study showed a difference in the work from students engaged in this process, resulting in improved writing as well as interactions amongst their peers. Reeves, Herrington, and Oliver have written several articles about creating authentic, real-world learning environments that can help guide this process for learning communities (see, for example, Reeves, Herrington, & Oliver, 2002).

Finally, in terms of supporting self-directed or self-regulated learning, the learning community environment should be "failure safe" in terms of working and communicating (Hill, 2002). Learners should feel free to express opinions and offer suggestions without fear of retribution. This will enable learners to set their own individual goals within the larger context, perhaps allowing for stretching beyond comfort zones into new areas.

Time

Time is perhaps one of the most precious resources that we have – and it is almost always in high demand. This is no different for those engaged in a learning community. There are a variety of strategies that can be used to assist the learner with time.

Reassuring the learner that someone is "out there" (Hill, 2002) is of prime importance. This can occur in a variety of ways, ranging from direct contact with the individual learner to sharing news with the larger community on a regular basis. This will further reinforce the idea of presence that is so important for a learning community (Tu, 2004).

Finding ways to help the learner to manage their time is also important. While social interdependence is key to a learning community, it is important to recognize that there are other things beyond the learning community. Not only can the learner establish strategies for managing the time given to the community (e.g., engaging in interactions 1–2 hours a day), they can also be encouraged to set priorities in terms of how they will participate. This is a hallmark of a self-directed learner (see Song & Hill, 2009, for additional information), and a good characteristic to reinforce in a learning community.

Technology

The technology that can be used to facilitate learning communities continues to evolve and grow. The latest tools (i.e., Web 2.0 and 3.0 technologies) continue to reinforce and strengthen the sociocultural context in which learning communities operate. The technology also continues to enable a stronger social presence easier and quicker. Tools like blogs and wikis enable outreach and collaborative knowledge building with millions around the globe in a matter of seconds.

A few long-standing strategies (Hill, 2002) related to the technology may prove beneficial. First, no matter whether the learning community is face-to-face or online, formal or informal, providing a well-organized structure that enables efficient interaction is important. It is also critical to ensure that there are multiple ways to engage in the learning environment so that everyone can find a way that works best for him/her. Finally, if the learning community is completely technology-supported, finding ways to minimize the glitches and providing 24/7 support is critical.

Perhaps the biggest challenge with the technology resides in how best to use it to facilitate a *learning* community vs. simply a community of learners. The distinction is more than semantic and will be an important consideration moving forward with the continued growth of learning communities.

Moving into the Future with Learning Communities: Conclusions and Recommendations for Further Research

Learning communities are founded on the adaptation of a well-known phrase: we can learn from the company we keep (Hill, 2002). As demonstrated in the strategies and techniques section, building a learning community takes care and nurturing. It is also a process that continues to evolve, particularly as new ways of establishing community are enabled. This provides a rich context for ongoing research. A few questions to consider include:

- Is it possible to enable transformative learning experiences for members of the learning community? A few scholars have explored the possibilities of transformative learning and learning communities (see, for example, Jenlink & Jenlink, 2008; Ryman *et al.*, 2009), but this is a recent trend. More research is needed to better understand what might be possible.
- What role does culture play in a learning community? As with transformative learning, some research has been done in this area (see, for example, Hudson, Hudson, & Steel, 2006; Uzuner, 2009), but more work is needed to gain a fuller understanding of how culture helps to support and/or challenge the learning community.
- Is it possible to have "too many" learners in a learning community? Some of the informal learning communities enabled through social networking technologies range in the tens of thousands in terms of members. Is this too many to enable the kinds of sharing and building of understanding that has been discussed here? Is it too many to enable

transparency of communication that leads to awareness (Dalsgaard & Paulsen, 2009)? Continued exploration is needed to look at the effectiveness of these environments from a learning perspective.

- How do we encourage and reward members of the community for their contributions, which are so critical to the learning community? Without the contributions of the individual members, the learning community will cease to exist. This brings to the fore the importance of social structures within the community (Cho *et al.*, 2005). Helping to encourage and motivate members is a key component needing further exploration.

Conclusion

Unlike some of the popular slogans urging us to "just do it," and advertisements by popular on-line course management tools that claim you can have an on-line course up in 15 minutes, web-based instruction (WBI) requires far more planning and development than what might at first be perceived. This is particularly true when it comes to building on-line community. By making use of specific strategies and techniques for community building in WBI, learners and instructors may have an easier time in adjusting and adapting to the required transformations for working in these environments, enabling the creation of effective virtual spaces for learning.

References

Allan, B., & Lewis, D. (2006). The impact of membership of a virtual learning community on individual careers and professional identity. *British Journal of Educational Technology, 37*(6), 841–852.

Barab, S. A., & Kirschner, D. (2001). Guest editor's introduction: Rethinking methodology in the learning sciences, *Journal of the Learning Sciences, 10* (1 & 2): 5–15.

Bielaczyc, K., & Collins, A. (1999). Learning communities in classrooms: A reconceptualization of educational practice. In C. Reigeluth (Ed.), *Instructional Design Theories and Models, Vol. II* (pp. 269–292). Mahwah, NJ: Lawrence Erlbaum.

Bird, K. A., & Sultmann, W. F. (2010). Social and emotional learning: Reporting a system approach to developing relationships, nurturing well-being and invigorating learning. *Educational & Child Psychology, 27*(1), 143–155.

Blaaka, G., & Cathrine, F. (2005/2006). A social and cultural approach to newcomers' workplace learning. International: Newcomers' learning process in two different knowledge communities. *Journal of Learning, 12*(2), 63-70.

Brown, J. S., & Adler, R. P. (2008). Minds on fire: Open education, the long tail and learning 2.0. *EDUCAUSE Review, 43*(1). Available online: http://www.educause.edu/EDUCAUSE+Review/EDUCAUSEReviewMagazineVolume43/MindsonFireOpenEducationtheLon/162420.

Brown, J. S., Collins, A., & Duguid, S. (1989). Situated cognition and the culture of learning, *Educational Researcher, 18*(1), 32–42.

Burgess, K. R. (2009). Social networking technologies as vehicles of support for women in learning communities. *New Directions for Adult and Continuing Education, 122,* 63-71.

Cho, H., Lee, J.-S., Stefanone, M., & Gay, G. (2005). Development of computer-supported collaborative learning in a distributed learning community. *Behaviour & Information Technology, 24*(6), 435–447.

Cook, D. L. (1995). Community and computer-generated distance learning environments. *New Directions for Adult and Continuing Education* (67), 33–39.

Coyle, D. (2007). Strategic classrooms: Learning communities which nurture the development of learner strategies. *Language Learning Journal, 35*(1), 65–79.

Dalsgaard, C., & Paulsen, M. F. (2009). Transparency in cooperative online education. *International Review of Research in Open and Distance Learning, 10*(3), 1–22.

Dierking, L. D. (1991). Learning theory and learning styles: An overview. *Journal of Museum Education,16*(1), 4–6.

Elvers, G. C., Polzella, D. J., & Graetz, K. (2003). Procrastination in online courses: Performance and attitudinal differences. *Teaching of Psychology, 30*(2), 159–162.

Espinoza, S. L. (2009). Practice activities in technological schools: Perspective of situated learning in communities of practice. *International Journal of Learning, 16*(1), 347–357.

Frazier, N. E. (2006). In the loop: One librarian's experiences teaching within first-year learning communities. *College and Undergraduate Libraries, 13*(1), 21–31.

Garrison, D. R. (1997). Self-directed learning: Toward a comprehensive model. *Adult Education Quarterly, 48*(1), 18–33.

Garrison, D. R., & Arbaugh, J. B. (2007). Researching the community of inquiry framework: Review, issues, and future directions. *Internet and Higher Education, 10,* 157–172.

Garrison, D. R., & Cleveland-Innes, M. (2005). Facilitating cognitive presence in online learning: Interaction is not enough. *American Journal of Distance Education, 19*(3), 133–148.

Garrison, D. R., Anderson, T., & Archer, W. (2010). The first decade of the community of inquiry framework: A retrospective. *Internet and Higher Education, 13,* 5–9.

Greyling, F. C., & Wentzel, A. (2007). Humanising education through technology: Creating presence in large classes. *South Africa Journal of Higher Education, 21*(4), 654–667.

Guldberg, K., & Pilkington, R. (2006). A community of practice approach to the development of non-traditional learners networked learning. *Journal of Computer Assisted Learning, 22,* 159–171.

Gunawardena, C. N., & Zittle, F. J. (1997). Social presence as a predictor of satisfaction within a computer-mediated conferencing environment. *American Journal of Distance Education, 11*(3), 8–26.

Hannafin, M. J., Hill, J. R., Land, S., & Lee, E. (in press). Student-centered, open learning environments: Research, theory, and practice. In Spector, M., Merrill,

D., Elen, J., & Bishop, M. J. (Eds.), *Handbook of Research on Educational Communications and Technology* (4th ed).

Hannafin, M. J., Hill, J. R., Oliver, K., Glazer, E., & Sharma, P. (2003). Cognitive and learning factors in Web-based environments. In M. Moore & W. Anderson (Eds.), *Handbook of Distance Education* (pp. 245–260), Mahwah, NJ: Lawrence Erlbaum.

Hartley, K., & Bendixen, L. D. (2001). Educational research in the Internet age: Examining the role of individual characteristics. *Educational Researcher, 30*(9), 22–26.

Hill, J. R. (2002). Strategies and techniques for community-building in Web-based learning environments. *Journal of Computing in Higher Education, 14*(1), 67–86.

Hill, J. R., Raven, A., & Han, S. (2007). Connections in Web-based learning environments: A research-based model for community building. In R. Luppicini (Ed.), *Online learning communities* (pp. 153–168). Greenwich, CT: Information Age Publishing.

Hudson, B., Hudson, A., & Steel, J. (2006). Orchestrating interdependence in an international learning community. *British Journal of Educational Technology, 37*(5), 733–748.

Jenlink, P. M., & Jenlink, K. E. (2008). Creating democratic learning communities: Transformative work as spatial practice. *Theory into Practice, 47*, 311–317.

Johnson, D. W., & Johnson, R. T. (2009). An educational psychology success story: Social interdependence theory and cooperative learning. *Educational Researcher, 38*(5), 365–379.

Johnson, D. W., Johnson, R. T., & Holubec, E. (2009). *Circles of learning: Cooperation in the classroom* (6th edn.). Edina, MA: Interaction Book Company.

Jonassen, D. H. (1995). Supporting communities of learners with technology: A vision for integrating technology with learning in schools. *Educational Technology, 35*(4), 60–63.

King, K. P. (2002). Identifying success in online teacher education and professional development. *Internet and Higher Education, 5*(3), 231–246.

Kirshner, D., & Whitson, J. A. (1997). Editors' introduction to situated cognition, In: D. Kirshner and J. A. Whitson (Eds.), *Situated cognition: Social, semiotic, and psychological perspectives* (pp. 1–16). Mahwah, NJ: Lawrence Erlbaum.

Komito, L. (1998). The Net as a foraging society: Flexible communities. *The Information Society, 14*, 97–106.

Land, S., Draper, D., Ma, Z., Hsui, H., Smith, B., & Jordan, R. (2009). An investigation of knowledge building activities in an online community of practice at Subaru of America. *Performance Improvement Quarterly, 22*(1), 1–15.

Lave, J., & Wenger, E. (1991). *Situated learning: Legitimate peripheral participation.* Cambridge, MA: Cambridge University Press.

Lim, D. H. & Kim, H. (2003). Motivation and learner characteristics affecting online learning and learning application. *Journal of Educational Technology Systems, 31*(4): 423–439.

Lock, J. V. (2006). A new image: Online communities to facilitate teacher professional development. *Journal of Technology and Teacher Education, 14*(4), 663–678.

Manning, G., Curtis, K., & McMillen, S. (1996). *Building community: The human side of work.* Cincinnati, OH: Thomson Executive.

Mocker, D. W., & Spear, G. E. (1982). *Lifelong learning: Formal, nonformal, informal, and self-directed.* Columbus, OH: ERIC Clearinghouse for Adult, Career, and Vocational Education, Ohio State University.

Moore, M. G. (1989). Three types of interaction. *American Journal of Distance Education, 3*(2). Available online: http://www.ajde.com/Contents/vol3_2.htm#editorial.

Moore, M. G., & Kearsley, G. (1996). *Distance education: A systems view.* New York: Wadsworth.

NielsenWire (2011). Led by Facebook, Twitter, global time spent on social media sites up 82% year over year. Available online: http://blog.nielsen.com/nielsenwire/global/led-by-facebook-twitter-global-time-spent-on-social-media-sites-up-82-year-over-year/.

Nieto, S. (1999). *The light in their eyes: Creating multicultural learning communities.* New York: Teachers College Press.

Oliver, M., & Shaw, G. P. (2003). Asynchronous discussion in support of medical education. *Journal of Asynchronous Learning Networks, 7*(1). http://www.aln.org/publications/jaln/v7n1/v7n1oliver.asp.

Pajares, F. (1996). Self-efficacy beliefs in academic settings. *Review of Educational Research 66*(4): 543–578.

Palloff, R. M., & Pratt, K. (1999). *Building learning communities in cyberspace: Effective strategies for the online classroom.* San Francisco, CA: Jossey-Bass.

Palloff, R. M., & Pratt, K. (2004). *Collaborating online: Learning together in community.* San Francisco, CA: Jossey-Bass.

Pea, R. D. (1993). Practices of distributed intelligence and designs for education, In: G. Salomon (Ed.), *Distributed cognitions: Psychological and educational considerations* (pp. 47–87). New York: Cambridge University Press.

Pea, R. D. (2004). The social and technological dimensions of scaffolding and related theoretical concepts for learning, education, and human activity, *Journal of the Learning Sciences, 13*(3), 423–451.

Petrides, L. A. (2002). Web-based technologies for distributed (or distance) learning: Creating learning-centered educational experiences in the higher education classroom. *International Journal of Instructional Media 29*(1): 69–77.

Reeves, T. C., Herrington, J., & Oliver, R. (2002). Authentic activities and online learning. In A. Goody, J. Herrington, & M. Northcote (Eds.), *Quality conversations: Research and Development in Higher Education*, Volume 25 (pp. 562–567). Jamison, ACT: HERDSA.

Robertson, J. (2011). The educational affordances of blogs for self-directed learning. *Computers & Education, 57*, 1628–1644.

Ryman, S., Hardham, G., Richardson, B., & Ross, J. (2009). Creating and sustaining online learning communities: Designing for transformative learning. *International Journal of Pedagogies and Learning, 5*(3), 32–45.

Salomon, G., (1993). No distribution without individuals' cognition: A dynamic interactional view. In G. Salomon, (Ed.), *Distributed cognition: Psychological and educational consideration* (pp. 111–138). New York: Cambridge University Press.

Scardamalia, M., & Bereiter, C. (1991). Higher levels of agency for children in knowledge building: A challenge for the design of new knowledge media. *Journal of the Learning Sciences, 1*(1), 37–68.

Scardamalia, M., & Bereiter, C. (2006). Knowledge building: Theory, pedagogy, and technology. In R. K. Sawyer (Ed.), *The Cambridge handbook of the learning sciences* (pp. 97–118). Cambridge, MA: Cambridge University Press.

Shea, P., & Bidjerano, T. (2010). Learning presence: Towards a theory of self-efficacy, self-regulation, and the development of a communities of inquiry in online and blended learning environments. *Computers & Education, 55,* 1721–1731.

Short, J., Williams, E., & Christie, B. (1976). *The social psychology of telecommunications.* London: John Wiley & Sons.

Sloan Consortium. (2004). *Entering the mainstream: The quality and extent of online education in the United States, 2003 and 2004.* Retrieved March 10, 2005, from http://www.sloan-c.org/resources/).

Song, L., & Hill, J. R. (2009). Understanding adult learners' self-regulation in online environments: A qualitative study. *International Journal of Instructional Media, 36*(3), 264–274.

Tu, C.-H. (2002). The measurement of social presence in an online environment. *International Journal on E-Learning, 1*(2), 34–45.

Tu, C.-H. (2004). *Online collaborative learning communities: Twenty-one designs to building an online collaborative learning community* Westport, CT: Libraries Unlimited.

Tu, C.-H., & McIsaac, M. (2002). The relationship of social presence and interaction in online classes. *American Journal of Distance Education, 16*(3), 131–150.

Tu, C.-H., Blocher, M., & Roberts, G. (2008). Constructs for Web 2.0 learning environments: A theatrical metaphor. *Educational Media International, 45*(4), 253–269.

Uzuner, S. (2009). Questions of culture in distance learning: A research review. *International Review of Research in Open and Distance Learning, 10*(3), 1–19.

Vygotsky, L. S. (1978). *Mind in society.* Cambridge, MA: Harvard University Press.

Wenger, E. (1998). Communities of practice: Learning, meaning, and identity. New York: Cambridge University Press.

Wenger, E. (2006). Communities of practice: A brief introduction. Available online: http://www.ewenger.com/theory/.

Whipp, J. L., & Chiarelli, S. (2004). Self-regulation in a web-based course: A case study. *Educational Technology Research and Development, 52*(4), 5–22.

Wilson, B. G., Ludwig-Hardman, S., Thornam, C. L., & Dunlap, J. C. (2004). Bounded community: Designing and facilitating learning communities in formal courses. *International Review of Research in Open and Distance Learning, 5*(3). Available online: http://www.irrodl.org/content/v5.3/wilson.html.

Yang, Y.-F., Yeh, H.-C., & Wong, W.-K. (2010). The influence of social interaction on meaning construction in a virtual community. *British Journal of Educational Technology, 41*(2), 287–306.

12 What is a Community of Practice and How Can We Support It?

Christopher Hoadley

One of the most important concepts in social or situated learning theory is the notion of a community of practice. The concept, like the concept of constructivism or the concept of zones of proximal development, has been used both as an explanatory framework for learning and as a metaphor for how instruction should take place. In this chapter, I first describe some basic history of the concept of communities of practice and some of the theoretical assumptions underlying it. Next, I examine some of the key processes identified as producing and sustaining communities of practice. I compare and contrast the notion of communities of practice with other social learning approaches or knowledge communities. And finally, I describe some of the techniques people have used to support communities of practice through technology.

Defining Communities of Practice

The term community of practice is usually attributed to Lave and Wenger's groundbreaking book on situated learning (Lave & Wenger, 1991), although the term was simultaneously in use by Brown and Duguid who worked with Lave and Wenger (Brown & Duguid, 1991), and can be traced back to work by Julian Orr (1990) and even earlier to Edward Constant (1987). Over time, the concept of community of practice has evolved from a descriptive one (Lave, 1987; Lave & Wenger, 1991) to a more prescriptive one (cf., Wenger, McDermott, & Snyder, 2002); Cox has a helpful analysis of how Orr's original work was discussed differently over time as focus moved from description to prescription (Cox, 2007). It is helpful to examine the earlier notion of community of practice, and the theories of knowing, learning, and technology that led to its emergence before discussing the question of whether a community of practice is a learning phenomenon or an instructional strategy.

What is a community of practice? Two definitions stem from Lave and Wenger's 1991 work, what I will term the feature-based definition, and the process-based definition.

Feature-Based Definition of Community of Practice

The first, feature-based definition comes from the words themselves: a community that shares practices. Anthropological perspectives on technology adoption, knowledge management, and learning had come to view that learning was not a property of individuals and the representations in their heads (the cognitive view), but rather a more relational property of individuals in context and in interaction with one another (the situated view). Orr's work on Xerox photocopy repairmen described a situation in which knowledge was not handed off, but co-constructed, by technicians who could not rely on manuals, standard operating procedures, or what they had been taught formally. Instead, through the construction and sharing of stories, and through joint problem solving, the repairmen were able to come to understand far more about how to repair copiers than the manuals could provide. This example of innovation and learning contradicted a more instructivist characterization in which experts or researchers would generate knowledge, which would then be transmitted to learners. Rather, the copy repair provided an example of learning which was situated in the context of problem solving; which was largely related to tacit knowledge, that could only be made explicit through social processes in the context of an actual problem; and which was indicative of the difficulty of attributing "knowing" to a single individual in the setting. While studying practices, their meanings and contexts, and their persistence, prevalence, and scope is a core part of anthropology, Orr's work, and later Lave and Wenger's, presents a key insight; namely, that knowledge, and therefore learning, were embedded in cultural practices. This insight was tied to earlier work in science and technology studies.

Previously, Constant (1987) had argued that the combination of "practice" and "community" was the best grain size at which to describe knowledge. Constant considered the question of knowledge management and innovation, and highlighted how both organizational perspectives on knowledge and systems perspectives on knowledge were limiting when considering technological innovation. Rather, he highlighted how knowledge was embedded in practices, and how communities of practitioners who shared practices might be the correct unit of analysis to examine knowledge. Coming from a history of science/knowledge management perspective, the issue of individual knowledge in the head was never central for Constant; instead the question was at what social granularity would studying knowledge (especially innovative knowledge) make sense. One of the obvious choices in Constant's purview would have included the firm or organization as holder of knowledge; this would connect to the idea of organizational knowledge management in companies. Another, which Constant explicitly considered, was the socio-technical system. Actor-network theory and activity theory (see Chapter 10) are both examples of theories at the grain size of system, where the scope of consideration is the scope of connected people and tools (e.g., a mainframe computer and all its users); of course, the difficulty is deciding what constitutes sufficient connection and therefore where the boundaries of a system lie. A third grain size which is not explicitly discussed by Constant but which also would have been reasonable is the grain size of a culture; however, cultural knowledge tends to describe commonalities across large groups of people, indeed some define the boundaries of culture by shared knowledge. The grain size of culture is not the most useful for studying noteworthy knowledge which is not evenly distributed, i.e., not useful for studying innovative or high-leverage knowledge.

As Brown and Duguid (1991) put it, some knowledge is "sticky" while other knowledge is "leaky". That is to say, some knowledge tends to reside within certain groups of people despite organizational or personal pressure to distribute it better: for example, the highly technical knowledge of an experienced computer user, which is quite difficult to distribute widely even though it may be of high value to others; or best practices in public health, which are easy in many cases to convey to people ("wash your hands," or "don't smoke") but which might "bounce off" the target population—this type of knowledge could be called "sticky" knowledge because it is difficult to spread around. Leaky knowledge is the opposite; an example might be an innovation that a company would like to keep as a trade secret, but which spreads like wildfire despite all efforts to the contrary. Brown and Duguid point out that knowledge can be both sticky and leaky simultaneously, spreading easily in some ways while not in others. Constant's conclusion in reaction to this situation, taken up by Brown and Duguid, is that the natural "range" or spread of knowledge can be described by looking at communities of people who share practices. The practice is important because it identifies knowledge with something people "do" as part of their culture, profession, or avocations. (As any teacher will attest, knowing without doing seems nearly impossible; whatever learning residue exists rarely sticks.) And, as another key insight, Constant says a practice is not enough to specify where knowledge lives, because disconnected groups may share a practice or even a set of practices, but if they are not in contact (harkening back to the idea of a community as a group of people in communion with each other), the meanings of those practices will not be the same. Simply put, knowledge equals practice in authentic contexts by communities. Various theorists have taken stronger and weaker stances on whether knowledge (or its analog) can actually exist in individuals at all, with Lave and Wenger taking the most strident view, stating that the community of practice is "an intrinsic condition for the existence of knowledge"; clearly, this idea of knowledge-as-situated is very different from the school-oriented notion of knowledge-in-the-head.

This connects with one of the central problems of the individualist perspective on learning, the transfer problem. On an individual level, learners may appear to know something (for instance, a skill for solving a math problem), but then fail to apply that knowledge in a context different from the one in which they learned the skill. What appears to be a puzzling defect when examined at an individual level becomes more sensible when looked at as a systemic property of a group of people who all share certain practices. Thus, learning mathematics becomes less a process of inscribing certain facts in the brain, and more one of becoming a person who practices mathematics. Certainly, we can see how this makes sense in specialized professions; a professional mathematician in graduate school learns how to do mathematical research "in communion with" other mathematicians. But it can also be true for young students learning arithmetic. Barab and Duffy (1998, see also Chapter 2), following Senge, described this as "practice fields"—practice in the dual sense of practicing piano, as well as in the sense of a sociocultural practice—in which learners have a practice that is authentically shared by people at a similar stage of learning, even if it is not professional-grade practice. Are minor-league baseball teams "authentic" baseball? What about little league? The idea of practice fields gives us a way to think about these examples— they represent communities that share practices, and in each case there is a possibility of identifying with that community and its behaviors, and becoming more central to its practices. The major league rookie, and the new entrant to little league, both share the opportunity to participate legitimately in the baseball practices of their respective communities, and to gradually identify more and more with those practices.

Thus, we see that the feature-based definition of a community of practice entails some fairly important ideas for educators. To sum up, the anthropological view of knowledge and situated learning identifies not knowledge structures in the head (as with cognitive constructivism), nor behaviors conditioned by an environment (as with behaviorism), but rather as a property lying somewhere between individuals and cultures, involving practices in context. Lave and Wenger's description of naturally occurring communities of practice, for instance the apprenticeship of tailors, highlights the importance of learning being situated in authentic practice contexts or practice fields. Educators, then, must either help embed learners in supportive authentic contexts, or create quasi-authentic contexts in which they can "do" the knowledge that is desired; mere regurgitation is not enough.

Defining Communities of Practice as a Process

The second, process-based definition of community of practice, put forth by Lave and Wenger as a description of the process of knowledge generation, application, and reproduction, is that communities of practice are groups in which a constant process of legitimate peripheral participation takes place. Through legitimate peripheral participation, learners enter a community and gradually take up its practices. Initially, people may participate in tangential ways, but over time, they take up more and more of the identity of group membership and centrality, and more and more of the central practices of the group. While later work on legitimate peripheral participation has often focused on participation in the form of discursive practice (e.g., Kilner, 2004; Senge, 1990), this practice can take any form (consider a community of practice of traditional dance, for instance). Lave and Wenger identify the reproduction (and evolution) of knowledge through the process of joining and identifying with communities as the central and defining phenomenon within a community of practice.

Again, this notion of learning has profound educational implications. For one, in the community of practice view, learners must have access to experts, and must either perceive themselves to be members or aspire to membership in a community in which expert practices are central; contrast this with the ways students are segmented into grades or levels within schools. Secondly, there is a bootstrapping problem; if learners are to enculturate themselves by joining a community of practice, it must already exist, with some sort of common history and an identity (Barab & Duffy, 1998). Third, there must be space in an educational system for legitimate peripheral participation. Often, schools emphasize uniformity in behaviors that may delegitimize the participation of those who are more peripheral. To take a concrete example, if a student wishes to "lurk" in class more before eventually identifying enough to speak, they need to have a space in which it is legitimate to be on the periphery of classroom discussion. Similarly, in a lecture format a student may have no opportunity to participate in any practice related to the knowledge at hand. A strict division of labor between a teacher lecturing and a student completing exercises robs the student of any opportunity to participate in a meaningful way. This process seems unlikely to allow a student to develop any sort of identification with the authentic practices of the classroom, much less the world outside the classroom.

Communities of Practice vs. Other Knowledge Communities

As mentioned earlier, the idea of a community of practice has broadened considerably since it was popularized by Lave and Wenger and Brown and Duguid. While Constant initially used it as a descriptor of a type of knowledge, and Lave and Wenger used it as an explanatory theory describing the naturally occurring processes underlying all knowledge and learning, writings since then have often altered the concept in two ways. The first shift has been from communities of practice as an endemic phenomenon that occurs naturally to one that can be explicitly created and fostered, whether by a teacher, a chief information officer, or a community organizer. The second change, linked with the first, is away from the anthropological and social aspects of the community of practice and towards the physical manifestation of communities of practice via external representations and explicit rules, i.e., technology platforms which instantiate a particular way of supporting or fostering community of practice. This is analogous to the idea of constructivism as a learning theory gradually being transformed into constructivism as a description of a family of teaching strategies (as explored elsewhere in this volume). It is entirely reasonable to want to understand pedagogical implications of a good learning theory, but it is important that we are careful to distinguish between theory and design. To advance social theories of learning, we need to remember some of the different assumptions and implications of different explanatory theories, and try to remember the role of designer/ educators in implementing educational strategies when they use those theories to create learning environments.

For example, the terms knowledge-building community and community of practice are sometimes used interchangeably; or occasionally with one as a special case of the other (e.g., Hoadley & Kilner, 2005). In this volume, knowledge-building communities are discussed as a framework for understanding social learning environments. The two concepts appear similar, but we can highlight several key differences. Most notably, a knowledge-building community is intentional, that is, the goal of the community (or of the organizers of the community) is explicitly on learning and building knowledge, whereas Orr's copier repairmen had a different goal, which was to do their jobs and to be comfortable within their professional identity. Learning was an incidental, instrumental aspect of that process. Contrast this with Scardamalia and Bereiter's emphasis on the transformative power of a learner developing and setting her own agenda for knowledge construction (Scardamalia & Bereiter, 1991); they argue that agency becomes a key driver of the community learning process, where a copier repairman might have limited agency in setting the agenda of his or her own day, much less the agenda of the community of other repairmen. A second difference between the two is the source and nature of authenticity. While it is presumed in both cases that a learner who is successful will be increasingly identified with the community's practices as something they do and that defines their own lives, a knowledge-building community may be investigating questions that derive from an individual's curiosity, or from a teacher's initial agenda-setting. A community of practice that occurs naturally will not typically have a learning goal; these will emerge depending on the evolution of the community's function and role within society. Practice fields may allow more preparatory types of learning to take place than those in professional practice, but ultimately little league has to be fulfilling enough on its own to survive, even if it might lead to the major leagues. Knowledge-building communities may not be limited in this way. Hoadley and Kilner (2005) argue that once a knowledge-building community is up and running, it does constitute a community of practice, one in which the core practice is an inquiry one.

Knowledge-building communities are just one example of many different kinds of communities that may be compared and contrasted with communities of practice. Unfortunately, terminologies are not always consistent; while "communities of learners" may have a more technical definition, the phrase may also be used more generically. Other terms which may have varying definitions include "knowledge networks", "communities of interest", and even "communities of practice" itself. However, despite the lack of common terms, it's helpful to examine some of the dimensions in which different configurations of groups of people and learning activities can be classified. Andriessen (2005) undertook a review of the literature and attempted to create a taxonomy of types of "knowledge communities" (his attempt to create an umbrella term to encompass all communities that support or generate knowledge) based on both published accounts and extraction of key features of archetypical knowledge communities. Several key distinguishing features of different types of knowledge communities were identified, including whether or not they have common purpose, whether they have commitment to a shared deliverable ("contract value"), whether there is a defined membership, the formality or informality of the group (for instance, whether there are formal rules, meeting schedules, a coordinator, etc.), composition (heterogeneous or homogeneous), degree of interaction or reciprocity, whether the community has a strong identity, whether it crosses or lies within formal organizations, whether it is geographically distributed or not, and to what degree the interaction within the group is technologically mediated. After assembling this list of features, Andriessen did, in essence, a factor analysis, and then clustered archetypical communities that had combinations of these features.

Andriessen found two correlated sets of characteristics that he used to produce two key dimensions of variability among knowledge communities. The first dimension he termed "connectivity", and it boiled down to the degree of social connectedness of the members, primarily relying on identity and degree of interaction. We might treat it as the "are these people all part of a social group?" test. The second dimension Andriessen identified was "institutionalization," which comprised contract value (deliverables), shared purpose, defined membership, composition, and formalization. One might think of it as "are these people part of a formal, goal-oriented team?" (Interestingly, geography, size, whether a group was intra- or inter-organizational, and whether or not a group was technologically mediated were not found to correlate with how communities were classified.) After plotting the communities in this two-dimensional space, Andriessen identified five clusters. With low connectivity and institutionalization, he found interest groups, groups of people with some shared interest but no real cohesion. He termed groups with moderate connectivity but low institutionalization "informal networks" and included in this group what Wenger termed "communities of interest" and what Brown had termed "networks of professionals". In the category of high connectivity but low institutionalization, which Andriessen calls "informal communities", he includes most definitions of community of practice, including the classic Lave and Wenger definition. In the case of high institutionalization, Andriessen termed high connectivity groups "strategic communities," and in this case he included highly structured, purposefully created communities of practice such as some corporate project teams (we might envision a school-based knowledge-building community in this category). Finally, in the case of low connectivity and high institutionalization, Andriessen finds a gap in the knowledge communities literature, but posits including "communities" such as participants in a formal Delphi process, in which cycles of surveys and summaries are used to construct a common consensus among experts without significant person-to-person contact.

One can use Andriessen's dimensions to consider educational knowledge communities as well. Where a naturally occurring community of practice might be low institutionalization and high connectivity, an ongoing study group might be high connectivity and low-to-moderate institutionalization, a university graduate student support group mailing list might be moderate-to-high institutionalization but low connectivity, and so on. Perhaps because Andriessen's review was grounded more in the information technology and knowledge management literature, a dimension that appears to be absent is the degree to which learning is a goal vs. other professional outcomes. Clearly one of the biggest differences between knowledge-building communities and communities of practice is the degree to which the core practice or value of the community is a learning practice as opposed to some other authentic professional or livelihood-related practice, and we might imagine expanding Andriessen's taxonomy into three dimensions. This would allow us to consider what might be the "educational" version of each of his categories: what, for instance, would be the "educational" equivalent of a loose-knit community of interest? In any case, the distinctions between types of communities are relevant in instructional design, since issues like the degree of connectivity expected between learners or the degree of formality and institutionalization may change the character of the community, and thus may profoundly impact the type of learning processes we might expect to take place in that community. If a group of university students in a large lecture participate in a discussion board in their course management system, will they truly be a high connectivity community? Though the teacher might label the group a "community of practice," the students' identification with the group, their ability to share a common practice with their peers, and so on may not reach the threshold to allow the process of enculturation and legitimate peripheral participation to take place.

Technology and Communities of Practice

The ties between technology and communities of practice run deep; as previously described, Orr, Constant, Brown and Duguid, and Lave and Wenger all had ties to knowledge management in the 1990s which was a de facto technology endeavor. One of the key drivers of technology adoption in the corporate space was the sense that information was a strategic asset for companies, and that its value was increased not only through the calculating aspects of computation, or even the transmission and copying aspects of computer-based information, but more importantly through technology's support of information routing, filtering, and transformation (e.g., Taylor, 1986). More recently, networked technology has allowed communication to become increasingly time and place independent, with ever richer communication channels, to the point where Andriessen found that distributed vs. face-to-face was not a primary issue in his taxonomy of the literature on knowledge communities (Andriessen, 2005). Wenger's more recent work, with White and Smith, has emphasized the role technology can play in providing a platform for a community of practice (Wenger, White, & Smith, 2010). Although one can conceive of technology supporting either the community, or the shared practice, or both, typically scholars have investigated technology's role in supporting the community (i.e., communication) rather than the practice itself. For example, an online discussion board might be used to support hobbyist quilters worldwide. In that case the technology is supporting the communication among the quilters, but presumably doesn't support the quilting itself. On the other hand, if the quilters used software that helped them lay out a quilt design in advance, that would be an example of technology supporting the practice. One can easily imagine that such software would also allow quilters in different locations to collaborate on designing a quilt; this would be an example of the technology supporting both the communication and the practice. To be clear, we can conceive of any artifact or cultural invention to be a technology (Hutchins, 1995), but the technologies which have been the primary focus of education and community of practice researchers are information and communication technologies, i.e., computers and their ilk.

What are some of the ways in which technology can support a community of practice? Hoadley and Kilner (2005), after Hoadley and Kim (2003), identify three areas of technology affordance relevant to communities of practice including content, process, and context (CPC). The content affordance refers to the representational abilities of technology, including the ability to store and manipulate information in a variety of formats (e.g., multimedia affordances, search, data processing, etc.), to transmit representations across distance or allow time-shifting (for instance, in asynchronous collaboration), and the ability to support human representational capacity (for example, allowing a writer to quickly and easily edit text in a word processor, as opposed to using a typewriter or writing longhand). The process affordance refers to technology's ability to scaffold a particular task, activity, or sequence of actions; for example, an enterprise technology in a company might constrain and implement a particular business process by helping route documents to allow an invoice to be paid, or a learning tool might guide a student through the steps of an inquiry cycle in science class. The third affordance, context, refers to the ability of technology to shift the social context of the user. For instance, an online forum might allow people with similar practices to form a community at a distance, a discussion tool might support more gender equitable discussion by allowing anonymity, or a social networking tool may allow someone to communicate with a much broader audience than face-to-face communication. These three affordances are ways in which technology tools may be deployed or designed to add value or improve learning generally, and a community of practice specifically.

Several books on communities of practice focus not on the naturally occurring variety described by Lave and Wenger, but rather on the community of practice as a goal for both educators, managers, or even scientists (e.g., Dixon, Allen, Burgess, Kilner, & Schweitzer, 2005; Kimble, Hildreth, & Bourdon, 2008; Olson, Zimmerman, & Bos, 2008; Saint-Onge & Wallace, 2003; Wenger, 1998; Wenger *et al.*, 2002). We must be careful to distinguish between a community of practice as a phenomenon (naturally occurring or otherwise), versus an intended or designed learning environment, versus the tools used to support a community of practice that interacts primarily online.

For educational designers, the key question is how technology might support either the formation or the continuation of a community of practice in which desired learning takes place. Recognizing that one can neither force a community nor a set of practices, what are some techniques in which technology is used to foster a learning-oriented community of practice? Below, I describe four such techniques, including linking others with similar practices; providing access to shared repositories; supporting conversation within a community; and providing awareness of the context of information resources. These four strategies follow four of the target areas in the C4P model of communities of practice identified in Hoadley and Kilner (2005). This model, created by Kilner and colleagues who run the CompanyCommand online community of practice for soldiers (Kilner, 2004), envisions the structure of an online community of practices as consisting of four factors—content, conversation, connections, and information context—supporting a common purpose. As noted previously, the community of practice may or may not be particularly task-oriented, and indeed the canonical models identified by Lave and Wenger are more oriented towards communities whose only shared purpose is to conduct the practices that help define that community (e.g., a tailors' community of practice has a shared purpose of tailoring, a community of practice of doctors has a shared purpose of practicing medicine, and so on). While many techniques are possible to support communities of practice with technology, I list these four strategies both because they cover the four c's in the C4P model, and because they are illustrative of common ways people support communities of practice with technologies.

The first technique for using technology to support a community of practice is linking people with others who have similar practices. As discussed above, sharing a practice is not enough to form a community of practice—the practitioners have to have what Andriessen termed connectivity. Social networking tools ranging from the more open, like Facebook (anyone can join), to the more closed, like the US Military's CompanyCommand (restricted to US military company commanders), can help what Kilner *et al.* termed "connections". This may include locating other people who share similar practices, which is especially important if novice or peripheral participants don't readily know who are the more central members of the existing community. For example, a Facebook group might be set up for automobile restoration hobbyists and professionals. People might gradually sign up for the group, but then develop individual relationships with others in the community, perhaps "friending" them, and using features like the NewsFeed to deepen the relationship through greater awareness of each other's lives, and so on. Other platforms might have features like corporate directories or profiles that allow like-minded individuals to find one another, and so on.

A second technique for using technology to support communities of practice is to provide some sort of shared repository of information resources. While a simplistic view of knowledge might think that this repository is the knowledge of the community, the community of practice view sees such repositories as simply information that is used by the community in its practices (where the knowledge truly resides). For example, corporate knowledge management systems might contain an information repository for sales contacts. Members of the community of practice that conduct sales would presumably use and maintain this repository as part of their practices in selling products to customers, and if the repository were designed to allow it, might help more peripheral members of the sales team to have access to some of the practices of more expert salespeople. Or, a community of practice of university students in a writing course might use a wiki as a shared repository for references and drafts of papers, with access to each other's work (supporting, again, legitimate peripheral participation, perhaps in the form of reading each other's work in preparation for class discussion). In the C4P model, this would be a way of supporting content.

A third technique is directly supporting communication by providing tools for discussing with others. This is, perhaps, the most common use for technology in communities of practice: supporting, as C4P terms it, conversation. Examples could range from a bulletin board used globally by members of a support group for a rare disease, to commenting tools for blog posts in a password-protected blog for members of a professional association, to an online videoconferencing tool used for informal consultation among doctors on difficult medical cases. Obviously, people can have conversations relevant to a community of practice in person or via written form on paper, but if the people are geographically distributed or need structure to discuss effectively, Internet-based technologies readily serve to allow new possibilities for conversation. Conversation need not look like the traditional threaded discussion tools. For instance, a more exotic form of technology supporting conversation might be using a virtual world like Second Life to generate a context in which people can communicate—a participant in a virtual conference might use their avatar's body language like sitting in rows in front of a virtual podium, or moving through a more cocktail-party-like arrangement of avatars to help structure textual chat.

A fourth technique used to support communities of practice with technology is providing awareness in a community of the information context of various resources. For example, an online bookstore might provide automated recommendations that would help a member of a community uncover what sorts of books are typically read by the same people, or the history (editing log) in a tool like Wikipedia might provide information about how an encyclopedia entry came into being, and perhaps even the goals or attitudes of the various editors of that page over time. In the C4P framework, this is helping establish the information context for shared information resources.

These four techniques correspond to one for each of Kilner *et al.*'s C4P framework, but they are by no means an exhaustive list of ways technology can use content, process, and context affordances to change or support communities of practice. Rather, they are a few of the more commonly applied techniques in each area of C4P. For instructional designers attempting to create or select a technology platform for a community of practice, there is no one correct or optimal technology which will allow a community of practice to thrive. "Community of practice" is not the name of a particular software genre. Instead, any tool or set of tools which support a group of people working in a community through shared practices can be the platform for a community of practice, whether it is a wiki, a blog, a virtual world, a course management system, or simply telephones and email. Again, the C4P model, and the CPC framework can help identify aspects of the community to be supported, and affordances of technology that can address these aspects.

Summary

A community of practice is an important theoretical construct that underlies a particular model of learning, namely, learning in which people, through a process of legitimate peripheral participation, take up membership in and identity with a community which serves as the home of these shared practices. While knowledge communities can take many forms (communities of interest, knowledge-building communities, Delphi groups, etc.), communities of practice typically have a degree of informality (low to moderate institutionalization, making them a community and not an organization), and high connectivity (rather tight social relationships between members of the community, and a relatively high degree of identification with the group). Communities of practice rely on situated theories of knowledge, i.e., the idea that knowledge is a property enacted by groups of people over time in shared practices, rather than the idea that knowledge is a cognitive residue in the head of an individual learner.

Educators and instructional designers may capitalize on the communities of practice model by trying to instantiate or support communities in which desired practices reside, and allowing learners to engage through the process of legitimate peripheral participation. While no manager, teacher, or designer can create a community of practice by fiat, such communities can be supported or fostered through a variety of means, many of which involve providing technologies that support the community. Technology has affordances that allow it to represent content, scaffold processes, and shift the user's social context. These affordances can be applied to support one or more of the key aspects of the functioning of a community of practice: connections, conversations, content, and information context.

References

Andriessen, J. H. E. (2005). Archetypes of knowledge communities. In P. van den Besselaar, G. De Michelis, J. Preece & C. Simone (Eds.), *Communities and technologies* (pp. 191–213). Milan: Springer.

Barab, S., & Duffy, T. (1998). *From practice fields to communities of practice* (p. 31). Bloomington, IN: Center for Research on Learning and Technology. CRLT Technical Report 1–98, http://crlt.indiana.edu/publications/duffy_publ3.pdf [accessed July 10, 2011].

Brown, J. S., & Duguid, P. (1991). Organizational learning and communities-of-practice: Toward a unified view of working, learning, and innovation. *Organization Science, 2*(1), 40–57.

Constant, E. W., II (1987). The social locus of technological practice: Community, system, or organization? In W. E. Bijker, T. P. Hughes & T. J. Pinch (Eds.), *The social construction of technological systems* (pp. 223–242). Cambridge MA: MIT Press.

Cox, A. (2007). Reproducing knowledge: Xerox and the story of knowledge management. *Knowledge Management Research and Practice, 5*(1), 3–12.

Dixon, N. M., Allen, N., Burgess, T., Kilner, P., & Schweitzer, S. (2005). *CompanyCommand: Unleashing the power of the army profession.* West Point, NY: Center for the Advancement of Leader Development & Organizational Learning.

Hoadley, C., & Kilner, P. G. (2005). Using technology to transform communities of practice into knowledge-building communities. *SIGGROUP Bulletin, 25*(1), 31–40.

Hoadley, C., & Kim, D. E. (2003). Learning, Design, and Technology: Creation of a design studio for educational innovation. In A. Palma dos Reis & P. Isaías (Eds.), *Proceedings of the IADIS International Conference e-Society 2003* (pp. 510–519). Lisbon, Portugal: International Association for the Development of the Information Society, IADIS.

Hutchins, E. (1995). *Cognition in the wild.* Cambridge, MA: MIT Press.

Kilner, P. G. (2004). The Con-4P Model of Learning Design for Professional Communities. In J. Nall & R. Robson (Eds.), *Proceedings of E-Learn 2004* (pp. 1307–1311). Norfolk, VA: Association for the Advancement of Computing in Education.

Kimble, C., Hildreth, P. M., & Bourdon, I. (2008). *Communities of practice: Creating learning environments for educators.* Charlotte, NC: Information Age Pub.

Lave, J. (1987). *Cognition in practice.* New York, NY: Cambridge University Press.

Lave, J., & Wenger, E. (1991). *Situated learning: Legitimate peripheral participation.* New York: Cambridge University Press.

Olson, G. M., Zimmerman, A., & Bos, N. (2008). *Scientific collaboration on the Internet.* Cambridge, MA: MIT Press.

Orr, J. E. (1990). Sharing knowledge, celebrating identity: Community memory in a service culture. In D. Middleton & D. Edwards (Eds.), *Collective remembering* (pp. 169–189). Newbury Park, CA: Sage Publications.

Saint-Onge, H., & Wallace, D. (2003). *Leveraging communities of practice for strategic advantage.* Boston: Butterworth-Heinemann.

Scardamalia, M., & Bereiter, C. (1991). Higher levels of agency for children in knowledge building: a challenge for the design of new knowledge media. *Journal of the Learning Sciences, 1*(1), 37–68.

Senge, P. M. (1990). *The fifth discipline: the art and practice of the learning organization* (1st edn.). New York: Doubleday/Currency.

Taylor, R. S. (1986). The value-added model. In R. S. Taylor (Ed.), *Value-added processes in information systems* (pp. 48–70). Norwood, NJ: Ablex.

Wenger, E. (1998). *Communities of practice: Learning, meaning, and identity.* Cambridge, UK: Cambridge University Press.

Wenger, E., McDermott, R. A., & Snyder, W. (2002). *Cultivating communities of practice: A guide to managing knowledge.* Boston, MA: Harvard Business School Press.

Wenger, E., White, N., & Smith, J. D. (2010). *Digital habitats: Stewarding technology for communities.* Portland, OR: CPSquare.

Part 3

Theoretical Perspective for Investigating Learning Environments

13 Learning Environments as Emergent Phenomena

Theoretical and Methodological Implications of Complexity

Michael J. Jacobson and Manu Kapur

There are various theories from which to ground systematic inquiry into *learning environments,* which is, of course, the core enterprise of this volume. But which has primacy: "learning," or "environment?" Risking the charge of theoretical reductionism, we suggest that discussions of theory in this area tend to argue for the primacy of the first or the second. As an example of the first, Piagetian (1980) constructivism views learning as changes in the individual associated with processes of assimilation and accommodation in response to a changing ecology or environment, whereas the second is exemplified by socio-cultural perspectives such as Vygotsky (1978). Other scholars have discussed, analyzed, contrasted, compared, not to mention championed or criticized various instantiations of these camps. (The interested reader should consult the special issue in *Cognitive Science* [Norman, 1993] and papers in *Educational Researcher* [Anderson, Reder, & Simon, 1997; Greeno, 1997] to sample this debate over the past nearly two decades.)

A goal of this chapter is not to further that debate, but to reconceptualize it by considering the implications for theory and methodology of a third locus: "learning-environments." We argue that environments in which learning occurs are in fact complex systems with particular properties and processes; we discuss these further below.

Bar-Yam (2003) has characterized the study of complex systems as not being about "trees" or a "forest" but rather "forest-trees." By this, he means that complexity scientists often rapidly shift or oscillate their theoretical vantage points to understand relevant properties across different levels of a complex system—such as a micro level of "trees" or a macro level of "forest"—that would not be salient by attending solely to the properties of a micro or macro level, such as shade on the forest ground from clusters of trees that helps bacteria in the soil survive that are essential for individual trees to survive.

In this chapter, we discuss how conceptual perspectives and methodologies being employed in the study of complex physical and social systems may be used to inform research in the learning sciences involving learning environments. In particular, we explore the notion of *complex learning-environment systems*, which we believe has the potential to advance theory by bringing principled consideration of feedback interactions within and across different levels of learning systems and attendant collective properties that emerge, and that in turn then feedback and constrain or shape interactions at micro, mezzo, and macro levels in systems of learning.

What is Complexity?

Scientific study of the behavior of complex systems over the past three decades has led to insights about the world that classical approaches tended to over-simplify or to ignore (Bar-Yam, 2003). Briefly, complex systems consist of elements or agents that interact with each other and their environment often based on simple rules. Feedback interactions within and across levels of the system result in self-organization, with emergent patterns forming at mezzo and macro levels of the system. There is also a dialectical co-existence of linearity and nonlinearity in the behavior of complex systems, such as the linear predictability of seasons that emerges out of the nonlinear and probabilistic nature of day-to-day weather. Another key characteristic of complex systems is that collective properties arise (i.e., emerge) from the behaviors of the parts, often with properties that are not exhibited by those parts. Examples of complex systems include adaptation of white blood cells to invading bacteria, emotional and cognitive brain behaviors out of the interaction of individual neurons, the flocking formation of individual birds, dynamic equilibrium in ecosystems out of individual predator–prey interactions, segregation patterns in cities out of individual choices in places to live, and so on.

An important question to be asked is: Has the study of complex systems yielded findings or insights that are different than those from theoretical, research, and disciplinary perspectives of scientific fields such as physics, biology, chemistry, and so on? This is an issue discussed in the recent book by Melanie Mitchell (2009), in which she considers what are perhaps the most significant contributions of research about the characteristics of complex systems. She notes that there have been new ways of conceptualizing complex problems that challenge longer-term scientific assumptions. For example, chaos has demonstrated that intrinsic randomness of a system may not be necessary for the overall behaviors of the system to look random; recent findings in genetics challenge the centrality of the role of genetic change in evolution; and chance and self-organization are being viewed as dynamics that challenge the centrality of natural selection in evolution. Mitchell also notes the importance in both scientific communities and the general population of ways of thinking that include nonlinearity, decentralized control, networks, hierarchical levels in systems, statistical representations of information, and so on.

We next consider how complexity ideas are now being incorporated into research in the learning sciences related to the study of learning environments.

Complex Systems and Research on Learning Environments

There has been a shift in the learning sciences and related fields over the past decade from earlier work on learning concepts about complex systems to the application of perspectives about complex physical and social systems to understanding learning processes and environments (for an overview, see Jacobson & Wilensky, 2006). One indication of this latter trend is reflected in the use of complexity concepts by researchers who are studying learning environments. For example, in the present volume, the DeVane and Squire chapter (Chapter 10) discusses current views of activity theory, and mentions Michael Cole's 5th Dimension, which is a technology-enhanced learning environment for after-school programs. Key design features of 5th Dimension are that it is a *decentralized* and *nonlinear network* of activities ranging from digital games to reading stories that students interact with. Note there is no explicit mention of complexity in Cole's papers nor in Chapter 10, yet key conceptual perspectives of decentralized processes and nonlinearity from complex systems research are being used (which is consistent with Mitchell's point above).

There are other complexity perspectives being used in learning environments research that we believe have important implications beyond just an enriched technical vocabulary for researchers. Bereiter and Scardamalia (2005) have argued that:

> As complex systems concepts such as self-organization and emergence make their way into mainstream educational psychology, it becomes increasingly apparent that there are no simple causal explanations for anything in this field. In general, what comes out of a sociocognitive process cannot be explained or fully predicted by what goes into it. Creative works, understanding, and cognitive development are all examples of complex structures emerging from the interaction of simpler components (Sawyer, 1999, 2004). Learning itself, at both neural and knowledge levels, has emergent properties.
>
> (Pribram & King, 1996,
> in Bereiter and Scardamalia, 2005, p. 707)

The critique of simple causal explanations made by Bereiter and Scardamalia centers on the construct of emergence, which are properties emerging from the interaction of simpler components. We believe that the construct of emergence is centrally important for the study of learning environments that has important methodological and theoretical implications. To consider these implications, in the next section, we first "unpack" perspectives about emergence more fully and then in the following sections we discuss its implications for methodology and theory for the study of learning environments.

Emergence in the Learning and Cognitive Sciences

Interest in emergence is a recent area for cognitive and learning scientists (Clancey, 2008; Goldstone, 2006). Existing theories of cognition and learning (e.g., Hutchins, 1995; Lemke, 2000) detail how cognition propagates once structured and organized, but for a theory of its emergence that does not presuppose these structures *ab initio*, we argue for the need of complexity theory perspectives mentioned above, with the particular relevance of the work of Epstein and Axtell (1996) into complexity in the social sciences.

This need also stems from the cumulative effect of empirical research indicating that inter-subjective processes at the local (individual) level yield cognitions—such as opinions (Isenberg, 1986), generation of abstract representations (Schwartz, 1995), representation and schema learning (Rumelhart, Smolensky, McClelland, & Hinton, 1986), group dynamics (Kapur, Voiklis, & Kinzer, 2008), knowledge building (Bereiter & Scardamalia, 2005), among others—that differ both in complexity and kind from those produced by any collaborating agent or those expected from the central tendency among collaborators (Vallabha & McClelland, 2007). Moreover, these cognitions emerge spontaneously, without forethought or awareness among collaborating agents (Goldstone, 2006). Apparently, both the individual and the group learn, complexity theory posits that this learning is at once distinct, dialectical, and emergent— which is a direct challenge to views of simple causal mechanisms critiqued by Bereiter and Scardamalia above.

The concept of emergent behavior is, however, rather paradoxical. On the one hand, it arises from the interactions between agents in a system (e.g., individuals in a collective). On the other hand, it constrains subsequent interactions between agents and in so doing, seems to have a life of its own independent of the local interactions (Kauffman, 1995) and therefore, cannot be reduced to the individual agents (or parts) of the system (Lemke, 2000). For example, a traffic jam emerges from the local interactions between individual drivers; at the same time, it constrains the subsequent local interactions between these individuals. Traffic jams, once under way do seem to have a life of their own—such as the backwards propagation of a traffic jam (i.e., a clump of cars)—and these emergent patterns cannot be reduced to the behavior of the individual drivers since they are generally moving forward. Similarly, structures (norms, values, beliefs, lexicons, and so on) within social networks emerge from the local interactions between individual actors, and then, once emerged, these structures constrain the subsequent local interactions between these actors (Lemke, 2000; Watts & Strogatz, 1998).

More pertinent to educational psychology and the learning sciences, Schwartz (1995) showed how the collaborative burden of establishing common ground resulted in the emergence of abstract representations that dyads used to solve novel problems, and how the likelihood of such emergence was significantly greater for groups than for individuals. Schwartz argued that while these representations emerged from the individual interactions, they could not be reduced or attributed to the individuals in the dyad. Furthermore, once these representations emerged, they shaped subsequent interaction between the dyad members. Finally, the abstract nature of these representations was argued to be a function of the need to represent and coordinate multiple features of the problem into a common representation. Kapur's work on productive failure (Kapur, 2009, 2010) further underscores the role emergent representations play in affording attention to critical features of the problem, and how representational diversity positively influences what students learn from collaborative problem solving (Kapur & Bielaczyc, 2011). Similarly, research on inter-subjective meaning making (Stahl, Koschmann, & Suthers, 2006) and knowledge-building communities (Bereiter & Scardamalia, 2005) underscores the emergent nature of learning.

It has been observed that an emergent phenomenon is its own shortest description (Bar-Yam, 2003; Kauffman, 1995), which has important methodological implications for the study of learning environments as complex systems with emergent properties (Voiklis, Kapur, Kinzer, & Black, 2006). For example, if one could roll back time, evolution may not (probably would not according to Dawkins, 1986) unfold in the way that it actually did; the shortest description of the phenomenon is the actual trajectory of the evolution of that phenomenon. In other words, when we come to learn or understand something over time, the same trajectory of learning may not unfold if we were somehow able to go back in time and start all over again. Therefore, it becomes fundamentally important to understand how macro-level behaviors emerge from and constrain micro-level interactions. Understanding the "how," however, requires an understanding of important principles in complexity.

Principle 1: Linearity and Nonlinearity Can Co-exist in Complex Systems

Perhaps it is best to illustrate this principle with a simplified example. Consider the brain as a collection of neurons (agents). These neurons are complex chemical systems themselves, but they exhibit simple binary behavior in their synaptic interactions that are often modeled as *linear*, probabilistic functions (or rules). This type of emergent behavior, which illustrates complexity at the individual micro level resulting in simplicity at the collective mezzo level, is called *emergent simplicity* (Bar-Yam, 2003). Put another way, *nonlinear* chemical reactions can result in a *linear*, global behavior.

Further, these simple (binary) synaptic interactions at a mezzo level between neurons collectively give rise to complex *nonlinear* macro level brain "behaviors"—memory, cognition, learning, and so on—that cannot be seen in the behavior of individual neurons, nor in the micro level chemical reactions. In other words, from the *linear* mezzo level synaptic interactions emerge complex, *nonlinear* behaviors such as memory, cognition, and so on. Simplicity at the individual level that yields complexity at the mezzo level is *emergent complexity* (Bar-Yam, 2003). Still, once cognitive structures emerge across levels through feedback mechanisms, these structures constrain the very linear, synaptic interactions between neurons that they emerged from (Epstein & Axtell, 1996; Kauffman, 1995). It is important to note here that this is just an example to illustrate the notions of emergent simplicity and emergent complexity. A host of other co-evolving factors—social, cultural, and environmental—are also critical for behaviors such as consciousness and cognition to emerge. Indeed, McClelland (2010) argues that:

> I don't think that anyone who emphasizes the importance of emergent processes would deny that planful, explicitly goal-directed thought plays a role in the greatest human intellectual achievements. However, such modes of thought themselves might be viewed as emergent consequences of a lifetime of thought-structuring practice supported by culture and education.
>
> (Cole & Scribner, 1974, p. 753)

The distinction between emergent simplicity and complexity is critical, for it demonstrates that a change of scale or levels (micro to mezzo to macro) can be accompanied with a change in the type (simplicity versus complexity) of behavior. "Rules that govern behavior at one level of analysis (the individual) can cause qualitatively different behavior at higher levels (the group)" (Gureckis & Goldstone, 2006, p. 1).

An important implication of this principle for research involving learning environments is that we do not necessarily have to seek complex explanations for complex behavior; such behavior may very well be explained from the "bottom up" via simple, minimal information, such as utility function, decision rule, or heuristic contained in local interactions (Nowak, 2004). To emphasize, this is not to say that these rules are deterministic, depriving humans of any form of agency or deliberate, goal-directed activity. In fact, it is quite the opposite; these rules are context-sensitive and probabilistic, and should be seen as explanatory constructs and relations developed by researchers to explain a complex phenomenon.

Thus conceived, the distinction between emergent simplicity and complexity is different from the traditional notions grounded in linearity wherein one would expect the macro phenomenon to be commensurate with the micro phenomenon. The failure of this logic requires a re-examination of the core notion of linearity.

Linearity is broadly conceived both as a *mathematical operator* as well as a *functional relationship*. A linear operator is essentially an additive operator (Bertuglia & Vaio, 2005). For example, traditional analytical methodologies such as linear differential equations and statistical modeling, regardless of their mathematical sophistication, are essentially linear operators. They work well for closed, linear systems (or approximations thereof) where the whole is equal to the sum of its parts, thus allowing one to break a system into its components or parts, study the parts individually, and then add the parts together to form the whole. However, applying the linear operator and its associated methodologies to the study of emergent behavior in open systems is *fundamentally problematic* because emergent properties, by definition, cannot be obtained and analyzed no matter how one adds the parts.

Linearity may also be conceived as a functional relationship, such as constant proportionality or a straight line. When applied to model a causal relationship, linearity restricts one to phenomena in which the effects are proportional to their causes. This is because linearity tends to treat small changes or perturbations as temporally transient without any long-term effects. However, emergent behavior often exhibits nonlinear global effects *even if the local action is linear*. As we demonstrated above, linearity and nonlinearity can co-exist in a system, and thus one cannot assume that global effects are proportional to their local causes. In fact, small linear changes or perturbations such as El Nino can and often do have large, nonlinear effects, which is metaphorically illustrated as the so-called "butterfly effect" that the seminal climate research of Edward Lorenz (1963) demonstrated nearly half a century ago. Therefore, important nonlinear relationships among variables across scales and hierarchies may be missed entirely, or worse, be inappropriately and inaccurately modeled linearly since that is only what the linear method can handle (Holland, 1995).

However, it is *not* the case that understanding emergent behavior requires that we make a "conceptual shift" from linearity to nonlinearity. Rather than characterizing the distinction between simple and complex systems in terms of dichotomies such as linear versus nonlinear, we propose that perhaps a more productive characterization of complexity, and of emergent behavior, lies not in emphasizing these dichotomies but in collapsing them. We argue that complexity is better characterized as a *dialectical co-existence of linearity and nonlinearity*. The complexity of emergent behavior comes from the co-existence of linearity and nonlinearity across and within multiple levels or scales of an open system. Indeed, because of this, complex systems exhibit seemingly opposing properties and behaviors: randomness and order, predictability (e.g., attractors, highly connected nodes or hubs) and unpredictability, coherence and incoherence, stability and instability, centralization and decentralization, and so on. It is not one or the other, it is *both* (Kauffman, 1995).

Consider an example to illustrate this point: the micro and macro dynamics of gases. Gas particles interact with each other based on well-defined laws of conservation of energy and momentum. Both are linear laws. Yet, the motion of the gas is evidently nonlinear and complex. Throwing dye into a gas chamber easily reveals the nonlinearity of diffusion paths. Thus the dynamics of gases as a complex system emerges from local linear interactions governed by well-defined, linear laws. Yet, the main global behavior of the gas—diffusion—is nonlinear. Furthermore, the nonlinear global behavior perpetuates the very linear local interactions between gas particles that it emerged from. Given this, are gas dynamics linear? The answer is *both*. The point we stress is that an emergent phenomenon such as diffusion in gases is best characterized as the dialectical co-existence of linearity and nonlinearity. It is interesting to note that other global properties of gases such as pressure and volume behave in perfectly linear ways according to the gas law equations, which only reinforces this important point.

Principle 2: Explanations of an Emergent Phenomenon are Causal

Causality, full or conditional, is merely the idea of relating effects to their causes that may be one or many, sequential or simultaneous. It is important not to confuse causality with linearity. Seeking a relation between causes and effects does not necessarily imply that the relation is linear. Historically, the mathematical tools available to us were largely linear in nature. As a result, the mathematical education of physical and social scientists primarily consisted of linear mathematical tools. For example, calculus, linear differential equations, statistical models such as regression, multi-level modeling, variance modeling, and so on, are all mathematical tools that *model relationships between causes and effects in a linear manner*. Thus, if the primary tool for relating causes with effects has, for the better part of our scientific history, been linear, then over time, it is not surprising that the notion of causality has become synonymous with linearity, when in fact it should not be the case.

The confounding of causality with linearity is so strong that the mere mention of causality invites strong reactions from researchers with commitments to qualitative methods for describing complexity. This is unfortunate because even descriptive methods must explain the causal mechanisms of a complex phenomenon (diSessa, 1993). To argue that qualitative descriptions of a complex phenomenon are never causal reveals a misconception of the dynamics of complex systems. This is because a study of emergent behavior requires that we employ upward causation to explain how emergent behavior arises from the local interactions, as well as downward causation to explain how global behavior, once emerged, constrains, or shapes the subsequent local interactions. Any explanation of the dynamics of complex systems, therefore, will necessarily have to explain upward and downward causations (Lemke, 2000). Whether one does it qualitatively, quantitatively, or computationally does not make an explanation any less causal, for if it is not causal, then it is not describing the necessary causations, and hence falling short of explaining the dynamics. Furthermore, that we are seeking upward and downward causal relations does not mean all relations between causes and effects have to be modeled using linear, mathematical tools. Indeed, complexity scientists often—of necessity—combine linear and nonlinear methods to explain the upward and downward causation as they study complex physical, biological, and social systems.

Principle 3: Any Explanation of an Emergent Phenomenon is Reductive

Reduction is merely the idea of seeking the minimum amount of description of a phenomenon that can explain the phenomenon. Whether we are speaking of theoretical, methodological, or ontological reduction, it is important not to confuse reduction with linearity. For example, in order to describe the behavior of a gas at different combinations of pressure, volume, and temperature, one does not need to actually describe the motion at the atomic or particle level. The gas law equations suffice as sufficient (i.e., reductive) descriptions of this phenomenon in a minimal manner. However, as we noted above, historically the scientific notion of what it means to explain is so deeply situated in mathematics (or a methodological reduction of observation to mathematical tools) that the predominant way of deriving reductive explanations has been in the form of linear mathematical tools.

It was a rejection of such (linear) reduction that led, in part, to the development of the qualitative paradigm that prides itself in not being reductive when describing a complex phenomenon. However, to maintain that qualitative descriptions of a complex phenomenon are not reductive represents a misconception of complexity. As argued earlier, learning as a complex phenomenon is its own shortest description. Therefore, any explanation, be it quantitative, qualitative, or computational, used alone or in combination, will necessarily be reductive (Kapur, Hung, Jacobson, Voiklis, & Victor, 2007). Bearing this albeit brief conceptual unpacking of emergence in mind, we now turn our attention to methodologies for how one might seek understandings of emergent behavior such as in "learning-environments" in a principled manner.

Methodological Implications

From the preceding section, it follows that if learning is conceived as a complex, emergent phenomenon, then methods for understanding and explaining learning must necessarily be causal and reductive. This means that the issue is not causality or reduction per se. The real methodological challenge lies in dealing with the dialectical co-existence of linearity and nonlinearity in the dynamics that result in learning. To this end, we need to examine existing methodologies in educational research to see if and how they may be used, and whether we need to consider methodologies that are currently little used in learning environments.

Broadly speaking, existing methodological approaches fall into one or more of three categories: (a) *experimental*, (b) *descriptive*, and (c) *design* (Suthers, 2006). For the purposes of our argument, however, the three categories may be reduced to two. This is because the third category—the design-based approaches—at the compositional, methodological level (as opposed to the theoretical level) uses methods that are typically descriptive, though sometimes integrative (descriptive cum experimental) to understand and explain learning. Design researchers offer rich accounts of an iterative exploration of the possibility space of designs; once promising or effective design features are identified, experimental methods may be used together with descriptive methods to document and explain the emergence of learning in collaborative settings (Barab & Squire, 2004). At the methodological level however, one could reasonably posit that the design approach, in the final analysis, typically resorts to descriptive or integrative (descriptive cum experimental) approaches to gain and explain phenomenological understandings (Bielaczyc & Collins, 2010). For the purposes of this chapter, therefore, it suffices that we examine the experimental and descriptive approaches in terms of their usefulness and limitations in studying learning and environments as an emergent phenomenon.

Experimental Approaches

Experimental (including quasi-experimental) approaches are pervasively used in educational research (Kapur & Kinzer, 2007; Suthers & Hundhausen, 2003). They typically seek to establish causal or quasi-causal explanations of design or intervention effects versus control or comparison conditions. Reductive quantification of qualitative interactional data into categories followed by counting and aggregation, and then linear statistical modeling, typify this approach. While this approach allows one to draw aggregated-level interpretations and conclusions about relationships between manipulated variables and their effects, it may be criticized for over-simplifying the complexity of interactional dynamics in educational groups. Still, it serves a valuable purpose as a method for making quantified causal or quasi-causal generalizations, especially as a complement to descriptive methods (Stahl *et al.*, 2006).

To examine if the experimental approach is sufficient for explaining the emergence of learning, we need to ascertain if and how it can deal with the dialectical co-existence of linearity and nonlinearity of the dynamics that result in learning. Unfortunately, because the major tools for mathematical modeling (e.g., differential equations, statistical modeling) are fundamentally *linear* tools, they cannot measure up to the methodological challenge of explaining an emergent phenomenon. As noted earlier, linear (additive) methods work by breaking a system into its components or parts, studying the parts individually, and then adding the parts together to form the whole. However, an emergent phenomenon, as discussed above, cannot be analyzed by "adding up the parts." Furthermore, critical information is lost when heterogeneous actors (parts) are aggregated or averaged into factors (Eidelson, 1997). As Holland (1995) explains, "Nonlinearities mean that our most useful tools for generalizing observations into theory—trend analysis, determination of equilibria, sample means, and so on—are badly blunted" (p. 5).

The historical predominance of linear tools and methodologies is perhaps best captured by Bertuglia and Vaio (2005):

> Despite the fact that linear models are, in reality, an exception in the panorama of models that we can construct to describe reality, they have received particular attention, above all in the past, for a variety of reasons. One reason is that the mathematical education of scientists, particularly those that study natural sciences, has been focused on linear mathematics for at least three centuries ... On the one hand, the reason for this was that linear mathematical techniques are simpler than those nonlinear ones ..., and on the other hand (perhaps above all), because linear mathematics is undoubtedly easier to grasp immediately than nonlinear mathematics. A second reason for this leaning towards linear mathematics is that there are several cases in which linear models provide effective descriptions of natural phenomena; the brilliance of the latter is such that it overshadows the other cases, the majority, in which linear models are not applicable and lack adequate descriptive techniques.
>
> (Bertuglia & Vaio, 2005, p. 241)

Therefore, traditional experimental approaches and their underlying assumption of linearity fail to capture let alone model emergent behavior of complex phenomena. This is not to suggest that we abandon their use altogether. For example, linear statistical modeling techniques may be valuable for analysis of dimensions of a complex system in which linearity is manifest. Still, this requires understanding the limitations of applying linear methods to study an emergent phenomenon and thus that one must exercise caution and humility in what can be accomplished by using these approaches.

Descriptive Approaches

One of the fundamental orientations in recent educational theory is the social-participatory construction of meanings as an inter-subjective, in-situ phenomenon (Koschmann *et al.*, 2005; Stahl *et al.*, 2006). Past research in this area has focused on the emergent meaning-making process through descriptive approaches designed to gain rich, data-driven, bottom-up understandings of the phenomenon as it unfolds. These methods include conversation analysis (Sacks, Schegloff, & Jefferson, 1974), discourse analysis (Johnstone, 2002), narrative analysis (Hermann, 2003), and so on. Because one could use these methods at multiple scales of a phenomenon (e.g., conversation or discourse analysis at a micro level, and perhaps narrative analysis at a macro level), when used together, they may provide an ecologically valid understanding of an emergent phenomenon.

Even so, limitations of descriptive methods have been well articulated, such as an inability to establish generalizations of interventions and design decisions as well as an over-emphasis on theory building as opposed to theory application (Stahl *et al.*, 2006). In addition, from a complexity perspective, even descriptive methods are reductive when used to explain emergent phenomena. Recall that an emergent phenomenon is its own shortest description, thus the difference between an experimental and descriptive approach is not that the former is reductive and the latter is not. Instead, *it is the degree of reduction that is different,* with descriptive methods being less reductive than experimental methods. Different levels of reduction lead to different kinds of explanations and understandings, and both can be insightful and important (Suthers, 2006).

Furthermore, the sheer spatial–temporal scale of an emergent phenomenon limits (but does not negate) the usefulness of in-depth, descriptive analysis, which, by definition, requires that one focus on a humanly-manageable portion of the spatial–temporal landscape, which is the entire space and time over which the phenomenon unfolds (Eidelson, 1997). For example, if one is examining authorial dynamics in Wikipedia using descriptive methods, then the choice of the method itself limits the scope of what one might choose for an in-depth study, perhaps one or a few articles. This, of course, would not pose any problems if the spatial–temporal landscape of Wikipedia (and large-scale collective dynamics in general) was uniform so that an understanding of a small part may be applied uniformly to the whole. Unfortunately though, this is rarely the case for emergent phenomena.

From a temporal standpoint, emergent behavior often occurs through *abrupt phase transitions* that tend to happen in a narrow temporal band of a phenomenon's evolution (Kauffman, 1995). A descriptive analysis likely makes it difficult (though not impossible) to detect this in a consistent and reliable manner (Kruse & Stadler, 1993). Similarly, large-scale dynamics can display drastically different characteristics in different parts of their spatial–temporal landscape. An in-depth description of a small part of that landscape, while informative and meaningful in its own right, does little if what one is really seeking is an understanding of the entire landscape. For example, large amounts of snow fell on the east coast of the United States in the winter of 2010, even though the average global temperature has been steadily rising since the mid-twentieth century. Further, large portions of the landscape may appear highly orderly, yet the seeds of chaotic and emergent behavior may be located in a small part. This is certainly exemplified in the linear order seen in climate sequences of seasons of winter–spring–summer–autumn in North America, even though there may be a colder day in spring than a particular winter day in Denver. Again, a descriptive analysis may make it difficult to detect this in a consistent and reliable manner (Kruse & Stadler, 1993). Still, an army of descriptive studies large enough to be distributed over varied portions of the spatial–temporal landscape of the phenomenon may yet prove to be highly useful provided one could somehow coordinate and integrate these efforts into a meaningful whole.

Finally, there is one limitation that cuts across both experimental and descriptive approaches, which is each of these approaches is largely limited to *explaining and understanding what has already emerged* (Epstein & Axtell, 1996). For example, once patterns or organizations (e.g., opinions, norms, convergence in group discussions) emerge, they can be subjected to experimental methods to explain aggregate-level relationships. At the same time, descriptive methods can be employed to gain thick descriptions and understandings of the trajectory of evolution that led to emergent organizations. However, if one could unwind time, *the same trajectory may not have unfolded even if one started with similar initial conditions* (Kauffman, 1995). Part of what makes an emergent pattern irreducible and therefore its own shortest description is its high sensitivity to initial conditions.

Consequently, to understand an emergent phenomenon, one needs to understand and explain not only the trajectory of evolution that *actually* unfolds but also the possibility space of trajectories of evolution that *could* unfold (Huang & Kapur, 2007). One has to go no further than the weather system to exemplify this. If researchers seeking understandings of the emergent dynamics of weather patterns were restricted mainly to experimental and descriptive approaches, they may not have been able to understand the possibility space of trajectories that a weather system may take in its evolution; a realization that was instrumental in the development of chaos theory (Gleick, 1987). Simply put, while it may be highly likely that it will be warm and sunny tomorrow (depending upon where one is), there is also a good chance it could rain, and even a slight chance of a major thunderstorm. Social dynamics and learning are probably even more complex than weather dynamics. Thus, relying mainly on experimental and descriptive approaches places limitations on a quest to seek understandings of the possibility space over which an emergent phenomenon may unfold.

Moving Forward

Realizing that experimental and descriptive approaches each have something to offer, researchers have called for greater integration of these approaches moving forward (Suthers, 2006). We second this call. However, as we have argued, both the experimental and the descriptive approaches—alone or combined—have limitations as methodologies for understanding learning environments. We see combining the two to be a necessary step; yet, that alone is insufficient (Huang & Kapur, 2007). The inherent complexities of "learning-environments" as an emergent phenomenon place limits even on an integrative approach (Epstein & Axtell, 1996; Holland, 1995).

In the light of our focus on explaining learning as an emergent phenomenon, this sets up an imperative for a methodology that not only builds on the experimental and descriptive methodologies but also is able to appropriately investigate learning from the "bottom up." *Agent-based modeling* and *models* (we use ABMs to refer to both agent-based modeling—i.e., creating new computational models—and the use of existing agent-based models) provide a methodological *complement* that is increasingly being used not only in the natural sciences (Jackson, 1996) but also in economics (Arthur, Durlauf, & Lane, 1997), sociology (Watts & Strogatz, 1998), socio-cultural psychology (Axelrod, 1997), organizational science (Carley, 2002), just to name a few. Grounded in complexity theory, agent-based modeling is providing significant theoretical and empirical insights into the dynamics of complex systems (Eidelson, 1997). Note however that we are not making the naïve claim that the integration of ABMs into our methodological toolkit will somehow solve our methodological problems in ways that experimental and descriptive methods cannot. Instead, cognizant of the fact that there are inherent epistemic and methodological limits to what an integrated—experimental, descriptive, and computational—approach can achieve, we argue that computational ABMs when integrated with experimental and descriptive approaches can potentially reveal insights that may otherwise remain elusive, much like how descriptive methods can reveal insights into a phenomenon that may not be possible with the use of experimental methods alone. With this in mind, we now briefly describe agent-based modeling, instantiate the methodology by giving examples from past research (including our own), and further consider its methodological potential for understanding the dynamics of the complexity of learning environments.

Agent-based Modeling

Over the past two decades, computational agent-based models (ABMs) and modeling have emerged as important tools for scientists seeking to understand complex physical, biological, and social phenomena (Eidelson, 1997). In fact, evidence from computational ABMs is increasingly being argued and endorsed as a third legitimate source of scientific evidence, a third way of doing science (Axelrod, 1997); the other two being direct observation and mathematical manipulation (Jackson, 1996). It is not surprising then that computational ABMs are being used pervasively in the natural and the social sciences (as we have discussed earlier). It is only recently, though, that researchers in the learning and educational sciences have begun to explore the use of computational ABMs (Abrahamson & Wilensky, 2005; Blikstein, Abrahamson, & Wilensky, 2006; Goldstone, 2006; Jacobson & Wilensky, 2006). However, their potential and use in the learning sciences more generally and in the study of "learning-environments" in particular remains largely unexplored. Therefore, a brief description of computational ABMs is in order, although it is not possible, within the constraints of a single manuscript, to provide a comprehensive account of ABMs. Instead, we hope to provide a conceptual basis and highlight the methodological issues in the process (for a fuller treatment of ABMs, the reader may consult several excellent texts: Axelrod, 1997; Epstein & Axtell, 1996).

ABMs shift the focus from *factors* to *actors* (Macy & Willer, 2002); one no longer has to investigate phenomena with the assumption of homogeneous actors that are then aggregated into factors. Instead, researchers can more appropriately maintain the *diversity* of agents in a population as *heterogeneous* actors, each with its own set of genetic and cultural traits, often using *simple rules* of behavior (Axelrod, 1997). ABMs leverage the cardinal principle of complexity, which is the principle of *dynamical minimalism* (Nowak, 2004): simple rules at the local level can sufficiently generate complex emergent behavior at the collective level (Bar-Yam, 2003). Requiring complex explanations for complex behavior is not an epistemological necessity (Casti, 1994; Kapur, Voiklis, & Kinzer, 2008); complex collective behavior may very well be explained via simple, minimal information (e.g., utility function, decision rule, or heuristic, contained in local interactions). Repeated updating of local interactions can generate the phenomenon over time from the "*bottom up*" (Nowak, 2004). Heterogeneous actors interacting with each other over *space* and *time* give rise to emergent global structures and patterns and these, in turn, dialectically shape and constrain the subsequent interactions between agents. ABMs represent these emergent behaviors from the "bottom up" by computationally simulating the interactions between individual agents and letting the system evolve *in silico* (Epstein & Axtell, 1996). So, rather than positing emergent structures *ab initio*, ABMs seek to generate and understand the possibility space of how these structures emerge in the first place and shape the very local behaviors they emerged from (for a review, see Vallacher & Nowak, 2004). Thus, one is no longer restricted to an analysis of static equilibria in social phenomena—an analysis of the already emerged—or of analyses based on simplifying assumptions of homogeneous agents as aggregated factors. With ABMs, there is the methodological potential of taking a principled, pro-active, and process-oriented analysis of the dynamics that result in emergence.

It is important to reiterate that the argued potential of ABMs no longer remains a mere theoretical proposition because ABMs are increasingly being used to model the dynamics of emergent behavior by researchers in the physical and social sciences. For example, consider the computational ABM of Social Impact Theory (Nowak, Szamrej, & Latane, 1990), which simulates how polarized clusters naturally emerge in public opinion. Building on previous theory and empirical evidence, an ABM for social influence operating via two interlocking, dialectical mechanisms is hypothesized: the group influences each person, and each person influences the group. The intensity of the dialectic is derived from a function of three variables: group size, personal persuasiveness, and personal position in physical (or social) space. During the course of evolution (i.e., the iterative application of the social influence function to each group-on-person and person-on-group interaction), the simulation evolves from an initial random distribution of opinions into emergent organizations of islands (clusters) of minority opinion in a sea of majority opinion, which is an emergent organization of opinions not unlike that in the real world.

In the cognitive sciences, the rise of distributed connectionist models to explain a wide variety of cognitive constructs presents another example of an emergentist approach to modeling learning (Rumelhart, Hinton, & McClelland, 1986). The connectionist modeling approach has now been applied to model a wide variety of cognitive behaviors such as acquisition of schemas (Rumelhart, Smolensky *et al.*, 1986), category learning (Vallabha & McClelland, 2007), linguistic rules (Rumelhart & McClelland, 1986), and decision making (Usher & McClelland, 2001) (for an excellent review, see McClelland, 2010).

Other examples where ABMs have been used to model emergent behavior include investigations of theories of cognitive and psychological development (Abrahamson & Wilensky, 2005; Blikstein *et al.*, 2006), inter-generation cultural transmission and evolution (Boyd & Richerson, 2005), emergence of social conventions (Barr, 2004), lexical development in interaction (Hutchins & Hazelhurst, 1995), emergence of social norms (Fehr & Fischbacher, 2004) and belief systems (Watts, 2007), group path formation (Goldstone, Jones, & Roberts, 2006), among many others. In what follows, we consider three examples of the use of computational models in learning sciences research.

Example 1: Piaget–Vygotsky Model

We use this example to discuss the use of agent-based modeling to explore theoretical issues in the learning sciences that are also of relevance to "learning environments." Abrahamson and Wilensky (2005) have been involved with research in which agent-based modeling was used to provide computational visualizations of different theoretical explanations of how people learn. They developed the "I'm Game!" ABM using NetLogo (Wilensky, 1999) to create computational instantiations of Piagetian and Vygotskian theories of learning. The simulation uses the context of a group of children who are playing, which links to studies of playing and cognitive development by Piaget and Vygotsky as well as being relatively easy to proceduralize using NetLogo computer code. Essentially, "I'm Game!" is a "model-based thought experiment" in which synthetic learners are trying to improve their performance of playing marbles in three computational conditions. In the first condition, the Piagetian players try to improve their marble playing (i.e., learn) based on feedback on how close their marble was to the target (i.e., accommodation of schema from feedback), whereas the Vygotskian players in the second condition learn by imitation of other virtual players who are more successful at the marble task. A third Piagetian–Vygotskian condition was programmed in which the synthetic learners improved their marble playing by both feedback and imitation. There was also a "random" condition as a computational control treatment.

Abrahamson and Wilensky (2005) are careful to point out in their paper that this model of Piagetian and Vygotskian learning "are gross caricatures of these theoretical models" (p. 18); however, they also hope the simple agent rules programmed in the model "may be sufficient to generate data revealing interesting behavioral patterns at the group level" (p. 18). They conclude with an invitation for other researchers to use ABMs as catalysts for disciplinary discourse, such as by making changes to their model to allow computational investigations of different assumptions about the theories or to create different treatment conditions for new computational experiments.

Professor Jim Levin and members of the Laboratory of Comparative Human Cognition (LCHC) at the University of California, San Diego, accepted this invitation (Abrahamson, Wilensky, & Levin, 2007). The LCHC group had begun using NetLogo as a modeling environment for learning, and, in particular, to examine the Abrahamson–Wilensky (A-W) model of Piagetian and Vygotskian learning. They articulated a critique of the A-W implementation of the Vygotskian notion of the Zone of Proximal Development (ZPD) as having a "simplex" assumption that the less skilled of a pair of learners would change but with no changes to the more skilled member. Instead, the LCHC group argued that the ZPD is a dynamic or "duplex" construction in which there are changes by both the less skilled

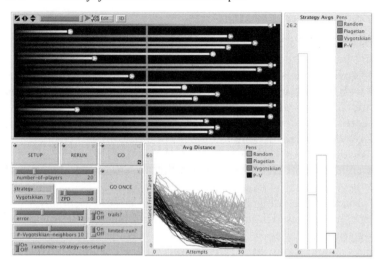

Figure 13.1 Screenshot from the NetLogo "I'm Game!" interactive simulation of learning (Abrahamson & Wilensky, 2005)

member (i.e., the learner) and the more skill person (i.e., the teacher). Levin made a relatively simple programming change in the model so that marble "teachers" would change based on their understanding of how their "students" performed (see Figure 13.2). For a full discussion of the model outcomes, see Abrahamson, Wilensky, and Levin (2007).

Example 2: Collaborative Learning in Classrooms

The research of Abrahamson, Blikstein, and Wilensky (2007) illustrates the use of agent-based modeling to provide analytical insights that complement and extend the descriptive techniques used to study a classroom learning environment. In this study, agent-based simulations were developed of students collaborating in a middle school mathematics classroom based on real classroom data. Running the simulation and comparing the outcomes with the data from the intervention validated the computer model. The model provided an isomorphic agent-based visualization of the collaborative interactions of the students, as seen in Figure 13.3. In addition, the model also generated emergent participation patterns similar to how individual students operated in roles within groups (such as "number crunchers," "checkers," or "assemblers") as well as some students who operated between groups as "ambassadors." Empirically, it was found that there were different types of mathematical activities associated with the different roles (e.g., "number crunchers" involved higher level mathematical thinking than "assemblers"), which in turn were related to mathematical achievement outcomes. The authors conclude that the functional resemblance of the real and simulated

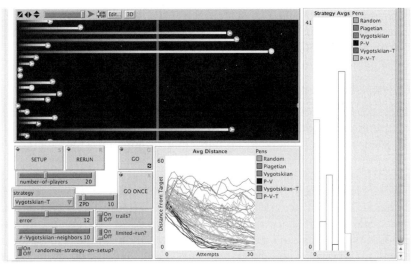

Figure 13.2 Screenshot from the A-W model modified by Jim Levin (Abrahamson, Wilensky *et al.*, 2007)

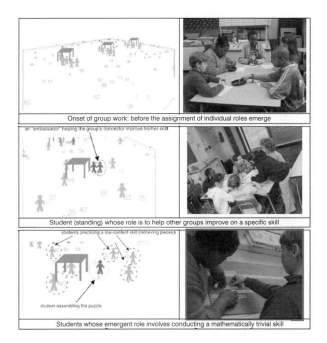

Figure 13.3 Three examples of computer simulation outcomes paired with classroom video data (Abrahamson, Blikstein *et al.*, 2007)

behaviors indicate that the model provides a "viable, if not complex, explanation for the emergence of the observed patterns" (Abrahamson, Blikstein *et al.*, 2007, p. 54).

Example 3: Markov Modeling of CSCL Groups

The second author's own research exploring the integrative use of computational models with experimental and descriptive methods has revealed what we believe to be important insights into the emergence of convergence in Computer-Supported Collaborative Learning (CSCL) group discussions. This work is part of an on-going research program and is available elsewhere (Kapur, Voiklis *et al.*, 2008; Kapur, Voiklis, Kinzer, & Black, 2006), so we only provide a brief description here. Grounding our work in complexity theory, we conceptualized convergence in in-group discussions as an emergent behavior arising from the transactional interactions between group members. Leveraging the concepts of emergent simplicity and emergent complexity (Bar-Yam, 2003), we hypothesized a set of theoretically sound yet simple rules to model the micro-level problem-solving interactions between group members, and then examined the resulting emergent behavior—convergence in their discussion. Employing a commonly used computational model in the form of a Markov walk, interactions between group members were conceptualized as goal-seeking adaptations that either help the group move towards or away from its goal, or maintain its status quo. Our analysis revealed novel insights into the emergence of convergence in group discussions. Specifically, our model, when applied to actual interactional data, suggested that groups tended to organize themselves into highly convergent or divergent regimes early in their discussion. Figure 13.4 shows the convergence curves of low- and high-performing groups solving well- or ill-structured problems.

Regardless of the type of problems, convergence curves clearly exhibit sensitivity of early exchange in the group discussions. The emergence of such sensitivity to early exchange meant that high or low quality member contributions had a greater positive or negative impact on the eventual group performance when they came earlier than later in a discussion. Consequently, eventual group performance could be predicted based on what happens in the first 30–40 percent of a discussion. Not surprisingly, we managed to demonstrate convergence to be a more powerful predictor of group performance than commonly used "coding and counting" measures in CSCL research (Suthers, 2006).

What is perhaps more important for the present purposes of illustrating ways in which ABMing approaches can enrich the understanding of different aspects of learning environments is that in all the examples thus far, simple agents interacting with each other using simple, linear rules could generate the emergent, nonlinear patterns that are surprisingly similar qualitatively to what we observe in social phenomena. With computational

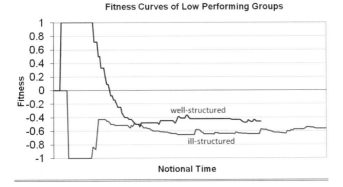

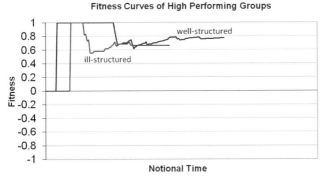

Figure 13.4 Convergence curves of low and high performing groups solving well-or ill-structured physics problems

ABMs, one has a method to deal with dialectical co-existence of linearity and nonlinearity. However, a skeptic could validly argue that ABMs also commit an over-simplification by reducing complex human behavior to computable agents so much so that it seems over-optimistic that the complexities of emergent behavior can be modeled successfully using ABMs. Advocates of ABMs would easily submit to this limitation. Indeed, they might make commitments to the notion that "all models are wrong, but some are better than others." However, we note that large-scale ABMs have been used to model large-scale phenomena, such as simulating traffic in large metropolitan areas with millions of travelers to assist urban planners (Balmer, Nagel, & Raney, 2004). The central idea here is that the integrative use of ABMs together with experimental and descriptive methodologies could result in interesting and plausible understandings of learning as an emergent phenomenon, understandings that may not otherwise be possible through descriptive and experimental methods alone.

Thus, verisimilitude—the plausibility of behavior and patterns—lends explanatory power to computational ABMs, as well as to other scientific methodologies. The notion of sufficiency of explanation is integral to scientific inquiry, although standards for what counts as sufficient vary across the fields, for example a *p*-value of "0.05 or less" is commonly accepted as sufficient to demonstrate a causal or correlational explanation. Concerning the explanatory power of ABMs, if simple mechanisms operating on minimal variables produce realistic phenomena in a simulated world, then perhaps the same simple mechanisms operating on the same minimal variables produce real phenomena in the real world (Nowak, 2004). Put another way, *what seems life-like could perhaps be like life* (Voiklis *et al.*, 2006). Thus, one could hypothesize theoretically-sound computational ABMs to perform computational experiments, and validate the results against theory and empirical data (Goldstone & Janssen, 2005; Jacobson & Wilensky, 2006). In so doing, computational ABMs push the very notion of what it means to *explain* a phenomenon, what Goldstone and Janssen (2005) refer to as a "proof-by-construction." Epstein and Axtell (1996) articulate this notion succinctly:

> What constitutes an explanation of an observed social phenomenon? Perhaps one day people will interpret the question, "Can you explain it?" as asking "Can you grow it?" Artificial society modeling allows us to "grow" social structures in silico demonstrating that certain sets of microspecifications are sufficient to generate the macrophenomena of interest. And that, after all, is a central aim. As social scientists, we are presented with "already emerged" collective phenomena, and we seek microrules that can generate them ... But the ability to grow them—greatly facilitated by modern object-oriented programming—is what is new. Indeed, it holds out the prospect of a new, generative, kind of social science.
>
> (Epstein & Axtell, 1996, p. 20)

While this may seem a somewhat over-enthusiastic endorsement, the ability of computational ABMs to model or "grow" an emergent social phenomenon from the "bottom up" does provide an ontological coherence between the method and its object of inquiry. Epistemological and, consequently, methodological debates within the scientific discourse about the nature of knowledge and knowing from computational ABM experiments increasingly lean in favor of using computational ABM as part of an integrated methodological tool-kit. Still, these debates suggest that computational ABM is not without its own set of limitations. For example, while verisimilitude proves essential to the theory-building efforts of those trying to understand an emergent phenomenon, clearly, an over-reliance on verisimilitude may strain one's evidentiary standards (Voiklis *et al.*, 2006). Because of this, there is a great need for phenomenological validation of results derived from computational ABMs (Goldstone & Janssen, 2005).

How might one achieve such phenomenological validation? Cioffi-Revilla (2002) suggests concrete steps for robust sensitivity and invariance analyses of computational ABMs to ensure that the simulated results are not merely "synthetic outcomes." Minimally, this may include examining the sensitivity and invariance of simulated results to *system size* (number of interacting agents), *agent geometry* (the structure of the spatial landscape on which agents interact, e.g., lattices), and *network topology*. Additionally, simulated results also need to be calibrated with respect to real-world phenomena. Phenomenological *time calibration* would help ascertain the correspondence between notional time (the number of iterations in the simulation) and referent time (e.g., hours, days, months, years, centuries). Phenomenological *magnitude calibration* would help ensure correspondence between simulated and real phenomena in terms of the magnitude or size or intensity of emergent behaviors. Phenomenological *distributional calibration* would help ensure that distributions (often power laws) that emerge in simulated phenomena parametrically correspond with those in the real phenomena. Finally, and most importantly, if ABMs are to make a significant contribution to our understanding of learning and learning environments, then there is a need to move beyond the behavioral level (how agents behave and what they do) to also model their capacities for learning. For this capability, we need agents that are self-modifying (e.g., genetic algorithms [Mitchell, 1996]; artificial life [Langton, 1995]) along theoretically important dimensions such as reflection, learning, use of tools, and so on.

As the field advances, this list of types of phenomenological validation for the study of "learning-environments" will grow, as well it should. It is hoped that a persistent conversation between advocates and skeptics will potentially generate new ideas for the validation of computational ABMs. Perhaps, over time, standards and metrics for what makes a *sufficient* explanation may emerge within this conversation. Still, we strongly believe that computational ABM alone is insufficient and that it cannot be done in isolation. One needs an integrative approach that builds on existing methodologies, although, as stated earlier, even such an approach will have unique advantages as well as limitations. For example, existing theoretical and empirical understandings (gained through methods experimental, descriptive, or both) could be used to articulate critical variables and interactional rules between individual agents in a collective. This, in turn, could be used to design agents and their interactional rules, which the computational ABMs could then simulate. Upon empirical validation, insights derived from the simulated collective behavior could in turn inform our theory-building efforts. Importantly, a repeated, iterative application of this process cycle is most essential and forms the thrust of our methodological position. It is through such an iterative process of *building from* and *validating with* theory and empirical data—an *iterative theory-building* cycle—that we seek a better understanding of learning as an emergent phenomenon.

ABMs are hypothesized from theory and empirical data. Computational experiments using ABMs, in turn, provide new insights, explain empirical data, and inform theory building.

The methodological approaches that have been used to study learning have yielded powerful—and often counter-intuitive—insights into our understanding of how people learn (Bransford, Brown, Cocking, & Donovan, 2000; Sawyer, 2006). However, embracing a theoretical perspective that environments in which learning occurs are inherently complex and that the phenomenon of learning emerges from various interactions and levels in complex learning systems that are dialectically linear and nonlinear potentially raises a great challenge for learning sciences researchers. We believe that augmenting the palette of research methodologies employed in learning environment research to also combine quantitative and descriptive approaches with ABM techniques has an enormous potential to reveal dimensions of learning and learning environments as emergent phenomena that lie currently beyond our ability in the field to systematically explore. Further, providing explanatory coherence for these new views of the processes of learning may well require new theoretical perspectives.

We note that in the history of the physical sciences, new instrumentation, and their attendant research methods, such as the telescope for Galileo or particle accelerators for modern high-energy physics, invariably led to theoretical breakthroughs that simply would not have been possible otherwise. Likewise, ABMs represent new instrumentation for learning environment researchers, and for the study of "learning-environments," which we argue could be used as part of an iterative theory-building cycle. Whether this might be a new kind of "generative" learning environment research field, as Epstein and Axtell (1996) aspire for the social sciences more generally, we do not know. Nevertheless, principled consideration of learning as an emergent phenomenon will, we firmly believe, yield generative conversations of central relevance to our field.

Theoretical Implications

We also believe that complexity perspectives such as attractors, scale-free networks, emergence, and so on have potentially important theoretical implications for learning environment research. For example, there has been a persistent theoretical "fault line" (diSessa, 2006) in the field for over two decades related to two competing theoretical views of knowledge representation and conceptual change: (a) "coherent knowledge" (CK) theories that conceptualize knowledge as being relatively stable and consistent, and (b) "knowledge-in-pieces" (KIP) theories in which ideas are viewed as fragmented and highly influenced by contextual cues and factors. Briefly, we suggest that these theories propose very different mechanisms for how knowledge is represented and changed. Theories of CK, such as the one articulated by Chi and colleagues (Chi, 1992, 2005; Chi, Slotta, & de Leeuw, 1994) propose that knowledge is represented as relatively stable (i.e., coherent) categories, and that learning involves processes of categorical elaboration for difficult-to-learn knowledge (e.g., many concepts in science), a process of re-categorization for conceptual change. In contrast, a KIP theory such as diSessa (2006) proposes that processes such as the activation of phenomenological primitives or "p-prims" are often unstable and influenced by situational cues and the development of coordination classes from p-prims.

Viewing knowledge representation and learning environments as complex systems, however, is predicated on the dynamic co-existence of both linearity and nonlinearity. This, in turn, means that there are both stable and unstable dynamics that will be manifest in the behavior of a complex cognitive knowledge system over time. We suggest that framing this learning environments debate about knowledge representation and conceptual change from complexity perspectives—such as work on scale-free networks (Barabasi & Bonabeau, 2003)—will reveal that CK and KIP theories have in fact focused on different aspects of the dynamics of evolving and changing cognitive knowledge systems, and that complexity perspectives might contribute to new theoretical advances in these areas. In other words, the co-existence of linearity and nonlinearity affords the possibility that knowledge representation and conceptual change can be both coherent and fragmented; instead of being either/or, it is both.

We are confident other researchers will find other ways in which complexity perspectives may help advance our theoretical understandings of learning environments. As we noted in the opening of this chapter, important theories to date about learning environments have generally embraced either Piagetian constructivism or Vygotskian socio-cultural perspectives, which we might characterize as theories that foreground either individual micro-level interactions of cognitive processes of individuals for the former and aggregate macro-level dynamics for the latter. Unfortunately, neither of these camps offers theoretically principled explanations for interactions across levels of a learning environment system. By this, we mean that socio-cognitive theories are weak at explaining emergent properties at the socio-cultural macro-level of a "learning-environment" system (see above); furthermore, socio-cultural descriptions do not articulate how macro-level structures set up feedback loops that might constrain and shape the micro-level behaviors of individual agents in the learning-environment. We believe complexity theories and conceptual perspectives can enrich our theories of learning environments and do so in ways that will also allow principled linking to new methodological approaches such as the use of agent-based modeling of learning environments we discussed earlier.

Conclusion

We have argued in this chapter that there are important conceptual and methodological implications for the study of learning environments that are raised by what might be called the complex systems framework. We use the term "framework" as it does not appear that there is a general "theory of complex systems" at this time (Mitchell, 2009). Rather, the multidisciplinary fields that study various types of complex systems use a set of conceptual perspectives or principles (e.g., multi-scale hierarchical organization, emergent patterning, dynamical attractors, scale-free networks) and methods of doing science (e.g., agent-based modeling, network analysis) that function as a shared framework for the discourse and representations used in the conduct of scientific inquiry. As such, various fields can formulate specific theoretical perspectives of relevance to the study of particular complex systems of interest that still share common elements due to their grounding in the complex systems framework.

Complexity perspectives also have epistemic implications for the study of learning environments. We suggest that many researchers seem to have a tacit epistemic frame that complex learning environments must have *complex explanations*—a complexity–complexity epistemic stance—and, a corollary view, that simple learning environments would have *simple explanations* or a simplicity–simplicity epistemic stance. However, we believe that complexity scientists have another epistemic frame, which is the apparent complexity in the behavior of many complex learning environments often has *simple explanations* based on the interaction of system elements based on relatively simple rules in conjunction with self-organization and emergent properties, and feedback mechanisms within and across different system levels and emergent. We call this the *simplicity–complexity* epistemic view.

Reifying such epistemic assumptions will, we believe, help researchers investigating "learning-environments" consider the theoretical and methodological viability of complexity (as well as competing theoretical views). However, some may find these approaches challenging. For example, someone holding a complexity–complexity epistemic stance may have difficulty accepting that a relatively simple agent-based model of a classroom-learning environment may be able to provide insights into important patterns and dynamics of learning in that context, such as in Abrahamson, Blikstein, and Wilensky's (2007) research discussed above.

In closing, we hope this chapter might stimulate interest in ways that theory and methods from the study of complex physical and social systems might enhance research investigating the dynamics and processes of "learning-environments." Important complexity constructs such as self-organization and nonlinearity have increasingly been finding their way into the conceptual discourse of research in the learning sciences in general and in the study of learning environments in particular. In contrast, there has been relatively little use of computational modeling techniques to complement traditional quantitative and qualitative methodologies that have heretofore been the sole lenses by which principled scientific inquiry into learning and learning environments has been conducted. Time will tell whether such conceptual and methodological enrichment is in fact warranted and accepted by the research community involved with the study of "learning," "learning environments," and "learning-environments." We suspect the answer will be yes, for reasons perhaps best articulated by Herbert Simon (1996, p. 1) in this way: "The central task of a natural science is to make the wonderful commonplace: to show that complexity, correctly viewed, is only a mask for simplicity; to find pattern hidden in apparent chaos."

Acknowledgements

This chapter incorporates ideas and material from earlier manuscripts (Jacobson *et al.*, 2010; Kapur & Jacobson, 2009). The insightful critical feedback on our earlier AERA symposium papers by Peter Reimann is gratefully acknowledged, as well as feedback from other readers of these manuscripts.

References

Abrahamson, D., & Wilensky, U. (2005). *Piaget? Vygotsky? I'm game!: Agent-based modeling for psychology research.* Paper presented at the Jean Piaget Society, Vancouver, Canada.

Abrahamson, D., Blikstein, P., & Wilensky, U. (2007). Classroom model, model classroom: Computer-supported methodology for investigating collaborative-learning pedagogy. In C. Chinn, G. Erkens & S. Puntambeka (Eds.), *Proceedings of the Computer Supported Collaborative Learning (CSCL) Conference* (Vol. 8, pp. 46–55). New Brunswick, NJ: Rutgers University.

Abrahamson, D., Wilensky, U., & Levin, J. A. (2007). *Agent-based modeling as a bridge between cognitive and social perspectives on learning.* Paper presented at the Annual Meeting of the American Educational Research Association, Chicago, IL.

Anderson, J. R., Reder, L. M., & Simon, H. A. (1997). Situative versus cognitive perspectives: Form versus substance. *Educational Researcher, 26*(1), 18–21.

Arthur, B., Durlauf, S., & Lane, D. (Eds.). (1997). *The economy as an evolving complex system* (Vol. II). Reading, MA: Addison-Wesley.

Axelrod, R. (1997). *The complexity of cooperation: Agent-based models of competition and collaboration.* Princeton, NJ: Princeton University Press.

Balmer, M., Nagel, K., & Raney, B. (2004). Large-scale multi-agent simulations for transportation applications. *Intelligent Transportation Systems, 8*, 1–17.

Bar-Yam, Y. (2003). *Dynamics of complex systems.* New York: Perseus Publishing.

Barab, S., & Squire, K. (2004). Design-based research: Putting a stake in the ground. *Journal of the Learning Sciences, 13*(1), 1–14.

Barabasi, A. L., & Bonabeau, E. (2003). Scale-free networks. *Scientific American, 288*(5), 60–69.

Barr, D. J. (2004). Establishing conventional communication systems: Is common knowledge necessary? *Cognitive Science, 28,* 937–962.

Bereiter, C., & Scardamalia, M. (2005). Technology and literacies: From print literacy to dialogic literacy. In N. Bascia, A. Cumming, A. Datnow, K. Leithwood & D. Livingstone (Eds.), *International handbook of educational policy* (pp. 749–761). Dordrecht, The Netherlands: Springer.

Bertuglia, C. S., & Vaio, F. (2005). *Nonlinearity, chaos, and complexity: The dynamics of natural and social systems.* Oxford, UK: Oxford University Press.

Bielaczyc, K., & Collins, A. (2010). Design research: Foundational perspectives, critical tensions, and arenas for action. In J. Campione, K. Metz & A. M. Palincsar (Eds.), *Children's learning in and out of school: Essays in honor of Ann Brown.*

Blikstein, P., Abrahamson, D., & Wilensky, U. (2006). *Minsky, mind, and models: Juxtaposing agent based computer simulations and clinical-interview data as a methodology for investigating cognitive developmental theory.* Paper presented at the annual meeting of the Jean Piaget Society, Baltimore, MD.

Boyd, R., & Richerson, P. J. (2005). *The origin and evolution of cultures.* Oxford University Press.

Bransford, J. D., Brown, A. L., Cocking, R. R., & Donovan, S. (Eds.). (2000). *How people learn: Brain, mind, experience, and school (expanded edition).* Washington DC: National Academy Press.

Carley, K. M. (2002). Computational organizational science: A new frontier. *Proceedings of the National Academy of Sciences, 19*(3), 7257–7262.

Casti, J. L. (1994). *Complexity.* New York: Basic Books.

Chi, M. T. H. (1992). Conceptual change within and across ontological categories: Implications for learning and discovery in science. In R. Giere (Ed.), *Minnesota studies in the philosophy of science: Cognitive models of science* (Vol. XV, pp. 129–186). Minneapolis: University of Minnesota Press.

Chi, M. T. H. (2005). Commonsense conceptions of emergent processes: Why some misconceptions are robust. *Journal of the Learning Sciences, 14*(2), 161–199.

Chi, M. T. H., Slotta, J. D., & de Leeuw, N. (1994). From things to processes: A theory of conceptual change for learning science concepts. *Learning and Instruction, 4,* 27–43.

Cioffi-Revilla, C. (2002). Invariance and universality in social agent-based simulations. *Proceedings of the National Academy of Sciences, 19*(3), 7314–7316.

Clancey, W. J. (2008). Scientific antecedents of situated cognition. In P. Robbins & M. Aydede (Eds.), *Cambridge handbook of situated cognition* (pp. 11–34). Cambridge, MA: Cambridge University Press.

Cole, M., & Scribner, S. (1974). *Culture and thought: A psychological introduction.* New York: Wiley.

Dawkins, R. (1986). *Blind watchmaker.* New York: Norton.

diSessa, A. (1993). Towards an epistemology of physics. *Cognition and Instruction, 10*(2), 105–225.

diSessa, A. A. (2006). A history of conceptual change research: Threads and fault lines. In R. K. Sawyer (Ed.), *The Cambridge handbook of the learning sciences* (pp. 265–281). Cambridge, UK: Cambridge University Press.

Eidelson, R. J. (1997). Complex adaptive systems in the behavioral and social sciences. *Review of General Psychology, 1*(1), 42–71.

Epstein, J. M., & Axtell, R. (1996). *Growing artificial societies: Social science from the bottom up.* Washington DC: Brookings Institution Press/MIT Press.

Fehr, E., & Fischbacher, U. (2004). Social norms and human cooperation. *Trends in Cognitive Sciences, 8,* 185–189.

Gleick, J. (1987). *Chaos: Making a new science.* New York: Viking Penguin.

Goldstone, R. L. (2006). The complex systems see-change in education. *Journal of the Learning Sciences, 15*(1), 35–43.

Goldstone, R. L., & Janssen, M. A. (2005). Computational models of collective behavior. *Trends in Cognitive Sciences, 9*(9), 424–429.

Goldstone, R. L., Jones, A., & Roberts, M. (2006). Group path formation. *IEEE Transactions on System, Man, and Cybernetics, Part A Systems and Humans, 36*(3), 611–620.

Greeno, J. G. (1997). On claims that answer the wrong questions. *Educational Researcher, 26*(1), 5–17.

Gureckis, T. M., & Goldstone, R. L. (2006). Thinking in groups. *Pragmatics and Cognition, 14*(2), 293–311.

Hermann, D. (Ed.). (2003). *Narrative theory and the cognitive sciences.* Stanford, CA: Center for the Study of Language and Information.

Holland, J. H. (1995). *Hidden order: How adaptation builds complexity.* Reading, MA: Addison-Wesley.

Huang, J. S., & Kapur, M. (2007). Diffusion of pedagogical innovations as a complex adaptive process – agent-based modeling as research method. In T. Hirashima & S. S. C. Young (Eds.), *Supporting Learning Flow through Interactive Technologies – Frontiers in Artificial Intelligence and Applications.* Amsterdam: IOS Press.

Hutchins, E. (1995). *Cognition in the wild.* Cambridge, MA: MIT Press.

Hutchins, E., & Hazelhurst, B. (1995). How to invent a lexicon: The development of shared symbols in interaction. In N. Gilbert & R. Conte (Eds.), *Artificial societies: The computer simulation of social life* (pp. 157–189). London: UCL Press.

Isenberg, D. (1986). Group polarization: A critical review and meta-analysis. *Journal of Personality and Social Psychology, 50,* 1141–1151.

Jacobson, M. J., & Wilensky, U. (2006). Complex systems in education: Scientific and educational importance and implications for the learning sciences. *Journal of the Learning Sciences, 15*(1), 11–34.

Jacobson, M. J., Wilensky, U., Reimann, P., Sengupta, P., Wilerson-Jerde, M., & Kapur, M. (2010). Learning about complexity and beyond: Theoretical and methodological implications for the learning sciences. In K. Gomez, L. Lyons & J. Radinsky (Eds.), *Learning in the Disciplines: Proceedings of the 9th International Conference of the Learning Sciences (ICLS 2010) – Volume 2, Short Papers, Symposia, and Selected Abstracts* (pp. 195–202). Chicago, IL: International Society of the Learning Sciences.

Johnstone, B. (2002). *Discourse analysis.* Oxford: Blackwell.

Kapur, M. (2009). Productive failure in mathematical problem solving. *Instructional Science, 38*(6), 523–550.

Kapur, M. (2010). A further study of productive failure in mathematical problem solving: Unpacking the design components. *Instructional Science, 39*(4), 561–579.

Kapur, M., & Bielaczyc, K. (2011). Designing for productive failure. *The Journal of the Learning Sciences*, DOI:10.1080/10508406.2011.591717

Kapur, M., & Jacobson, M. J. (2009). *Learning as an emergent phenomenon: Methodological implications.* Paper presented at the annual meeting of the American Educational Research Association, San Diego.

Kapur, M., & Kinzer, C. (2007). The effect of problem type on interactional activity, inequity, and group performance in a synchronous computer-supported collaborative environment. *Educational Technology, Research and Development, 55*(5), 439–459.

Kapur, M., Voiklis, J., & Kinzer, C. K. (2008). Sensitivities to early exchange in synchronous computer-supported collaborative (CSCL) groups. *Computers & Education, 51*(1), 54–66. Retrieved from http://dx.doi.org/10.1016/j.compedu.2007.04.007.

Kapur, M., Voiklis, J., Kinzer, C., & Black, J. (2006). Insights into the emergence of convergence in group discussions. In S. Barab, K. Hay & D. Hickey (Eds.), *Proceedings of the International Conference on the Learning Sciences* (pp. 300–306). Mahwah, NJ: Erlbaum.

Kapur, M., Hung, D., Jacobson, M., Voiklis, J., & Victor, C. D.-T. (2007). *Emergence of learning in computer-supported, large-scale collective dynamics: A research agenda.* Paper presented at the Computer Supported Collaborative Learning Conference, New Brunswick, NJ.

Kauffman, S. (1995). *At home in the universe: The search for laws of self-organization and complexity.* New York: Oxford University Press.

Koschmann, T., Zemel, A., Conlee-Stevens, M., Young, N., Robbs, J., & Barnhart, A. (2005). How do people learn? Members' methods and communicative mediation. In R. Bromme, F. W. Hesse & H. Spada (Eds.), *Barriers and biases in computer-mediated knowledge communication* (pp. 265–294). Boston: Springer-Verlag.

Kruse, P., & Stadler, M. (1993). The significance of nonlinear phenomena for the investigation of cognitive systems. In H. Haken & A. Mikhailov (Eds.), *Interdisciplinary approaches to nonlinear complex systems* (pp. 138–160). Berlin, Germany: Springer-Verlag.

Langton, C. (Ed.). (1995). *Artificial life: An overview.* Cambridge, MA: MIT Press.

Lemke, J. J. (2000). Across the scales of time: Artifacts, activities, and meanings in ecosocial systems. *Mind, Culture, and Activity, 7*(4), 273–290.

Lorenz, E. N. (1963). Deterministic nonperiodic flow. *Journal of Atmospheric Science, 20*, 130–141.

Macy, M. W., & Willer, R. (2002). From factors to actors: Computational sociology and agent-based modeling. *Annual Review of Sociology, 28*, 143–166.

McClelland, J. L. (2010). Emergence in cognitive science. *Topics in Cognitive Science, 2*(4), 751–770.

Mitchell, M. (1996). *An introduction to genetic algorithms.* Cambridge, MA: MIT Press.

Mitchell, M. (2009). *Complexity: A guided tour.* New York: Oxford University Press.

Norman, D. (1993). Cognition in the head and in the world: An introduction to the special issue on situated action. *Cognitive Science, 17*(1), 1–6.

Nowak, A. (2004). Dynamical minimalism: Why less is more in psychology. *Personality and Social Psychology Review, 8*(2), 183–192.

Nowak, A., Szamrej, J., & Latane, B. (1990). From private attitude to public opinion: A dynamic theory of social impact. *Psychological Review, 97*, 362–376.

Piaget, J. (1980). *Adaptation and intelligence: Organic selection and phenocopy* (S. Eames, Trans.). Chicago: University of Chicago Press.

Pribram, K., & King, J. (Eds.). (1996). *Learning as self organization*. Mahwah, NJ: Lawrence Erlbaum Associates.

Rumelhart, D. E., & McClelland, J. L. (1986). On learning the past tenses of English verbs. In J. L. McClelland & D. E. Rumelhart (Eds.), *Parallel distributed processing: Explorations in the microstructure of cognition* (Vol. II, pp. 216–227). Cambridge, MA: MIT Press.

Rumelhart, D. E., Hinton, G. E., & McClelland, J. L. (1986). A general framework for parallel distributed processing. In D. E. Rumelhart, J. L. McClelland & the PDP Research Group (Eds.), *Parallel distributed processing (Vol, 1: Frameworks)*. Cambridge, MA: MIT (Bradford) Press.

Rumelhart, D. E., Smolensky, P., McClelland, J. L., & Hinton, G. E. (1986). Parallel distributed processing models of schemata and sequential thought processes. In J. L. McClelland & D. E. Rumelhart (Eds.), *Parallel distributed processing: Explorations in the microstructure of cognition* (Vol. II, pp. 7–57). Cambridge, MA: MIT Press.

Sacks, H., Schegloff, E. A., & Jefferson, G. (1974). A simplest systematic for the organization of turn-taking in conversation. *Language, 50*(4), 696–735.

Sawyer, R. K. (1999). The emergence of creativity. *Philosophical Psychology, 12*(4), 447–469.

Sawyer, R. K. (2004). The mechanisms of emergence. *Philosophy of the Social Sciences, 34*, 260–282.

Sawyer, R. K. (Ed.). (2006). *Cambridge handbook of the learning sciences*. Cambridge, UK: Cambridge University Press.

Schwartz, D. L. (1995). The emergence of abstract dyad representations in dyad problem solving. *Journal of the Learning Sciences, 4*(3), 321–354.

Simon, H. A. (1996). *The sciences of the artificial*. Cambridge, MA: MIT Press.

Stahl, G., Koschmann, T., & Suthers, D. D. (2006). Computer-supported collaborative learning. In K. I. Sawyer (Ed.), *The Cambridge handbook of the learning sciences* (pp. 409–425). Cambridge, UK: Cambridge University Press.

Suthers, D., & Hundhausen, C. (2003). An empirical study of the effects of representational guidance on collaborative learning. *Journal of the Learning Sciences, 12*(2), 183–219.

Suthers, D. D. (2006). Technology affordances for intersubjective meaning making: A research agenda for CSCL. *International Journal of Computer-Supported Collaborative Learning, 1*(3), 315–337.

Usher, M., & McClelland, J. L. (2001). On the time course of perceptual choice: The leaky competing accumulator model. *Psychological Review, 108*, 550–592.

Vallabha, G. K., & McClelland, J. L. (2007). Success and failure of new speech category learning in adulthood: Consequences of learned Hebbian attractors in topographic maps. *Cognitive, Affective and Behavioral Neuroscience, 7*, 53–73.

Vallacher, R. R., & Nowak, A. (2004). Dynamical social psychology: Toward coherence in human experience and scientific theory. In A. W. Kruglanski & E. T. Higgins (Eds.), *Social psychology: Handbook of basic principles*. New York: Guilford Publications.

Voiklis, J., Kapur, M., Kinzer, C., & Black, J. (2006). An emergentist account of collective cognition in collaborative problem solving. In R. Sun (Ed.), *Proceedings of the Cognitive Science Conference* (pp. 858–863). Mahwah, NJ: Erlbaum.

Vygotsky, L. S. (1978). *Mind in society: The development of higher psychological processes*. Cambridge, MA: Harvard University Press.

Watts, D. J. (2007). *The collective dynamics of belief*. Paper available online at http://cdg.columbia.edu/uploads/papers/.

Watts, D. J., & Strogatz, S. (1998). Collective dynamics of "small world" networks. *Nature 393*, 440–442.

Wilensky, U. (1999). *NetLogo*. Evanston, IL: Center for Connected Learning and Computer-Based Modeling. Northwestern University (http://ccl.northwestern.edu/netlogo).

Contributors

Roger Azevedo is a Professor of Educational Psychology at McGill University. He is also a Senior Canada Research Chair in the area of Metacognition and Advanced Learning Technologies. His main research areas include examining the role of cognitive, metacognitive, affective, and motivational self-regulatory processes during learning with computer-based learning environments. He is the director of the Laboratory for the Study of Metacognition and Advanced Learning Technologies (http://smartlaboratory.ca/). He has published over 100 peer-reviewed papers in the areas of educational, learning, and cognitive sciences. He serves on the editorial board of several top-tiered educational psychology and instructional science journals. He is a fellow of the American Psychological Association and the recipient of the prestigious Early Faculty Career Award from the National Science Foundation.

Sasha Barab, PhD is the Pinnacle West Presidential Chair and a Founding Senior Scientist & Scholar in the Learning Sciences Institute at Arizona State University. He was previously the Director of the Center for Research on Learning and Technology at Indiana University. His current research involves the development of gaming environments designed to assist children in developing a sense of purpose as individuals, as members of their communities, and as knowledgeable citizens of the world. Central to this work has been a focus on the understanding of the value of transformational play. He is the principal investigator of the Quest Atlantis project, a highly successful educational game (for more information on QA, visit http://lacunagames.org/barab/rsrch_qa.html).

Reza Feyzi Behnagh is a doctoral student in Educational Psychology, Learning Sciences stream at McGill University, Montreal, Canada. He received his MA in Teaching English as a Foreign Language from Tarbiat Modares University, Tehran, Iran. His research interests include self-regulated learning, cognitive load, and computer-based learning environments.

Philip Bell pursues a cognitive and cultural program of research across diverse environments focused on how people learn in ways that are personally consequential to them. He is an Associate Professor of the Learning Sciences at the University of Washington, and he is Geda and Phil Condit Professor of Science and Mathematics Education, and he directs the ethnographic and design-based research of the Everyday Science and Technology Group. He also directs the University of Washington Institute for Science and Mathematics Education focused on coordinating P-20 education efforts across the university.

John B. Black   (black@tc.edu) is the Cleveland E. Dodge Professor at Teachers College, Columbia University in the Departments of Human Development, and Mathematics, Science, and Technology. He is Chair of the Department of Human Development, Coordinates the Program in Cognitive Studies and is the Director of the Institute for Learning Technologies. His current research focuses on research in cognition, especially grounded/embodied approaches and their application to improving learning, memory, understanding, problem solving and motivation.

Ben DeVane is an Assistant Professor of Digital Arts and Sciences at the Digital Worlds Institute at the University of Florida. He received his doctorate in Educational Technology from University of Wisconsin-Madison. His dissertation was a three-year ethnographic study of a game-based learning program for adolescent youth that examined how players' trajectories of identity formation influenced how they learned about history and geography. His current research looks at the design of learning games focused on topics like public health, science education and financial literacy.

Brian Dorn is an Assistant Professor at the University of Hartford, holding a joint appointment in Computer Science and Multimedia Web Design & Development. He conducts research primarily in the fields of computing education and human–computer interaction. Dorn received his PhD in Computer Science from the Georgia Institute of Technology in 2010.

Melissa Duffy is a doctoral student in the Learning Sciences program at McGill University. She received her MA in Educational Psychology from McGill University. Her research interests include self-regulated learning, achievement motivation, and epistemic beliefs.

Thomas M. Duffy is the Barbara Jacobs Chair of Education and Technology at Indiana University. His research and teaching focuses on the design of learning environments that support inquiry and problem solving in post-secondary education and training. His recent work focuses on the design of distance education environments based on work in cognitive science on how people learn.

Matthew Easter is an assistant research professor at the University of Missouri. He recently earned his doctorate in Educational Psychology from the University of Missouri. His research includes investigating how conceptual change theories relate to cognitive theories of motivation. Specifically, he has investigated how the environment and emotions can influence cognition and subsequently, motivational beliefs. He also assists in the development and study of online learning environments in the College of Engineering at the University of Missouri.

Cameron L. Fadjo is a Research Associate with the Institute for Learning Technologies and doctoral candidate in the Cognitive Studies in Education program at Teachers College, Columbia University. His research focuses on grounded embodied cognition, Instructional Embodiment, Computational Thinking, and Touch-based Gestural Interfaces. He is especially interested in how creating and exploring with interactive technologies improves learning, memory, understanding, and problem solving.

Mark Guzdial is a Professor in the College of Computing at Georgia Institute of Technology. He was the Director of Undergraduate Programs (including the BS in Computer Science, BS in Computational Media and Minor in Computer Science) until October 2007. Mark is a member of the GVU Center. He received his PhD in education and computer science (a joint degree) at the University of Michigan in 1993, where he developed Emile, an environment for high school science learners programming multimedia demonstrations and physics simulations. He was the original developer of the CoWeb (or Swiki), a widely used Wiki engine in universities around the world. He is the inventor of the Media Computation approach to learning introductory computing, which uses *contextualized computing education* to attract and retain students. He was vice-chair of the ACM Education Board, and still serves on that board, as well as on the ACM SIGCSE Board. He serves on the editorial boards of *ACM Transactions on Computing Education* and *Journal of the Learning Sciences*. His blog on Computing Education is active, with 200–300 page views per day.

Michael Hannafin (PhD, Arizona State University, Educational Technology) is the Charles H. Wheatley-Georgia Research Alliance Eminent Scholar in Technology-Enhanced Learning and Professor in the Department of Educational Psychology and Instructional Technology at the University of Georgia (UGA) where he directs the Learning and Performance Support Laboratory—an R&D organization that studies the potential for and impact of emerging technologies for teaching and learning. His background and prior work focused on the intersection of psychology, technology and education, where he developed and validated frameworks for teaching and learning. His current research focuses on the study of technology-enhanced teaching and learning environments—especially those that are open and student-centered in nature.

Jason Harley is a doctoral student in the Educational Psychology program (Learning Sciences stream) at McGill University. He received his MA in Educational Psychology and BA in Psychology at McGill University. His research interests include the study and measurement of affect and affective regulation, human–computer interaction, self-regulated learning and serious games.

Janette Hill earned her PhD in Instructional Systems Design from Florida State University, and has since held academic positions at the University of Northern Colorado and Georgia State University. Currently, she is a faculty member in the Department of Lifelong Education, Administration, and Policy at the University of Georgia (UGA) where she also serves as Department Head. Her current research focuses on the study of emerging/Web-based technologies, community building in virtual environments, resource-based learning, and information/knowledge management systems.

Christopher Hoadley is an Associate Professor and Director of the programs in educational communication and technology and digital media design for learning at New York University. He heads dolcelab, the Lab for Design of Learning, Collaboration, & Experience. Hoadley's research focuses on computer support for collaborative learning, especially unconventional technology applications for human empowerment. In 2008–2009, he served as a Fulbright scholar to India and Nepal.

Dirk Ifenthaler (ifenthaler@ezw.uni-freiburg.de) is Assistant Professor at the Department of Educational Science at the Albert-Ludwigs-University of Freiburg, Germany. Dr Ifenthaler's research interests focus on the learning-dependent progression of mental models, problem solving, decision making, situational awareness, and emotions. He developed an automated and computer-based methodology for the analysis of graphical and natural language representations (SMD Technology). Additionally, he developed components of course management software and an educational simulation game (SEsim – School Efficiency Simulation).

Michael J. Jacobson is a Professor and Chair of Education at the University of Sydney. He also is the Co-director of the Centre for Research on Computer Supported Learning and Cognition (CoCo), and Deputy Director, Institute for Innovation in Science and Mathematics Education. His research focuses on the design of learning technologies to foster deep conceptual understanding, conceptual change, and knowledge transfer in challenging conceptual domains. Most recently, his work has explored learning in agent-augmented virtual worlds and with agent-based modeling and visualization tools, as well as cognitive and learning issues related to understanding new scientific perspectives emerging from the study of complex systems.

David Jonassen is Curators' Professor at the University of Missouri where he teaches in the areas of Learning Technologies and Educational Psychology. Since earning his doctorate in educational media and experimental educational psychology from Temple University, Dr Jonassen has taught at the University of Missouri, Pennsylvania State University, University of Colorado, the University of Twente in the Netherlands, the University of North Carolina at Greensboro, and Syracuse University. He has published 35 books and hundreds of articles, papers, and reports on text design, task analysis, instructional design, computer-based learning, hypermedia, constructivism, cognitive tools, and problem solving. His current research focuses on the cognitive processes engaged by problem solving and models and methods for supporting those processes during learning, culminating in the book, *Learning to Solve Problems: A Handbook for Designing Problem-Solving Learning Environments.*

Manu Kapur is an Associate Professor of Curriculum, Teaching and Learning and a researcher in the Learning Sciences Lab (LSL) at the National Institute of Education of Singapore. He conceptualized the notion of *productive failure* and used it to explore the hidden efficacies in the seemingly failed effort of small groups solving complex problems collaboratively in an online environment. Over the past five years, Manu has done extensive work in mathematics classrooms to extend his work on productive failure across a range of schools in Singapore.

Janet L. Kolodner is Regents' Professor in the School of Interactive Computing at the Georgia Institute of Technology. Her research addresses issues in learning, memory, and problem solving, in computers and in people. She pioneered the computer reasoning method called case-based reasoning, a way of solving problems based on analogies to past experiences, and Learning by Design (LBD), an approach to promoting science in middle school based on case-based reasoning's model of learning. She is lead author on Project-Based Inquiry Learning (PBIS), a three-year middle-school science curriculum that incorporates LBD's approach. She is co-founder and former Executive Officer of the International Society of the Learning Sciences (ISLS, http://www.isls.org), and Founding and Emerita Editor in Chief of *Journal of the Learning Sciences.*

Susan M. Land is an Associate Professor and past Program Head of the Instructional Systems Program (Learning, Design, and Technology emphasis) in the College of Education at The Pennsylvania State University. She earned her Ph.D. from The Florida State University in Instructional Systems Design. Her research investigates frameworks for the design of open-ended, technology-rich learning environments. She studies learning environments and design connected to everyday contexts, mobile devices, social networking, and student-created design projects.

E. Michael Nussbaum is a Professor of Educational Psychology at the University of Nevada, Las Vegas. He researches the development of students' argumentation skills in science (in relationship to conceptual change) and social studies (in relation to controversial issues). His recent work on argument-counterargument integration has appeared in the *Journal of the Learning Sciences*, *Journal of Educational Psychology*, and in the *International Journal of Computer-Supported Collaborative Learning*. He is also the Principal Investigator on the Losing the Lake Project, which is developing educational technology on climate change. Dr Nussbaum received his doctorate in Psychological Studies from Stanford University in 1997.

Kevin Oliver (PhD, University of Georgia) is Program Coordinator and Associate Professor of Instructional Technology in the Department of Curriculum, Instruction, and Counselor Education at North Carolina State University. He conducts research on Web-based cognitive tools integrated in varied subjects such as science and history, and he is actively involved in evaluating several statewide technology initiatives including virtual schooling and one-to-one computing. He has taught online courses in NC State's Master's and Doctoral programs in IT for six years, and was recently involved in the design of a new Graduate Certificate in E-Learning.

Pablo Pirnay-Dummer (pablo@pirnay-dummer.de) is Assistant Professor at the Department of Educational Science at the Albert-Ludwigs-University of Freiburg, Germany. His research and publications are located in the area of language, cognition, learning, expertise and technology where his practical focus is on model based knowledge management and organizational learning. He developed the language-oriented model assessment methodology T-MITOCAR (Text Model Inspection Trace of Concepts and Relations) that is built to assess, analyze and compare individual and group models of expertise. He also developed the web-based training framework L-MoSim (Learner Model Simulation), including new approaches of automated tasks synthesis for complex problem solving.

Norbert M. Seel (seel@ezw.uni-freiburg.de) is chair of the Department of Educational Science at the Albert-Ludwigs-University of Freiburg, Germany. As a cognitive scientist he is concerned with mental model research, instructional design and media research. Dr Seel's work is rooted in quantitative empirical research methods. He has published several books and articles in these fields.

Ayelet Segal (segalayelet@gmail.com) has been exploring problems in Cognitive Psychology, Education and Interactive Media for over 15 years. Ayelet has a PhD (2011) in Cognitive Psychology and Education from Teachers College, Columbia University. Her research focuses on embodiment theory and gestural interfaces to promote cognition and learning. She also holds a Master of Arts in Interactive Media from Middlesex University in London. Ayelet has won several international awards and presented her research in numerous conferences.

Kurt Squire is an Associate Professor of Educational Communications and Technology at University of Wisconsin-Madison, co-director of the Games, Learning, and Society Initiative, associate co-director of the Education Research Challenge Area (ERCA) of the Wisconsin Institutes for Discovery (WIDS), and vice president of the Learning Games Network, a non-profit network expanding the role of games and learning. An internationally recognized leader in digital media and education, Kurt has delivered dozens of invited addresses across Europe, Asia, and North America and written over 50 scholarly articles.

Jakita O. Thomas, PhD is an Assistant Professor of Computer and Information Science at Spelman College in Atlanta, Georgia. Dr Thomas's research interests include promoting access to healthcare services for under-served populations, supporting the development of computational algorithmic thinking, and complex cognitive skills learning. She received a BS in Computer and Information Science with a minor in Mathematics from Spelman College, and a PhD in Computer Science from the Georgia Institute of Technology.

Gregory Trevors is a doctoral student in the Learning Sciences at McGill University. His research interests include issues in real-time learning processes, particularly as these relate to conceptual change and self-regulated learning in science domains.

Jonathan Vitale (Jmv2125@columbia.edu) is currently completing his dissertation research at Teachers College, Columbia University. Jonathan is a former high school math teacher and an undergraduate computer science and psychology major at the University of Pennsylvania. His research focuses on how emerging digital technologies may be used to promote mathematical learning. Jonathan develops learning and assessment tools with Adobe Flash.

Heather Toomey Zimmerman is a researcher who develops situated accounts of learning within and across informal settings to advance learning theory and educational practice. She uses ethnographic, interaction analysis, and design-based research methods to understand how families and youth learn ecological, environmental and earth sciences content and practices. She is an assistant professor in the College of Education at the Penn State University.

Index